D0097940

DATE DUE			
MAR 2 1992			
MAY 2 2 1992			

DEMCO 38-297

THE SPIRIT OF D. H. LAWRENCE

The Spirit of D. H. Lawrence

Centenary Studies

Edited by

Gāmini Salgādo
sometime Professor of English
University of Exeter

and

G. K. Das
Professor of English
University of Delhi

Foreword by

Raymond Williams

BARNES & NOBLE BOOKS
TOTOWA, NEW JERSEY

© the Estate of Gāmini Salgādo and G. K. Das 1988
Foreword © Raymond Williams 1988

All rights reserved. No reproduction, copy or
transmission of this publication may be made
without written permission

First published in the USA by
BARNES & NOBLE BOOKS
81 Adams Drive
Totowa, New Jersey 07512

ISBN 0–389–20665–2

Printed in Hong Kong

Library of Congress Cataloging-in-Publication Data
The spirit of D. H. Lawrence.
Includes index.
1. Lawrence, D. H. (David Herbert), 1885–1930 –
Criticism and interpretation.   I. Salgādo, Gāmini,
1929–1985.   II. Das, G. K.
PR6023.A93Z9238   1986   823'.912   86–17385
ISBN 0–389–20665–2

Contents

PR
6023
A93
Z92
1988

Foreword

RAYMOND WILLIAMS

Lawrence needed no centenary. No prompting of a date was required for him to be read and reread and continually discussed. Moreover, though he has remained a highly controversial figure, he has been, for two generations, a leading example, even at times a proud possession, of otherwise radically different movements in writing and thought.

Today, in his centenary year, he is still being presented with these different and even alternative emphases. He is a major instance – perhaps, as in Leavis, the last instance – of the great tradition in English fiction: at once a highly original but in a key sense traditional novelist, exploring the health and sickness of a culture and a society through detailed and intensive analysis of personal relationships. Or, in quite a different tone, he gives us the first major example of the English working-class novel, extending the boundaries of fiction to kinds of work and living conditions which the earlier tradition had been unable or unwilling to reach: the novelist, then, of working-class culture and the movement out of it through education and a more general mobility. Or, yet again, he is the pioneer of a new kind of understanding and presentation of sexuality, moving beyond the concerns alike of tradition and of class. In one common form of this view, it is not only the new sexuality as such, but its direct association with forms of feeling and thinking distinct from and opposed to received forms of rationality and enlightenment, that is seen as linking him not to the social novel of the mainline tradition but back to such figures as Blake and forward to a radically dissident sub-culture of our own time.

Can we say, consensually, that there is truth in each of these presentations? Not, usually, to those who are offering them. For quite apart from the deep-rooted attachments to the general positions which underlie the alternative presentations, there is the special problem that Lawrence is taken, again and again, not simply as an exemplary but as a campaigning figure. Indeed, he is often taken as in effect the private possession of this or that tendency. He is at once their justification, their promotional instance and, where necessary – which can produce the most curious results – the stick to beat the others with.

It is true that the rest of us can observe, in this process, an interesting selectivity of his writings. For those of the great tradition, *Women in Love*, and behind it *The Rainbow*, are the really important works. For those of the working-class novel, *Sons and Lovers*, such early stories as *Odour of Chrysanthemums*, the early plays and some fragmentary late writings, such as *Return to Bestwood*. For those of the third persuasion, *Lady Chatterley's Lover*, *The Plumed Serpent*, *Fantasia of the Unconscious* and other stories and essays of the 1920s. The works beyond these leading instances are typically either gathered into their orbit or seen as secondary, even preparatory, incidental or decadent.

Can we then say, consensually, that as against these selective interpretations Lawrence has to be seen as a whole? Perhaps, but it is doubtful if that plausible formulation will serve. The real question may be whether there is any whole, in that sense, to see. In an intensely productive but relatively short writing life, Lawrence undoubtedly went through certain periods and phases of emphasis. Yet, from any of the selective positions, elements can be traced, backwards and forwards, to illustrate alternative forms of continuity. The true wholes, the real figures in the carpet, turn out, on closer inspection, to be as radically selective as the more evident primary recommendations.

Yet what does this then commit us to saying? That, following some recent theory, this is an author who must be dissolved into a series of texts? No case known to me seems less likely as a plausible example of this procedure. Lawrence's fingerprint, in his most diverse kinds of writing, must be one of the most recognisable anywhere. That particular liveliness of voice – at once strongly oral and relentlessly, monologically persuasive – is by now imitable but remains unique. Indeed, there are many who will settle for prizing this extraordinarily direct and immediately involving style, leaving all further questions to the secondary interests of ideologues and moralists. It is a point of view, but a curiously abstract one. It is not only that it would have infuriated Lawrence to have his style separated from what he had to say. It is also that, in any steady consideration, the particular qualities of

Lawrence's writing seem inseparable from his specific stance within a complex cultural situation at a particular historical time. The writing is then an innovative response to the very experiences and issues which are made prominent, and general, in the selective interpretations and appropriations.

Two new conditions are now affecting our understanding of this already complex problem. The most evident is the remarkable process, now well under way in the Cambridge edition, of reissuing and in very many cases re-editing his works. Already some quite new material has been published, such as the second half of the novel *Mr Noon*, and there have been a number of interesting new letters. Work I have seen on the relations between the manuscripts and the published texts of his plays suggests that important new perspectives will be gained when this editing is complete. It is said, further, that even in what have been taken as the most reliable texts the new editions will contain much that is new and significant.

This process, much of it arising from Lawrence's publishing difficulties during his most mobile years, is important not only for what it may show us in the texts but for its evidence of the material and cultural conditions of this innovating and in the broadest sense unsettled writer. Nobody can yet say for certain whether the re-edited texts will in themselves make a significant difference to our specific readings of Lawrence. On what I have so far seen there is a great deal of local and specialist interest, but I take leave to doubt whether our general sense of the major works will be substantially affected.

What is certain, however, to come more clearly into view is the condition of Lawrence's whole project: the social and material demonstration of the constraints and opportunities he was working to, and the probable correlation of phases of this condition to what can otherwise be taken – and must still to some degree continue to be taken – as a simple development within the isolated and freely determined will of the author. The case of the unfinished *Mr Noon*, at a time of great need and difficulty after the publishing problems of the war years, with its abundant internal evidence of Lawrence's now exceptionally problematic and at once suspicious and mocking sense of his probable readers, is already illuminating in this way. More general changes in Lawrence's sense of who he was writing to and for, and within this of his understanding and self-definition as a writer, already clear from direct evidence, should become clearer when the new texts and the changes in texts are fully available.

The second condition which is affecting our understanding is of a less obvious but perhaps even more important kind. It has been common to read Lawrence within the perspective retrospectively labelled as modernism: often, in fact, with some difficulty, for in some of his most important writing he kept resolutely to traditional artistic forms, which he extended for his own purposes but which he was not often tempted to replace by, for example, quite differently organised and differently oriented fictions. In some of his later fiction, when in detail and in tone many quite new things are being done, there is even what seems a deliberate return, in some styles of narrative and address, to his nineteenth-century predecessors. Thus the question of modernism in Lawrence, which has to be related not only to his own important innovations but also to his settled and often bitter hostility to other kinds of contemporary experimental work, is already in itself complex.

Yet what is now happening is that the whole period and range of processes that have been labelled modernist is at an evident distance from many of his contemporary readers. The distance between 'modernism' and the actually modern is visibly widening, and may already, apart from some institutionalised continuities of assumption and procedure, have passed through a qualitative break. It is too early to be sure of the consequences of seeing modernism as a specific and now ended historical period. The crisis of terms is only one of the most obvious: to be 'modern' within a marked-off historical period, without any guarantee of continuity to what is significantly contemporary, is an ironic condition.

More to the real point, however, is the fact that one of the leading elements of that sense of 'the modern' and 'modernism' was a sense of a new and exciting, truth-bearing universality. In the rushing experiences of the twentieth century, this sense of novelty, of an effectively universal *avant-garde*, has lasted in some minds to a time in which we are celebrating the centenaries not only of the births but also of the deaths of so many of its leading figures. There are few, though there are some, signs of the diminution of the intrinsic power of this movement, though its radical diversities are now much more evident. The energy and significance of many of its particular works are not seriously in doubt. But there is something about the end of a period, and in particular the loss of its promotional value as the latest and most modern kind of work, which brings about many kinds of reconsideration.

Thus, to take just two examples, there is a real shift of emphasis, in relation to Lawrence, when consciously feminist readers go through the novels and essays again: not as texts of the most modern understanding of sexuality but as texts of a particular kind of masculine perspective; and moreover when this can be done not only with the single figure of Lawrence, but with a whole grouping of figures, from Freud to Strindberg, in whom certain historical and cultural patterns can be discerned. Simple amendments and reversals in readings of Lawrence are already significant and, of course, contentious. But the wider effect will come from the explorations, now well begun, into the whole structure of feeling which can be traced in these important writers and thinkers. To bring Strindberg and Lawrence together, for example, can be to enter on an astonishingly new set of problems and questions, for the similarities between many of their works and beliefs, and even the crises of their development as writers, have little if anything to do with influence, in the ordinary literary-historical sense, but seem to have everything to do with certain common factors in an underlying cultural condition within which, in different countries and at different times, these two writers of genius were working and changing.

Thus even a centenary is no time of steady summing-up. Radical changes are happening even while a developed scholarship and criticism deploys its increased understanding. Yet what we are now marking, within these changes, is the continuing importance of Lawrence, even though the perspectives and valuations are so varied, and perhaps because of this. In English culture, especially, the figure of Lawrence still looks quite central to what has happened, and also what has been projected but has failed to happen, in the culture which in so many respects we still share with him, over so long and disturbed a time.

There may be writers of whom standard, 'classical' accounts and valuations can be achieved, but if there are, Lawrence is not among them. Not only because, in the sadness of his early death, much of his project must be seen as unfinished, but also because, in the whole nature of that project, finish, settlement were never either the ends or the means, and the most critical modes accept this. It is then especially useful, given the occasion of a date, to see what a wide range of readers, as scholars or critics, now most want to say about this continually engaging figure: not, as it were, definitively but as a lively reading in progress.

1985

Preface

This book of essays commemorates the centenary of the birth of D. H. Lawrence, who was appropriately described by E. M. Forster as the 'greatest imaginative novelist of our generation'. The centenary – of a writer who wrote: 'I don't care whether I am great or small, rich or poor, or remembered or forgotten' – has been a memorable international event in 1985, having been celebrated widely in Britain, Europe, the USA and India. In visiting Nottingham and Eastwood in the beautiful harvest season of September ('best of all the months', according to Cyril Beardsall of *The White Peacock*) and participating in the vibrant international symposium at the University of Nottingham, one was left with a deep and unforgettable feeling that the spirit of Lawrence had indeed immortalised the spirit of this place. The spirit of Lawrence himself is less easily defined; perhaps it is best apprehended, through his works, as the ever-growing spirit of life itself in its most complete sense.

The essays contained in the present commemorative volume explore various aspects of that complex central theme. Specially written for this volume, they examine or re-examine, in the light of many newly-discovered biographical facts and with new critical insights, a wide variety of academic and intellectual issues – textual as well as polemical – concerned with Lawrence's 'thought adventure' into life. In attempting to establish his unique distinction as a creative writer, artist and thinker of our generation and of generations to come, they throw new light on several of his writings and on various controversial issues: his 'Counter-Romanticism', for example, his dialectics of sexual passion, his philosophy, religion, cosmology and vision of history, and his tormenting utopian ambition to bring about a new social revolution; in addition, two scholarly essays analyse what is called the 'Lawrence legend' in literature (fiction as well as poetry) written since his time.

It has been a matter of very deep shock and sorrow to me and to all those associated with the writing of this volume that my fellow-editor Gāmini Salgādo died in June 1985 and was not able to see the fruit of our collaborative effort through the past few years. His untimely death was a great blow to me personally; the book, at least, will now remain simultaneously a commemoration of the writer that Gāmini most dearly loved and a memorial to himself.

I should like to thank all the contributors for their scholarly support and for their warm-hearted and most patient cooperation. For advice, editorial assistance and other forms of help received in moments of crisis I am grateful to Frances A. Arnold, Alice K. Beebe, Gillian and John Beer, Peter Corbin, Bulbul Das, T. M. Farmiloe, Nick Furbank, Fred McDowell, A. N. Kaul, Vi Palfrey, Richard Parkinson, Valery Rose, Fenella Salgādo, Julia Steward and John Worthen.

My participation in the international Lawrence symposium held in the University of Nottingham was made possible by the kind invitation of the organisers – Professor J. T. Boulton, Dr Allan Rodway, Peter Preston, Peter Hoare and Allan Cameron – and by financial support from the British Council and Dr J. B. Pattnaik, the Chief Minister of Orissa. I express my indebtedness to them all.

I am also deeply grateful to Professor Raymond Williams for his foreword.

G. K. Dᴀs
Nottingham

Acknowledgements

The editors and publishers wish to thank the following who have kindly given permission for the use of copyright material:

the Estate of Helen Corke, for the extracts from *Neutral Ground* by Helen Corke.

Alfred A. Knopf Inc., for the extracts from *St Mawr* and *The Plumed Serpent* by D. H. Lawrence;

Laurence Pollinger Ltd and the Estate of Mrs Frieda Lawrence Ravagli, for the extracts from *Movements in European History* by D. H. Lawrence;

Laurence Pollinger Ltd, Virago Press Ltd and New Directions Publishing Corp., for the extracts from *Bid Me To Live* by H. D.;

Laurence Pollinger Ltd, the Estate of Mrs Frieda Lawrence Ravagli and Viking Penguin Inc., for the extracts from the following works:

Phoenix: The Posthumous Papers (1936), by D. H. Lawrence, edited and with an Introduction by Edward D. McDonald; copyright 1936 by Frieda Lawrence, renewed © 1964 by the Estate of the late Frieda Lawrence Ravagli.

Phoenix II: Uncollected Papers of D. H. Lawrence, edited by F. Warren Roberts and Harry T. Moore; copyright © 1959, 1963, 1968 by the Estate of Frieda Lawrence Ravagli.

The Collected Letters of D. H. Lawrence, edited by Harry T. Moore; copyright © 1962 by Angelo Ravagli and C. Montague Weekley, Executors of the Estate of Frieda Lawrence Ravagli; copyright 1932 by the Estate of D. H. Lawrence, and 1934 by Frieda Lawrence; copyright © 1933, 1948, 1953, 1954, and each year 1956–1962 by Angelo Ravagli and C. Montague Weekley, Executors of the Estate of Frieda Lawrence Ravagli.

The Letters of D. H. Lawrence, edited by Aldous Huxley; copyright 1932 by the Estate of D. H. Lawrence, © 1960 by Angelo Ravagli and C. Montague Weekley, Executors of the Estate of Frieda Lawrence Ravagli.

Kangaroo, by D. H. Lawrence; copyright 1923 by Thomas Seltzer, Inc.; copyright renewed 1951 by Frieda Lawrence.

Sons and Lovers, by D. H. Lawrence; copyright 1913 by Thomas Seltzer, Inc., all rights reserved.

Women in Love, by D. H. Lawrence; copyright 1920, 1922 by D. H. Lawrence; renewed 1948, 1950 by Frieda Lawrence.

John Thomas and Lady Jane, by D. H. Lawrence; Italian translation copyright 1954 by Carlo Izzo, Arnoldo Mondadori; English copyright © 1972 by the Estate of Frieda Lawrence Ravagli.

The Complete Plays of D. H. Lawrence, by D. H. Lawrence; copyright © 1965 by the Estate of Mrs Frieda Lawrence.

Aaron's Rod, by D. H. Lawrence; copyright 1922 by Thomas Seltzer, Inc.; copyright renewed 1950 by Frieda Lawrence.

Collected Poems, by D. H. Lawrence; copyright 1929 by D. H. Lawrence; copyright renewed © 1956 by Frieda Lawrence Ravagli.

The Complete Poems of D. H. Lawrence, collected and edited with an Introduction and notes by Vivian de Sola Pinto and F. Warren Roberts; copyright © 1964, 1971 by Angelo Ravagli and C. M. Weekley, Executors of the Estate of Frieda Lawrence Ravagli.

Fantasia of the Unconscious, by D. H. Lawrence; copyright 1922 by Thomas Seltzer, Inc.; copyright renewed 1950 by Frieda Lawrence.

Apocalypse, by D. H. Lawrence; copyright 1931 by the Estate of David Herbert Lawrence; Introduction by Richard Aldington; copyright 1932; copyright renewed © 1960 by the Viking Press, Inc.

Notes on the Contributors

Maurice Beebe, sometime Professor of English at Temple University in Philadelphia, was the Editor of *Journal of Modern Literature*. His many publications include a book on the artist-as-hero in fiction from Goethe to Lawrence, entitled *Ivory Towers and Sacred Founts*. He died in January 1986.

John Beer, Reader in English Literature at Cambridge University and Fellow of Peterhouse, is the editor of *'A Passage to India': Essays in Interpretation* and the author of *Coleridge the Visionary*, *The Achievement of E. M. Forster*, *Blake's Humanism*, *Blake's Visionary Universe*, *Coleridge's Poetic Intelligence*, *Wordsworth and the Human Heart* and *Wordsworth in Time*. His articles include ' "The Last Englishman": Lawrence's appreciation of Forster', in *E. M. Forster: a Human Exploration* (ed. Das and Beer).

James C. Cowan is the founder and former editor (1968–83) of *The D. H. Lawrence Review*. He is the author of *D. H. Lawrence's American Journey: a Study in Literature and Myth* and the compiler and editor of two volumes of bibliographical abstracts, *D. H. Lawrence: an Annotated Bibliography of Writings about Him*, vols I and II.

Keith Cushman, the author of *D. H. Lawrence at Work*, has published widely on twentieth-century literature. He has co-edited *The Letters of D. H. Lawrence and Amy Lowell, 1914–1925*.

G. K. Das is Professor of English at the University of Delhi, where he was Director of an international D. H. Lawrence centenary seminar in 1985. He was a Commonwealth Staff Fellow at Queens' College, Cambridge, a Senior Fulbright Visiting Scholar at Harvard University, and Professor and Head of Department of English at the University of Kashmir. He is the author of *E. M. Forster's India* and editor (with John Beer) of *E. M. Forster: a Human Exploration*.

Albert J. Devlin, Professor of English Literature at the University of Missouri-Columbia, has written widely on Southern American literature. His most recent work is *Eudora Welty's Chronicle: a Story of Mississippi Life*. He is now completing a bibliographical study of Southern literature.

P. N. Furbank, formerly Reader in Literature at the Open University, has published several books including *Samuel Butler 1835–1902*, *Italo Svevo: the Man and the Writer*, *Reflections on the Word 'Image'*, *E. M. Forster: a Life* and *Unholy Pleasure: or the Idea of Social Class*.

Holly A. Laird is an Assistant Professor of English at the University of Virginia. She obtained her Ph.D. from Princeton University and is currently preparing a book on the poetry of D. H. Lawrence.

Louis L. Martz is the author of *The Poetry of Meditation*, *The Paradise Within*, *Poet of Exile*, and other writings on seventeenth-century literature, and has edited the *Collected Poems of H. D., 1912–1944*. He has recently retired as Sterling Professor of English at Yale University.

Frederick P. W. McDowell, formerly Professor of English at the University of Iowa, has published books on Ellen Glasgow, Caroline Gordon and E. M. Forster, and has written widely on other authors. He is currently completing a book on Bernard Shaw's twentieth-century plays, and has written 'D. H. Lawrence and E. M. Forster in their Fiction' for a volume of essays on *Lady Chatterley's Lover*.

George A. Panichas, Professor of English at the University of Maryland since 1962, received his Ph.D. at the University of Nottingham, where he was a pupil of Vivian de Sola Pinto. The author of *Adventure in Consciousness: the Meaning of D. H. Lawrence's Religious Quest*, he has also written essays on Lawrence which are included in his two major books of literary and social criticism, *The Reverent Discipline* and *The Courage of Judgment*.

R. N. Parkinson is Senior Lecturer in English at Exeter University and has taught and lectured widely in Austria, Germany, France,

India and the USA. His critical study of Edward Gibbon was published in 1973, and he has published articles on Shakespeare, modern poetry and E. M. Forster. He is currently working on Pound, Eliot, modern poetry and the Scottish historian William Robertson.

F. B. Pinion, Litt.D. and a MASUA Distinguished Foreign Scholar, was Reader in English Studies and a Sub-Dean at the University of Sheffield. His books include *A D. H. Lawrence Companion*, similar publications on Hardy, Jane Austen, the Brontës, George Eliot, Wordsworth, T. S. Eliot and Tennyson, *Thomas Hardy: Art and Thought* and *A Commentary on the Poems of Thomas Hardy*.

Gāmini Salgādo was, until his death in 1985, Professor of English Literature at the University of Exeter. He had written widely on D. H. Lawrence, including *A Preface to Lawrence* and a short study of *Sons and Lovers*; he edited a collection of essays on *Sons and Lovers, Three Jacobean Tragedies, Three Restoration Comedies, Conycatchers and Bawdybaskets, Four Jacobean Comedies* and *The Elizabethan Underworld*. His publications include *Eyewitnesses of Shakespeare, Shakespeare and Myself* and *King Lear: Text and Performance*.

John B. Vickery is Professor of English and Chairman of the department at the University of California, Riverside. He is the author of *Robert Graves and the White Goddess, The Literary Impact of 'The Golden Bough'* and *Myths and Texts*.

J. R. Watson is Professor of English at the University of Durham, author of *Picturesque Landscape and English Romantic Poetry* and *Wordsworth's Vital Soul*, and editor of several anthologies, casebooks and texts, including *Everyman's Book of Victorian Verse*.

Kingsley Widmer's several hundred publications include eight books of literary and cultural criticisms: *The Art of Perversity: D. H. Lawrence's Shorter Fictions; Henry Miller; The Literary Rebel; The Ways of Nihilism: Herman Melville's Short Novels; The End of Culture: Essays on Contemporary Sensibility; Paul Goodman; Edges of Extremity: some Problems of Literary Modernism; Nathanael West*. He has taught at several institutions, in the USA and other countries, and is currently Professor of English at San Diego State University (California).

John Worthen teaches at the University College of Swansea. He is the author of *D. H. Lawrence and the Idea of the Novel*, and has edited *The Lost Girl*, *The Prussian Officer* and *Love Among the Haystacks* for the Cambridge Edition of Lawrence's works. He is currently engaged on the first volume of a new biography: *D. H. Lawrence: a Life*.

George J. Zytaruk, formerly President of Nipissing University College in North Bay, Ontario, Canada, and currently Professor of English there, is the author of *D. H. Lawrence's Response to Russian Literature*. He has edited *The Quest for Rananim: D. H. Lawrence's Letters to S. S. Koteliansky* and *The Collected Letters of Jessie Chambers*, and is co-editor with James T. Boulton of volume II of *The Letters of D. H. Lawrence*.

1

Lawrence's Autobiographies

JOHN WORTHEN

I

Lawrence is widely known to have been an autobiographical writer; it is less well known what that might mean. I shall suggest ways in which his novel *Sons and Lovers* (1913) is, and is not, autobiographical; and shall discuss the group of autobiographical essays he wrote in the late 1920s. What versions of his life did he create? What was he doing with autobiography?

Sons and Lovers had been recognised in 1913 as a sign that Lawrence's writing might draw upon his own life;[1] but an assumption that all his work was a kind of unwitting autobiography appears to date from the 1930s, and has been surprisingly influential. Middleton Murry had remarked in *Son of Woman* (1931) that 'there is, and can be, but one true life of Lawrence; and that is contained in his works';[2] T. S. Eliot's review of Murry's book had agreed that 'the whole history of Lawrence's life and of Lawrence's writing . . . is the same history';[3] and Richard Aldington wrote in his introduction to *Last Poems* (1932) that Lawrence's writing 'forms one immense autobiography' (*Poems*, p. 594).* Our problem is that there is a kind of truth in the idea, but a good deal of muddled thinking too. Biographers have often felt encouraged to treat Lawrence's fiction as if they were grave-robbers (or old-fashioned archaeologists, gleaning facts but asking no questions); we need a clearer notion than Murry's about Lawrence's involvement with his own work.

II

Lawrence more than once specifically referred to *Sons and Lovers* as autobiographical (*Letters*, I, p. 490; *Phoenix II*, p. 300), and it clearly does present a family very like his own, with a central character who goes through many of his own experiences. The conflicts between Lawrence's parents, for instance, bear close relation to the quarrels in the novel; and we know that Lydia Lawrence's mother love played an enormous part in the emotional life of her son, just as Mrs Morel's kind of love is deeply influential upon Paul. However, the novel makes some interesting adjustments to the family and to the central figure. Lawrence's sister Ada – the closest to him, in every sense, of his brothers and sisters – is transmuted into a man; and Arthur Morel is also reminiscent of Lawrence's eldest brother George, as well as of people outside the family altogether. A result of this is that Paul is more isolated within his family than we may guess Lawrence to have been. The Morel family has no context of grandparents, aunts and uncles; we know that these relations were important to the Lawrence family. Paul Morel himself, being an artist, has no interest in writing, and little enough in books; for the young Lawrence, nothing else was so important. Paul stays at work in Jordan's factory for the duration of the novel; Lawrence's equivalent experience lasted only three months, partly because of illness, but partly because of the way 'he longed for the teaching profession' (Neville, p. 40). From the age of seventeen, Lawrence was obviously going to become a teacher; his training and practical experience lasted from 1901 to 1911. Paul Morel's experiences with women, after Miriam, also seem very unlike those of the young Lawrence; the single, intensely serious affair with Clara Dawes replaces the multitude of different relationships Lawrence had with women as diverse as Alice Dax, Agnes Holt, Helen Corke, Louie Burrows and Marie Jones; and, of course, finally with Frieda Weekley. His elopement with Frieda had begun to answer some of the problems of his early life; Paul is left specifically 'derelict' after his mother's death, essentially tragic where his creator's life was not.

III

Lawrence's continual rewriting and revision of his work was in search not of formal or aesthetic perfection, but of what the work could really say: for the statue within the marble (*Letters*, II, p. 146). It is characteristic of his writing that an autobiographical novel like *Sons and Lovers* should have been as difficult to write as any other kind of novel. Jessie Chambers has recorded some of the vicissitudes of its early versions, and how Lawrence found himself unable to go on with it in October 1911.[4] Its earliest surviving version locates Miriam in an urban bourgeois family, and shows Walter Morel killing his son Arthur with a carving steel, for which he goes to prison, and dies shortly after his release. (Lawrence's uncle Walter – Arthur Lawrence's brother – actually had killed *his* son with a carving steel, and had been sent to prison briefly, so the episode is not simply fictional, but it constitutes an extraordinary intrusion of one kind of family experience into the experience of another family altogether.) Although one of his revisions to the novel was to include more of the real events (and members) of the Lawrence family, it was never simply an account of family life, of parents and childhood. It was concerned to create an attitude to these things, and not until its last writing did Lawrence find what Frieda called 'the hang of it' (*Letters*, I, p. 479).

The very first manifestation of the novel was probably the novel fragment starting 'There is a small cottage', dating from 1910.[5] This describes the girlhood of a woman who will almost certainly become a kind of Mrs Morel; the details are apparently all taken from Lydia Lawrence's memories of her early life. By the autumn of 1912, this rather sentimental writing had become an account of a woman who selects her sons as lovers: Mrs Morel is herself both creative and destructive. This version of Mrs Morel appears to have become clear to Lawrence only as he wrote the final version of the novel, though the destructive potential of the mother is presented alongside a kind of adoration of her not dissimilar to the saintly potential of the heroine of 'There is a small cottage'. The letter that Lawrence wrote to Edward Garnett upon finishing the novel takes the analysis still further, into an understanding of mother love; as Frieda had put it (proud of having helped introduce this kind of understanding), 'the mother is really the thread, the domineering note' (*Letters*, I, p. 479). But that understanding, in its turn, gave way in Frieda's conception – and probably in Lawrence's – to a sense of its inadequacy. 'You see I don't really believe in *Sons and Lovers*. It feels as if there were nothing *behind* all those happenings . . . only intensely felt fugitive things' (*Letters*, II, p. 151). We have a record of Lawrence's own view of the novel from nine years later:

Lawrence pensively watched [the workman], announcing that
he resembled his father – the same clean-cut and exuberant
spirit, a true pagan. He added that he had not done justice to
his father in *Sons and Lovers* and felt like rewriting it. . . . Now
he blamed his mother for her self-righteousness.   (Nehls, II,
p. 126)

Autobiography clearly was not his way of presenting truths about
his early life, but a way of *creating* a life; and like all fiction, that
creation might later be judged inadequate.

IV

Lawrence returned in 1926 to an extended series of accounts of
his parents and their differences. Over the years, there are
numerous records of conversations in which he described his
upbringing;[6] but at the end of his life he wrote a number of
explicitly autobiographical pieces which do much more than just
describe his early life; like *Sons and Lovers*, they make something
of it, and attempt to account for developments in his life in terms
of his upbringing. Simply to list them: the essays 'Getting On'
and 'Return to Bestwood', written in October–November 1926,
and themselves early drafts of the essay finally collected in
Assorted Articles (1930) as 'Autobiographical Sketch', but first
written in its final shape in January 1927 as 'Which Class I Belong
to', and later published as 'Myself Revealed'; the autobiographical
notes demanded by the French publisher Kra (written 18 July
1928); the essay 'Enslaved by Civilisation' (written in November
1928); and finally the essay 'Nottingham and the Mining
Countryside', written by the late summer of 1929. To these we
should add a number of poems in *Pansies* (1929), notably 'Red-
Herring', 'Climbing Up', and the sequence of five from 'A Rise in
the World' to 'Have Done with it', all written in November–
December 1928.[7]

The only part of Lawrence's life that the above deal with in any
detail is his very early experience. Even the notes for Kra spend
more than half their length describing his life between 1885 and
1910 – that is, before he had published a book. And when
protesting about having to provide such material, Lawrence told

Jean Watson that Kra should read *Sons and Lovers* and *The Rainbow* instead (letter of 18 July 1928): the novel about his early life, and (presumably) the schoolteaching sections of *The Rainbow*. It is also significant that the pieces all group together between the autumn of 1926 and the summer of 1929; like the three versions of the *Lady Chatterley* novel, they grew out of Lawrence's last visit to England during August and September 1926. England had first brought Lawrence a renewed sense of his own connection with it; on the Lincolnshire coast, he was happy to record that 'I like England again, now I am up in my own regions . . . there seems a queer, odd sort of potentiality in the people, especially the common people' (30 August 1926). A fortnight later, he was still feeling that 'I've got quite into touch with my native land again, here – and feel at home' (12 September 1926). That mood lasted only until he actually went to Eastwood and to Ripley, where he was staying with his sister Ada; between 13 and 16 September he saw the human results of the coal strike which was still going on.

> The strike has done a lot of damage – and there is a lot of misery – families living on bread and margarine and potatoes – nothing more. The women have turned into fierce communists – you would hardly believe your eyes. It feels a different place – not pleasant at all.   (15 September 1926)

A letter to Rolf Gardiner (3 December 1926) says rather the same kind of thing, and the essay 'Return to Bestwood' describes what he saw in detail. But it also shows him mourning the passing of the old-style collier, masculine and self-dependent. The fact that he sees striking colliers actually picking blackberries hits him particularly hard:

> when I was a boy, it was utterly *infra dig.* for a miner to be picking blackberries. He would never have demeaned himself to such an unmanly occupation. And as to walking home with the little basket – he would almost rather have committed murder. The children might do it, or the women, or even the half grown youths. But a married, manly collier! (*Phoenix II*, p. 258)

On the one hand, people are living on 'bread and margarine and potatoes'; on the other, Lawrence is shocked to find the colliers behaving 'as if there were a famine'. He has more invested in his creation of the old-fashioned 'manly collier' than is quite compatible with good sense.

But it is to the collier that he addresses himself when he tries to explain in what way the Midlands are still home for him. The colliers 'have, I think, an underneath ache and heaviness very much like my own. And it must be so, because when I see them, I feel it so strongly.' The same men castigated for picking blackberries are

the only people who move me strongly, and with whom I feel myself connected in deeper destiny. It is they who are, in some peculiar way, 'home' to me. I shrink away from them, and I have an acute nostalgia for them. (*Phoenix II*, p. 264)

The essay – written in Italy, after Lawrence's return there – attempts to create an 'England' unconnected with the 'England' he had been denouncing since 1914. It is to an *older* England that the essay starts to appeal; and his mother's belief in progress is seen as simply another blind alley leading away from such an England.

There is almost no mention of Lawrence's father in 'Return to Bestwood'. In the related essay 'Getting On',[8] however, he appears as a man who drinks, never goes to church, speaks only broad dialect, and is simply one of the 'common colliers'. Very much the same one-sided portrait of him appears in the final essay of this sequence, 'Myself Revealed'. Arthur Lawrence, however, could speak 'proper' English when he chose, or until his wife and family laughed him out of it (Neville, p. 50); according to May Chambers, he *did* attend chapel on rare occasions (Nehls, III, p. 554); according to almost all surviving testimony, although he frequently drank he was by no means notorious as a drinker. George Neville's account of him dressed in his Sunday clothes certainly distinguishes him from the 'common collier', and according to Neville 'he was quite a bit above the average collier of that district in those days' (Neville, pp. 50–1). But Lawrence's portrait makes him extraordinarily ordinary; what distinguishes him is simply his vitality.

One thing about Lawrence's childhood of which we can be certain is that he hated and disliked his father. We have his direct statement: 'I was born hating my father: as early as ever I can remember, I shivered with horror when he touched me' (*Letters*, I, p. 190). We have the independent testimony of people as different as May Chambers and George Neville, both of whom knew the Lawrence family well, and both of whom wrote memoirs of Lawrence in the 1930s – but whose memoirs remained unpublished until 1959 and 1981 respectively, after the deaths of them both. May Chambers remembered the young Lawrence sending out 'jagged waves of hate and loathing' at his father (Nehls, III, p. 570); George Neville remembered him repeating that his father '"is a beast, a beast to mother, a beast to all of us"' (Neville, p. 60). As late as 1911, when he was 26, Lawrence wrote to the local Congregational minister that his father was 'disgusting, irritating, and selfish as a maggot' (*Letters*, I, p. 220).

Yet of this attitude there is not a trace in 'Return to Bestwood' or 'Getting On' – or in any of the late autobiographical pieces: though we can find, of course, a direct equivalent to it in *Sons and Lovers*, where 'Paul hated his father' (*SL*, p. 61). In 'Getting On', Lawrence's father is not hostile 'till provoked, then he too was a devil'. The 'too' is significant; in these accounts, Lydia Lawrence is also a devil. The worst Arthur Lawrence does is to keep more money to himself than he should, given the difficulty of educating and clothing five children. Apart from that, he is just an ordinary collier – except for the vitality.

It is significant that in 'Getting On' it is Lawrence himself who is the heir to that vitality. 'I always had more vitality than all the rest put together,' he suddenly says towards the end of the essay. 'My very vitality wore me thin' – an odd account of a life which was also a history of ill health and finally tuberculosis. But, without ever being stated outright, the kind of sympathy with his father as 'pagan' which he had suggested in 1922 is here confirmed. It is not a personal, or filial, or even forgiving sympathy; the father remains a shadowy, drinking, charming pagan, but in so far as he represents a vitality, and a class, and an older England, then he is a hero. Lawrence's mother, whom he loved and respected, becomes a rather repressive bourgeois woman with her eye firmly fixed on the goal of 'getting on'. Such an account goes well beyond the restoration of a balance of sympathy, or the repayment of a debt of ingratitude; but these late essays are less concerned with what we might normally call 'autobiography' than with the creation of myth.

V

There is a strange prefiguring of this argument in *Sons and Lovers*. Paul Morel, sounding rather like the later essayist, insists on a distinction between the working class and the middle class. ' "From the middle classes one gets ideas, and from the common people – life itself, warmth. You feel their loves and hates." ' But Mrs Morel offers a devastating reply: ' "It's all very well, my boy. But, then, why don't you go and talk to your father's pals?" ' It is impossible to imagine Paul shouldering his way into the Palmerston Arms of an evening, and his reply recognises that: ' "But they're rather different." ' Mrs Morel is remorseless: ' "Not at all. They're the common people . . ." '; and Paul falters into silence: ' "But – there's the life" ' (*SL*, pp. 256–7). He has lost the argument, has been shown up as an amiable theoretician. In the late essays, it is Mrs Morel who loses the argument – or, rather, who is not allowed to argue; while Paul asserts an old England, an old working class, without fear of Mrs Morel's interruption.

George Neville's testimony about class is perhaps as near the truth of Lawrence's early years as we are likely to get: 'Lawrence never belonged to the working class in spirit' (Neville, p. 161). His need of them in later life is something else altogether. His early writing is characterised by a point of view rather like that of Paul Morel in the earliest surviving version of *Sons and Lovers*, who looks at a middle class morning-room and thinks it

> very beautiful to sit perfectly at peace, in a quiet room, taking tea with people of refined manners: no dinner boiling on the hob, no miner eating dinner noisily while other folk had tea, no jumping up and down to serve vegetables and puddings, no discord, no hopeless scotch in the conversation, no spots on the cloth.[9]

Paul's creator clearly knows such feelings well, and in no way disapproves of them; and we have only to read Lawrence's letters to Blanche Jennings and Grace Crawford between 1908 and 1911 to realise how easily he wrote from the position of the sophisticated middle classes. It is certainly not true that he actually came to prefer such a position; he was always a man divided between conflicting loyalties. But it is striking that his late autobiographical essays came to adopt a position at such a polar opposite. Between 1926 and 1929 he was establishing what 'home' now meant to him, and, in particular, the symbolic potential he had been coming to see in the life of his father.

VI

Arthur Lawrence had died on 10 September 1924, while his son was in New Mexico. He cannot have seen his son more than half a dozen times since 1912, and although Lawrence's letters and postcards to his sister Ada frequently asked after him, there is no reference to him in Lawrence's accounts of family gatherings in the intervening years. His death received a single mention in Lawrence's correspondence, in a strange letter about the coming of autumn in New Mexico. 'Did I tell you my father died on Sept. 10th, the day before my birthday? – The autumn always gets me badly, as it breaks into colours. I want to go south, where there is no autumn . . . The heart of the north is dead, and the fingers of cold are corpse fingers' (3 October 1924). His father's death is caught up in a complex rejection of death. But it cannot have been an accident that a novel – 'The Flying Fish' – which he began in February 1925, and which would have ended with 'regenerate man, a real life in this Garden of Eden' (Nehls, III, p. 226), was based upon the journey home of an expatriate and desperately ill Englishman from Mexico upon the death of his only surviving relative in England. The connection suggests a movement of imagination homeward to a long-abandoned England.

VII

The three autobiographical pieces which Lawrence wrote in 1928–9 carry the process of thought about parents through to its natural conclusion. The piece for Kra describes Lawrence as being tempted by 'the bourgeoisie' throughout his early life, but at school and university 'he instinctively recoiled away' from them; and in spite of the hopes of his mother ('from the bourgeoisie') that he would 'rise in the world, step by step . . . D. H. recoiled away from the world, hated its ladder, & refused to rise' (Nehls, III, pp. 232–3). Is this the same man who fulfilled the hopes of his mother by training as a teacher from 1901 to 1908? The Kra piece continues: 'He had bourgeois aunts with "library" & "drawing-room" to their houses – but didn't like that either – preferred the powerful life in a miner's kitchen' (Nehls, III, p. 233). The creator of Paul Morel observing the middle-class morning-room did not so simply prefer 'a miner's kitchen', and the man who wrote *A Collier's Friday Night* in 1909 showed the miner's kitchen of the Lambert household (very similar to the Lawrence household) crammed with books that Mr Lambert would not read – a constant reminder of the education which is offering his children new and welcome opportunities. The 'powerful life' in *that* kitchen shows Lambert behaving grossly, rudely, clumsily and (eventually) drunkenly; his university student son Ernest hates him in the same way as witnesses of quarrels in the Lawrence household remembered the young Lawrence hating: ' "I would kill him, if it weren't that I shiver at the thought of touching him." '[10]

Lawrence's essay 'Enslaved by Civilisation', written late in 1928, rejects even the process of education from which we can see Ernest Lambert profiting. Education is a matter of being 'forced to knuckle under', of being 'really broken in' (*Phoenix II*, p. 580); but Lawrence's father's generation, 'at least among the miners where I was brought up, was still wild'. His father was never made 'a good little boy'. But Lawrence's own generation was 'broken in . . . for a nation, for England, it is a disaster' (*Phoenix II*, p. 581). So the whole process of 'getting on' is decried and abandoned: a process which, so far as it meant his becoming a teacher rather than a miner, or a clerk, was something he had grasped at, as a young man. His father, whose idea of 'pit' as the proper career for his sons was rejected outright, becomes mythic, untamed, vital; Lydia Lawrence becomes a narrow-minded opponent of vitality.

The last of these essays, 'Nottingham and the Mining Countryside', was written shortly before Lawrence's forty-fourth birthday in September 1929. It describes the country of his upbringing in some detail; it makes no direct reference to his mother at all. She is absorbed in a general attack upon 'the collier's wife', who 'nagged about material things . . . It was a mother's business to see that her sons "got on" ' (*Phoenix*, p. 137). That reference to 'a mother' is as close as the essay comes to mentioning Lydia Lawrence. But the collier himself, sometimes directly 'my father', 'fled out of the house as soon as he could, away from the nagging materialism of the woman' (*Phoenix*,

p. 136). Colliers had 'an instinct of beauty. The colliers' wives had not.' Colliers loved flowers, but 'most women love flowers as possessions, and as trimmings'. Mrs Morel's beloved garden (*SL*, pp. 164–5) is forgotten.

Lawrence's myth-making could hardly go further. Again, his father is not presented as an individual; he is a symbol of the careless and independent male. Lawrence is using his family to help him construct one of those dualisms which had been the pattern of his thinking since at least 1914; and, this time, his father is unequivocally the symbol of old England itself: an old England suffering the 'disaster' of change. Lawrence is quite unconcerned with the feelings he himself had experienced about his parents. He desires myth and symbol.

VIII

In 1922, Rebecca West had met Lawrence in Florence, and was both shocked and amused to find him typing an article on the state of the town the very day he arrived. Later, she changed her mind about what he was doing:

> I know now that he was writing about the state of his own soul at that moment, which, since our self-consciousness is incomplete, and since in consequence our vocabulary is also incomplete, he could render only in symbolic terms; and the city of Florence was as good a symbol as any other. If he was foolish in taking the material universe and making allegations about it which were only true of the universe within his own soul, then Rimbaud was a great fool also. (Nehls, II, p. 66)

The point is well worth making, and it would be strange if, in his autobiographical pieces, Lawrence had adopted a naturalistic mode when it is clear from the rest of his writing that such a mode did not interest him. But we can still ask what it was about his final years that made Lawrence make such extraordinary symbols out of his own family.

IX

Lawrence's writing of the middle 1920s, when it is concerned with

England (as in the 'Nightmare' chapter of *Kangaroo*), is dismissive, angrily and fundamentally. But it is also clear that, the longer Lawrence spent away from England, and the more he hated it, the more he also experienced a deep sense of loneliness. He began to express this in 'Return to Bestwood' in 1926, and it reaches its conclusion in 'Myself Revealed': 'I don't feel there is any very cordial or fundamental contract between me and society, or me and other people. There is a breach' (*Phoenix II*, pp. 594–5). Seeing the colliers of the Erewash valley in 1926 – and with that residual feeling of guilt towards his father – he was encouraged to think of them as 'in some peculiar way, "home" to me' (*Phoenix II*, p. 264): a particularly poignant sensation, since he could no longer live in England himself, for reasons of health. His extraordinary and rather desperate patriotism, the feeling he had had since at least 1915 that 'I am English, and my Englishness is my very vision' (*Letters*, II, p. 414), seems to have worked with his isolation to encourage him in the formation of a new (and for him, final) myth about his English origins. In *The First Lady Chatterley* he created Parkin, his first totally working-class hero; his sense of loyalty to 'my working people' (*Phoenix II*, p. 595) was a preliminary way of trying to say in what way England was 'home'. But he would not be a great writer if he had not begun to subvert his own myth, after creating it. By the third *Lady Chatterley* novel, of 1927–8, Mellors is no longer purely working-class; and in 'Myself Revealed', Lawrence rejected the very security of belonging to the working class. For all his sympathy with them, he cannot live with them: they are 'narrow in outlook, in prejudice, and narrow in intelligence. This again makes a prison' (*Phoenix II*, p. 595). It may not be the voice of Mrs Morel; at least it is not simply Paul Morel. But rejecting the working class does not solve the problem of his own attachments. 'Myself Revealed' finds its solution in a theory of 'blood-affinity' which he *can* share with people, working-class or not; but it is only a theory. A man as desperately ill as was Lawrence, by 1928, not surprisingly could find no solution to the problem of his loneliness; and we must not underestimate the effect of his own illness upon his creation of warm, vital and vigorous Englishmen. But we should view these last autobiographical pieces as extraordinary and rather despairing recreations of a symbolic 'home' rather than as trustworthy records of the past; and my final concern is with the very nature of autobiography.

X

Autobiographical fiction, like all fiction, clearly exists as something *made*; it does not deal with truths, or facts, or conclusions, but is itself a construct; it cannot be taken off the shelf, ready-made, by an author in need. But at least some non-fictional autobiography exists in exactly the same way, so that in it we no more hear the indisputable voice of its author than we do in a work of fiction. When we read an autobiographical piece by Lawrence, even one entitled 'Myself Revealed', the only voice of Lawrence that we hear is a created voice; all voices are constructs, all autobiographies (to put it another way) are fictions. An autobiography by Lawrence makes something of the facts in the same way as does fiction drawing upon real life.

When Lawrence rewrote the history of his own early life around the figure of Paul Morel, and made Paul's life in some ways so unlike his own, he was in a way recognising that there was no 'truth' to be told about his early life, but that there was some inner problem to be investigated. Just as an intelligent critic might point out that *Sons and Lovers* is organised around the damage done to Paul by his mother's emotional life, so (for Lawrence) a Paul not particularly interested in books and with no conception of a career is rather more suitable for such an investigation than is a Paul with ambitions to be a teacher, who goes to university and becomes an author. Such a Paul suggests a much more independent figure – one capable of evolving his own life; and if Lawrence himself (in spite of his successful career) did not feel that he was such a person, we can see the attraction for him of a fictional creation in which the 'damage' done to Paul affects only his love life; Lawrence himself may have felt much more deeply undermined.

So though we cannot read Lawrence's autobiographies as if they told the true story of his life, we are able to turn to the *creating* which they involve: to the selection and alteration lying beneath the construct. And since he created a number of autobiographical accounts of his life, we are enabled to see him as a man conscious of 'my life as moving on phase by phase' (*Letters*, I, p. 239), as he put it in 1911. His work tells us about his life not because it is the kind of extended (though unwitting) commentary upon it of the kind suggested by Middleton Murry, but because it continually visits and revisits the areas of his experience which most deeply concerned him; it regularly revisits the buried life. Carl Baron has rightly suggested that all Lawrence's novels explore 'the same fundamental material as *The White Peacock*', and that 'in essence all Lawrence's main problems were present before he ever put pen to paper' (Neville, p. 2). We need not assume that Lawrence's fiction is primarily a function of his psychological make-up in order to accept that there are mysterious subterranean connections between the novels. If *Sons and Lovers* investigates emotional damage, loveless marriage and an upbringing distorted by love and hate, then it is true that identical problems had already appeared, much more naively and in some ways more revealingly, in *The White Peacock*. The latter is in no sense a conventionally autobiographical novel, but there are ways in which it is as revealing as any of Lawrence's autobiographical writings about his deepest early concerns. One of Lawrence's greatest achievements as a writer is in continually making articulate what in most people is never known, let alone admitted. He wrote in 1923 how 'we can only go forward step by step through realisation, full, bitter, conscious realisation' (*Phoenix II*, p. 358). He can make such realisations possible for others even when he himself is not fully conscious of them; that, however, was one of the powers he ascribed to his 'demon' – 'to say things I would much rather not have said: for choice' (*Poems*, p. 849).

NOTES

* The following abbreviations are used in the text and indicate the edition cited:

Letters   *The Letters of D. H. Lawrence*, ed. James T. Boulton, 7 vols (Cambridge University Press, 1979–).

Nehls   *D. H. Lawrence: a Composite Biography*, ed. Edward Nehls, 3 vols (Madison: University of Wisonsin Press, 1957–9).

Neville   George H. Neville, *A Memoir of D. H. Lawrence*, ed. C. Baron (Cambridge University Press, 1981).

Phoenix   *Phoenix*, ed. Edward D. McDonald (London: William Heinemann, 1936).

Phoenix II *Phoenix II*, ed. Warren Roberts and Harry T. Moore (London, 1968).

Poems   *The Complete Poems of D. H. Lawrence*, ed. V. de S. Pinto and W. Roberts, 2 vols (London, 2nd edn, 1967).

SL   D. H. Lawrence, *Sons and Lovers* (London, 1913).

Some cited letters have not yet been included in the Cambridge Edition, and these are identified by date only.

1. *D. H. Lawrence: the Critical Heritage*, ed. R. P. Draper (London, 1969) p. 63.
2. J. M. Murry, *Son of Woman* (London, 1931) p. 21.
3. *Critical Heritage*, ed. Draper, p. 362.
4. E. T. [Jessie Chambers], *D. H. Lawrence: a Personal Record* (London, 1935) p. 190.
5. Holograph MS, University of California at Berkeley, Roberts–Vasey E392a.
6. For example, Nehls, I, pp. 114–15, 136–7, 271; II, pp. 268, 411–12, 417–18; III, pp. 22–3, 37, 130–2, 216–17, 245, 266, 276.
7. The piece included in *Phoenix* as 'Autobiographical Fragment' by E. D. McDonald was written in October–November 1927 for Lawrence's friend S. S. Koteliansky, who planned an 'Intimate Series' of books in which established authors would reveal intimate things about themselves. The series failed to materialise; McDonald gave the piece its title in 1936.
8. Holograph MS, University of Cincinatti, Roberts–Vasey E144.
9. Holograph MS, University of Texas, Roberts–Vasey E373d.
10. *The Complete Plays of D. H. Lawrence* (London, 1965) p. 522.

2

'The country of my heart': D. H. Lawrence and the East Midlands Landscape

J. R. WATSON

Landscape, however, is different. Here the English exist and hold their own. But, for me, personally, landscape is always waiting for something to occupy it. Landscape seems to be *meant* as a background to an intenser vision of life, so to my feeling painted landscape is background with the real subject left out.[1]

Lawrence is writing of pictorial art, in the Introduction to the Mandrake Press Edition of his paintings written in 1929. He has been criticising the lack of imaginative consciousness in English painting, the denial of the instincts and the intuition; landscape becomes something in which the English have always delighted, because 'it is a form of escape for them, from the actual human body they so hate and fear':

Landscape is background with the figures left out or reduced to a minimum, so let it stay back. Van Gogh's surging earth and Cézanne's explosive or rattling planes worry me. Not being profoundly interested in landscape, I prefer it to be rather quiet and unexplosive.[2]

Lawrence – as so often – is writing dogmatically, piquantly, with the considered breadth of his argument sacrificed to the stabbing, hard-punctuated sentences of the polemicist. And, as so often happens in these essays, the description of his own views has had to be simplified, so that it is in a way very characteristic of Lawrence, both true and not true (see his admission of 'impressionism and dogmatism' in a letter of 1909: 'Suddenly, in a world full of tones and tints and shadows I see a colour and it vibrates on my retina. I dip a brush in it and say, "See, *that's* the colour!" So it is, so it isn't').[3] His theoretical writings abound in such is/is not moments: the summary cuts down the reality to a size which is manageable, and in so doing loses what is found in the novels, the dense and complex relationship between the whole person, body, mind and spirit, and the external world – that relationship of 'an infinite complexity' which Wordsworth talked of in the Preface to *Lyrical Ballads*. So when Lawrence writes of landscape as 'background with the real subject left out' and of himself as 'not being profoundly interested in landscape', we must understand this as true in a certain sense only: in that he is more interested in the 'real subject', in the relationship between nature and man. We must trust the tale, not the artist, and see what happens to landscape in Lawrence's novels; and when we do so, we must interpret his remarks about landscape in the context of a wider and more generous understanding. They become part of a declaration of wholeness, in which landscape and nature become part of a certain sensitivity, what Lawrence himself called 'real intuitional awareness and solid instinctive feeling'.[4] This total apprehension of the external world becomes much more than an acquaintance with surroundings: it includes a creative interaction between the internal and external world which is a total experience, involving mind, body and accumulated understanding. In this process, the great enemy is division, some kind of mechanical pigeon-holing: landscape seen and not felt or understood, is the result of man functioning with the eyes only, like tourists ('poor English and Americans', Lawrence called them) in front of the Botticelli Venus:

> They stare so hard; they do so *want* to see. And their eyesight is perfect. But all they can see is a sort of nude woman on a sort of shell on a sort of pretty greenish water.[5]

In the same way the mind can become separated from a total intuitive awareness: 'The very statement that water is H_2O is a mental *tour de force*. With our bodies we know that water is *not* H_2O, our intuitions and instincts both know it is not so. But they are bullied by the impudent mind.'[6] So when Lawrence says that he is not profoundly interested in landscape, he is speaking of land-scape, country shaped to be seen by the eye, and he is asserting the primacy of something more important than the experience of the bodily eye (as did Wordsworth and Coleridge before him). We can have some inkling of what this was in the letter to Rolf Gardiner, written from exile in Florence in December 1926. It is too long to quote in full, but it celebrates the places of Lawrence's youth – Hucknall, Newstead Abbey, Watnall and above all Eastwood:

> Go to Walker St – and stand in front of the third house – and look across at Crich on the left, Underwood in front – High Park woods and Annesley on the right: I lived in that house from the age of 6 to 18, and I know that view better than any in the world. Then walk down the fields to the Breach, and in the corner house facing the stile I lived from 1 to 6. And walk up Engine Lane, over the level-crossing at Moorgreen pit, along till you come to the highway (the Alfreton Rd.) – turn to the left, towards Underwood, and go till you come to the lodge gate by the reservoir – go through the gate, and up the drive to the next gate, and continue on the *footpath* just below the drive on the left – on through the wood to Felley Mill (the *White Peacock* farm). When you've crossed the brook, turn to the right through Felley Mill gate, and go up the footpath to Annesley. Or better still, turn to the right, uphill, *before* you descend to the brook, and go on uphill, up the rough deserted pasture – on past Annesley Kennels – long empty – on to Annesley again. That's the country of my heart.[7]

In his mind's eye, Lawrence can see it all: it goes back to a time before Florence, and New Mexico, and Australia, and London, before all those layers of experience were superimposed on the Bert Lawrence of Eastwood. The letter goes on to describe walk after walk, a criss-crossing of paths which are also the paths of memory and love. For Lawrence, the great traveller, this is the country of the heart – not the country of the eye – and it is curiously, quintessentially English: 'it's real England,' he wrote, 'the hard pith of England'.[8] He was torn apart by his memories of this England and the one which he found during his visit to Derbyshire earlier in 1926: 'I was at my sister's in September, and we drove round – I saw the miners – and pickets – and policemen – it was like a spear through one's heart. I tell you, we'd better buck up and do something for the England to come, for they've pushed the spear through the side of *my* England.'[9]

'*My* England': the possessive goes deep, down into the deepest self. 'Men are only free when they are doing what the deepest self likes', and to get down to it 'takes some diving';[10] in the essay from which this comes, 'The Spirit of Place', Lawrence connects this deep freedom with a sense of homeland and community:

> Men are free when they are in a living homeland, not when they are straying and breaking away. . . . Men are free when they belong to a living, organic, *believing* community, active in fulfilling some unfulfilled, perhaps unrealised purpose. Not when they are escaping to some wild west. The most unfree souls go west, and shout of freedom.[11]

He returns to the landscape of the heart in one of his last and most attractive essays, 'Nottingham and the Mining Countryside', written in 1929 and published after his death. It describes the landscape with feeling and an almost uncanny accuracy, catching its complexity – the strange mixture of the old and the new, the beautiful and the ugly – and stamping upon it the impress of his own emotion. It is full, too, of a lament for what is happening in 1929; but it also looks back in love to the unique 'feel' of the place as he had known it as a child and a young man:

> It is hilly country, looking west to Crich and towards Matlock, sixteen miles away, and east and north-east towards Mansfield and the Sherwood Forest district. To me it seemed, and still seems, an extremely beautiful countryside, just between the red sandstone and the oak-trees of Nottingham, and the cold limestone, the ash-trees, the stone fences of Derbyshire. To me, as a child and a young man, it was still the old England of the forest and agricultural past; there were no motor-cars, the mines were, in a sense, an accident in the landscape, and Robin Hood and his merry men were not very far away.[12]

Then came the big mines, the miners' dwellings, the churches and chapels, 'so that life was a curious cross between industrialism and the old agricultural England of Shakespeare and Milton and Fielding and George Eliot'.[13] The essay, which goes on to talk about the real tragedy of England as 'the tragedy of ugliness',[14] is a wonderful example of Lawrence's quicksilver darting intelligence at work on a known and familiar scene, showing the landscape

not only as it is but how it came to be so, in order that the reader
may understand it more fully. For Lawrence himself it was a kind
of possession, *his* England, the East Midlands, the hard pith of
England, a possession in description. Jessie Chambers described
this in *D. H. Lawrence, a Personal Record*, remembering a trip to
Skegness with Lawrence pointing out the features on either side:
'It was more than merely *seeing* those landmarks; it was a kind of
immediate possession, as though to have missed seeing them
would have been to lose an essential moment of life.'[15]

It is with this apprehension of the East Midlands landscape in
mind that I wish to examine briefly the settings of some of
Lawrence's early novels, beginning with *The White Peacock*. Jessie
Chambers described the young Bert Lawrence's way of infusing
everything around him with his own vitality and charm, and this
is evident on almost every page of the novel. It has been called
'callow' by some critics,[16] but the other side of this callowness is a
lovely openness to the world around, especially to the
Nottinghamshire–Derbyshire landscape in different seasons. It is
a kind of openness which (as Roger Ebbatson has shown)[17] comes
down from Richard Jefferies, but which represented something
very important for Lawrence at the time. Although he tried to
laugh off the book's excesses ('all about love – and rhapsodies on
Spring scattered here and there – heroines galore – no plot – nine-
tenths adjectives – every colour in the spectrum descanted upon –
a poem or two – scraps of Latin and French – altogether a sloppy,
spicy mess'),[18] Lawrence was undoubtedly struggling to express
something about the world around him, and wanting to say
something through the description of that world. Of the second
version of the novel he told Jessie Chambers: 'Everything that I
am now, all of me, so far, is in that.'[19]

What is this 'everything'? Criticism of *The White Peacock*, with
the hindsight of an acquaintance with Lawrence's later work, has
fastened on the gamekeeper Annable as a significant point in the
novel. But Annable's role is nugatory in comparison with the
descriptions of nature and place in the novel. Lawrence is
producing his 'sloppy, spicy mess' with its rhapsodies on spring,
because that is what concerns him as it relates to the characters
(Annable included). The main plot of Lettie, George, Leslie and
Meg, with Cyril and Emily as onlookers, is worked out against a
natural background which is both visual and symbolic. Robert E.
Gajdusek, in his strong defence of *The White Peacock*,[20] has

explored the symbolism of the natural things – the lake, the birds, the rabbits, the peacock itself: he argues that the novel is concerned with the making of a new religion, an earth-related pagan revitalisation of a Christian idealism. If this is the case – and Gajdusek can point to an intricate scaffolding of image and symbol – then Lettie and George both fail in different ways. Lettie becomes a dominating, refined woman, while George becomes stupid and feeble through drink. (Gajdusek's theory that he achieves a sort of Pyrrhic victory seems, to me, too consoling.) At the end of the novel, he appears to Cyril 'like a tree that is falling, going soft and pale and rotten, clammy with small fungi' (p. 494). The lovely September afternoon cannot affect him, and there is a poignant contrast between his decay and the healthiness of Tom and Arthur:

> Tom climbed the ladder and stood a moment there against the sky, amid the brightness and fragrance of the gold corn, and waved his arm to his wife who was passing in the shadow of the building. Then Arthur began to lift the sheaves to the stack, and the two men worked in an exquisite, subtle rhythm, their white sleeves and their dark heads gleaming, moving against the mild sky and the corn. (pp. 494–5)

This final scene contains echoes of the lovely passage earlier in the novel in which Cyril breaks off the narrative in order to describe September (the fact that the narrative can be so interrupted is itself significant). It is appropriate that this should come immediately after the conversation between George's father and the squire, punctuated with whisky, in which they discuss the problem of the rabbits. The rabbits make farming impossible: they destroy the corn and ruin the grass, and the squire, who sells dead rabbits at a shilling each in Nottingham, is unwilling to do anything about it. Then comes:

> I was born in September, and love it best of all the months. There is no heat, no hurry, no thirst and weariness in corn harvest as there is in the hay. If the season is late, as is usual with us, then mid-September sees the corn still standing in stook. The mornings come slowly. The earth is like a woman married and fading; she does not leap up with a laugh for the first fresh kiss of dawn, but slowly, quietly, unexpectedly lies

watching the waking of each new day. The blue mist, like
memory in the eyes of a neglected wife, never goes from the
wooded hill, and only at noon creeps from the near hedges.
. . .
   Afternoon is all warm and golden. Oat sheaves are lighter;
they whisper to each other as they freely embrace. The long
stout stubble tinkles as the foot brushes over it; the scent of the
straw is sweet. When the poor, bleached sheaves are lifted out
of the hedge, a spray of nodding wild raspberries is disclosed,
with belated berries ready to drop; among the damp grass lush
blackberries may be discovered. Then one notices that the last
bell hangs from the ragged spire of fox-glove.   (pp. 89–91)

The sense of work, companionship, and hope, are all strong at this
point; and Cyril here, as elsewhere, is a figure who throughout
the novel is aware of the circumambient universe in a way that
makes him the eyes and ears for all the other characters. The word
'circumambient' is, of course, Wordsworth's, but it is Lawrence's
too:

Man's life consists in a connection with all things in the
universe. Whoever can establish, or initiate, a new connection
between mankind and the circumambient universe is, in his
own degree, a saviour. Because mankind is always exhausting
its human possibilities, always degenerating into repetition,
torpor, *ennui*, lifelessness. When *ennui* sets in, it is a sign that
human vitality is waning, and the human connection with the
universe is gone stale.[21]

Cyril's position here as the chief mediator between man and the
external world is one of the minor difficulties of *The White Peacock*:
the narration is interrupted to allow for his description, which
then has to be held in the memory as a background to the action.
It is springtime, for instance, when the gamekeeper is buried:

Ah, but the thrush is scornful, ringing out his voice from the
hedge! He sets his breast against the mud, and models it warm
for the turquoise eggs – blue, blue, bluest of eggs, which cluster
so close and round against the breast, which round up beneath
the breast, nestling content. You should see the bright ecstasy
in the eyes of a nesting thrush, because of the rounded caress
of the eggs against her breast!

What a hurry the jenny wren makes – hoping I shall not see her dart into the low bush. I have a delight in watching them against their shy little wills. But they have all risen with a rush of wings, and are gone, the birds. The air is brushed with agitation. There is no lark in the sky, not one; the heaven is clear of wings or twinkling dot.

Till the heralds come – till the heralds wave like shadows in the bright air, crying, lamenting, fretting forever. Rising and falling and circling round and round, the slow-waving peewits cry and complain, and lift their broad wings in sorrow. They stoop suddenly to the ground, the lapwings, then in another throb of anguish and protest, they swing up again, offering a glistening white breast to the sunlight, to deny it in black shadow, then a glisten of green, and all the time crying and crying in despair.   (p. 238)

Such natural life forms an important presence in the novel, affecting all the characters: they have a relationship with the weather, with the natural life, with the seen landscape, with beauty and casual destruction. A wild dog savages sheep, and is killed; a baby chick walks into the fire and is burned: such episodes suggest a certain natural indifference to joy and sorrow, a persistence of place alongside the coming and going of the people of Nethermere (the title of the first chapter). Leslie and Lettie marry and have children, and George drinks himself into helplessness after his marriage to Meg. Only Cyril seems to escape from the enclosing grasp of family life: Lettie becomes preoccupied with the baby, Meg with her children and her drunken husband, Alice with Percival Charles. The natural world continues, like some more benevolent Egdon Heath: *The White Peacock* lacks the dark centre of Hardy's novel, but in many ways the landscape performs a similar function. As Lawrence was to write in his 'Study of Thomas Hardy':

What matters if some are drowned or dead, and others preaching or married: what matter, any more than the withering heath, the reddening berries, the seedy furze, and the dead fern of one autumn of Egdon? The Heath persists.[22]

In *The White Peacock*, Cyril plays the part of the returning native, coming back, like Clym, from France. Sitting in the train on the way to Charing Cross, he watches the evening sun glitter on the stubble of the cornfields, and remembers that it is George's birthday. George is no St George – in fact the name may be an ironic contrast, and George's socialist phase an impudent sideswipe at Ruskin's Guild of St George – but Cyril's departures and returns emphasise the Englishness of the place and of the novel. George, who is considering emigration, says 'you feel somebody in your own countryside, and you're nothing in a foreign part, I expect' (p. 99). Cyril offers a different perspective on the valley when he leaves and becomes alienated from it:

> Nethermere was no longer a complete, wonderful little world that held us charmed inhabitants. It was a small, insignificant valley lost in the spaces of the earth. The tree that had drooped over the brook with such delightful, romantic grace was a ridiculous thing when I came home after a year of absence in the south. The old symbols were trite and foolish.   (p. 406)

So Cyril becomes a *spectator ab extra*, watching Tom and Arthur instead of working with George in the field as he did earlier. And one of the most powerful forces in *The White Peacock* is time. ('The long voyage in the quiet home was over; we had crossed the bright sea of our youth . . . It was time for us all to go, to leave the valley of Nethermere whose waters and whose woods were distilled in the essence of our veins'; p. 361.) The 'children of the valley', as they are called (p. 361), have to grow up and leave: 'growing up' and 'leaving' become two sides of the same process. Childhood and youth must be left behind, and all that remains is a view of the landscape in which Cyril is no longer a participator and which the others have lost in different ways. The final chapter is entitled 'A Prospect among the Marshes of Lethe', a title which underlines the poignancy of the change – not just for Cyril and George, but for them all.

So *The White Peacock*, which is so intricately constructed (as Gajdusek has shown), is also a novel with a dewy-fresh awareness of something fragile and precious, the love which men and women have for each other in youth, and the feeling which they have for the landscape which is the setting for that love and becomes inextricably connected with it. Men and women, seasons and weather, land and sky, become indistinguishably part of a single world; and critics who dismiss the novel are, I believe, ignoring its ability to render the process of maturity as involving both loss and gain.

The authentic representation of adolescent experience is poignant and vital; for Cyril, the exile, is a forecast of Lawrence's own progress, that wandering over the earth in search of a sky that was not so old, and air that was newer, an earth that was not so tired.[23] Again and again he returned to the East Midlands, sometimes imaginatively in his novels, sometimes in the flesh. His actual visits aroused powerfully mixed feelings. No doubt he had changed, but so had the places of his youth:

> The old sheep-bridge where I used to swing as a boy is now an iron affair. The brook where we caught minnows now runs on a concrete bed. The old sheep-dip, the dipping-hole, as we called it, where we bathed, has somehow disappeared, so has the mill-dam and the little water-fall. It's all a concrete arrangement now, like a sewer. And the people's lives are the same, all running on concrete channels like a vast cloaca.[24]

In *The White Peacock*, the characters change and the landscape remains; at other times, Lawrence is deeply conscious that an industrial–agricultural landscape is continually changing. *Sons and Lovers* and *The Rainbow* are both concerned with this, in different ways. *Sons and Lovers* begins with a description of Bestwood, and of the way in which the little mines, or gin-pits, which had been worked since the seventeenth century, were succeeded in the Victorian period by large concerns. With the big mines came the railway, the blocks of houses, the pit-heads set among the cornfields. The present is superimposed on the past, the buildings are put down on the natural landscape:

> Carston, Waite and Co found they had struck on a good thing, so, down the valleys of the brooks from Selby and Nuttall, new mines were sunk, until soon there were six pits working. From Nuttall, high up on the sandstone among the woods, the railway ran, past the ruined priory of the Carthusians and past Robin Hood's Well, down to Spinney Park, then on to Minton, a large mine among corn-fields; from Minton across the farm-lands of the valleyside to Bunker's Hill, branching off there, and running north to Beggarlee and Selby, that looks over Crich

and the hills of Derbyshire; six mines like black studs on the countryside, linked by a loop of fine chain, the railway.

(pp. 35–6)

The landscape is here something which is known and familiar (the place names are important here) and, above all, understood: we discover how the present landscape came to be as it is, what changes lay behind it, what its history was. Even today, the landscape of the Nottinghamshire–Derbyshire border is the same kind of broken semi-industrial scene, with buildings interspersed with field and farmland. It contains within itself, as Lawrence saw so clearly, the central change of modern England, the movement from agrarian openness and small-scale cottage industry to a fully industrialised environment. The landscape is thus the setting, as it was in *The White Peacock*, but it is no longer a landscape to be loved and left, but a landscape to be lived with, to be explored and rediscovered, above all to be felt – not as a place to be loved so much as an ever-present force, part of the accumulation of experience which is the miraculous achievement of *Sons and Lovers*: that sense of a family's life, how it came to be as it is, how it develops and changes, and of a child's life, for Paul and Miriam especially, growing into some kind of maturity.

The landscape is *there*, in the East Midlands, *then*, at the end of the nineteenth century; and Paul finds himself responding to everything – the flowers, the fields, the pit – as it is in this particular place and at that time. And as this landscape reflects the central tension between the older countryside and modern industrialisation, so Paul's upbringing encompasses both his father's primitivism and his mother's aspirations. The novel is central, not only to Lawrence's own consciousness, but to his perception of what England was – in the middle of England, 'the quintessentially English Midlands – and Paul Morel, as Lawrence himself recognised (in his letter to Edward Garnett),[25] is a central English figure. The landscape and the life in it are one, and it is significant that in 'Nottingham and the Mining Countryside' Lawrence expresses this unity by the word 'life': 'the life was a curious cross between industrialism and the old agricultural England'.[26] To Paul, the landscape is his experience: the pit which seems alive, the church at Alfreton filled with flowers on the Bank Holiday walk, the gardens, the farm. As a painter, he sees the landscape with a painter's eye, and in Lincolnshire talks to Miriam about his love for horizontals:

> how they, the great levels of sky and land in Lincolnshire, meant to him the eternality of the will, just as the bowed Norman arches of the church, repeating themselves, meant the dogged leaping forward of the persistent human soul, on and on, nobody knows where; in contradiction to the perpendicular lines and to the Gothic arch, which, he said, leapt up at heaven and touched the ecstasy and lost itself in the divine. Himself, he said, was Norman, Miriam was Gothic.   (p. 229)

The comparison is adolescent and artificial. Later in the novel, Paul moves beyond this kind of experience on the second visit to Lincolnshire with Clara as they swim in the sea at daybreak; and his love-making with Clara is linked with elemental forces, the emotion 'strong enough to carry with it everything' –

> reason, soul, blood – in a great sweep, like the Trent carries bodily its back-swirls and intertwinings, noiselessly. Gradually the little criticisms, the little sensations, were lost, thought also went, everything borne along in one flood. He became, not a man with a mind, but a great instinct. . . . Just as he was, so it seemed the vigorous, wintry stars were strong also with life.   (pp. 431–2)

The river, the stars, flowers, fields, all these are part of Paul's experience, and of that of the other characters in *Sons and Lovers*. For them landscape is life, inextricably bound up with parenthood, with love, with the growth of the mind and the understanding. *The Rainbow* is different. It begins with landscape, with what is perhaps the most famous piece of descriptive writing in the whole of Lawrence's work. After it, we are told of the history of the place, the building of the canal in 1840, the coming of the railway, the opening up of the big mines, and the Marsh Farm itself, something left over from before the industrial revolution:

> Still the Marsh remained remote and original, on the old, quiet side of the canal embankment, in the sunny valley where slow water wound along in company of stiff alders, and the road went under ash-trees past the Brangwens' garden gate.
> But, looking from the garden gate down the road to the right,

there, through the dark archway of the canal's square aqueduct, was a colliery spinning away in the near distance, and further, red, crude houses plastered on the valley in masses, and beyond all, the dim smoking hill of the town.   (p. 46)

All this sounds somewhat similar to the landscape of *Sons and Lovers*, as indeed it is. But the important thing to notice is that this is the opening part of the *second* section of Chapter 1. It comes after the description of the Brangwens living for generations on the Marsh Farm. feeling the soil in their blood and bones, listening for the seasons, looking up from their work to see the church tower at Ilkeston. Before we learn the history of the place, therefore, Lawrence is describing the powerful primitive relationship between man and the land, as experienced by generations of Brangwens in that spot. It is the prelude to a novel in which the landscape does what it does in *Sons and Lovers*, and much more: not only is it *there*, landscape as life, but it is set against the pattern of individual lives, landscape as power. It is the force of the landscape, accumulated over centuries, that pulses in the blood of Tom, Anna and Ursula, making them what they are: they are shaped and possessed by a power greater than themselves, shown in Tom's need to marry a Polish lady and engage the blood of the Brangwens with something foreign; in Anna's dancing before the fire; and in Ursula's particular kind of authenticity, which causes her to reject incomplete solutions, relationships with Winifred, or Skrebensky, or schoolteaching, or college life. It is this power which is manifested in certain celebrated moments of the novel, as when Tom takes the child Anna to see the cows feeding, or Will and Anna gather the sheaves of corn, or Ursula destroys Skrebensky on the sands. It is this power, too, which lies behind the final vision of the novel: for the only conclusion which will satisfy Ursula is one in which the place, that place where the Brangwens have lived for centuries, is transfigured. She gropes 'to find the creation of the living God' (p. 547), and sees the rainbow standing on the earth, the covenant of God with man made manifest in the East Midlands. Nothing less will do, for Ursula feels the pull of something stronger than any of the human relationships in the book – the blood of the Brangwens and the blood-tie to place and to the earth.

In the space available, I can say only a few words about *Women in Love*. If landscape is life in *Sons and Lovers*, and landscape is power in *The Rainbow*, landscape in *Women in Love* becomes a part of the great unexplained other, that world which is not ourselves: it becomes less important as landscape, and less concerned with the past becoming present. The main characters relate to the world around them in ways which make them seem unimportant, and yet they are foregrounded in ways which make them seem profoundly representative of the age in which they live. It is as though their consciousness, their awareness of being particular men and women in a particular place at a particular time, is vitally present in the novel but also held within a greater world. Lawrence described it best himself, in the 'Study of Thomas Hardy':

> Upon the vast, incomprehensible pattern of some primal morality greater than ever the human mind can grasp, is drawn the little, pathetic pattern of man's moral life and struggle, pathetic, almost ridiculous. The little fold of law and order, the little walled city within which man has to defend himself from the waste enormity of nature, becomes always too small, and the pioneers venturing out with the code of the walled city upon them, die in the bonds of that code, free and yet unfree, preaching the walled city and looking to the waste.[27]

In *Women in Love*, the major characters are free and yet unfree: free to marry and cast off, free to force a horse to stand by a level crossing when a train goes by. Yet they are unfree, too: Gudrun dancing before the cows, Birkin throwing stones into the water to shatter the image of the moon, Gerald walking out into the snow – each of them is insignificant against 'the vast, unexplored morality of life itself':

> what we call the immorality of nature, surrounds us in its eternal incomprehensibility, and in its midst goes on the little human morality play, with its queer frame of morality and its mechanised movement; seriously, portentously, till some one of the protagonists chances to look out of the charmed circle, weary of the stage, to look into the wilderness raging around.[28]

So the landscape of *Women in Love* is a crucial element of the novel. It is not described in set pieces, but it is always present: in the Crichs' home, Shortlands, at Breadalby 'standing among the softer, greener hills of Derbyshire', in the forest, on the train journey to Innsbruck. It can be terrible and destructive, as it is at the water-party; it can be beautiful and deadly, as it is in the Alps. It is always *there* in the novel, outside and beyond the characters, unfathomable and wonderful, providing another perspective against which we must view human life 'as we live it in our self-aggrandised gravity'.[29]

In his relationship with the circumambient universe, a character such as Birkin is the fullest example of a feeling for natural landscape which began with Cyril in *The White Peacock*. It is humbling for us to contemplate his particular kind of self-aggrandised gravity: and beyond him we recognise a greater, more inexplicable world. As Lawrence said of Hardy,

> this is the quality Hardy shares with the great writers, Shakespeare or Sophocles or Tolstoi, this setting behind the small action of his protagonists the terrific action of unfathomed nature; setting a smaller system of morality, the one grasped and formulated by the human consciousness within the vast, uncomprehended and incomprehensible morality of nature or of life itself, surpassing human consciousness.[30]

The incomprehensible morality of life itself is Lawrence's object to record: it is in this light that landscape becomes 'background with the real subject left out'. Like man's morality and human systems, it is limited, circumscribed; yet so it is, so it is not – it is also part of the way in which Lawrence's novels so vividly recover for the reader those inarticulate gestures which we all have towards the other, to that which is greater than ourselves. Beginning in the East Midlands, the middle of England, Lawrence steadily forces us to see the landscape, and in our seeing to become aware of the nature of mankind in all its greatness and all its absurdity.

NOTES

1. 'Introduction to These Paintings', in *Phoenix*, ed. Edward D. McDonald (London, 1936) p. 561.
2. Ibid.
3. *The Letters of D. H. Lawrence*, ed. James T. Boulton (Cambridge, 1979) I, p. 129.
4. *Phoenix*, ed. McDonald, p. 560.

5. Ibid., p. 557.
6. Ibid., p. 574.
7. *The Collected Letters of D. H. Lawrence*, ed. Harry T. Moore (London, 1962) II, p. 952.
8. Ibid., p. 953.
9. Ibid., p. 952.
10. D. H. Lawrence, *Selected Literary Criticism*, ed. Anthony Beal (London, 1956) p. 301.
11. Ibid., p. 301.
12. *Phoenix*, ed. McDonald, p. 133.
13. Ibid., p. 135.
14. Ibid., p. 137.
15. E. T. [Jessie Chambers], *D. H. Lawrence, a Personal Record* (Cambridge, 1980) pp. 38–9.
16. F. R. Leavis describes *The White Peacock* as 'painfully callow' (*D. H. Lawrence: Novelist*, p. 19) and Keith Sagar calls the early novels 'callow and conventional' (*The Art of D. H. Lawrence* (Cambridge, 1966) p. 19).
17. Roger Ebbatson, *Lawrence and the Nature Tradition* (Brighton, 1980).
18. *Letters*, ed. Boulton, I, p. 44.
19. E. T., *Personal Record*, p. 82.
20. Robert E. Gajdusek, 'A Reading of *The White Peacock*' in *A D. H. Lawrence Miscellany*, ed. Harry T. Moore (Carbondale, Ill., 1959) pp. 188–203.
21. 'Aristocracy', in *Phoenix II*, ed. Warren Roberts and Harry T. Moore (London, 1968) p. 478.
22. *Phoenix*, ed. McDonald, p. 415.
23. *Letters*, ed. Moore, II, p. 481.
24. *Phoenix*, ed. McDonald, p. 822. It is probable that Lawrence is remembering Ruskin's description of Carshalton pools in the opening pages of *The Crown of Wild Olive*; Lawrence would have known the spot from his days at Croydon. See *The Complete Works of John Ruskin*, ed. E. T. Cook and Alexander Wedderburn (London, 1903–12) XVIII, pp. 385–6.
25. *Letters*, ed. Boulton, I, p. 477.
26. *Phoenix*, ed. McDonald, p. 135.
27. Ibid., p. 419.
28. Ibid.
29. Ibid.
30. Ibid. For other treatments of this subject, see Claude M. Sinzelle, *The Geographical Background of the Early Works of D. H. Lawrence* (Paris, 1964), and Ian G. Cook, 'Consciousness and the Novel: Fact or Fiction in the Works of D. H. Lawrence', in *Humanistic Geography and Literature*, ed. Douglas C. D. Pocock (London, 1981).

3

The Extension of Metaphor to Scene and Action, Chiefly in Lawrence's Early Novels

F. B. PINION

Aristotle asserted in his *Poetics* that command of metaphor constitutes 'the mark of genius' in a writer. It certainly suggests liveliness of interest and of imaginative response. More than any other modern literary form, the novel allows scope for its extension. It would be wrong to claim that the extended metaphor is a characteristic of all great novelists, yet it is found in many writers of fiction. To cite those who readily come to mind, it occurs both inventively and poetically in the more mature Jane Austen; frequently in scenes by Charlotte and Emily Brontë; and both in scene and action in novels by George Eliot and Thomas Hardy. On a small scale it may be seen in those warped trees at Wuthering Heights which denote the winds of hatred and revenge that prevail during the earlier part of Emily Brontë's story. In an action of a chapter's length (most of the threshing-scene at Flintcomb-Ash), it presents with reference to a late crisis in Tess's life nothing less than Hardy's tragic philosophy. To use George Eliot's terms, the view of life which he there expresses is incarnate and aesthetic, an integral part of a scene which is vividly and dramatically realisable in its more restricted, non-metaphysical dimensions.

In George Eliot's fiction, the extended metaphor usually relates to character or human situation. Lawrence also uses it in this more normal artistic mode, but he is most strikingly brilliant in the invention of metaphorical scenes and actions which express his convictions as the priest of love. The metaphor is informed with meaning that gives key images a quasi-symbolic connotation, especially by force of recurrence in variant forms. Such writing is particularly characteristic of that fecund period when creativity of ideas was stimulated by fruition of love with Frieda Weekley and by the novelty of colourful scenes in the Alps and northern Italy. Their fictional effect is to be found in *Sons and Lovers*, *The Rainbow* and *Women in Love*.

Before Lawrence met Frieda, his ideas on love and sexual fulfilment had been repeatedly expressed in metaphorical imagery, in poems as well as in his first two novels, *The White Peacock* and *The Trespasser*. During the period of fecundity already referred to (1912–16), when he wrote poems, plays and version after version of his novels, this expression of his private symbolism was further elaborated and enriched, some of it deriving from Meredith's 'Love in the Valley' in conjunction with the Tennyson lyric which probably supplied its title. 'Come down, O maid, from yonder mountain height' associated not only love with the valley but death with snowy peaks and ravines in the Alps, both correlatives providing, subconsciously perhaps, the seed for those metaphorical scenes which bring *Women in Love* to its climax. Tennyson's accompanying lyric, in the seventh part of *The Princess*, contains the line, 'Now droops the milkwhite peacock like a ghost', which suggested the title of Lawrence's first novel.

Lawrence attributed a devitalising connotation to Tennyson's image, and he gives it definition in two scenes. A peacock flies from the Hall and perches on the neck of a sculptured angel; its screech seems to tear 'the dark sanctuary of twilight', causing primroses and violets to waken and gasp with fear. When Annable frightens it off, he discovers that it has fouled its perch. The neighbouring graveyard and ruined, infested church are redolent of death. In this composite image he sees the life-destroying vanity of the lady he had married; aesthetically he had been like Greek statues to her, but she refused to have children, and became 'souly', accepting him as 'her animal', a degradation to which he submitted for a year before leaving her. The main story of *The White Peacock*, rather like that of *Wuthering Heights*, turns on Lettie's self-betrayal, which makes her marry for social status and reject the man to whom she is naturally drawn. His life is ruined, but she attains a pavonine splendour, in the portrayal of which, one after another, her hand, face, bosom and shoulder are revealed white in moonlight. Here, rather than in the earlier scene (where little imaginative cogency is found in the suggestion that Annable's wife may have been a *white* peacock because she was not altogether culpable), Lawrence's metaphorical description gets under way; the whiteness presents a denial of life. Lettie is another Lady Crystabel or Lady of Shalott, her existence a small indoor one 'with artificial light and padded upholstery. Only occasionally, hearing the winds of life outside, she clamoured to be out in the black, keen storm.'

The moon is a dead satellite reflecting the light of the sun; a white moon for Lawrence represents inhibited or 'spiritual', idealised love, the 'self-aware-of-itself' as opposed to the spontaneous self. Three short poems, 'Aware', 'A Pang of Reminiscence' and 'A White Blossom' (with reference to Jessie Chambers), depict it blanching as it rises to shine, 'the first white love of my youth, passionless and in vain'. In 'Study of Thomas Hardy' Lawrence asks how Jude could 'take with his body the moonlit cold body of a woman who did not live to him, and did not want him'. The heroine of *The Trespasser* is sympathetic to Siegmund, but her responses are passionless. White is the key colour in the scene which introduces her; white moonlight makes Siegmund think of her. His passion is denoted by the burning sun, but it is his destiny to see her ivory face, and the white transport of the sea, as they stand 'folded together, gazing into the white heart of the night'. While he thinks of the separation that must end their brief holiday, the fiery gold of the rising moon is outpoured; he then turns to Helen and finds her face 'white and shining as the empty moon'.

White lilies provide another emblem of passionless love or affection. It is employed rather infelicitously in 'Lilies in the Fire' (a poem written with Helen Corke in mind, as were 'And Jude the Obscure and his Beloved' – a forerunner of 'Passing Visit to Helen' – and *The Trespasser*). The inception of that spiritual bondage which inhibits the post-adolescent love of Paul Morel in *Sons and Lovers* is vividly presented when Mrs Morel is shut outside by her drunken husband, and her dedication to the child within her is externalised in the garden scene. She stands 'as if in an immense gulf of white light, the moon streaming high in face of her'; in her perturbed state, 'seared with passion', she sees the tall white lilies reeling in the moonlight. She puts her hand into one of the pollen bins, drinks a deep draught of the scent, and seems to melt like scent into the air. The child melts with her 'in the mixing-pot of moonlight', and she remains with the lilies and her surroundings, 'all swum together in a kind of swoon'. Metaphorically the passage expresses a fertilisation, the prenatal establishment of the psychic bond between Paul and his mother which outlasts her life.

In *Sons and Lovers* the sex-awareness which was an inhibiting factor in Lawrence's early love for Jessie Chambers (as he makes clear in 'A State of Funk') is translated into the frustrating spirituality of Miriam. The scent of lilies and narcissi among the Easter decorations in Alfreton Church makes her soul glow. She is drawn to Paul; all his latent mysticism quivers into life, and he becomes 'a prayer along with her'. Sex-consciousness fills her with shame; she shrinks from it in 'convulsed, coiled torture'. Here Lawrence alludes to the 'serpent in her Eden'. The Fall did not occur when Adam first 'knew' Eve, but when 'knowledge-poison' entered their consciousness, Lawrence tells us in his essay on *The Scarlet Letter*; 'the mind and the spiritual consciousness of man simply *hates* the dark potency of blood-acts', he continues. Emphasis on blood-consciousness, the dark self as opposed to the light (the mental or spiritual), begins in *Sons and Lovers*. In the darkness of the firs, before Miriam sacrifices herself to him, Paul says, 'I like the darkness. I wish it were thicker – good thick darkness.' Her sacrifice fails, and day for Paul seems a white shadow. 'To be alive . . . was *not-to-be*'; supremely, it was 'to melt out into the darkness and sway there, identified with the great Being', as he felt during his first consummation with Clara Dawes. Fittingly, therefore, the urge which tempts Paul to relinquish Miriam for the physically attractive Clara is imaged in a garden behind which a dusky half-moon sinks behind a dark sycamore. He is drawn to a white row of madonna lilies. They are flagging, but their scent is intoxicating. He then catches another perfume, 'raw and coarse', and finds that it comes from purple irises which stand 'stiff in the darkness' as he touches 'their fleshy throats and their dark, grasping hands'. The physicality of their sexual overtones is as obvious as it is, with reference to Gerald Crich and Gudrun who meet there, in the 'turgid fleshy' water-plants which rise out of the mud by the edge of the lake in *Women in Love*.

'The Spinner and the Monks' (*Twilight in Italy*), which was written about the time when Lawrence was proof-reading *Sons and Lovers*, contains perhaps the most exquisite of his metaphorical scenes, a memorable expressoin of that fullness of love which Paul Morel never attains. After meeting the spinner high above a lake, Lawrence continues his climb in the late afternoon, and sees in the shadow just below him two monks walking backwards and forwards 'with a strange, neutral regularity'. Never looking up, they fail to see the rosy incandescence of a snow-capped ridge beneath the emerging moon. In the 'shadowless light of shadow' they know neither the darkness nor the light. 'Neither the blood nor the spirit spoke in them, only the law, the abstraction of the average.' Repeating the mystical thought of *Sons and Lovers*, Lawrence asserts the oneness of eternal 'not-being' and eternal being, and sees the ecstasy of consummation in the rosy snow shining over a darkened earth. The old spinner does not know 'the yielding up of the senses, which happens under a superb moon'. Lawrence asks where one can find the supreme ecstasy that makes 'single abandon of the single body and soul' an 'ecstasy under the moon':

> Where is the transcendental knowledge in our hearts, uniting sun and darkness, day and night, spirit and senses? Why do we not know that the two in consummation are one; that each is only part; partial and alone for ever; but that the two in consummation are perfect, beyond the range of loneliness or solitude?

This is the kind of ecstasy that the girl Anna enjoys as she responds bodily and spiritually to a large golden moon, which makes her 'drift and ebb like a wave' in the scene where she and Will Brangwen set up the oat sheaves. They work rhythmically for a time, 'in tune' until harder notes enter.[1] These hardening notes are a prelude to the metaphorical flood which the eponymous rainbow presupposes. With the banning of *The Rainbow*, Lawrence found it necessary to repeat his message through new media in *Women in Love*, and so vehemently did the subject move him that he was prepared to change the title of his novel to 'Day of Wrath'. He believed that true love is based on natural responses, following the rhythm of the year and of the universe; forced or exploited, sexual activity is 'reductive' or debilitating. *Twilight in Italy* supplies the key to much of his imagery on the subject. In 'The Lemon Gardens' Aphrodite, born of the sea and 'queen of the senses', is associated with the 'white-cold ecstasy of darkness and moonlight'; 'goddess of destruction, her white, cold fire consumes and does not create'. The imagery of this cold fire scintillates in terms of felinity, phosphorescence and electricity. (In *Fantasia of the Unconscious* we learn that the cold white fire of the moon shows an 'almost malignant apartness', her 'struggle into fierce, frictional separation'.) Sensual gratification becomes the conscious aim of the assertive self, whereas in the ecstasy of genuine love, self is lost in infinity. The main tenor of Lawrence's writing was that no wholeness or sanity was possible in civilisation until right relationships were established between men and women.

The account of Will Brangwen's courtship of Anna contains premonitory hints: his 'catlike' quality and the 'electric state' of his passion are twice referred to; his eyes shine like a bird's, utterly without depth; they have the hard brightness of the hawk's; he is possessive and demanding. In the harvest scene 'his will drummed persistently'; it is seen in his striding as he changes the rhythm of his work and drives Anna to meet him; it is felt in the twanging insistence when he commands her to set her sheaf down first in order that he can embrace her. As he does so, he thinks of her 'All the night in his arms . . . All the night for him'. Suddenly he finds he wants her, but she loosens herself from him, and insists on returning home. He does not rest until he has secured Tom Brangwen's consent to their marriage; as he discusses it, he looks at his uncle with 'bright inhuman eyes, like a hawk's'. His name is no accident: 'his will was set'; 'he was like a gleaming, bright pebble, something bright and inalterable'. After the early ecstasy of marriage, 'his will was coiled like a beast', and Anna 'realized that her life, her freedom, was sinking under the silent grip of his physical will'. She is the ark that saves him from the flood he dreads; when she refuses him, he seeks sexual gratification in the Park at Nottingham. To keep him, Anna complies with his demands. 'There was no tenderness, no love between them any more, only the maddening, sensuous lust for discovery and the insatiable, exorbitant gratification in the sensual beauties of her body.' Love is reduced to 'a sensuality violent and extreme as death'.

That this unfulfilled man should seek compensation in church duties and ritual, and experience a kind of mystical communion within the Gothic 'womb' of Lincoln Cathedral, elicits no surprise; yet, since 'there was a darkness in him which he *could* not unfold, which would never unfold in him', it is strange that Lawrence attributes to him (in an image derived from Haeckel) a disillusionment which gives him a sense of God in the wide universe: 'He thought of the ruins of the Grecian worship, and it seemed, a temple was never perfectly a temple, till it was ruined and mixed up with the winds and the sky and the herbs.'

The role played by Will as the object of Lawrence's moral offensive is sustained by Skrebensky in the next generation. Meeting him in her adolescence, Anna's daughter Ursula thinks him wonderful, 'one such as those Sons of God who saw the daughters of men, that they were fair'.[2] When she recovers from her disillusionment at the end of *The Rainbow*, she hopes that one of the Sons of God will come from the Infinite, and that she will hail him. In *Women in Love* she finds 'one of the Sons of God from the Beginning' in Birkin, and he finds in her 'one of the first most luminous daughters of men'. Ursula and Skrebensky's first love begins in self-assertion, on which Lawrence comments: 'Wherein was something finite and sad, for the human soul at its maximum wants a sense of the infinite.' Skrebensky sees a bargee with wife and child looking wistfully at Ursula, in soul-and-body worship of body and soul, and wonders why he himself wants her 'only just physically'. This is the prelude to a wedding party at the Marsh and another harvest scene by moonlight. The former creates 'a kind of flame of physical desire', and one girl, 'chill and burning as the sea' (a faint echo of the Aphrodite passage in 'The Lemon Gardens'), makes witty remarks, appreciation of which causes her to glint like phosphorescence. The 'deep underwater' created by waves of dance music, with shadowy couples passing and repassing the fire, suggests 'the depths of the underworld, under the great flood'. When the music stops, Ursula sees a great white moon 'looking at her over the hill'. She wishes for its coolness and liberty and brightness, and is 'cold and hard and compact of brilliance as the moon' towards Skrebensky. After a few more dances, they go towards the new corn stacks, which he sees, with something like terror, glimmering in a moon-conflagration of cold, whitish steely fires; she then, 'cold as the moon and burning as a fierce salt', destroys him in a kiss, which is 'hard and fierce and corrosive as the moonlight'. She is sorry for him, and the next morning they attend church, where she glances at the Bible and, ironically, has little patience with the idea of a god who promised that 'the waters shall no more become a flood to destroy all flesh'.

Skrebensky has to leave England for the Boer War. Six years later he is on leave again before being posted to India. His embraces make Ursula 'dark' and 'will-less'; 'her whole soul was implicated with Skrebensky', but what was he? – 'a dark, powerful vibration that encompassed her'; she did not know 'the young man of the world, but the undifferentiated man he was'. During their unlicensed honeymoon they are 'sensuous aristocrats, warm, bright, glancing with pure pride of the senses'. For a time she is 'fiercely jealous of his body', but there has been a 'hopeless fixity' about him from the first, and their union inevitably nurtures its 'germ of death'.

> He aroused no fruitful fecundity in her. He seemed added up, finished. She knew him all round, not on any side did he lead into the unknown. Poignant, almost passionate appreciation she felt for him, but none of the dreadful wonder, none of the rich fear, the connection with the unknown, or the reverence of love.

She does not wish to marry him or accompany him to India, but consents to spend a week with him on the Lincolnshire coast. In the evenings a passion for the unknown comes over her, and she walks along the shore at dusk, alone. 'The salt, bitter passion of the sea, its indifference to the earth . . . its attack, and its salt burning, seemed to provoke her to a pitch of madness, tantalizing her with vast suggestions of fulfilment' until, 'for personification, would come Skrebensky . . . whose soul could not contain her in its waves of strength, nor his breast compel her in burning, salty passion'.

While they are walking together one evening, Ursula suddenly looks up and sees a great whiteness ahead, the moon 'incandescent as a round furnace door' emitting a 'high blast of moonlight, over the seaward half of the world, a dazzling, terrifying glare of white light'. He feels himself 'fusing to nothingness', but she thinks it wonderful, wanting to go she knows not where. Suddenly she clutches Skrebensky with 'the strength of destruction', and his heart melts in fear from her 'fierce, beaked, harpy's kiss' until it seems that she has 'the heart of him'. Then she entices him, and he leads her to a dark hollow among the sandhills. She insists on going to a slope 'full under the moonshine' (clearly Lawrence attaches great importance to this), where she lies 'motionless, with wide-open eyes looking at the moon'. He comes 'direct to her, without preliminaries'. Ursula plays the role of Aphrodite, queen of the senses and goddess of destruction with her cold, white, consuming fire. 'The fight, the struggle for consummation' is 'terrible'. He feels as if 'the knife were being pushed into his dead body'. When she rises there is 'no moon for her, no sea'. They are like two dead people, and Skrebensky marries his colonel's daughter within two weeks. 'He had no soul, no background', Lawrence comments.

Ursula's willed destructive sexuality kills her natural responses temporarily. She had realised in an inspirational flash during an unenlightened chemistry lecture at college that oneness with the infinite is the key to vital living, and that 'to be oneself' is 'a supreme, gleaming triumph of infinity'. Undoubtedly the moon during the climactic scene with Skrebensky appears in an aspect consonant with the tenor of Lawrence's imagery; so too must the sea (the destructive Aphrodite of the senses was born of the sea foam), the probable explanation occurring in *The Crown*, where Lawrence holds that corruption is necessary for higher developments, and 'divine' because it will break down 'deadened forms' and 'release us into infinity'. He finds such divine corruption in the swan (and the snake), which he associates with 'the dead beauty of the moon', 'the cold white fire of flux', and 'the salt, cold burning of the sea'. Ursula's renewal of life and hope, reflecting Lawrence's hopes for mankind, are signalled by the rainbow at the end of the novel.

In Ursula's two moonlight crises, as well as in the darkness of the ecstasy which 'undifferentiated man', personified in Skrebensky, awakens in her, we have glimpses of those larger, non-human forces in humanity which Lawrence told Edward Garnett, in a letter of 5 June 1914, he was trying to present in *The Wedding Ring* (the Ursula–Skrebensky story), rather than characters in the more conventional sense. These moonlight scenes indicate that the presentation can be far more mythopoeic than realistic, even when it intensifies the feelings by which individuals are carried away. In a discarded prologue to *Women in Love*, Lawrence refers to the inhuman cry of gulls. It is Ursula's cry when she is driven to express her abhorrence of merely physical love in the way most likely to be understood by Skrebensky; it is also the cry of her sister Gudrun in the rabbit scene where a 'hellish recognition' is exchanged between her and Gerald Crich. Ursula has higher aims; Gudrun is inexorably damned.

The banning of *The Rainbow* in 1915 caused Lawrence to renew his crusade in *Women in Love*, which was completed in 1917. Through the sustained interweaving of the fortunes of two couples, Ursula and Birkin, Gudrun and Crich, he makes a more effective contrast between a progress in love's fulfilment and the development of a reductive passion than he does in *The Rainbow*, where fulfilment is achieved in the first of its three generations, favourably related to nature though threatened by industrialism. In *Women in Love*, industrial overtones are more intense and pervasive. Writing to Lady Ottoline Morrell (27 December 1915, after his return to England) on the subject he had most at heart, Lawrence speaks of the perfect relations he finds between men and women, and their 'very perfection of passion', in the Ajanta frescoes, contrasting this with the 'very one-sided thing' we call passion, based chiefly on hatred and the will to power. 'The strange, dark, sensual life, so violent, and hopeless at the bottom, combined with this horrible paucity and materialism of mental consciousness' which made him so sad that he could scream generated the vitriolic condemnation of the *Wille zur Macht*, sexual and industrial, which he concentrated in Gerald Crich and his relationship with Gudrun.

The sexuality of Gerald and Skrebensky is associated with horses, and each is a masterful rider. The way in which the former forces his terrified Arab mare to confront the clanking engine at the railway crossing exemplifies his will-power, and appeals strongly to the sexual imagination of Gudrun, who screams with challenging applause, in a gull-like voice which is heard in later scenes. When they next meet, by the edge of the lake, more premonitory Lawrentian signals – whiteness, electricity, phosphorescence – are flashed with reference to Gerald. She seems to be 'a soft recipient of his magical, hideous white fire' in the hellish alliance that they mutually recognise in the rabbit scene. The alliance is abhorrent to them both, but she has determined to strike the last blow. Their love is linked with death, literally and spiritually, from the outset. At the end, when Birkin views Gerald's dead body, he is reminded of a dead stallion: a 'mass of maleness, repugnant'. Gudrun's reductiveness extends cynically beyond the physical; she has no values. Her soul houses 'a pungent atmosphere of corrosion, an inflamed darkness of sensation, and a vivid, subtle, critical consciousness, that saw the world distorted, horrific'. When she has finished with Crich, she seeks the 'ultimate', nihilistic reduction in Loerke, with whom she can engage in the 'mystic frictional activities of diabolic reducing down, disintegrating the vital organic body of life'.

The Tennysonian conjunction of the snowy Alps with death

was confirmed by impressions which Lawrence described in another *Twilight in Italy* essay, 'The Return Journey'. Valley beds were like deep graves; the 'glamorous snow' of the mountain peak was 'the very quick of cold death'. This idea informs those Alpine scenes where the last sorry act of the Gerald–Gudrun drama is performed. Ursula hates the 'ghastly glamour' of the snow, and the 'unnatural feelings it makes everybody have'; she wishes to have done with 'the snow-world, the terrible, static ice-built mountain tops', and see the 'dark earth' below, smell its fecundity, and feel the sunshine 'touch a response in the buds'. Lawrence's spiritual death and life overtones are clear. The 'blind valley' or 'great cul-de-sac of snow and mountain peaks' which Gudrun and Gerald reach enraptures her but makes him feel alone. When she sees the rosy summits 'glistening like transcendent, radiant spikes of blossom in the heavenly upper-world' (a scene reminiscent of 'The Spinner and the Monks'), she knows how 'immortally beautiful' these 'great pistils of rose-coloured, snow-fed fire in the blue twilight of the heaven' are, but they are not of her world; she is 'debarred, a soul shut out'. Her one wish is to climb this wall of 'white finality' and find her consummation in the 'frozen centre of the All'. In her see-saw contest with Gerald, she treats him with 'diabolic coldness'; he wonders why he is left 'with the ice-wind blowing through his heart' while she surveys the 'rosy snow-tips'. She turns to Loerke, who finds the breath of being in art but regards life as a bagatelle. Gerald, slave of his will and life-denier, toils upward to his death in freezing wind and snow. He is reduced to 'the frozen carcase of a dead male', a 'block of ice'.

The ooze and mud in which the 'turgid fleshy' water-plants grow by the meeting-point of Gerald and Gudrun were in Lawrence's mind when he wrote the passage in *The Crown* on the swan and the divine corruption which leads to higher forms of life. It is 'a fearful flower of corruption' when we turn to 'cold, bygone consummations', he continues. Two discussions in *Women in Love* (chs xiv, xxviii) suggest the thought in its earlier development: the 'flux of corruption' generates 'the living desire for positive creation'; sea-born Aphrodite is associated with 'the first spasm of universal dissolution', and marsh-flowers – and Gerald and Gudrun – with 'the process of destructive creation'. *Fleurs du mal* – 'flowers of mud' – are white and phosphorescent, lilies being specified. Birkin prefers 'roses, warm and flamy'.

Expressing Lawrence's ideal marriage relationship at
writing, Birkin emphasises the basic need for 'the
knowledge'. 'You've got to learn not-to-be, before you ↵
being', he tells Hermione, whom he accuses of wanting to enjoy
passion consciously, as if reflected in a mirror – 'that Lady of
Shalott business'. His theory of a union in the unknown, beyond
womanly feelings, is too impersonal for Ursula; he loathes the
idea of subservience in marriage, fulfilment in which, he holds,
creates purity and singleness of being, the self being maintained
'in mystic balance and integrity – like a star balanced with another
star'. Their love does not blossom quickly or easily. Ursula, he
feels, wishes to be dominant, a Magna Mater; and his protest
against her 'assertive *will*' is expressed in the 'Moony' scene.
Significantly, as Ursula approaches the mill-pond, she observes
the moon watching her with a 'white and deathly smile'. Birkin
curses Cybele, the Magna Mater of the ancients, and casts stones
in an effort to destroy the moon image on the water. First it sways
distorted, shooting out fiery arms like a cuttlefish; then flakes of
fire contend with dark waves; later, flakes of scattered white seem
like rose petals blown far and wide. Birkin watches the moon reform in the intertwining heart of the rose, and stones it until the
white centre has vanished and only a darkening confusion
remains. Then Ursula sees the heart gathering again, until a
ragged rose, trying to be 'whole and composed, at peace', forms
on the tremulous water. It is not perfect, but it contrasts
favourably with the dead husks of flowers that Birkin had thrown
on the pond, saying 'There wouldn't have to be any truth, if there
weren't any lies'; and it prefigures eventual fulfilment in love.
Soon after completing *Women in Love*, Lawrence clarified the rose
image in the essay 'Love'. Stressing the spiritual as well as the
physical, he asserts that sensual passion is 'the only fire that will
purify us into singleness'. The rose is a state of transcendence
when lovers achieve 'perfect singleness' in equilibrium. Dark
waves and fire combine with the emerging rose to give
metaphorical unison in the mill-pond scene.

Lawrence adapts images to his evolving philosophy; they do
not form a set of counters or recurring fixities. Clearly, the moon
has various shades of meaning. The darkness of blood-
consciousness is more constant, but there is a vast difference
between the darkness that Will Brangwen cannot escape and the
dark knowledge of sensuality which Lawrence postulates in love.

To sustain the realisation of this physical consciousness in fiction is difficult. In describing the bliss of Ursula with Skrebensky after his long absence, Lawrence continually repeats the images of darkness and fecundity, but the darkness, literal and figurative, allied with the fecundity, allows little permutation, and repetitive redundancy (tautological at times) indicates the uncriticality of Lawrence's spontaneous insistence. A similar tendency is perceptible in 'Excurse', where Birkin rides with Ursula in the darkness to Sherwood Forest, and their consummation in love brings 'the knowledge which is the death of knowledge'. His 'pure Egyptian concentration in darkness' as he drives like a Pharaoh 'seated in immemorial potency', knowing what it is to be potent in the 'deepest physical mind', is risible.

The extension of metaphor to scene and action creates fascinating imaginative facets in some of Lawrence's later short stories and *novelle*, where it is not always allied to his major prepossession. In no novel did he return to this more seriously than in *The Plumed Serpent*, which supplied a code, both in thought and in expression, to the theme that engendered his most creative imagery. After conversion to the worship of Quetzalcoatl (the winged serpent god uniting earth and sky, the sensual and the spiritual), Kate attains blood-communion with Cipriano and the universe. As the old Eve of the Western world and the Aphrodite of consciously-willed, frictional sensuality give way within her to a kind of prelapsarian grace, she discovers a sense of reconciliation with the snake which has been traditionally associated by the Christian Church with the sinfulness of sex (and is implicit in Miriam's 'coil of torture'). The oncoming of this *vita nuova* has its outward and visible confirmation both in the countryside and on the lake, with the renewal of nature and the approach of a boat like that of Dionysus 'coming with a message, and the vine sprouting'. Kate can hardly remember the waste land of her old life, 'the dry rigid pallor of the heat, when the whole earth seemed to crepitate viciously with dry malevolence: like memory gone dry and sterile, hellish'.

NOTES

1. Perhaps the scene was purposively distorted long after being sown in Lawrence's mind by Meredith's 'Love in the Valley':

O the golden sheaf, the rustling treasure-armful!
O the nutbrown tresses nodding interlaced!
O the treasure-tresses one another over
Nodding! O the girdle slack about the waist!

2. This image was mediated by Charlotte Brontë: see *Shirley*, xii, xxvii (the romantic pre-Flood story 'La Première Femme Savante'); also Genesis, vi.1–4.

4

Lawrence's Counter-Romanticism

JOHN BEER

Simply to glance through the list of books and articles about D. H. Lawrence which have appeared since the Second World War is a dizzying experience. For a man whose effective writing career lasted little more than twenty years, the amount of work he produced is in itself astonishing, and the range of themes within that body has facilitated endless cross-connections in the minds of critics and scholars.

Yet one also senses a bewilderment. Although Lawrence is immediately attractive, he is not easy to apprehend in his wholeness. Despite the excellence of many studies, the reader is likely to be left unsatisfied, feeling that some essential elements have escaped the net. This is not an effect of the necessary exclusions which one expects when reading all good criticism; it is, rather, a sense that statements made about Lawrence's work turn out not to be justified in relation to large areas of it. Large claims have been made for Lawrence as a social realist, for example. With his incomparable picture of English provincial society in *Sons and Lovers* and his deeper probing in *The Rainbow*, he can be seen as a protagonist of those who believe the full strength of English culture to lie in the traditional values of its working and lower middle classes, and his frankness in sexual matters as representative of a larger honesty in dealing with English life as a whole. Yet no one who knows British society well would claim that either *The Rainbow* or *Women in Love* presents a true picture of it as a whole, in any 'naturalistic' sense. It is, of course, accurate on important points. The detail of the social background is correct, often brilliantly so, but what takes place against that background belongs to the artist's imagination. The picture of the Brangwens contains elements of implausibility; nor would one go for an accurate commentary on the mining industry to *Women in*

Love: neither management nor staff would recognise themselves in that portrayal. It is in *Sons and Lovers* that one finds the accurate and the typical in both cases; yet we know that *The Rainbow* and *Women in Love* are the greater achievements.

Another major contribution to Lawrence criticism, by F. R. Leavis, took this approach in its stride and transcended it. Protesting against T. S. Eliot's placing of him as displaying the 'crippling effect upon men of letters of not having been brought up in the environment of a living and central tradition', Leavis contended that this was quite untrue: the nonconformist chapel of Lawrence's time had been 'the centre of a strong social life, and the focus of a still persistent cultural tradition'; in addition, Lawrence had been able to make full use of the opportunities available by then at a provincial university.[1] Yet the thrust of his criticism took him well beyond such matters. The Lawrence whom he valued most, the Lawrence of *Women in Love* and *St Mawr*, was a writer displaying his greatness not primarily through the strength of his grasp on English society, but through the working of a subtle and complex intelligence, manifesting itself in the intensity and complexity of his best writing.

Leavis makes his case; but as he does so, we find ourselves wondering in turn about the appositeness of his title, *D. H. Lawrence: Novelist*, since the qualities he turns out to be describing apply not specifically to the novel, but to writing or art in general. When one applies the formal criteria of novel criticism to Lawrence's works of fiction, in fact, they do not automatically emerge in the first rank. His handling of characters or of plot is often rather loose; and if we take as our guide the range of *human* insight displayed, there is still room for disappointment. One critic has pointed out that in his major novels, it is usually the impersonal that triumphs.[2]

In view of such bewilderments it may be better to approach Lawrence from a different point of view, beginning, not ending, with that word 'impersonal'. There is a sense in which such a characterisation must be taken seriously, indicating an important element in his art. It is associated with a paradoxical element in the numerous biographical studies. Lawrence is presented as being deeply engaged with his companions – often polemically so.[3] The resulting arguments and battles are absorbing. Yet when we turn from them to the work that he was producing at the same time, we sense a disparity. There was an intensity in his human relationships, just as there was an intensity in his writing, but they were not of the same kind, or devoted to the same objects. He could sometimes draw upon incidents from real life in his novels, yet increasingly the impression created by the novels is that their central running thread consists not of events, or even of people, but of an internal meditation (if something so lively and free-flowing can be properly so described) carried on in his own mind.

It is clear, certainly, that he early began to move towards a very distinctive view of the world, which set him apart from those around him. While participating spiritedly in the life of his family and the group of friends who constantly visited them, he was evolving his own sense of things. He would have disclaimed any straightforward ordering of his ideas, since this was alien to his purpose. Writing to his fiancée Louie Burrows in 1911, he asserted that he would never be able to share all his ideas with her, but continued: 'it's a philosophy that, shared, would be aggravated to abstruseness and uselessness'.[4] Occasionally he could be a little more forthcoming. Writing in December 1909 to a lecturer at Nottingham, nicknamed 'Botany' Smith, he had said,

> Life seems to me barbarous, recklessly wasteful and destructive, often hideous and dreadful: but on the whole, beautiful . . . I owe you a debt. You were my first live teacher of philosophy: you showed me the way out of a torturing crude Monism, past Pragmatism, into a sort of crude but appeasing Pluralism.   (*Letters*, I, p. 147)

The terms here are not lightly chosen; they are terms which were particularly topical during the period when he was awakening mentally. To discover what he meant by a 'torturing crude Monism', for example, we may turn to a book which we know he read as a young man,[5] Ernst Haeckel's *The Riddle of the Universe at the Close of the Nineteenth Century*. Published in England in 1900, this was influential among those who were trying to come to terms with the world created by nineteenth-century science. Haeckel's position was of straightforward monism: he believed that the natural order was the sole reality of the universe, and that the aim of human beings must therefore be to understand nature, together with man's part in it. Haeckel was so excited by the developments of science, in terms not only of Darwin's theories but of the extraordinary profusion among living things that was simultaneously being revealed by the microscope, that he felt confident in giving nature such centrality. Writing from within German society, he saw himself aligned with those who were fighting against Catholicism, extending the Protestantism of the Reformation into this final phase where Nature took the place of God and where morality, though necessary, would be seen as embodying principles of *human* morality, deduced from knowledge of nature itself and fashioned in conformity with what was to be discovered there.

Such a philosophy carried the compulsiveness of a firm logical body of thought: it also represented a development from those doctrines of Kant, influential throughout the nineteenth century in Germany, which found their most succinct formulation when he described how one could look up to the starry heavens or contemplate the moral law within one's own nature, and discover the same majestic order in both.[6] Haeckel adopted a similar duality of thinking, which in the Kantian version had provided a firm basis for the position of writers such as George Eliot, but simplified it further. For him it was enough to look up to the starry heavens above and to contemplate the wonders revealed in the depths of the microscope.[7]

Why should Lawrence have found so simple and understandable a position 'crude' or 'torturing'? Presumably because, despite its immediate attractiveness, it wound human beings more firmly into a sense that they lived in the grip of inexorable laws. The cruelties, as well as the wonders of nature, must be seen as inescapable. Haeckel's book ends with a quotation from Goethe:

> By eternal laws
> Of iron ruled,
> Must all fulfil
> The cycle of
> Their destiny.[8]

However invigorating these lines so long as one thought of that destiny as an upward progress, they offered little consolation to those who found themselves victims of such laws.

Lawrence's reference to his subsequent 'pragmatism' suggests that he found one answer to this problem in William James, another favourite writer of his in youth.[9] James's principle that in philosophy an allowance must be made for the validity of personal experience – that if, for example, the hypothesis of God's existence worked for someone, that person was justified in believing it – helped to liberate his readers from the bonds of law by simply transferring the focus of their attention to individual human experience.

When Lawrence refers to a further movement into a 'crude but appeasing pluralism', similarly, it is likely that he is referring to William James's more recent book *A Pluralistic Universe*. Published in 1909, the year of Lawrence's letter to Smith, James's lectures had the avowed aim of offering some way out of the monist position which, he suggested,

> insists that when you come down to reality as such, to the reality of realities, everything is present to *everything* else in one vast instantaneous co-implicated completeness – nothing can in *any* sense, functional or substantial, be really absent from anything else, all things interpenetrate and telescope together in the great total conflux.　(p. 322)

The actual state of things in which we live, James argued, meant that

> However much may be collected, however much may report itself as present at any effective centre of consciousness or action, something else is self-governed and absent and unreduced to unity.　(p. 322)

James's goal, in other words, was to deliver human beings from the sense of living under the shadow of a vast absolute which imprisoned them in its categories, and restore them to a universe where they could, legitimately, deal with each situation to the best of their abilities, and in the light of the ideas available to them at the time.

Lawrence's acknowledgement that 'Botany' Smith had helped him to reach this latest position suggests that his progress had been assisted by something more than a sequence of philosophical arguments. Indeed, it may not be illegitimate to suppose that the subject Smith taught had something to do with the matter. The incident in *The Rainbow* where Ursula, who has been listening to the argument that life might consist in no more than a complexity of physical and chemical activities, following the same pattern as other complexities in nature, looks into a microscope and suddenly grasps the existence of an alternative principle – that self is a oneness with the infinite, and that to be oneself is a 'supreme, gleaming triumph of infinity' – is pivotal in the novel's intellectual structure.[10] At this moment, moreover, one has a strong suspicion that Lawrence is describing something that has happened to himself; and one can see that such an apprehension, however firmly Lawrence's own, might well have grown out of contact with an enthusiast for botany. For Ursula, to see that a cell exists in its own infinity was to find a key to the significance of all life, including human life; as she did so, she was delivered into a pluralistic universe, where existence in a common infinity paradoxically allowed each self to flourish in its own individuality – and in the process guaranteed the full quality of that individuality.

The paradox here is of the same order as that which underlies Coleridge's principle, 'Everything has a life of its own, and we are all one life',[11] where the biological analogue lies in a speculation that the whole of animated nature might consist of organic harps, trembling into thought at the impact of 'one intellectual breeze, / At once the Soul of each, and God of all'.[12]

Yet there was an important difference. As soon as one moves beyond Coleridge's formulation to the larger context of his thought, one sees that he was surrounding it with assumptions concerning the nature of human affections. The joint perception of the life in each and the one life in all ministered to Coleridge's belief in the sovereignty of love: it was love that provided the link between the two kinds of perception and informed every individual act of perception of either kind. For Lawrence, on the contrary, as the remainder of *The Rainbow* shows, the experience is liable to be isolating and distancing. Intimacy and sympathetic affection are not concepts that one readily associates with him: affection when it comes has a sardonic overtone, and often does not seem to come at all. There are strong indications that in the years afterwards, Lawrence felt himself to be in an unreal world, surrounded by human beings living according to false gods and false ideas. His main problem, in fact, was to retain a profitable contact with human society, whether in actuality or in the writing of his novels. This extended even to his most intimate relationships. Despite his closeness to Frieda, there were some elements in his outlook which he could not feel that she shared. Shortly after they were married, he wrote, in a moment of semi-humorous

bitterness, 'Would I had married a microscope: I could have kept
my eye on it and my heart in my pocket, and been called
blessed' – a statement which may have had more literal meaning
than one would at first sight suspect. While fulfilling his need for
a vital physical relationship, the marriage to Frieda was in other
respects dislocating to him as an imaginative artist. There is a
telling incident in *Kangaroo* when Lovat's wife asks him

> 'Who is there that you feel you are with, besides me – or who
> feel themselves with you?'
> 'No one', he replied. And at the same moment he looked up
> and saw the rainbow fume beyond the sea. But it was on a dark
> background, like a coloured darkness. The rainbow was always
> a symbol to him – a good symbol: of this peace. A pledge of
> unbroken faith, between the universe and the innermost. And
> the very moment he said 'No one,' he saw the rainbow for an
> answer.[13]

Lawrence's reference to the rainbow as 'a pledge of unbroken
faith, between the universe and the innermost' places him with
unexpected directness in a tradition that again leads back to the
early Romantics, this time to Wordsworth's lines beginning 'My
heart leaps up when I behold/A rainbow in the sky'. The source
of 'natural piety' which Wordsworth had celebrated there was just
such a 'pledge of unbroken faith'.

By Lawrence's time, the connotations of such a 'natural faith'
had become a part of the sub-Romantic ethos. Encouraged by
certain elements in Wordsworth's poetry, and notably the lines in
'Tintern Abbey' describing

> that serene and blessed mood
> In which the affections gently lead us on, –
> Until, the breath of this corporeal frame
> And even the motion of our human blood
> Almost suspended, we are laid asleep
> In body, and become a living soul:
> While with an eye made quiet by the power
> Of harmony, and the deep power of joy,
> We see into the life of things
>
> (ll. 41–9)

various nature writers had come to find their own version of an 'unbroken faith, between the universe and the innermost' revealed in moments of peace and harmony.

Lawrence knew this tradition well. There is a moment of the kind in *Sons and Lovers*, when Paul and Miriam go to see a wild rose bush on a quiet summer evening:

> In bosses of ivory and in large splashed stars the roses gleamed on the darkness of foliage and stems and grass. Paul and Miriam stood close together, silent, and watched. Point after point the steady roses shone out to them, seeming to kindle something in their souls. The dusk came like smoke around, and still did not put out the roses.[14]

For Miriam it is a moment of communion and worship in the midst of nature. Paul shares that sense to some extent, but also feels 'anxious and imprisoned': as soon as he is away from the scene and her, he begins to run as fast as he can.

The story of *Sons and Lovers* is partly the story of a young man who finds himself forced to leave such experiences behind him and move into another area of psychic experience, delighting in nature's vital energies rather than its moments of trance. ('Turning sharply, he walked towards the city's gold phosphorescence, towards the faintly humming, glowing town, quickly.')[15] Lawrence's use of the rainbow image must be seen in a fuller context, therefore. His introduction of an actual rainbow into his novel *The Rainbow* is sometimes criticised as sentimental – naturally so to anyone familiar with its use in Pre-Raphaelite painting and so on. But at the end of the novel it is given a more vital status by Ursula's final vision of a rainbow that is 'arched in the blood' of humanity. The rainbow of *Kangaroo*, similarly, is a rainbow that reveals itself against a dark background and across ruffled waves, 'a tall fume far back among the clouds of the sea-wall' which recalls for Lovat a time when in the midst of a dismal scene with pouring rain he had seen a rainbow spanning Sydney Harbour – 'A huge, brilliant, supernatural rainbow, spanning all Sydney'.[16]

For Lawrence it is not the straightforward sight of a rainbow as such that is comforting; it is rather the awareness that there is little in the order of things that might logically lead one to expect something so beautiful in nature – which contends against such miracles. Wordsworth, too, had that sense. In a manuscript passage that Lawrence would not have known, where he was tracing the 'analogy betwixt/The mind of man and nature', he recalled an occasion when he saw a scene of fierce tumult during a storm on Coniston, 'Mist flying up and down, bewilder'd showers,/Ten thousand thousand waves, mountains and crags,/And darkness, and the sun's tumultuous light', – and then, over all, a 'large unmutilated rainbow . . . Immovable in heav'n . . . With a colossal stride bridging the vale'.[17]

In reading Wordsworth, and particularly in reading *The Prelude*, we are often aware of undertones which counterpoint and give further definition to those images of peace which are typically 'Wordsworthian'. In *The Prelude*, the experiences in which such images are impressed on the heart regularly follow times of unusual energy or directed attention: it is in the relaxation from effort, not in some straightforwardly passive state, that the experience of revelation comes.[18] The resulting sense of a total process preserves such passages from charges of sentimentality or softness.

Here, as elsewhere, one is conscious of striking points of resemblance between the personalities and experiences of Wordsworth and Lawrence. Similar forces in the two men were simply being apprehended and organised differently. Wordsworth, although passionate, was fearful of the effects of his energy, and even more wary of delivering himself into a fixed or static universe of law. He seized with relief upon the mediating elements in the natural world to which his affections could hold. Lawrence, on the other hand, while attracted by such a mediating world of affection, also felt stifled by it, breaking out to find his natural world of discourse in those expressions of energy which Wordsworth treated with reserve. It was at the moment when he could sense his own imaginative energies in unison with those in nature that he felt most at home in the world.

This in turn made him a divided man. Within his own family circle in youth, and in that circle as it extended itself to immediate friends, he could be extremely affectionate. But in more solitary moments, and in his growing awareness of nature, he found himself rebelling against the nineteenth-century ideal of relationships based centrally on affection; hence the crucial tension in the relationship with Jessie Chambers. His visits to her home at Haggs Farm made him aware of the full range of natural life, its cruelties and harshness as well as its charms and tendernesses;

he also became aware that, if he were looking for points of correspondence between the natural and the human, those differing factors in external nature could speak to very different elements in the psyche. It was one thing for the affections to be nourished by contact with nature on a calm summer evening, quite another for human instincts to find themselves in rapport with the instincts of wild creatures. Wordsworth had solved this problem by presupposing that the life of instinct was properly cultivated in childhood and youth, to be left behind once one entered adulthood and the sphere of moral responsibility. Lawrence could not adopt that assumption. In his pluralistic universe, the role of the instincts, particularly in sexual life, was altogether more significant. The relationship with Jessie Chambers was the stage of a cruel drama, therefore. Jessie was his ally as he sought to find his identity as a writer: against the other 'Pagans' and his mother, who believed that if he were to achieve fame as a writer he would be lost to their little society, and who therefore fought against her cultivation of him, she kept his work and encouraged him to submit it for publication.[19] But the same process of cutting himself off from his own group, which she encouraged, was also setting up a division in himself between that affectionate intellectual self which was drawn to her and the instinctual sexual self which could not be satisfied by such a relationship. The first signs of such a tension appeared as early as 1906, during the summer before Lawrence's entry into college. He formulated it to Jessie in terms of his lack of sexual feeling for her, defining it in the memorable sentence, 'The trouble is, you see, I'm not one man, but two. . . . One man in me loves you, but the other never can love you'.[20] While he apologised to her for the 'perverse' element in himself, it is clear that he was also coming to acknowledge that that perversity might represent an important element in his whole nature. And the recognition of two natures in Lawrence was not confined to himself: it was evident to perceptive observers. Ford Madox Hueffer (later Ford), for example, who knew him best in the years 1909 and after, contributed a similar impression:

if the God Pan did look at one round a trunk one might well feel as one felt when the something that was not merely eyesight peeped out at you from behind Lawrence's eyes.
For that was really what the sensation was like – as if

something that was inside – inhabiting – Lawrence had the job of looking after him. It popped up, took a look at you through his pupils and, if it was satisfied, sank down and let you go on talking. . . . Yes, it was really like that: as if perhaps, a mother beast was looking after its young.

It was not so bad an impression, founded as it was on the peculiar, as if sunshot tawny hair and moustache of the fellow and his deep-set and luminous eyes. He had not, in those days, the beard that afterwards obscured his chin – or I think he had not. I think that on his holiday he had let his beard grow and, it having been lately shaved off, the lower part of his face was rather pallid and as if invisible, whereas his forehead and cheeks were rather high-coloured. So that I had had only the impression of the fox-coloured hair and moustache and the deep, wary, sardonic glance . . . as if he might be going to devour me – or something that I possessed.

always at first, for a second or two, he seemed like the reckless robber of hen-roosts with gleaming eyes and a mouth watering for adventure and then, with the suddenness of a switched-off light, he became the investigator into the bases of the normal that he essentially was.[21]

Various of Lawrence's own statements at this time draw a similar analysis of his own nature. In May 1910, when it seemed as if he might after all be going to marry Jessie Chambers, he wrote to Helen Corke about the feeling of inertness which this recognition induced. 'I seem to have no will: it is a peculiar dull, lethargic state I have never known before.'

Till Saturday I shall merely wait in lethargy: I can do no other. Yet I have a second consciousness somewhere actively alive. I write 'Siegmund' – I keep on writing, almost mechanically: very slowly, and mechanically. . . .
   Muriel will take me. She will do me great, infinite good – for a time. But what is awake in me shivers with terror at the issue. (*Letters*, I, pp. 159–60)

At the end of that year, when he had become engaged to Louie

Burrows, he wrote to her in different terms, being now more aggressive on behalf of his writing self:

> I am very much afraid indeed of disappointing you and causing you real grief for the first time in your life. It is the second me, the hard, cruel if need be, me that is the writer which troubles the pleasanter me, the human who belongs to you. Try, will you, when I disappoint you and may grieve you, to think that it is the impersonal part of me – which belongs to nobody, not even to myself – the writer in me, which is for the moment ruling.   (Ibid., p. 214)

To other people he put the point differently again, making it clear that he foresaw a marriage in which Louie Burrows would have only a partial share of him. To his sister Ada he wrote: 'Don't be jealous of her. She hasn't any share in *your* part of me. You and I – there are some things which we shall share, we alone, all our lives: you know, also, that there is more *real* strength in my regard for you than there is for Louie.'[22] In this case, he was thinking primarily of his mother's death and of their previous experiences with his father, which, he thought, had given them a more tragic view of life than Louie, living with her own, better-knit family, could possibly imagine. This was not the only area Louie could not share, however, as a letter to Helen Corke makes clear:

> The common everyday – rather superficial man of me really loves Louie. Do you believe that? But do you not think the open-eyed, sad critical, deep seeing man of me has not had to humble itself pretty sorely to accept the imposition of the masculine, stupid decree. There is a decree for each of us – thou shalt live alone – and we have to put up with it. We may keep real company once in our lives – after that we touch . . . now and again, upon someone else – but do not repose.   (*Letters*, I, p. 240)

The rest of the letter shows that his ideas rested upon a further ideological basis: the laws of life and of nature were made for 'the unseeing, unintelligent mass', but it was also possible to 'step out of the common pale' and find new laws suddenly reigning. He returned to the matter in July, speaking of his love for her: 'Some of you I should always love. Then again, I must break free. And I *cannot* marry save where I am not held. . . . I love Louie in a certain way that doesn't encroach on my liberty, and I can marry her, and still be alone. I must be so, if I marry – alone in soul, mostly' (*Letters*, i, p. 285).

The realignment of himself which Lawrence was trying to make is not difficult to understand. Having recognised himself to be a divided man with Jessie, he had still hoped to preserve a relationship of intensified sensibility with her, leaving his instinctive self and his creative self to look after themselves. But after his mother's death he knew this to be impossible: to live wholly in sensibility would be to perpetuate a part of the relationship with his mother which, after her tragic death, he could never re-enter. Instead, he was now trying an opposite expedient: a relationship of physical fulfilment with Louie Burrows which would neither tax his sensibility nor restrain him from continuing with artistic creation.

Neither relationship could be satisfactory. In his writing, after all, which was now to be conceived as essentially impersonal, he was trying to reconcile sensibility and instinct; to live on one rather than the other would leave his writing impoverished. With Louie, moreover, the 'passion' was coarse-grained: there was little subtlety in her vitality. If he had married her he would have been false to the intelligence which had informed the writing of *The White Peacock* – where an implicit sympathy with the broad, unrefined vitality of George Saxton was matched by a still more evident recognition of its shortcomings.[23]

There had been times when he could ride happily on the crest of a variegated personality, as when, in the early days of his relationship with Louie, he had written, 'I wish you'd tell me which of my epistolary styles you prefer: the gay, the mocking, the ironic, the sad, the despairing, the elevated, the high romantic, the didactic, the emphatic, the bullying, the passionate, the disgraceful or the naive, so that I can be consistent' (*Letters*, i, p. 217). The death of his mother and its aftermath had increased his sense of self-division, however, and one suspects that the attack of pneumonia at the end of the year was either connected with, or at least subsumed within itself, the resulting psychic conflicts. By early February, he was writing to Louie to break off their engagement on the grounds of his ill health. Soon afterwards, Ada Lawrence wrote to her urging her to accept the situation. She referred to the 'flippant and really artificial manner' which

Lawrence had recently adopted, commenting: 'It's surprising how very much changed Bert is since his illness, and changed for the worse too, I think.'[24]

Whatever one makes of all this, it is evident that Lawrence had found himself in a false situation which he was no doubt wise to escape. In the process, he saw himself as 'a sort of impersonal creature, without heart or liver, staring out of a black cloud'.[25] Yet there was also a swift reaction on his part. A fortnight later he was back in Eastwood making love lightheartedly at a dance; six weeks later he had fallen in love with Frieda Weekley.

The love for Frieda represented a further reorientation of himself, this time enabling the passionate element in his personality, which empathised with the instinctive in nature, to find full expression for the first time. His subsequent letters were full of delight at new freedom and at the wonder of his love. But this new kind of relationship was not without its own divisiveness; he and Frieda fought as well as making love, and the emergent dark side to his personality which Ada had noticed issued from time to time in blind rages, lending a shadow to some of his subsequent pronouncements about human affairs. To give rein to the instinctual might at times be liberating, but it could also issue in fierce destructiveness.

This is not the place to trace all the complexities of Lawrence's later personality; attention is drawn simply to the part which his subconscious powers continued to play. In January 1912, for example, just before the end of his engagement to Louie, he wrote to Edward Garnett:

I can never decide whether my dreams are the result of my thoughts, or my thoughts the result of my dreams. It is very queer. But my dreams make conclusions for me. They decide things finally. I dream a decision. Sleep seems to hammer out for me the logical conclusions of my vague days, and offer me them as dreams. It is a horrid feeling, not to be able to escape from one's own – what? – self – daemon – fate, or something. I hate to have my own judgments clinched inside me involuntarily. But it is so. (*Letters*, I, p. 359)

'What tosh to write. I don't know what ails me', he continued; but it was certainly not an isolated reflection, for many years later, in 1928, he returned to the theme when he wrote a preface (never

to appear as such) for his *Collected Poems*. There he talked of
certain poems which he had begun writing at about the age of
twenty which haunted him and made him feel guilty.

> In those early days – for I was very green and unsophisticated
> at twenty – I used to feel myself at times haunted by something,
> and a little guilty about it, as if it were an abnormality. Then the
> haunting would get the better of me, and the ghost would
> suddenly appear, in the shape of a usually rather incoherent
> poem. Nearly always I shunned the apparition once it had
> appeared. From the first, I was a little afraid of my real poems –
> not my 'compositions', but the poems that had the ghost in
> them. They seemed to me to come from somewhere, I didn't
> quite know where, out of a me whom I didn't know and
> didn't want to know, and to say things I would much rather
> not have said: for choice . . . To this day, I still have the uneasy
> haunted feeling, and would rather not write most of the things
> I do write – including this note. Only now I know my demon
> better, and, after bitter years, respect him more than my other,
> milder and nicer self. . . . I must have burnt many poems that
> had the demon fuming in them. The fragment *Discord in
> Childhood* was a long poem, probably was good, but I destroyed
> it. Save for Miriam, I perhaps should have destroyed them all.
> She encouraged my demon. But alas, it was me, not he whom
> she loved. So for her too, it was a catastrophe. My demon is not
> easily loved: whereas the ordinary me is. So poor Miriam was
> let down. Yet in a sense, she let down my demon, till he
> howled. And there it is. And no more *past* in me than my blood
> in my toes or my nose is past.   (*Collected Poems*, II, pp. 849–50)

That last reference to the blood is a reminder that Lawrence's
belief in the demon was associated with his sense of a 'blood-
consciousness' in the body, a belief which he expressed memorably
in a letter to Bertrand Russell in December 1915:

> Now I am convinced of what I believed when I was about
> twenty – that there is another seat of consciousness than the
> brain and the nerve system: there is a blood-consciousness
> which exists in us independently of the ordinary mental
> consciousness, which depends on the eye as its source or
> connector. There is the blood-consciousness, with the sexual

connection, holding the same relation as the eye, in seeing, holds to the mental consciousness. One lives, knows, and has one's being in the blood, without any reference to nerves and brain. This is one half of life, belonging to the darkness. (*Letters*, II, p. 470)

Quoting this letter nearly forty years later, Russell commented: 'This seemed to me frankly rubbish, and I rejected it vehemently, though I did not then know that it led straight to Auschwitz.'[26] In expressing himself so vehemently he may have been recalling some expressions of extravagant hatred in Lawrence's other letters of the time, resulting from his black moods,[27] but the larger context of Lawrence's ideas was far from that of Nazism. In Germany, references to a blood-consciousness were linked closely with militarism and aggression, expressing themselves through the technology of war, whereas Lawrence's philosophy was based rather on a vision of independent growth in individuals and free communication between them, grounded in the inward life of nature and criticising those forces of industry and war which followed a mechanical and inhuman logic of their own.

The individuality of Lawrence's position is more evident in an earlier statement to Ernest Collings, which links naturally to those speculations about the self over the microscope which had appeared in *The Rainbow*:

My great religion is a belief in the blood, the flesh, as being wiser than the intellect. We can go wrong in our mind. But what our blood feels and believes and says, is always true. The intellect is only a bit and a bridle. What do I care about knowledge. All I want is to answer to my blood, direct, without fribbling intervention of mind, or moral, or what not. I conceive a man's body as a kind of flame, like a candle flame forever upright and yet flowing: and the intellect is just the light that is shed onto the things around. And I am not so much concerned with the things around – which is really mind – but with the mystery of the flame forever flowing, coming God knows how from out of practically nowhere, and being *itself*, whatever there is around it, that it lights up. (*Letters*, I, p. 503)

Such speculations did not take place in an intellectual void. Materials for them can be traced in an article in the *Hibbert Journal* for October 1911, which Lawrence passed round to various of his friends. This piece, entitled 'Creative Evolution', was by A. J. Balfour: it had been written in reaction to Bergson's *Creative Evolution*, and attempted to look at his theories sympathetically while preserving a sceptical attitude. Lawrence may well have valued it particularly for its account of Bergson's idea of consciousness, which corresponded to his own in so far as it presupposed a primitive consciousness which had passed into a state of division as human beings became civilised: 'The primordial consciousness falls, as it were, asunder. On the one side it rises to an ever fuller measure of creative freedom; on the other, it lapses into matter, determinism, mechanical adjustment, space.'[28] In Bergson this second sphere was seen as corresponding to the domain of reason:

> reason is at home, not with life and freedom, but with matter, mechanism, and space – the waste products of the creative impulse. We need not wonder, then, that reason should feel at home in the realm of matter; that it should successfully cut up the undivided flow of material change into particular sequences which are repeated, or are capable of repetition, and which exemplify 'natural laws'. (p. 12)

Such beliefs correspond fairly closely to those which we have traced in Lawrence himself. His conception of the rational self as fitted to handle the dead products of life simply takes the process a stage further from Bergson's contention that it had been evolved to help human beings cope successfully with matter. When Bergson is cited as supposing that 'free consciousness pursues no final end, it follows no predetermined design . . . It follows no designs, it obeys no laws' (p. 14) the language, as well as the ideas being expressed, look forward directly to Lawrence's assertion concerning the poetry of 'the immediate present' which he was coming to see as an alternative to the poetry of 'perfected bygone moments, perfected moments in the glimmering futurity' associated with the 'treasured gem-like lyrics of Shelley and Keats'. The free verse of the 'instant moment', he would assert,

> has no goal in either eternity. It has no finish. It has no satisfying stability, satisfying to those who like the immutable. None of this. It is the instant; the quick; the very jetting source

of all will-be and has-been. the utterance is like a spasm, naked contact with all influences at once. It does not want to get anywhere. It just takes place.   (*Phoenix*, p. 221)

There is no evidence that Lawrence was ever a disciple of Bergson's. On the contrary, after reading one of his books in 1914, he wrote: 'Bergson bores me. He feels a bit thin.'[29] Bergson's writing did not have the thrust and excitement that Lawrence himself believed to be present in the workings of the primordial consciousness. But this does not mean that Lawrence did not look gratefully to him for support in his own views.

In particular, such writings fostered Lawrence's belief in an art of process his unwillingness to rest in finished products. And this is perhaps the most crucial matter of all. One reason that he is so often misread (creatively or otherwise) is that it is easy to take particular passages here and there and impose upon them a pattern of one's own. One can, for instance, take the imagery of violence in the novels and trace a pattern that might seem to be dominant. Or one can concentrate on the imagery of energy through his work until he is seen as dissolving the whole world into its component electrical relationships.

To do so, however, is to lose sight of the fact that Lawrence's larger philosophy is continually acting to create particular patterns of process in, through, or over such imagery. Such patterns are to be traced, for instance, in his sense of the organism as subsisting within its own energy. The violence of energy is for him an essential element in the universe of life, but it is an energy which finds its true form only in association with life, realising itself fully in shaping the beautiful forms of living beings or of their spontaneous moments. This in turn helps to illuminate certain elements in Lawrence's art, such as his love of flowers. His delight in spring flowers, linking naturally with the main tradition of romanticism, might appear strangely sentimental. The indications are, however, that he was being true to further implications of that tradition as they had developed in England during the nineteenth century, differentiating them from other European theories of the organic. Those theories had concentrated mainly on vegetable growth, focusing therefore upon the unity in diversity to be seen in the growth of a vegetable, realising the 'idea' that had always been implicit in its seed. They were inevitably conservative in nature, since they encouraged the concept of an evolution which took place according to inward laws. To interfere with such natural workings out, whether in the vegetable creation or in society at large, could be seen, therefore, as destructive. All that might be countenanced was something in the nature of a pruning, which must take strict account of the organism in question and its natural form of development.

Throughout the nineteenth century, however, a further undercurrent had to do with qualities such as 'energy', 'vitality' or 'animation'. Devotion to the traditional organic would logically end in an entranced meditation, but there was a growing sense that life consisted in something more than a simple unfolding. The energies of animals and birds, particularly as displayed in their flights or movements of play, witnessed to different forces.

Such awareness is to be found in many places. It is there in Blake's visual imagery of flames and serpents;[30] it is there, as we have seen, in Wordsworth's *Prelude*, with its moments of high insight following upon unusually intense fits of energy. Later in the century, it expressed itself more directly in impulses for energetic action or in Arnold's demand for literature that will 'animate'.[31]

For Lawrence it was not just the display of energy as such that marked the operation of life; certain particular qualities in that display were to be seen as essential. To express this connection, he devised a particular dialect: words such as 'quick', 'flickering', 'glancing', and so on, hint at qualities that can be caught only in movement and are essentially elusive and fugitive. But this very elusiveness made it hard for him to give this conception adequate expression. In his work it often defines itself rather through *antitype, negative implication* or, at best, *partial illustration*.

A good example of antitype is to be found in the famous scene in which Birkin stones the moon on the water until there are only 'a few broken flakes tangled and glittering broadcast in the darkness, without aim or meaning, a darkened confusion, like a black and white kaleidoscope tossed at random'. Yet even as he watches, satisfied, the reverse process begins inexorably to take effect:

> Gradually the fragments caught together re-united, heaving, rocking, dancing, falling back as in panic, but working their way home again persistently, making semblance of fleeing away when they had advanced, but always flickering nearer, a

little closer to the mark, the cluster growing mysteriously larger and brighter, as gleam after gleam fell in with the whole, until a ragged rose, a distorted frayed moon was shaking upon the waters again, reasserted, renewed, trying to recover from its convulsion, to get over the disfigurement and the agitation, to be whole and composed, at peace.[32]

The brilliance and power of the writing here have often been commented upon. It should also be noted, however, that the passage harshly tenders the ambiguity of Lawrence's vision. What presents itself in recalcitrant opposition to Birkin's will is cold and circular; but in the process of its recalcitrance it turns first into a disorder of scattered energies, then into an analogue of organic process as the lights become flowerlike. What is happening on a cold reading of the scene is the re-establishment of a blank disc of light; in the energy of the interplay of forces between man and water, on the other hand, there is appearing something which must lie at the heart of all growth, an interweaving that is at once dance and flower. Had Wordsworth been writing this passage, it would have been the sight of the re-established moon that would have been revelatory, its beauty being impressed upon the heart in the moment of peace after agitation; for Lawrence, the beauty cannot be established so firmly: it is essentially elusive, fleeting.

For an example of negative implication, we might turn to another scene in *Women in Love*, this time the triangular exchange when Ursula looks on as Rupert Birkin shows Hermione the red ovary flowers on some catkins.

'From those little red bits, the nuts come; if they receive pollen from the long danglers.'
'Little red flames, little red flames,' murmured Hermione to herself. And she remained for some moments looking only at the small buds out of which the red flickers of the stigma issued.
'Aren't they beautiful? I think they're so beautiful,' she said, moving close to Birkin, and pointing to the red filaments with her long, white finger. . . .
Her absorption was strange, almost rhapsodic. Both Birkin and Ursula were suspended. The little red pistillate flowers had some strange, almost mystic-passionate attraction for her.[33]

To see the stigma as little red flames might seem to be peculiarly Lawrentian, an authentic recognition of the energies of the vegetable creation; yet the stress in this chapter is clearly on Hermione's inauthenticity, and there is no good reason for Lawrence to move against that by compromising so central a theme. The implication must be rather that in electing the flame-image and concentrating upon it so exclusively, Hermione is indulging in a paradoxical act of fixation which reveals her consciousness as held in an old stereotyping. To see the stigma with Birkin, as 'flickering', on the other hand, is to keep the flame-imagery from fixation, to acknowledge its importance without allowing that to take over.

Apart from this, the particular quality of Lawrence's vision of nature is revealed also in the very guardedness of his assertions: as in one incident of what might otherwise seem to be total physical consummation:

> He stood on the hearth-rug looking at her, at her face that was upturned exactly like a flower, a fresh, luminous flower, glinting faintly golden with the dew of the first light. And he was smiling faintly as if there were no speech in the world, save the silent delight of flowers in each other. Smilingly they delighted in each other's presence, pure presence, not to be thought of, even known. But his eyes had a faintly ironical contraction.[34]

The afflatus in the writing, signalled by repetition where there is no corresponding movement in the sense and by the archaic 'save' brought in for quieting effect, is compensated by the ironic expression in Birkin's eye. Even at the height of love there will be dislocation, a hint of overwriting in the expression, a failure to underwrite in the observed and observing eye, which will preserve it from being stamped too fixedly into experience.

By Lawrence's time the invocation of an ironical or sardonical note had become necessary if his imagery of flowering were to be guarded against the associations of sentimentality which had accreted round it in sub-Romantic texts. In the early stages of Romanticism, when that threat had been less present, the existence of a guarding counter-force can still be traced, particularly in a fascination with energy. Blake is the most obvious figure here, and it is no accident that he is the English writer with whom

Lawrence is most frequently associated. Jessie Chambers records his enthusiasm for Blake's work as early as 1905, when Lawrence was particularly intent on painting;[35] and it was for Blake's paintings that he later expressed his enthusiasm: 'Blake paints with real intuitional awareness and solid instinctive feeling. He dares handle the human body, even if he sometimes makes it a mere ideograph. And no other Englishman has even dared handle it with alive imagination' (*Phoenix*, p. 560). He also responded to the poetry, however, as various allusions to it show,[36] his one negative comment, 'I am never very fond of abstract poetry, not even of Blake', betraying admiration even in the moment of criticism.[37]

In some ways Lawrence was too close to Blake to be able to discuss him profitably. When he turned to the other Romantics, his divided self could respond, with an alternation of hostility and respect, to the force and counter-force which we have traced.

In many aspects, of course, he rejected their influence as harmful. The concept of the 'child of nature', for example: 'The simple innocent child of nature does not exist: if there be an occasional violet by a mossy stone in the human sense, a Wordsworthian Lucy, it is because her vitality is rather low, and her simple nature is very near a simpleton's.'[38] Yet he could also see Wordsworth in a different light, as one of those who 'slit the fabric' in which human beings customarily cocoon or screen themselves from the true nature of things: 'The joy men had when Wordsworth, for example, made a slit and saw a primrose! Till then, men had only seen a primrose dimly in the shadow of the umbrella. They saw it through Wordsworth in the full gleam of chaos' (*Phoenix*, p. 256). That acknowledgement of a concealed energy in Wordsworth was matched in the terms of his respect for other poets. He resisted the swooning towards death in Keats and still more the tendency to male abstractness in Shelley, yet numbered their odes, along with the Immortality Ode of Wordsworth, among the 'lovely poems which after all give the ultimate shape to one's life'.[39] In Keats, he acknowledged, 'the body can still be *felt* dissolving in waves of successive death', and his hostility to Shelley for declaring to the skylark 'Bird thou never wert' was qualified by a recognition that the last line of the same stanza, 'In profuse strains of unpremeditated art' is 'the tumbling sound of a lark's singing, the real Two-in-One'.[40] When he visited Lerici in 1913 he was particularly mindful of Shelley's brilliant use of metre; in 1916 he went so far as to nominate him and Swinburne as our greatest poets and fantasised about a tea-party to which he would invite the two of them along with Herodotus and Flaubert.[41] But he believed that Shelley's drowning was not really an accident ('he was always trying to drown himself – it was his last mood'), and his main judgement was that 'Wordsworth, Keats, Shelley, the Brontës, all are post-mortem poets'.[42]

From that list Coleridge's name is absent. The absence might well be significant, since the counter-spirit that is observable in Coleridge's work is closer to Lawrence's vitalism than is that in any other English Romantic poet. The 'one Life within us and abroad' of 'The Eolian Harp', which is present also in many of the conversation poems, manifests itself very openly in *The Ancient Mariner*, while the serpent-imagery of 'Christabel' has thematic links with the 'serpent of secret shame' in Lawrence's writings.[43] From the first, Coleridge had drawn back from the full implications of devotion to the 'one Life'. Even in 'The Eolian Harp' he introduced a reproof for such speculations from his betrothed; in later years he retreated from them except in scattered moments.

Lawrence can hardly have been unaware of such implications in the poetry, which he read enthusiastically in his youth. Jessie Chambers recalls how during the winter of 1908 they walked over frozen snow to the ruins of Beauvale Abbey. 'It was a day of brilliant sunshine, and the three of us perched in a tree that leaned over a pond, while Lawrence read Coleridge's *Christabel*.'[44] From time to time he adopted well-known lines from *The Ancient Mariner*; in 1928 he recalled the year after his mother's death as one in which everything collapsed 'save the mystery of death, and the haunting of death in life'.[45] The Mariner's vision of the water-snakes ('Blue, glossy green, and velvet black,/They coiled and swam; and every track/Was a flash of golden fire') is of a vividness which looks forward directly to Lawrence's language; one also recalls his lines in 'Snake': 'And I thought of the albatross,/And I wished he would come back, my snake.'[46]

Such references, along with Birkin's ready citation of the 'Woman wailing for her demon lover' in *Women in Love*,[47] make it clear that, like many writers, he had Coleridge's poems of the supernatural at his fingertips; but how well did he know the rest of Coleridge's works? The presence of an otherwise striking phrase in a letter of 1909, 'Ah, woful when!' from 'Youth and

Age', is explained as soon as one knows that the poem was one of two by Coleridge in the *Golden Treasury* which, said Jessie Chambers, was a 'kind of Bible' to them in earlier years,[48] but there are one or two other hints that he read and responded to Coleridge's poetry as a whole, the most striking being in his poem 'Catullian Hendecasyllabics',[49] which is a close translation from a part of Friedrich von Matthison's 'Milesisches Märchen':

> Hear, my belovéd, an old Milesian story! –
> High, and embosom'd in congregated laurels,
> Glimmer'd a temple upon a breezy headland;
> In the dim distance amid the skiey billows
> Rose a fair island; the god of flocks had blest it.
> From the far shores of the bleat-resounding island
> Oft by the moonlight a little boat came floating,
> Came to the sea-cave beneath the breezy headland,
> Where amid myrtles a pathway stole in mazes
> Up to the groves of the high embosom'd temple.
> There in a thicket of dedicated roses,
> Oft did a priestess, as lovely as a vision,
> Pouring her soul to the son of Cytherea,
> Pray him to hover around the slight canoe-boat,
> And with invisible pilotage to guide it
> Over the dusk wave, until the nightly sailor
> Shivering with ecstasy sank upon her bosom.

Certain features of this poem are close to those of Lawrence's 'The Man who Died'. The man who comes in his canoe to visit a lonely priestess on her island at night has points of resemblance with Lawrence's Christ figure who arrives to find love with a similar priestess and later departs in a boat across the water. One suspects that Coleridge's poem, with its subdued erotic appeal, may have lingered in Lawrence's subconscious to provide the central idea for his tale: certainly the setting of the priestess's temple, as he describes it, is remarkably similar:

> The woman who served Isis stood in her yellow robe, and looked up at the steep slopes coming down to the sea, where the olive-trees silvered under the wind like water splashing. She was alone save for the goddess. And in the winter afternoon the light stood erect and magnificent off the invisible sea, filling

the hills of the coast. She went towards the sun, through the grove of Mediterranean pine-trees and ever-green oaks, in the midst of which the temple stood, on a little, tree-covered tongue of land between two bays.[50]

The resemblances between the two descriptions are those of a *gestalt* rather than of detail, clearly; one might also dwell profitably upon the differences between them. The verbal sequence, 'embosom'd', 'embosom'd', 'her bosom', in Coleridge's poem presents an imagery of enclosed and affectionate love which is not paralleled in Lawrence's tale. What is more significant, however, is the sense of slightly dangerous speculation in Coleridge's poem. Lawrence's more open exploration of the idea, that of a man visiting the priestess of love with whom he finds ideal physical fulfilment, is deliberately made to challenge the Christian ethos from which Coleridge keeps it carefully segregated. Coleridge's translation does no more than indulge what is repressed in his own poetry; in Lawrence's tale that repressed element has returned to dominate.

Coleridge's counter-Romanticism was never more than a subdued element. It could not be allowed to challenge belief in the moral law. Lawrence's statement, 'with should and ought I have nothing to do',[51] would have been impossible to him. As a result such strands in his work run out into private conversations, isolated notebook entries, footnotes to his published works, and so on. Lawrence, by contrast, begins his explorations at the point where Coleridge leaves off, being willing to contemplate unafraid the fact that a full relationship between the unconscious powers in the human mind and those in nature must take account of violence as well as calm.

He could do so more readily because in his time the element of sensibility in Romanticism had been overplayed to the point of being played out. The cultivation of states of entrancement had led to the 'dreaming woman',[52] that typical figure in the society of Lawrence's time which he found so disturbing, negating as she did the possibility of more vital and energetic relationships between men and women. In the same way he found the negative quality in *A Passage to India* at once authentic and inadequate: 'The day of our white dominance is over, and no new day can come till this of ours has passed into night. Soit! I accept it. But one must go into the night ahead of it . . . the dark ahead and the silence into which we haven't yet spoken our impertinent echoes.'[53] The imagery here foreshadows that of 'Bavarian Gentians', where the energy of the flower becomes a torch to guide him into the darkness;[54] it also suggests something of the increasing greyness which he felt to be surrounding the play of energies in the world.

Something of what was now at stake is to be seen in one of his last stories, 'The Flying Fish', which plays cleverly in a series of ideas around a single theme: that human beings in the white civilisations live in a 'lesser day', ignoring that 'great day' which is also the great deep from which they have drawn and to which they must return. The hero is himself called Day, he comes from a family of Days who have lived in Daybrook for generations. He is on the way home from the decadence of his life in South America to resume the family home. But it is what he sees on the voyage home that focuses the story's themes. His sight of flying fish leaping together comes as a final revelation of powers unrealised by human beings:

> This is the purest achievement of joy I have seen in all life: these strong, careless fish. Men have not got in them that secret to be alive together and make one like a single laugh, yet each fish going its own gait. This is sheer joy – and men have lost it, or never accomplished it. . . . It would be wonderful to know joy as these fish know it. The life of the deep waters is ahead of us, it contains sheer togetherness and sheer joy. We have never got there.   (*Phoenix*, p. 795)

The language that Lawrence uses here is spirally repetitive in the manner of much of his prose, recalling what 'Botany' Smith had told him long before – that he was obsessed rather than possessed by his ideas.[55] The method of the whole story, with its interlocking of the idea of 'the greater day' through various elements in space and history, enables him to put that obsessive quality to unusually good use, however, making it an imitative form for the interplaying movement of the flying fish themselves. Perhaps in producing that vision of interweaving energies he was recalling, whether consciously or subconsciously, Coleridge's similar vision of the water-snakes, just as Coleridge himself, voyaging to Malta, saw a myriad of insect activity in the shadow of his ship: 'scattered Os, rapidly uncoiling into serpent spirals', and wrote how hard it was to express 'the Life and time-mocking Motion of that Change, always Os before, always Spirals, coiling, uncoiling, *being*'.[56]

The last word is a most important one. Somewhere in the process of those coilings and uncoilings, Coleridge glimpsed a key to the nature of being itself. In the same way, Lawrence had found release from the tyranny of the microscope as an instrument for fixing objects when he saw that even in the simplest cell there lay a complex interplay of energies, which as a human he could recognise also in himself.

The fact that Lawrence did not set Coleridge among those who denied the 'essential instinctive-intuitive body' may well reflect a recognition of his 'one Life' as a power similar to that which he honoured in his work. Perhaps he regarded Coleridge's work primarily as an unsolved riddle, containing attractive elements that he would have liked to investigate further. The only firm clue that we have lies in a letter he sent to Amy Lowell in 1914: 'And don't talk about putting me in the safe with Keats and Shelley. It scares me out of my life, like the disciples at the Transfiguration. But I'd like to know Coleridge when Charon has rowed me over.'[57]

NOTES

1. F. R. Leavis, *D. H. Lawrence: Novelist* (1955) pp. 306–8.
2. See W. T. Andrews, 'Laurentian Indifference', *Notes and Queries*, ccxiv (1969) pp. 260–1.
3. A good representative account may be found in, e.g. Knut Merrild, *A Poet and Two Painters* (1938) *passim*.
4. *The Letters of D. H. Lawrence*, ed. James T. Boulton (Cambridge University Press, 1979) i, p. 251.
5. E.T. [Jessie Chambers], *D. H. Lawrence: a Personal Record* (1935) p. 112 (hereafter referred to as E.T.).
6. Immanuel Kant, Conclusion to *Critique of Practical Reason* (1788).
7. Ernst Haeckel, *The Riddle of the Universe* (1900) p. 344, *passim*.
8. J. W. von Goethe, 'Das Göttliche'.
9. E.T., p. 113.
10. D. H. Lawrence, *The Rainbow* (1915) ch. xv, p. 412.
11. S. T. Coleridge, *Collected Letters*, ed. E. L. Griggs (1956–71) ii, p. 864.
12. S. T. Coleridge, 'The Eolian Harp', ll. 47–8, in *Poetical Works*, ed. E. H. Coleridge (Oxford, 1912) i, p. 102.
13. D. H. Lawrence, *Kangaroo* (1923) ch. viii, p. 171.
14. D. H. Lawrence, *Sons and Lovers* (1913) ch. vii, pp. 160–1.

15. Ibid., end.
16. Lawrence, *The Rainbow*, end.
17. W. Wordsworth, *The Prelude*, ed. E. de Selincourt (2nd edn, 1959) pp. 623–4.
18. See my *Wordsworth in Time* (1979) ch. ix.
19. George Neville, *A Memoir of D. H. Lawrence (The Betrayal)* (1981) pp. 42–3, 188–9, quoting 'Early Days', ms 1.
20. E.T., p. 136.
21. Ford Madox Ford, *Mightier than the Sword* (1938) pp. 109–10, 106–7, 112.
22. *Letters*, ed. Boulton, i, p. 231.
23. See D. H. Lawrence, *The White Peacock* (1911) ch. iii, p. 43, and my discussion in *E. M. Forster: a Human Exploration*, ed. G. K. Das and J. Beer (1979) p. 247.
24. *Letters*, ed. Boulton, i, p. 361n.
25. Ibid., p. 366.
26. Bertrand Russell, *Portraits from Memory and other Essays* (1956) p. 107.
27. See, e.g., *Letters*, ed. Boulton, ii, p. 340.
28. A. J. Balfour, 'Creative Evolution', *Hibbert Journal* x (1911) p. 12.
29. *Letters*, ed. Boulton, i, p. 544.
30. See my discussion in 'Blake, Coleridge and Wordsworth (etc.)', in *William Blake: Essays in Honour of Sir Geoffrey Keynes*, ed. M. D. Paley and M. Phillips (1973) pp. 234–9.
31. See the letter of 30 November 1853 in *Letters of Matthew Arnold to Arthur Hugh Clough*, ed. H. F. Lowry (1932) p. 146.
32. D. H. Lawrence, *Women in Love* (1921) ch. xix, p. 260.
33. Ibid., ch. iii, p. 39.
34. Ibid., ch. xxiii, p. 329.
35. E.T., pp. 62–3.
36. For further discussion, see H. T. Moore, *Life and Works of D. H. Lawrence* (1951) p. 313.
37. *The Collected Letters of D. H. Lawrence*, ed. H. T. Moore (1962) ii, p. 872.
38. 'On Human Destiny', in *Phoenix II*, ed. Warren Roberts and Harry T. Moore (London, 1968) p. 624.
39. Ibid., p. 597.
40. *Phoenix*, ed. Edward D. McDonald (London, 1936) pp. 561–2, 459, 478.
41. *Letters*, ed. Boulton, i, pp. 63, 105, 120; ii, p. 654.
42. Ibid., ii, p. 115; *Phoenix*, ed. McDonald, p. 552.
43. 'The Reality of Peace (ii)', *English Review*, xxiv (1917) p. 518 (*Phoenix*, ed. McDonald, p. 677). Cf. my discussion in *Coleridge the Visionary* (1959) p. 156.
44. E.T., p. 115.
45. Unpublished foreword to the *Collected Poems* of 1928: *Collected Poems*, ed. V. de S. Pinto and W. Roberts (1964) ii, p. 851.
46. Ibid., i, p. 349.
47. Lawrence, *Women in Love*, ch. iii, p. 44.
48. *Letters*, ed. Boulton, i, p. 132; E.T., p. 99.
49. Coleridge, *Poetical Works*, i, p. 307.
50. *The Tales of D. H. Lawrence* (1934) p. 1116.
51. E.T., p. 184.

52. See D. H. Lawrence, *The Trespasser* (1912) ch. IV, p. 35. The allusion is to Rachel Annand Taylor's poem 'The Epilogue of the Dreaming Women', in *The Hours of Fiammetta* (1910); see *The Trespasser*, ed. E. Mansfield (Cambridge, 1981) pp. 236, 18.
53. See the unpublished letter to Forster of 23 July 1924, quoted in part by me in *E. M. Forster*, ed. Das and Beer, p. 256.
54. *Collected Poems*, ed. Pinto and Roberts, II, p. 697 (cf. p. 955).
55. E.T., p. 76.
56. S. T. Coleridge, *Notebooks*, ed. K. Coburn (1957–) II, p. 2070.
57. *Letters*, ed. Boulton, II, p. 223.

5

The 'strange and fiery' Course of *The Fox*: D. H. Lawrence's Aesthetic of Composition and Revision

ALBERT J. DEVLIN

How shall we read *The Fox*? This question has persisted through a half-dozen reissues of Lawrence's popular tale and has continued to separate critics who take both a formal and a thematic direction. As formal artifice, *The Fox* appealed to F. R. Leavis because of 'the fulness, depth, and unambiguous clarity' that Lawrence brought to his theme of 'youthful love'. 'One of the supreme things among the major tales', *The Fox* 'can hardly seem involved in any . . . questionable generality of intention'.[1] For Ian Gregor, this encomium provides only a sceptical point of departure. In his reading, *The Fox* is beset by puzzling shifts of emphasis and by radical discontinuity in the presentation of character. These 'equivocations', Gregor warns, produce a dismaying 'fissure between the violence of the catastrophe and the events which lead up to it'.[2]

Critics who focus more intently upon thematic issues also find little agreement. In 1931 John Middleton Murry attached special biographical importance to *The Fox*. By his account, the years 1916–18 had been 'a veritable nightmare' for Lawrence. Feeling besieged on all fronts, Lawrence indulged 'his appetite towards disintegration and death, his mood of loathing and hatred for all mankind'.[3] Presumably, *The Fox* breaks this deathly hold; although composed in the winter of 1918, it is a springtime book that registers new 'victory for life'.[4] More recently, Keith Sagar has extended the duration of Lawrence's 'nightmare' and has accordingly given *The Fox* quite different status. The years 1917–24 mark a time of 'withering vision' when Lawrence exhibited 'moral and artistic uncertainty or even perversity'. *The Fox*, then, is not 'filled with the promise of spring', as Murry thought, but with the apparent sanction of murder.[5]

At first this record of disagreement may be alarming. Can *The Fox* have artistic integrity and coherence if it generates the staunchly held antithetical positions of Leavis and Gregor or of Murry and Sagar? The answer is yes, although the operative conception of artistic integrity will have much wider boundaries of definition than, say, the formalist critic usually allows. With Blake, Yeats, Joyce and Faulkner, D. H. Lawrence is fundamentally a systemic writer whose work is marked by a circulation of meaning among discrete texts. As Keith Sagar notes in his *Calendar* of Lawrence's work, this writer 'never stood still. . . . He was continually incorporating his latest experiences and testing his latest ideas in his work, continually pushing outwards the frontiers of his life and work.'[6] Clearly, questions of artistic integrity as they pertain to Lawrence cannot long evade genetic and intertextual study. A full treatment of *The Fox* along these lines would include all the texts that Lawrence wrote between 1916, when he completed a first draft of *Women in Love*, and late 1921, when he produced the third and final version of *The Fox*, and would explore the manifold personal experiences and alternating states of mind that compose this time of 'nightmare'. The present remarks must, of course, be more selective. It is my sense, however, that *England, My England* (1922), *The Lost Girl* (1920) and *Aaron's Rod* (1922) can be the most useful texts in helping to define the artistic integrity of *The Fox* and perhaps to answer the readerly question that precedes these remarks. Firstly, however, a description of *The Fox* itself and of the circumstances of composition is needed in order to focus critical attention.

In December 1918, Lawrence wrote to Katherine Mansfield from Mountain Cottage in Derbyshire, and reported completion of 'the fox story – rather odd and amusing'.[7] The impetus of this first draft of *The Fox* derives from Lawrence's visits to Grimsbury Farm earlier in 1918 when he and Frieda lived in Berkshire. There, like March and Banford, the fictional proprietors of Bailey Farm, Violet Monk and Cecily Lambert lived precariously as amateur agriculturalists. They were visited as well by a soldier on leave, specifically by Cecily Lambert's brother, who undoubtedly contributed to the characterisation of Henry Grenfel, March's wilful suitor.[8] This first draft of *The Fox* became widely available only in 1959, when Harry T. Moore published a transcription and a facsimile reproduction of the manuscript in *A D. H. Lawrence Miscellany*. Lawrence next took up *The Fox* in July 1919, pruning and tightening this 'odd and amusing' tale for publication in *Hutchinson's Story Magazine*.[9] The final version of *The Fox* was completed in November 1921 in Taormina, Sicily. Writing from the Villa Fontana Vecchia, Lawrence told Earl Brewster, an American friend, that he had 'put a long tail to "The Fox", which was a bobbed short story. Now he careers with a strange and fiery brush.'[10] Several days later, in correspondence with Thomas Seltzer, Lawrence further specified his enthusiasm and sense of artistic breakthrough. *The Fox* is 'so modern, so new: a new manner', he claimed.[11]

When *The Fox* was published in March 1923 in collection with *The Ladybird* and *The Captain's Doll*, this novella had been extended to nearly three times the length of the original story. The original story ended with Henry Grenfel's abrupt proposal of marriage to March, her mystical acceptance, Banford's muted dismay, and then the factual report of marriage followed by Henry's departure 'in ten days['] time'.[12] The 'long tail' that Lawrence attached to *The Fox* in 1921 begins with the above proposal scene, but Nellie March is now granted resistance to the 'curious power' of Henry's voice, and the scene itself dissolves inconclusively when Jill Banford calls from the house, ' "Are you out there?" '[13] Thereafter the mutual struggle of Henry, March and Banford is expanded and intensified until it concludes with the death of Banford. On 16 February 1918, Lawrence wrote gloomily to Mark Gertler about the treachery of modern history: 'Nowadays one can do nothing but glance behind to see who now is creeping up to do something horrible to the back of one's neck.'[14] Lawrence's lament seems to anticipate with no little irony of reversal the fate ordained for 'the Banford', an exemplar of decadent modernity. Henry Grenfel 'gave two swift, flashing blows, in immediate succession. . . . No one heard the strange little cry which the Banford gave as the dark end of the bough swooped down, down on her. No one saw her crouch a little and receive the blow on the back of the neck' (p. 173).

As this description indicates, *The Fox* was not the product of one sustained creative endeavour. Instead its composition was spread over three years that were tumultuous even by Lawrence's standards. Lawrence left England on 14 November 1919.

Thereafter, 'the spirit of pilgrimage by which he lived' (the phrasing is L. D. Clark's) drew Lawrence south to Italy, specifically to Florence, Rome and Capri, before he and Frieda settled in March 1920 at the Villa Fontana Vecchia in Taormina. But even the relative stability of their two-year residue in Sicily was upset by wandering to Syracuse, Malta and Sardinia, and, more distantly, to Italy, Germany and Austria. Lawrence's travel between 1919 and 1921 undoubtedly broadened his range of experience and heightened his normally avid response to new people and places, further enriching the personal and cultural matrix of *The Fox*. Its growth during this period from an 'odd and amusing' tale into one that Lawrence thought 'so modern, so new', has not, however, been treated carefully by critics, especially by those who take formalistic exception to Lawrence's work. This transformation merits careful study because it contains implicit evidence of Lawrence's artistic integrity and control. As noted above, *England, My England*, *The Lost Girl* and *Aaron's Rod* can best guide this developmental study of thematic issues which appear and mature in the 'strange and fiery' course of *The Fox*.

The collection *England, My England* emerges directly from Lawrence's thinking about the First World War. Lawrence, of course, shuddered as did other sensitive Englishmen at 'the torn dead' of Ypres and the Somme. Moreover, Lawrence's personal and artistic freedom was curbed drastically by his enforced residence in England from 1915 until the Armistice. Stephen Spender has not exaggerated the bitterness of Lawrence during these years: 'The hatred in his war letters is that of a man who thinks that he is the only live thing left on the world and who regards everyone and everything else as wishing to kill him.'[15] Lawrence also reserved other, more complex and aesthetically productive moods for the war. By Lawrence's account, 'the *will* to war', that he placed 'at the bottom of almost every Englishman's heart' and 'at the bottom of every German's' (*Letters*, II, p. 233), confirmed the pervasive sickness of European society and pointed urgently to the need of spiritual regeneration. 'The fact of resurrection is everything, now', Lawrence warned in October 1915: 'whether we dead can rise from the dead, and love, and live, in a new life, here' in England (*Letters*, II, p. 420). Paradoxically, Lawrence does not, however, exclude war itself from creativity. 'Love', he explained in November 1915, 'is the great creative process, like Spring', while war 'is a great and necessary disintegrating autumnal process'

(*Letters*, II, p. 424). Lawrence's complex response to European history between 1914 and 1921 not only provides the source and structure of *England, My England*, and by extension of *The Fox*, but also reveals the indispensable terms of his artistic integrity and control.

Of the ten stories collected in *England, My England*, six precede the first draft of *The Fox* in date of composition: 'The Primrose Path', 'England, My England', 'The Horse Dealer's Daughter', 'Samson and Delilah', 'Tickets, Please' and 'The Blind Man'. The remaining stories, including 'Wintry Peacock', 'Fannie and Annie', 'Monkey Nuts' and 'You Touched Me' were probably completed between January and June 1919. Composed and printed in 1915, the title story echoes ironically the patriotism of William Ernest Henley: 'What have I done for you,/England, my England?' he asks in full nineteenth-century pride of Empire. In quite another vein, Lawrence claimed that his story 'should do good, at the long run' (*Letters*, II, p. 636), for instructing Britons in the harsh necessity that the First World War would smash 'the old, stable, measured, *decent* England'[16] of memory. In 'England, My England' this heritage is recalled by a lush pastoral landscape, by evocation of earlier, more vital phases of national life, and by the doomed Evelyn who knows instinctively the shortness of his time. Married to Winifred, the daughter of a forceful businessman, Evelyn tends a 'flamy' garden in a remote part of England that 'had no context, no relation with the world'.[17] But when Evelyn is killed in the Great War, a fate to which he submits in a 'seethe' of destruction, Lawrence dooms both his pastoral occupation and the cultural values of old English breeding that adhere to Evelyn. Triumphant at the end of 'England, My England' are Winifred, the wilful mother, and her father, for whom prosperity and patriotism are subtly entwined. Together they project an anti-pastoral ideal of modernity that grips the English landscape with disintegration and death.

As the title story and the first in order of collection, 'England, My England' earns its prominence by recording symbolically the death of the traditional 'English consciousness' (in Stephen Spender's phrase) and by forecasting what Lawrence termed 'the chaos and the orgy of ugly disintegration which is to come'.[18] The bitter fruit of this 'autumnal process' is everywhere present in the stories which compose *England, My England*. In 'Wintry Peacock', the landscape itself is crafted by Lawrence to pronounce death and devastation upon wartime Europe. 'I felt I was in a valley of the dead', the narrator notes, as he surveys the 'glistening shroud' of snow, the trees 'black and thin looking like wire' and the 'sky above sombre, heavy, yellowish-dark'. Even the commonest arrangements of society undergo a corresponding deterioration. In 'Tickets, Please', Lawrence admits that riding on Midlands cars 'is always an adventure', but because this is wartime, 'the drivers are often men unfit for active service: cripples and hunchbacks', whose trains commonly 'come to a dead halt in the midst of unbroken blackness'.[19] Lawrence, however, is most sensitive to the disruption and disorder of sexual relations in these harmful days. The deliberate Winifred, the coy Mrs Nankervis ('Samson and Delilah'), Annie, the vengeful tram-girl ('Tickets, Please'), the shrewish Mrs Goyte ('Wintry Peacock'), the profoundly self-conscious Isabel Pervin ('The Blind Man'), and finally Miss Stokes, a bold, importuning land-girl ('Monkey Nuts'), are unified by the urgency, assertion or violence that they reveal in addressing the men of *England, My England*. This reversal of roles, Lawrence would note in *Fantasia of the Unconscious* (1923), signifies the barrenness and derangement of the age. Not only do men and women remain unfulfilled in their passional lives, but society also lacks the purposive energy generated by the 'deep, magical sex-life'[20] of receding memory. Their mutual alienation from 'the tremendous unknown forces of life' (*Letters*, II, p. 218) – a phrase that Lawrence used with full cultural import in September 1914 – measures accurately the contraction of life in wartime England.

Probably the latest story in date of composition in *England, My England*, 'You Touched Me' not only exposes the malady of the age but also gives the most advanced statement of Lawrence's search for 'pure relationships and living truth', the 'new shoots of a new era' (*Letters*, II, pp. 633, 426) that would indicate 'resurrection'. Emmie and Matilda, the aging daughters of Ted Rockley, live 'grey and dreary' lives in the waning days of their father's pottery works. 'In their quiet, melancholy way, the two girls were happy', Lawrence affirms, until this passive condition is upset by the return of their adopted brother Hadrian after the signing of the Armistice. This self-possessed 'charity boy' is inspired quite accidentally to pursue both his stepfather's wealth and his elder daughter's promise of marriage. Thinking to touch the sleeping face of her dying father, Matilda touches instead the brow of Hadrian and awakens him to a vision of 'unknown things'. Thereafter the story is made taut by Ted Rockley's imperative that Matilda marry Hadrian lest she be excluded from his considerable wealth. Her capitulation is sealed by a reluctant kiss: ' "Kiss him,' the dying man said. Obediently, Matilda put forward her mouth and kissed the young husband.' Cryptic and at least on the surface unpalatable, 'You Touched Me' moves nonetheless toward the regeneration of those immured in modern life. His 'man's figure, laconic, charged with plebian energy',[21] identifies Hadrian as the power needed to banish sentimental, domestic or maternal varieties of love, and to restore a proper relation between the vying, confounded sexes of *England, My England*. Probably composed in June 1919, 'You Touched Me' stands in complex relation to *The Fox*: its plot or design clearly bears the imprint of the first draft of December 1918, while its extremity, even its cruelty, anticipates Lawrence's later revision.

The first draft of *The Fox* is a unique, irrecoverable instance of temperament, circumstance, and execution. But while its appearance in December 1918 may not have been predictable, Lawrence's story nonetheless speaks in one rhythm with the adjoining stories of *England, My England* and betrays the same formative concerns and hopes engendered by the First World War. The links between the first draft of *The Fox* and the stories of *England, My England* need only brief enumeration here. The argument of the title story, that the First World War marks the end of old England and forecasts a time of 'ugly disintegration', is ratified by the ironic pastoral of Bailey Farm – the hens do not lay, a heifer 'refused absolutely' (p. 28) to be corralled, and the landscape is uniformly 'black' (p. 34) when winter comes in Berkshire. In addition, wartime restraints on hunting have increased the 'evil' of the fox until he becomes 'a demon', plundering 'the hens under the very noses of March and Banford' (p. 30). As Nellie March trudges through this ironic version of pastoral, she reveals a symptomatic disquietude that aligns her conceptually with the troubled women of *England, My England*. Her 'consciousness was, as it were, held back' (p. 31) from vital contact with the unknown self. The arrival of Henry Grenfel fulfils the prophecy of renewal conveyed by March's earlier encounter with the fox, and thus begins 'the great creative process' of love that Lawrence foresaw. Banford's resistance to this creativity is scarcely developed in the first draft of *The Fox*, although her incipient role as Magna Mater to Henry evokes the

deranged sexuality of *England, My England.* Had Lawrence not
recognised the potential of his material, the 'odd and amusing'
tale that he completed in 1918 might have been added to *England,
My England,* for their main lines of cultural conception and artistic
rendering are nearly congruent. Neither is intelligible apart from
its source in England's precipitous fall into the First World War
and Lawrence's hope for 'resurrection'. This early history of *The
Fox* partially answers the opening question, but a more satisfactory
answer must await examination of Lawrence's motives in revising
a relatively untroubled story of 'youthful love'. How to read the
expanded version of *The Fox* of 1921 that Lawrence found 'so
modern, so new', depends upon further study conducted along
intertextual lines. Such criticism will cause us to reflect upon
Lawrence's underlying integrity of motive and to recognise his
true achievement of ends in *The Fox.*

The elements of complication that give *The Fox* its 'strange and
fiery' momentum were ordained by Lawrence's personal experience
and tested aesthetically in *The Lost Girl* (1920) and *Aaron's Rod*
(1922). For Lawrence, the doctrine of 'resurrection' simply means
to keep vital company with the indwelling godhead. As he
explained to Gordon Campbell in September 1914, 'we want to
realise the tremendous *non-human* quality of life –

> it is wonderful. It is not the emotions, nor the personal feelings
> and attachments, that matter. These are all only expressive, and
> expression has become mechanical. Behind us all are the
> tremendous unknown forces of life, coming unseen and
> unperceived as out of the desert to the Egyptians, and driving
> us, forcing us, destroying us if we do not submit to be swept
> away. (*Letters*, II, p. 218)

Lawrence's doctrine of 'resurrection', which is at once the
source of his fictional characterisation and of his vision of personal
and cultural well-being, remained constant throughout his life
and profuse writing. What changed regularly, and often drastically,
was Lawrence's estimation of recalcitrant, reactionary powers that
hinder the creative 'forces of life'. Lawrence's historical faith that
war, although 'hideous', was 'a great and necessary disintegrating'
process that precedes renewal, at least partially sustained him
through 1915. Thereafter Lawrence was progressively disillusioned
by the war's length, by England's stubborn defence of antiquated

political, social and economic values, and especially by the rise of
unworthy leadership in Lloyd George and other 'fleas and bugs of
righteous militarism'.[22] By 1917 Lawrence had abandoned any
hope that 'a new state' committed to 'the highest good of the *soul*'
(*Letters*, II, p. 366) would emerge from the testing of national wills.
Instead, as he told Waldo Frank in July, 'I believe the deluge of
iron rain will destroy the world here, utterly: no Ararat will rise
above the subsiding iron waters'.[23] Temperamentally, Lawrence's
mood in 1918 vacillated between weary resignation – 'I sit in bed
. . . and wait for the Judgement Day' – and murderous revenge –
'I've got quite a lot of murder in my soul: heaven knows how I
shall ever get it out'.[24] What remained constant, however, was
Lawrence's feeling of entrapment in England, 'like a wild cat in a
cage',[25] and his will to leave now that 'the orgy of ugly
disintegration' would be complete. Whether *Rananim*, Lawrence's
promised land, lay to the east, south or west, in Palestine, Italy or
America, Lawrence was adamant in March 1919 that he was 'quite
at the end of everything' in England.[26] To be sure, his faith in 'the
power to live and be one's own self'[27] was not destroyed, but
between the outbreak of war in 1914 and his departure for Italy in
1919, Lawrence learned bitterly the strength of domestic, social
and political forces that stood in resistance to 'resurrection' and
renewal. This knowledge was distilled into *The Lost Girl* (1920),
Aaron's Rod (1922) and especially *The Fox*, which best dramatises
what Lawrence termed 'the great articulate extremity of art'.[28]

In their respective chronologies, *The Lost Girl* and *Aaron's Rod*
bracket the years of the First World War and thus detail social
England during a critical period. Alvina Houghton, the 'lost girl'
of the title, is the daughter of James, the irrepressible entrepreneur
of Woodhouse, which is modelled closely upon Lawrence's native
Eastwood. In the pre-war years, Woodhouse is the usual
microcosm of English piety, class restriction, materialism, and a
relentless if now largely ineffectual mechanism. After a brief
struggle, the thirty-year-old Alvina is liberated from this grey
Midlands world by Ciccio, her dark Italian lover, who happens
upon Woodhouse in his travels with the Natcha-Kee-Tawara,
Lawrence's philosophic variety troupe. Their sudden marriage
and equally abrupt departure for Italy in November 1914 allow
Lawrence to rehearse his own last bitter, if wistful, view of
receding England, 'like a long, ash-grey coffin slowly submerging.
. . . It seemed to repudiate the sunshine, to remain unilluminated,

long and ash-grey and dead.'[29] In *Aaron's Rod* there is no
resurrection for post-war England. Recognised by his fellow
miners as 'a man of peculiar understanding', Aaron Sisson knows
that 'nothing was changed' by the war. Not only does 'the
unspeakably familiar' pall of marriage, children and labour cover
Britain, but also post-war society is threatened by 'a new menace',
the long-awaited peace which merely discharged 'the violence of
the nightmare . . . into the general air'.[30] Accordingly, all
conditions of men, including the privileged capitalist, the
Bohemian poseur, and the miner in the 'Royal Oak', betray 'a
neurasthenic haste for excitement' (p. 11) and thus remain
impervious to 'resurrection'. Against the same 'ugly disintegration'
that Lawrence observed, Aaron Sisson holds a 'hard, inviolable
heart' (p. 40) and a 'cold diabolical consciousness' (p. 19), before
leaving his importunate wife and children to travel in Italy. Its
'brutal way was better', he realises, than 'the cosy brightness of a
real home' (p. 205) in England.

Working 'very spasmodically', Lawrence completed *Aaron's Rod*
in May 1921 after more than three years' effort; by contrast, *The
Lost Girl* was written in eight weeks in the spring of 1920, and was
published that autumn. Each work is quite different in tone and
intention, but they share the same autobiographical pattern of
disillusion, critique of post-war England, and departure for the
more authentic fields of Italy, and thus represent Lawrence's first
and most nearly sustained treatment of these exceedingly personal
materials. In projecting Lawrence's vision of social destruction,
The Lost Girl and *Aaron's Rod* establish a conceptual framework
and a distinctive authorial tone; in sum, a voice of extremity
mated to the exigencies of the day that is heard still more urgently
in *The Fox*.

At the centre of the conceptual framework that Lawrence
established in *The Lost Girl* and *Aaron's Rod* is the act of submission.
As a form of relationship, submission was invested by Lawrence
with values that indicate the inimical temper of the age. In 'the
fatal year 1914' (p. 262), Alvina Houghton is besieged by Dr
Mitchell, a typical modern lover whose 'imperious condescension'
(p. 257) is mocked by his delicate bowels, before she submits to
the dark, mysterious Ciccio. 'Strange fine black hair, he had, close
as fur, animal' (p. 129), Lawrence chants, in projecting a lover
destined to free Alvina from the 'permanent fact' (p. 143) of
English atrophy and death. The 'cat-like look in his derisive eyes'

(p. 159) not only measures Ciccio's contempt for the wilful, domestic love ideal that pervades England, but also elicits from Alvina her painful submission to a hitherto 'unknown beauty': 'the spell was on her, of his darkness and unfathomed handsomeness. And he killed her. He simply took her and assassinated her. . . . Yet all the time, his lustrous dark beauty, unbearable' (p. 202).

The 'seethe of excitement' (p. 266) of the war awakens Alvina's spirit and arms her to resist Dr Mitchell's promise of comfort and security. In *Aaron's Rod*, however, this fortunate fall has lost its paradoxical virtue and has emerged as the nullity of post-war England. In 'More Pillar of Salt', a chapter remarkable for its sustained, purposive cruelty, Aaron Sisson thwarts the 'cunning' (p. 154) female will of his wife. To 'the iron of her threat', to Lottie's tears, reproaches, and finally to her 'wifely tenderness', Aaron answers with silence, irony and sarcasm, before departing into 'a black unconsciousness' (pp. 121–2) of restored isolate being. His refusal to submit to the presumed 'life-centrality of woman' (p. 155), which by 1921 summarises for Lawrence the mistaken tenor of the age, augers submission to what the author later termed in *Fantasia of the Unconscious* (1922) 'the great centres of dynamic consciousness'.[31] When Aaron Sisson bows in recognition to this long-denied power, Lawrence exults that 'he had got it back, the male godliness, the male godhead' (p. 250). In effect, Aaron Sisson has been assimilated to 'the tremendous unknown forces of life' that Lawrence described in 1914: 'driving us, forcing us, destroying us if we do not submit to be swept away'.

In expanding *The Fox*, Lawrence developed the inherent tensions of Banford, March, and especially Henry who enacts the autobiographical pattern of disillusion, critique and departure. His disillusion may be dated from a scene in which Henry overhears Banford and March through their bedroom door. Henry is 'a beastly labourer', Banford warns, who only covets Bailey Farm. 'Oh, we *did* make a mistake when we let him stop. We ought never to have lowered ourselves. And I've had such a fight with all the people here, not to be pulled down to their level.' Henry turns from the door with eyes 'so round and wide that he seemed to see the whole night' (pp. 144–5). Thereafter Henry speaks as pariah, no less vulnerable to censure than the fox that he kills in abnegation. 'And suddenly it seemed to him England was little and tight, he felt the landscape was constricted even in the dark' (p. 146), formerly an ambience congenial to the huntsman. Later, when March recants her marriage promise, Henry knows intuitively that 'society was on top of him, and he must scheme' to have 'his doom, his destiny, and his reward' (pp. 166–7). Henry's vitalistic scheming and his critique of post-war England are naturally inseparable, but the final consequence of Henry's expanded role in *The Fox* is the promise of departure. Following Lawrence's inclination for the west, a dream of transcendence that competed with eastern and southern expressions, Henry has taken March to Cornwall where they contemplate passage to 'the West, Canada, America': 'To leave this shore! He believed that as they crossed the seas, as they left this England which he so hated, . . . she would go to sleep. She would close her eyes at last and give in to him' (pp. 178–9).

It is this drama of submission and the collateral issue of Banford's death that make *The Fox* 'so modern, so new', and ordain the 'strange and fiery' course of its development. By assimilating Henry Grenfel to the fox, Lawrence not only recapitulates the characterisation of Ciccio but also lodges an important statement concerning the source of motivation in personal and social relations. In *Fantasia of the Unconscious*, an occult and sometimes insouciant book written in June 1921, Lawrence made clear the import of imagery long prominent in his work. Keen, predatory, and concentrated in vision, such animals as 'cats, wolves, tigers, [and] hawks' have exemplary value because they live 'chiefly . . . from the great voluntary centres' where assertiveness and independence are formed. 'The narrowed vision of the cat, the single point of vision of the hawk – these we do not know any more',[32] Lawrence concludes, in an age dominated by mental consciousness and addicted to ideals and conventions. Henry's immediate antecedents in the mode of male power are Hadrian, Ciccio and Aaron Sisson, but in *The Fox* the resultant drama of submission inspires Lawrence to explore the most subtle and extreme recesses of this infinitely complex theme.

The subtlety of *The Fox* is best demonstrated by Lawrence's inconclusive treatment of the theme of submission. Whereas Ciccio does not waver in his hard, insentient masculinity and Alvina falls a ready prey to the Italian's 'lustrous dark beauty', both March and Henry only partially transcend their discontents in addressing the 'unknown forces of life'. Throughout *The Fox*,

March veers precariously between the rationalised pole of Banford's consoling conventionalities and the vulpine pole of Henry's sensual will. But neither the death of Banford nor the subsequent marriage of Henry and March entirely relieves her dilemma of how to be. Indeed, the apparently didactic conclusion of *The Fox* succeeds only in holding up to March both the haunting memory of Banford and the equally compelling presence of Henry. 'Instead of her soul swaying with new life, it seemed to droop, to bleed, as if it were wounded', the conformation, Lawrence concludes, 'of a woman who has died in the old way of love, and can't quite rise to the new way' (p. 175). soon after their marriage, Henry brings March to his native village in Cornwall, a region that Lawrence knew well and that he reserved for special significance. 'Cornwall . . . isn't really England, nor Christendom', he told Bertrand Russell in January 1916. 'It has another quality: of King Arthur's days, that flicker of Celtic consciousness before it was swamped under Norman and Teutonic waves' (*Letters*, II, p. 505). But the savage idyll of Henry's marriage recoils ironically upon Lawrence's vitalistic hero. Henry 'had won her', but 'he had not yet got her' (p. 175). To the extent that March retains 'her independent spirit', Henry 'chafed, feeling he hadn't got his own life. He would never have it till she yielded and slept in him. Then he would have all his own life as a young man and a male' (pp. 178–9). Lawrence's inconclusive treatment of the theme of submission does not reflect imprecision, uncertainty or violation of the 'logical architectural limits'[33] of his material. By temporising, Lawrence acknowledges instead its inherent complexity. The imperfect encounter of Henry and March not only indicates the temper of the age but also dramatises in terms that we know to be psychologically valid the halting effect of history upon human motivation.

The 'strange and fiery' course of *The Fox* leads irresistibly to the extremity of Banford's death. Among several critics, Keith Sagar has deplored this necessity, which Lawrence appears to equate with 'the fox's taking of a hen'. Sagar warns further of 'the danger of seeking too close an identification between what humanity lacks and what gives splendour to the beasts'.[34] These reflections are not easily dismissed, but at the same time they do not address with precision the internal cogency of Henry's action. His willed murder of Banford should be approached simultaneously from several avenues of perception. Firstly, after Banford is apprised of

Henry's proposal, her wilful maternalism evolves quickly and inevitably into a virulent regard for the young man that is predicated upon class consciousness and upon attendant moral, economic and social ideals. Conceived in the same wilful–spiritual mode as Winifred ('England, My England'), Emmie Rockley ('You Touched Me') and Miss Frost (*The Lost Lady*), 'the Banford' brings to ultimate expression and practice what Lawrence termed in *Fantasia* 'the automatism of ideals and conventions'.[35] We should read in this character's formation Lawrence's measurement of contemporary resistance to renewal and 'resurrection'. Henry's willed murder of Banford is too well known to be restaged here. What needs more precise identification, however, is the appropriate category for understanding this deed of extremity. In October 1916 Lawrence praised the 'horrible and terrifying' quality of Mark Gertler's painting *Merry-Go-Round*. Its 'combination of blaze, and violent mechanised rotation and complete involution' proceeded from 'an ecstasy of destructive sensation' that constituted at the same time 'a real and ultimate revelation' of modern perversity. 'I must say, I have, for you, reverence', Lawrence told Gertler, 'the reverence for the great articulate extremity of art'.[35] In 1917 Lawrence employed a similar aesthetic of destruction to explain his own work to Waldo Frank. *The Rainbow*, he admitted, was 'a destructive work, . . . a kind of working up to the dark sensual or Dionysic or Aphrodisic ecstasy, which does actually burst the world, burst the world-consciousness in every individual'.[37] The expanded version of *The Fox* of 1921 is governed by the same crux of aesthetic ideas and emphases. Henry's murder of Banford is a bursting of the 'world-consciousness' so that the more subtle circulations of the isolate soul may stimulate both personal and cultural 'resurrection'. Neither the modernity of *The Fox* nor the 'strange and fiery' course of its development can be understood apart from this artistic cooperation with the overarching process of destruction and creation, Lawrence's unfailing signature of 'the tremendous unknown forces of life'.

These remarks tend to validate F. R. Leavis's judgement that *The Fox* 'can hardly seem involved in any . . . questionable generality of intention'. During its lengthy period of composition, *The Fox* was urged forward by social and historical factors that reveal Lawrence's complex literary situation. In part at least, this answers the question of how we shall read *The Fox* by employing a historical imagination to reconstruct the contextual values of this remarkable tale. But at the same time, the contextual values provided by history and registered in the texts that precede *The Fox* can help to focus the related question of Lawrence's aesthetic integrity and control. Beginning with *England, My England* and culminating in *The Fox*, Lawrence's artistic conscience was engaged progressively by the deepening intensities of Georgian England and Europe at large. At each point in the composition, revision and expansion of *The Fox*, Lawrence fulfilled the inner necessity of his material by selecting the approximate image, symbol and design. This fidelity to the peculiar intensities of the age encompasses what Lawrence meant by morality in art. In his *Study of Thomas Hardy*, Lawrence asserted that art 'must give fair play all round. . . . if it be really a work of art, it must contain the essential criticism on the morality to which it adheres'.[38] In projecting March's final wavering state, Lawrence has recognised the inherent antinomy of his material, submitting the vital truth of Henry's sensual will to the corrosive memory of Banford. But Lawrence's fairness does not produce mere stasis; instead, it allows the artist to resist conceptualisation and render honourably 'a vast living universe' of potentiality. 'Each thing', Lawrence stated in 'Art and Morality', 'streams in its own odd, intertwining flux, and nothing, not even man nor the God of man, nor anything that man has thought or felt or known, is fixed or abiding. All moves.'[39] The extremity of *The Fox*, lodged principally in the sacrifice of Banford, provides the inevitable climax of Lawrence's engagement with the apocalypse of modern history. Perhaps our access to *The Fox* depends finally upon the recognition that D. H. Lawrence posits no substantial differences between artistic integrity, morality and life itself. This aesthetic does not promise even a narrow bridge of *rapprochement* with formalist criticism, but it may help to place the apparent discontinuities of *The Fox* within a richer and more comprehensive realm of intentionalism.

NOTES

1. F. R. Leavis, *D. H. Lawrence: Novelist* (1955; reprinted New York: Alfred A. Knopf, 1956) pp. 321, 332.
2. Ian Gregor, '*The Fox*: a Caveat', *Essays in Criticism*, IX, (1959) p. 17.

3. John Middleton Murry, *Son of Woman* (New York: Jonathan Cape & Harrison Smith, 1931) pp. 105, 112.
4. Ibid., pp. 124–5.
5. Keith Sagar, *The Art of D. H. Lawrence* (Cambridge University Press, 1966) pp. 116–17.
6. Keith Sagar, *D. H. Lawrence: a Calendar of his Works* (Austin: University of Texas Press, 1979) p. vii.
7. Letter to Katherine Mansfield, 10 December 1918. Because an edition of Lawrence's letters is in preparation, only the date and recipient will be noted for correspondence not yet printed in *The Letters of D. H. Lawrence*, ed. James T. Boulton, 7 vols (Cambridge University Press, 1979–81). References to the Cambridge Edition will be included parenthetically in the text.
8. See *D. H. Lawrence: a Composite Biography*, ed. Edward Nehls (Madison: University of Wisconsin Press, 1957) I, pp. 463–7, and Paul Delany, *D. H. Lawrence's Nightmare* (New York: Basic Books, 1978) pp. 347, 355.
9. This printing was first reported by Brian H. Finney, 'The Hitherto Unknown Publication of Some D. H. Lawrence Short Stories', *Notes and Queries*, CCXVII (February 1972) pp. 55–6.
10. Letter to Earl Brewster, 16 November 1921.
11. *D. H. Lawrence: Letters to Thomas and Adele Seltzer*, ed. Gerald M. Lacy (Santa Barbara: Black Sparrow Press, 1976) p. 29.
12. *A D. H. Lawrence Miscellany*, ed. Harry T. Moore (Carbondale: Southern Illinois University Press, 1959) p. 48.
13. *Four Short Novels* (New York: Viking, 1965) pp. 132–33. All quotations from *The Fox* follow the Viking edition; page references are included parenthetically in the text.
14. Letter to Mark Gertler, 16 February 1918.
15. 'D. H. Lawrence, England and the War', in *D. H. Lawrence: Novelist, Poet, Prophet*, ed. Stephen Spender (New York: Harper & Row, 1973) p. 72.
16. Letter to Mark Gertler, 5 December 1916.
17. Quotations follow the first printing of 'England, My England', *English Review*, XXI (October 1915).
18. Letter to Lady Cynthia Asquith, 25 November 1916.
19. Quotations follow the first printings of 'Wintry Peacock', *The Metropolitan* (August 1921) and 'Tickets, Please', *Strand* (April 1919).
20. D. H. Lawrence, *Fantasia of the Unconscious* (1922; reprinted with *Psychoanalysis and the Unconscious*, New York: Viking, 1960) p. 123.
21. Quotations follow the first printing of 'You Touched Me', *Land and Water*, 29 April 1920.
22. Letter to Mark Gertler, 16 February 1918.
23. Letter to Waldo Frank, 27 July 1917.
24. Letters to S. S. Koteliansky, 20 January 1918, and Montague Sherman, 21 February 1918.
25. Letter to Mark Gertler, 16 March 1918.
26. Letter to John Middleton Murry, 6 March 1919.
27. Letter to Lady Cynthia Asquith, 1 July 1919.
28. Letter to Mark Gertler, 9 October 1916.

29. D. H. Lawrence, *The Lost Girl*, ed. John Worthen (1920; reprinted Cambridge University Press, 1981) p. 294. Later citations follow the Cambridge edition; page numbers are noted parenthetically in the text.
30. D. H. Lawrence, *Aaron's Rod* (1922; reprinted New York: Viking, 1961) pp. 1–7. Later citations follow the Viking edition; page numbers are noted parenthetically in the text.
31. Lawrence, *Fantasia*, p. 74.
32. Ibid., p. 102.
33. Kingsley Widmer, *The Art of Perversity* (Seattle: University of Washington Press, 1962) p. 63.
34. Sagar, *The Art of D. H. Lawrence*, p. 117.
35. Lawrence, *Fantasia*, p. 105.
36. Letter to Mark Gertler, 9 October 1916.
37. Letter to Waldo Frank, 27 July 1917.
38. See *Phoenix: the Posthumous Papers of D. H. Lawrence*, ed. Edward D. McDonald (New York: Viking, 1936) p. 476.
39. See ibid., p. 525.

6

'Pioneering into the wilderness of unopened life': Lou Witt in America

FREDERICK P. W. McDOWELL

St Mawr is one of Lawrence's richest fictions and it continually expands in the mind. It is primarily parable, and Lawrence's development of his fable and his establishing of its archetypal and mythical dimensions provide its essential fascination and challenge. Three critics have recently related this novella to Lawrence's contemporaneous experiences in Europe and America. Richard Poirier discerns in Lawrence's heroine, Lou Witt, an attempt to find renewal in the wilderness; such 'visionary possession of America', according to Poirier, is an insistent theme in American literature.[1] Tony Tanner and James C. Cowan refer the tale to Lawrence's own intense, if somewhat ambiguous, reactions to America and to New Mexico.[2] Following the lead of these critics, I shall focus upon Lou Witt's sojourn in New Mexico, despite the fact that it forms a relatively brief, though brilliant, coda to the rendition of her life in English society. I shall also consider St Mawr, the impetuous stallion, and Morgan Lewis, his groom, as tutelary presences who give Lou guidance, through their examples, of the course that she should follow in America after her recoil from 'modern' pseudo-sophistication.

I wish, furthermore, to emphasise the unity of the tale and to dispel the notion that there is a break between its European and American sections. Though St Mawr and Lewis figure only in the first episode in America – in Texas – and do not accompany Lou to her final haven in New Mexico, Lawrence nevertheless unifies his novella in subtle ways. Foreshadowings of Lou's reactions in America occur in the English part of the tale; and common motifs and images make it a coherent whole. The intensity of Lou's quest for awareness reveals also a close link between Lawrence's

92

protagonist and himself. His revulsion from the British middle and upper classes after he returned from America to visit England in 1923 is parallel to Lou's ('I feel the English much more my enemies than the Americans'),[3] and his turning from them in order to establish a fresh regimen for the spirit in America is prototypic of Lou's progression.

Even if there are overtones of Lawrence in her actions and thoughts, she remains an authentic fictional personage. From the beginning she is partly an outsider as an American expatriate, but in the course of the tale she renounces any plans to identify with her adopted British milieu. Her voyage westward is in some sense, therefore, a return to her native roots. With something of a shock of recognition, she realises that she has at last found a place where she can achieve a new perspective and a meaningful fruition of her powers. In words echoing those of Brigham Young when he first saw the Salt Lake country, she says of her ranch at first glance: 'This is the place.' If, as Lawrence thought, America as a whole may oppress by its materialistic fervour and its crude assertion of will, the American West at least has reserves for the soul that are lacking in a worn-down Europe and in an England where 'the dead hand of the war lay like a corpse decomposing',[4] even over the Shropshire countryside.

When Lou Witt first sees the stallion, St Mawr, he seems to be looking at her 'from another world'. On fuller knowledge after she buys him for her effete artist-husband Rico Carrington (a baronet from Australia), her uncanny feeling that St Mawr is in truth the denizen of a country alien to England intensifies; and she determines, if at all possible, to forsake the shallow 'society' of bourgeois and aristocratic England in order to enter the universe that St Mawr by native authority inhabits: 'When he reared his head and neighed from his deep chest, like deep wind-bells resounding, she seemed to hear the echoes of another darker, more spacious, more dangerous, more splendid world than ours, that was beyond her. And there she wanted to go' (pp. 26–7). Lou's pilgrimage to America reveals an attempt to discover in the actuality the invisible and inaudible world wherein the horse dwells with regal splendour. She also exemplifies the Anglo-Saxon myth that in a wilderness one can undergo a spiritual transformation, as Lawrence himself apparently did in New Mexico: 'I think New Mexico was the greatest experience from the outside world that I have ever had. It certainly changed me for ever. . . . In the magnificent fierce morning of New Mexico one sprang awake, a new part of the soul woke up suddenly, and the old world gave way to a new.'[5] Both Lou and Lawrence illustrate the reorientation that the European sensibility must try to attain as it confronts the primitiveness of unspoiled America. Such a reorientation Lawrence described in 'Fenimore Cooper's Leatherstocking Novels': the Europeans came to America, Lawrence said, '1. To slough the old European consciousness completely. 2. To grow a new skin underneath, a new form.'[6] Lou realises that 'half-way across from our human world to that terrific equine twilight' (p. 20) represents no easy step for her to take; the old consciousness will not yield easily to the new and yet there is no turning back for a person who has seen the light – as she has done in her visionary apprehension of St Mawr. She nerves herself to take this step in the course of the parable, to grow in America this 'new skin'; and she is the only one in her immediate circle who is prepared to do something so decisive. She is a wanderer between two worlds, one that is most certainly dead and the other that it is difficult to bring into being. Writing to Catherine Carswell from America in 1924, Lawrence, as it were, spoke for himself and his heroine as they both tried to adapt to the strange, disturbing Southwest: 'It was good to be alone and responsible. But also it is very *hard* living up against these savage Rockies. The savage things are a bit gruesome, and they try to down one. – But far better they than the white disintegration' (*CL*, p. 814).

From the first, St Mawr's 'power, his alive, alert intensity, his unyieldingness' (p. 14) had affected Lou, and he begins almost at once to exert over her his magnetic influence. She responds to the Promethean aspect of the horse, who with pride and defiance brings to her perception the gift of a divine fire. The Promethean aspect of St Mawr Lawrence emphasised by his use of fire-images in limning the stallion's figure and power: the stallion 'burns with life', 'a dark, invisible fire seemed to come out of him', he stands 'looming like a bonfire in the dark', and 'in his dark eye, that looked, with its cloudy brown pupil, a cloud within a dark fire, like a world beyond our world, there was a dark vitality glowing, and within the fire, another sort of wisdom' (pp. 49, 12, 31, 26). To Lou, St Mawr is emphatically a bringer of light into the outer darkness of her present situation in Europe. By taking him to America, she saves him from the enmity of Rico and his friends who want to geld him; to these people, not only the apparent viciousness but the coursing life of the horse is an affront. Lou leaves St Mawr on the family ranch in Texas, as she embarks upon a new existence in the further West. But the positive force and vitality of St Mawr, his self-sufficiency, and his disdain of the ordinary, the conventional and the trivial guide her in her search for a firmer identity when she settles in New Mexico. She has thus found in St Mawr the dynamic attributes that Lawrence associated with the horse as a mythical presence, as 'the symbol of surging potency and power of movement, of action, in man'.[7]

Lawrence forged the link between St Mawr and Lou Witt in New Mexico by his use of fire-images – hitherto associated with St Mawr – to describe Lou's sense of dedication and envisioned mode of existence there. She will follow a sexless routine until a truly vital man appears for her. Until then she will remain in an interim state which she compares to that of the Vestal Virgins, 'the Virgins of the holy fire in the old temples' serving 'the hidden fire' (p. 139). She will hold herself aloof from men just as St Mawr has held himself distinct from animal contact in England and just as Natty Bumpo in *Deerslayer* would remain 'alone' rather than 'be dragged into a false heat of deliberate sensuality. . . . His soul is alone, for ever alone. So he would preserve his integrity, and remain alone in the flesh. It is a stoicism which is honest and fearless' (*SCAL*, p. 90).

The unleashing of St Mawr's sexual powers in America hints of some such fulfilment in the future for Lou, though in America she now adopts, somewhat paradoxically perhaps, the same remoteness sexually that had characterised him in England. After she defines her role as Vestal Virgin in terms of the fire-images betokening the quickening power upon her soul of St Mawr, despite his actual absence from New Mexico, she also regards the desert and mountain scenery that surrounds her in terms of such images. In this landscape there is a version of that other world that had emanated to her from the eyes of St Mawr: 'It seemed to her that the hidden fire was alive and burning in this sky, over the desert, in the mountains. She felt a certain latent holiness in the very atmosphere, a young spring-fire of latent holiness, such as she had never felt in Europe, or in the East' (p. 140).

In St Mawr from the beginning Lou finds, intertwined with his free abandon, an element of the demonic and a potentiality for evil as for the positive. It is as if the savage force and the stark sensuality which Lawrence attributes to the African statue in Halliday's apartment in *Women in Love* are implicit in St Mawr. There is as much to fear as to admire in him. So in her second vision of St Mawr, after the accident at the Devil's Chair when Rico is injured by refusing to give him rein as he shies at a dead snake, the stallion seems to her, for the moment at least, an evil presence. Nevertheless, the person – like Lou or her mother – who views an authentic presence like St Mawr's in a true perspective, will realise that moral categories resist simplistic definition and that some manifestations of evil are more reprehensible than others. If the violence of St Mawr can bring disaster, it is the result of a natural cause (the snake), and it lacks the flabbiness, the betrayal, the deceit and the hypocrisy of the people in Lou's immediate social milieu who are the ones most implicated in her vision of evil. In St Mawr there are forthrightness, directness and honesty, all qualities lacking in those people she knows most intimately. She decides that St Mawr cannot be wholly evil, or even intrinsically so, in comparison with the men whom he has been bred to serve, men unlike those in the past with whom he would have felt affinity, men 'who had a flickering, rising flame of nobility in them. . . . But now where is the flame of dangerous, forward-pressing nobility in them?' (p. 75). Such nobility is lacking, certainly, in the people she knows best. Therefore, the horse with its 'brave spirit', she concludes, cannot be 'mean'.

The vitality of St Mawr is apparently inseparable not only from nobility but from truculence. If St Mawr nourishes life, he carries with him a smouldering resentment. His having been in servitude to unworthy men has fostered his 'slavish malevolence' and has diminished his life-enhancing aspects. And if his vitality remains with her in New Mexico, the malevolence in the inspiriting landscape suggests that the stallion's spirit is present in full ambivalence, in its terror-infusing as in its exalting influence. In Europe the example of St Mawr had inspired Lou in her wish 'to get her life straight from the source' as animals do; but she finds this a formidable undertaking in America, more formidable perhaps than of which, even by the end of the tale, she can have any just conception. She will undoubtedly have to weather anew some of the hardships and frustrations undergone by the New England woman, the wife of the trader who had been a former owner of the ranch that Lou purchases. These are hardships and frustrations of which Lou is not fully conscious, since they are directly recounted by the narrator. Actually, they comprise a test of what she will have to survive, and are not an ironic deprecation of her naiveté, as one critic has alleged.[8] And so if there is a 'latent holiness' in the atmosphere and if the ranch becomes a 'blessed' and a 'sacred' place to her, then she is yet alive to the 'certain cruelty' of 'the great desert-and-mountain landscape' (p. 134), to aspects of this country that will provide the greatest challenge to her received Christian values. Like the New England woman, Lou will have to learn to live in 'a world before and after the God of Love' (p. 151), in an America 'tense with latent violence and resistance' (*SCAL*, p. 73). Temporarily at least, Lou's world will be one from which sex is absent because meaningful emotional expression has become impossible for her in a superficial, pleasure-loving society. The pine tree which is the guardian of her ranch is an evocative symbol for her present bleak but genuine mode of existence: 'a passionless, non-phallic column rising in the shadows of the pre-sexual world, before the hot-blooded ithyphallic column ever erected itself' (p. 146). As the pioneer woman before her, Lou will become increasingly conscious of 'the animosity of the spirit of place . . . like some serpent-bird for ever attacking man, in a hatred of man's onward-struggle towards further creation' (p. 152).

By his example, St Mawr has encouraged Lou to examine herself, to break through to a new awareness, and to struggle uncompromisingly toward 'increased illumination'. As a result of her vision of evil at the time of the accident to Rico, Lou is desperate as to how best to handle her situation, but decides that she at least can no longer be passive. Rather, she must struggle to achieve a sense of integrity as a human being, and, above all, she must struggle to prevent her new illumination from fading:

> The individual can but depart from the mass, and try to cleanse himself. Try to hold fast to the living thing, which destroys as it goes, but remains sweet. And, in his soul fight, fight, fight to preserve that which is life in him from the ghastly kisses and poison-bites of the myriad evil ones. Retreat to the desert, and fight. But in his soul adhere to that which is life itself, creatively destroying as it goes: destroying the stiff old thing to let the new bud come through. The one passionate principle of creative being, which recognises the natural good, and has a sword for the swarms of evil. Fights, fights, fights to protect itself. But with itself, is strong and at peace. (pp. 71–2)

Lou's sentiments are analogous to those that Lawrence expressed in a contemporaneous letter, when he also emphasised the importance of strenuous effort: 'One fights and fights for that living something that stirs way down in the blood, and *creates* consciousness' (*CL*, p. 843).

From the first, St Mawr had impressed Lou with the need to hold by her sense of the fitting and never to give way or to give in. On the ride to the Devil's Chair in Shropshire, overlooking the habitats of the ancient Celts, Lou identifies with 'the old fighting stock' that had once dwelt among the Welsh hills, and she decides that the people accompanying her on this ride are anaemic in comparison to these sensitive and imaginative peoples of long ago. In America Lou settles at her ranch, Las Chivas, as 'new blood to the attack' upon the subversive influences that surround it. Even to maintain intact her identity, she will learn that she will have to struggle against those very forces that also can promote a sense of well-being and renewal. She will have to commit herself to overcome the 'sordidness' of the primitive as such, in order to capture the 'inward vision' and the 'cleaner energy', and to 'win from the crude wild nature the victory and the power to make another start' (pp. 153–4). Her renunciation of European 'civilisation' does not allow for passivity. Lou, accordingly, adopts the Lawrentian posture in America: 'As for the fight – subtly and eternally I fight, till something breaks in me' (*CL*, p. 764).

The courage that she finds so admirable in the ancient Celts and in St Mawr is the quality which she emulates in New Mexico, again attesting to the surviving influence upon her there of St Mawr. Courage is the attribute that is most electrifying in St Mawr, the attribute most lacking in the decadent people surrounding Lou, and the attribute that she comes to value most as it enables her to forge a new philosophy. It is from St Mawr that Lou derives the strength to recast her life and to cut herself off from the pleasures and the futilities of a polite society; as a life-serving force, he is not afraid to destroy if he must do so in order to create anew. St Mawr gives her, in short, the power to resist the bogus and the determination to achieve a significant order of being by an active assertion of her powers, whatever the cost in immediate ease. In boldness, defiance, endurance, self-sufficiency and vigour, St Mawr had seemed to her the only genuine embodiment of 'Pan', the elemental life-principle, that she had encountered in England. When she reaches New Mexico, the landscape possesses a strange animistic energy as if its most significant aspect lies behind the outward phenomena that compose it. She finds 'Pan' in New Mexico, not in a human being but in the sublime landscape, though she is also awaiting a man who may truly embody the strength of that god. Lawrence had asserted in 'Pan in America' that in America 'we can still choose between the living universe of Pan, and the mechanical conquered universe of modern humanity'.[9] In effect, Lou has made this choice, difficult as it has been for her to implement. In America, in short, she can catch a glimpse of the god Pan by opening her 'third eye', her sharpened sensory powers which her English acquaintance Cartwright had described as indispensable for catching sight of this god. Pan, whom Lou had found in England in St Mawr alone, has been transferred from him to inhere in the spreading New Mexican landscape, another instance of the stallion's presence with Lou in America. Like St Mawr, Lou is now able to immerse herself in a world of primaeval nature. The New England woman, who had fought in vain to impose order upon wild nature at the ranch, had also discovered that 'the landscape lived, and lived as the world of the gods, unsullied and unconcerned' (p. 148) – a world, that is, where a god-like animal like St Mawr would naturally take his place. The gods that the New England woman had found in 'those inner mountains' were, however, 'grim and invidious and relentless, huger than man, and lower than man' (p. 153), seemingly replicas of the haughty and imposing and masterful St Mawr himself. If Lou can be regarded as following a course parallel to that of the New England woman, then she also reaches this disquieting realm of the unseen and its supernal deities where she had envisioned St Mawr as being.

In England, Lou had hoped to find a 'pure, animal man' who by his elemental nature would be 'part of the unseen', but had not done so. For such a man she is waiting at the end of the tale, much as Ursula Brangwen hopes for fulfilment in *The Rainbow* from 'a son of God' who will come to her at a later time. For Ursula as for Lou, the stallion is a symbol of the fierce strength of life that is both inspiriting and destructive, but rigorous and harsh in any case. One remembers that the stampeding horses at the end of *The Rainbow* cause Ursula's child by Anton Skrebensky to miscarry, while they also presage renewal for her. It requires much courage for Lou to cut herself off from the existence that she has known and enjoyed superficially for many years; and it is this element in her character that some critics neglect when they either identify her with the shallowness of the world that she learns to criticise or else regard her as an unpleasant person because of her uncompromising attitudes towards those who had formerly been her friends.[10] She does not possess a full measure of this courage until she knows St Mawr; but she then develops the power to resist 'the pasteboard society' around her rather than being engulfed by it.

In America, Lou is convinced of the truth of the revelations that came to her as she and her mother were bringing St Mawr to America to escape emasculation. On board ship in the Gulf of Mexico, she is impressed with the beauty and grace of the porpoises: 'The marvellous beauty and fascination of natural wild things! The horror of man's unnatural life, his heaped-up civilisation!' (p. 128). Even in America, where there are stores of freshness and vitality, she must be alert to escape the tawdry; the second-hand intensities and superficialities of the Texas cowboys and ranch-owners, the tourist ambience of Santa Fe, the Mexicans of Santa Fe, the 'lurking, invidious Indians', in short, the 'great weight of dirt-like inertia' (p. 140) enveloping the country.

In the quotation cited in the middle of the preceding paragraph, Lou expresses the rationale behind her escape from British society. She gives over the forms, manners, customs, conventions and expectations of this closed world for the openness of America (Mrs Witt finds far greater cohesion in English life than in America), and she ardently attempts to reach 'the successive inner sanctities of herself' that are for her 'inviolable' (p. 139). Like Whitman, as Lawrence described him, Lou is 'pioneering into the wilderness of unopened life' (*SCAL*, p. 253). She reaches a spiritual maturation in America despite the asceticism that she imposes upon herself, or perhaps because of it. She reacts with the fullness of the self to attain the firmest integration of the powers of the self; she reacts with intensity to the cosmic forces, and recovers some of the wonder that she had felt passing out of her life in England, where she had said: 'Oh, no, mother, I want the wonder back again, or I shall die' (p. 50). The elemental quickened man whom she hopes sometime to meet would also 'breathe silence and unseen wonder'.

Lou at last knows what she wants in America and is apparently on her way to achieving it at the end of the novella: 'She wanted to be still: only that, to be very, very still, and recover her own soul' (p. 137). Lou thus perceives the necessity of attaining for herself the emancipated inner being that Lawrence describes in 'Whitman': 'The soul wishes to keep clean and whole. The soul's deepest will is to preserve its own integrity, against the mind and the whole mass of disintegrating forces' (*SCAL*, p. 262). To regain the wonder and to recast her own soul, she needs the free spiritual climate of the American wilds; here she can submit to what she finds her contemporaries in Europe incapable of attaining, 'the hard, lonely responsibility of real freedom' (p. 73), the true liberty that Americans can attain if they once discover it and try to fulfil its demands: 'IT [*sic*] being the deepest *whole* self of man, the self in its wholeness, not idealistic halfness' ('The Spirit of Place', in *SCAL*, p. 10). In New Mexico, Lou can expect, she thinks, to see the meaningless appurtenances of her previous life dissolve, and to gain strength from identifying with 'the wild spirit' that has waited for her here for so long, a spirit that will not be gentle with her but will force her to become alive: 'But it's something big, bigger than men, bigger than people, bigger than religion. It's something to do with wild America' (p. 138). Lawrence may well be dramatising here, through Lou, his own emotions as he penetrated into the culture of the North American Indian and found there a vibrant religious sensibility: 'For the whole life-effort of man was to get his life into direct contact with the elemental life of the cosmos'.[11] Such is the thrust of Lou Witt's own adjustment to her strange adoptive land.

Lou's association in England with three of the central characters in the novella – her mother, Phoenix and Lewis – also helps her to prepare for her sojourn in America, and unifies the tale acceptably though perhaps not so strongly as some critics would have wished. From her mother, Lou acquires the habit of independent thinking and of a self-sufficiency based upon the honest, rational judgement of the people about her. As an agent for the exposure of the shallow and the sham, Mrs Witt is a powerful and perceptive iconoclast; but except for helping to save St Mawr and her appreciation of Morgan Lewis, she is a destructive force, never having learned the secret of 'creatively destroying'.

As for Phoenix, he confirms Lou in her desire 'for the more absolute silence of America' after flashy British life has spread its pall upon her; and when he tries to persuade her to take St Mawr there, she sees in her mind's eye 'that country, with its dark, heavy mountains holding in their lap the great stretches of pale, creased, silent desert that still is virgin of idea, its word unspoken' (p. 78). She sees in anticipation, therefore, the reality as she later finds it; she has an intuition that in a country so new, anything might yet be possible, even rebirth for the soul. Phoenix arouses Lou's admiration for his stoic isolation, his continual struggle to assert himself, his 'peculiar courage of an inherited despair' (p. 77), and his 'unyielding' resistance. But he is less a hero in the final analysis than he is an opportunist, and a sexual opportunist most of all. From him Lou learns also that admirable qualities can be blighted by too much exposure to the dehumanising pressures of contemporary life. He lacks, finally, the self-sufficiency that characterises Morgan Lewis and Lou Witt, so that when he is in New Mexico he seems to Lou to be no more complete a person than is her husband Rico.

Of these people in England who influence her later, it is Morgan Lewis who gives her most. Like St Mawr, he instructs by example; and like St Mawr, he is striking by his air of mystery, of being, like him, the denizen of another world at a distance from this one. As even the similarity of their names might indicate, Lou and Lewis are the people most closely allied in the novella by intangible ties, though differences in class and education separate them. Because of the barriers erected by civilisation, the time is not yet ripe for any consecrated relationship between them, as it is for the risen Christ and the Priestess of Isis in 'The Man Who Died'. Lou recognises something extraordinary in Lewis, a fully developed instinctive consciousness; and she declares to her mother that, unlike most other men she knows, he has 'a good, intuitive mind' (p. 49), the only genuine sort, and a sort capable of great insight. Because there is something of the unspoiled animal in him, he has a distinction lacking in most other modern men: his phosphorescent 'wildcat' eyes and his luxuriant hair suggest an intelligent, healthy animal, and he has a close understanding of the primordial St Mawr. The animal life in him has not gone awry, and puts him still in touch with unseen powers. As a result, the narrator associates him with the god Pan on the ride to Oxford to save St Mawr. As he walks his horse quite naturally 'in the shadow of the wood's edge', he is at home seemingly in 'the darkness of the old Pan' (p. 102). Lou's identification with Pan as he is subsumed in both St Mawr and the American landscape can, therefore, be extended to include

Lewis as one other embodiment of the old god; and like St Mawr, Lewis is with Lou in spirit in New Mexico, though like St Mawr he is physically absent from her.

Lewis has the self-sufficiency by nature that Lou later attains, an indifference born of self-possession and not, as with Mrs Witt, of cynicism. He is a man who keeps to himself, conscientiously preserving his sense of identity against the inroads that others try to make upon it. It is for this reason that he resists Mrs Witt when she proposes marriage to him. When he comes to London after delivering St Mawr to safety, he impresses Lou as having about him 'a quality of eternity' (p. 119), which derives from his having accepted the role that destiny has allotted him. At this point he registers upon her as an extraordinary man, 'an aristocrat, unaccessible in his aristocracy. But it was the aristocracy of the invisible powers, the greater influences, nothing to do with human society' (p. 119). There is even some suggestion in him of the fiery disposition of St Mawr, but in him the fires are muted. The cold fires of the moon and the falling star, with which he is associated, might connect him with the stallion and with the latent fires in the mountains of New Mexico; the image used to describe his anger at Mrs Witt for her insistence when she proposes to him links him again tacitly with St Mawr and the West, 'an anger congealed cold like lava' (p. 107).

Lou can sympathise at this point with Lewis's aversion to physical contact since such contact for both of them in the past has had none of the healing quality of touch, celebrated as the proximate cause for Lady Chatterley's renewal in *Lady Chatterley's Lover*. Lewis regards physical touch as a spiritual encroachment; and he recoils from all suggestion of intimacy as having about it a potentially degrading aspect. Like that of the risen Christ initially in 'The Man Who Died', his would be the cry, *'Noli me tangere'*. Lewis's passionate renunciation of sensuality points to Lou the path that she will take, when in New Mexico she elects an interim life of enforced chastity. In the talk with him in London, moreover, she expresses sentiments with which he would agree, that men and women must now stay apart from one another since they have hurt each other so much in the past: they must learn once again to be gentle with others, as they do seemingly in Lawrence's last works of fiction.

The worth of *St Mawr* has led to continuing controversy, but a consensus is now emerging that it is a work of notable stature, rising superior to incidental flaws. Lawrence has imagined a fable in which he dramatises with insight the dilemma of a sensitive modern woman in a world that seems to be increasingly without value. Through the symbolic thrust of St Mawr and of the Western landscape, Lou reaches a new understanding of the self. In my view, her sincerity and her dedication make of her progression toward awareness an achieved and searching work of art. In its furthest reaches it is prophetic, in its denunciation of the barren contemporary scene, and, too, in its intimations of the process by which modern man may encounter renewal and salvation. Lou's expectations at the end of the novella do not include a present fulfilment with another person, a situation which she accepts with resignation. But she is a forerunner of those later characters who can fulfil their personal aspirations as well as their spiritual ones: Lady Chatterley, Mellors, the risen Christ and the Priestess of Isis. She demonstrates that a secure sense of the self is a needed preliminary for regeneration. For all these individuals, the readiness is all. Lou is herself ready for the full transfiguration that eludes her in *St Mawr*.

NOTES

1. Richard Poirier, *A World Elsewhere: the Place of Style in American Literature* (New York: Oxford University Press, 1966) pp. 40–50.
2. Tony Tanner, 'D. H. Lawrence in America', in *D. H. Lawrence: Novelist, Poet, Prophet*, ed. Stephen Spender (New York: Harper & Row, 1973) pp. 170–96; and James T. Cowan, *D. H. Lawrence's American Journey* (Cleveland: Case Western Reserve, 1970) pp. 81–96, *passim*. I agree with most of the judgements expressed by Alan Wilde in 'The Illusion of St Mawr: Technique and Vision in D. H. Lawrence's Novel', *PMLA*, LXXIX (1964) pp. 164–70.
3. *The Collected Letters of D. H. Lawrence*, ed. Harry T. Moore (New York: Viking, 1962) p. 765; hereafter designated as *CL*.
4. '*St Mawr*' and '*The Man Who Died*' (New York: Vintage Books, n.d.) p. 59; hereafter references will be made to this edition at appropriate places in the text.
5. 'New Mexico', in *Phoenix: the Posthumous Papers of D. H. Lawrence*, ed. Edward D. McDonald (New York: Viking, 1936) p. 142.
6. *Studies in Classic American Literature* (New York: Thomas Seltzer, 1923) p. 76; hereafter designated as *SCAL*.
7. D. H. Lawrence, *Apocalypse* (New York: Viking, Compass edn, 1966) p. 98.
8. Michael Ragussis, 'The False Myth of *St Mawr*: Lawrence and the Subterfuge of Art', *Papers on Language and Literature*, XI (1975) pp. 195–6.

9. *Phoenix*, ed. McDonald, p. 31.
10. See J. I. M. Stewart, *Eight Modern Writers* (Oxford: Clarendon Press, 1963) p. 570, and R. P. Draper, *D. H. Lawrence* (New York: Twayne, 1964) p. 131.
11. 'New Mexico', in *Phoenix*, ed. McDonald, p. 146.

7

The Second Lady Chatterley

LOUIS L. MARTZ

It is a pity that one of Lawrence's best novels should have appeared under the inappropriate title *John Thomas and Lady Jane*. Of course we are told that this is the title that Lawrence preferred; and it is true that in his letters of 1928 he was doggedly insisting upon this title, instead of *Lady Chatterley's Lover*.[1] But the change of title does not refer to the second version, finished in 1927; it refers to the drastically different third version, for which the title *John Thomas and Lady Jane* might in some ways seem appropriate, since it is only in the third version that these names are used. The change in title represented an act of defiance, motivated, as Lawrence tells us, by Juliette Huxley's dislike of the final manuscript. She 'read the MS. and was *very* cross, morally so', Lawrence reports, and then she 'suggested rather savagely I should call it: *John Thomas and Lady Jane*'. 'Many a true word spoken in spite', he adds, 'so I promptly called it that. Remains to be seen if Secker and Knopf will stand it.'[2] But later he decided, or was persuaded, to use the names only as a subtitle; and finally he agreed to expunge even the subtitle from the proofs of the first, Florentine edition.[3]

The point to remember is that Lawrence never contemplated any title other than *Lady Chatterley's Lover* for his second version, a title that he thought 'nice and old-fashioned sounding', and hence apparently, in his view, highly appropriate to this novel, for which Lawrence in his letters shows a remarkably old-fashioned and protective affection: 'To me it is beautiful and tender and frail as the naked self is, and I shrink very much even from having it typed.'[4] The phrase 'old-fashioned sounding' is perhaps a valid clue to the peculiar composition of this version, and a key to its essential difference from the novel that Lawrence ultimately printed. In the second version, Lawrence returned to the tradition of George Eliot and Thomas Hardy, both of whom, in their own ways, had written novels of sexual conflict involved with problems of class. *Adam Bede* and *Tess* are the immediate precursors of what is best called (as in the Italian translation) *The Second Lady Chatterley*.[5] It is as though Lawrence had asked himself: how would a novel in this English tradition have developed if George Eliot and Thomas Hardy had been able to present the explicit details of sexual experience and all the language that the common characters really would have used? Such an approach would explain why Lawrence could compose his 'English novel' so 'patiently',[6] sitting amid the trees and flowers of the Tuscan countryside, and remembering the country of his youth which, as he tells Earl Brewster, he had revisited in 1926 with affection and a strange feeling of hope:

> Curiously, I like England again, now I am up in my own regions. It braces me up: and there seems a queer, odd sort of potentiality in the people, especially the common people. One feels in them some odd, unaccustomed sort of plasm twinkling and nascent. They are not finished. And they have a funny sort of purity and gentleness, and at the same time, unbreakableness, that attracts one.[7]

Thus, after experimenting with the draft of the short novel that we know as *The First Lady Chatterley*, Lawrence proceeded to flesh out a full novel of character in the nineteenth-century tradition, with Constance, Clifford and Parkin developed into fully-motivated, fully-realised characters who stir a sympathetic response and draw the reader gradually into a story that deals with the basic problems of English and Western society in the 'tragic age'[8] following upon the First World War. In the third version, however, which was written after months of miserable illness, the novel becomes a bitter polemic against a dead society, interspersed with glimpses of the fugitive happiness available to two alienated figures who find their lonely consolation in sexual love.

The difference is clear in Connie's motor trip through the Midland landscape, a long passage occupying some ten pages near the middle of the last two versions, a position that allows the passage to act as a revelation of each novel's basic themes and attitudes. In both the scene is dismal, dreary, blackened,

oppressive; but in *The Second Lady Chatterly*, the scene has still
some life, as in Lawrence's letter to Brewster:

> Yet, gradually, it came to have a certain hold over her. It was
> sad country, with a grey, almost gruesome sadness. Yet it was
> not dead. It was alive, labouring under a queer, savage weight
> of dismalness and acquiescence. It was not cowed nor broken,
> either. No, the very ugliness seemed to have preserved a manly
> relentlessness in the men, a sort of slow, smouldering courage
> of death and desperation. But no hope. No immediate
> hope.   (*2LC*, p. 150)[9]

Is there then some hope in the future? Connie, looking at the
colliers 'going home from the pit, in their underworld grey
clothes, with underworld grey faces,' is overcome with 'fear and
dread':

> The future! The far future! Out of the orgy of ugliness and of
> dismalness and of dreariness, would there, could there ever
> unfold a flower, a life with beauty in it? . . . After all this that
> existed at present was gone, smashed and abandoned,
> repudiated for ever – could the children of miners make a new
> world, with mystery and sumptuousness in it? Her own
> children's children, if she had a child to Parkin? She shuddered
> a little, at the awful necessity for transition.   (*2LC*, pp. 156–7)

The word 'transition' marks the basic difference between the
last two versions, for in Connie's relation to Parkin lies the basis
of the transition, the possibility of a sympathy, even a love,
between individuals of the now severed classes. That is why
Parkin, however rebellious, must still be one of the people, must
be seen living with his mother and the Tewsons, must speak their
dialect consistently. Connie herself makes the point neatly in *The
First Lady Chatterley*, when she says that she 'must not try to
make' of Parkin, 'even in the mildest form, a gentleman. It would
only start a confusion. No! She must not even try to make him
develop along those lines, the lines of educated consciousness.
She must leave him to his own way. His instinct was against
education. His instinct made him refuse to speak King's English,
even to her' (*1LC*, p. 53).[10] And again, a few pages later in this
version, as she thinks of the impossibility of her becoming a

'working man's wife': 'He would probably begin speaking King's English – and that would be the first step to his undoing. No no! He must never be uplifted. He must never be brought one stride nearer to Clifford' (*1LC*, p. 62). And yet in the third version, Lawrence proceeds with every step in Parkin's undoing.

In the second version, which clings to this initial principle of Parkin's creation, Connie thinks of Parkin with a mingling of compassion and desire as she drives through the region, while her feelings flow out to embrace the whole 'disfigured countryside, and the disfigured, strange, almost wraithlike populace. . . . Ugliness incarnate, they seemed. And yet alive!' (*2LC*, p. 157). And as her feelings embrace the scene, she is able to express her struggling hope in the words of one of Lawrence's most moving and beautiful visions of prophecy:

> She shuddered again at the thought of them: and even her Parkin was one of them. Creatures of another element, they did not really live, they only subserved the coal, as the steel-workers subserved the steel, the workers in the potteries, the clay. Men not men, but merely the animae of coal and steel, iron and clay. Strange fauna of the mineral elements, of carbon and iron and silicon!
>
> If ever they did emerge, it would be with weird luxuriance, something in heavy contrast to what they were now. From ugliness incarnate, they would bring forth, perhaps, a luxuriant, uncanny beauty, some of the beauty that must have been in the great ferns and giant mosses of which the coal was made: some of the beauty of the weight and the resistance of iron, and the blueness of steel, and the iridescence of glass. When at last they had risen from subservience to the mineral elements, and were really animate, when they really *used* the iron, for the flowering of their own bodies and anima, instead of, as now, being used by it. Now the iron and the coal used them, not they the iron and the coal. (*2LC*, p. 158)

In the third version of the novel, however, all this atmosphere of sympathy and tenderness and half-hope is extinguished: the last paragraph above is removed, while some of its details are absorbed into an expansion of the earlier paragraph that sees the men as 'fauna of the mineral elements'. Now Lawrence concludes: 'They had perhaps some of the weird, inhuman beauty of minerals, the lustre of coal, the weight and blueness and resistance of iron, the transparency of glass. Elemental creatures, weird and distorted, of the mineral world! They belonged to the coal, the iron, the clay, as fish belong to the sea and worms to dead wood. The anima of mineral disintegration!' (*3LC*, pp. 146–7).[11]

In the third version, Connie's love for a man of the people is unable to spread out over the landscape and the populace, for Parkin has been transformed into Mellors, a grammar-school boy, a lieutenant (almost a captain) in the army, a man who can, and frequently does, speak 'King's English,' a man who has lived in India and Egypt – 'quite the gentleman, really quite the gentleman!' as Ivy Bolton says (*3LC*, p. 133) – and thus a man deracinated from the region, the people and the language of his birth. Lawrence stresses the significance of the change:

> She felt again in a wave of terror the grey, gritty hopelessness of it all. With such creatures for the industrial masses, and the upper classes as she knew them, there was no hope, no hope any more. . . .
> Yet Mellors had come out of all this! – Yes, but he was as apart from it all as she was. Even in him there was no fellowship left. It was dead. The fellowship was dead. There was only apartness and hopelessness, as far as all this was concerned.   (*3LC*, pp. 140–1)

Thus the love affair loses the basic function in the novel which Lawrence seems to have discovered near the very close of his first, experimental version, as he tries to sum up the direction in which his thoughts are moving. Connie, he writes, 'wanted to pity Parkin and be maternally kind to him, keeping her deeper self shut off and the mysterious stream that can flow all the time between man and woman walled back'. This is the 'stream of desire' which, he adds, 'is the stream of life itself'. 'It is that which unites us. It is that, even, which makes a nation a nation: the soft, invisible desire of people making a great swarm like a hive of bees. The clue is some unconscious, living idea which draws multitudes of men in a stream of desire' (*1LC*, p. 198). Therefore in *The Second Lady Chatterley*, the love affair must constantly be related, not only to birds, beasts and flowers, but also to the novel's prophetic hope for a new civilisation, replacing the one that the war has left in ruins. For the war is only the precipitating, immediate cause of the disaster: the true cause lies deeper, in the barriers of class and industry that sever the flow of life.

In all three versions, Clifford is treated not simply as a wounded victim of the war, but also as a man wounded in his psyche by his upper-class breeding and position. As Lawrence explains rather awkwardly in the first draft, through the thoughts of Constance:

> She thought she had loved Clifford. And she *had* loved him. But, she knew it now, not with her heart. Her heart had never wakened to him, and left to him, never would have wakened. No, not if he had never been to the war at all. – His terrible accident, his paralysis or whatever it was, was really symbolical in him. He was always paralysed, in some part of him. That part in a man which can wake a woman's heart once and for all was always dead in him. As it is dead in thousands of men like him. All the women who have men like him live with unawakened hearts. (*1LC*, p. 69)

Although this idea underlies all three versions, the treatment of Clifford in the second version is remarkably different from that in the other two, where Clifford's 'symbolical' function is stressed throughout, and stressed with particular bitterness in the final version. But in *The Second Lady Chatterley*, in accord with its mode as a novel of character in the English tradition, the symbolical function of Clifford emerges only tacitly and gradually, while for most of the novel Lawrence makes a great effort to hold the reader's sympathy with Clifford, as the victim of a disaster that has wounded a whole society. The presence of the war, as a constant memory, is kept before us persistently, by dozens of large and small reminders, in a way that is not characteristic of the other two versions. The war thus runs through the second version like a disease in the stream of life. This is part of the naturalistic action and motivation of this version: the suffering has a realistic cause.

In keeping with this naturalistic mode, the breaking of Connie's relationship with Clifford is gradual, as, more and more, the frustration of her natural instincts drains her vitality, and the constant tending of Clifford becomes an unbearable burden. And when at last a nurse is hired, we are told that Clifford 'resented' the change 'deeply'. 'It made a cleavage through his feeling for her, that she had relinquished his wrecked body into the hands of a stranger. He never any more felt the close oneness between himself and his wife.'

> Constance knew, but did not really mind. It was a relief to her. That other oneness had almost destroyed her. Sometimes, upstairs, she would sing to herself the song: 'Touch not the nettle!' It has a refrain: 'for the bonds of love are ill to loose'. She had never quite understood that, till lately, when she was trying to extricate herself from the intense personal love that was between her and Clifford.   (*2LC*, p. 79)

Lawrence is distinguishing an 'intense personal love' from a sexual love – but in the third version even this kind of intense love is gone. Indeed, the handling of the revised passage here is indicative of the ways in which, throughout the final version, Lawrence goes about removing all sympathy from Clifford and trivialising the 'love' that once existed between the pair. Now, we hear, Clifford, 'never quite forgave Connie for giving up her personal care of him to a strange hired woman'. It is one thing to 'resent'; something else never to forgive. It is one thing to remember Clifford's 'wrecked body'; quite something else to speak of 'personal care', as in a nursing home. And finally, it is one thing to resist turning one's body over to a stranger; but there is an added element of class antagonism in resisting the attention of a 'hired woman'. 'It killed, he said to himself, the real flower of the intimacy between him and her. But Connie didn't mind that. The fine flower of their intimacy was to her rather like an orchid, a bulb stuck parasitic on her tree of life, and producing, to her eyes, a rather shabby flower' (*3LC*, p. 76). After this, the bonds of love may still be 'ill to loose', but they come apart much more easily.

In the second version the loosing of these bonds is shown to be disastrous for Clifford: 'It was Connie's gradual abandonment of all her intimate duties towards him, that had finally hardened Clifford's heart, and cut him off from her, emotionally' (*2LC*, pp. 134–5). The relation with Parkin has now begun, and Clifford feels the change, though not knowing the cause. But he notices when, for the first time, she forgets to kiss him goodnight:

> He gazed angrily at the door-panels, too angry to ring as yet for Mrs Bolton. Ah well! Let the last vestiges of the old love

disappear! He could not make love to her! and therefore she was withdrawing every tiny show of love. She forgot, no doubt. But the forgetfulness was part of her whole intention.

Ah well! He was a man, and asked charity from nobody, not even his wife! He was a net-work of nerves, it is true, and suffered terrible nervous torments of fear and gloom, dread of death, dread of the future. (*2LC*, p. 135)

Throughout the middle of the second version, Clifford's suffering and torment are borne in upon us, especially in the episode where Connie returns from a visit with Parkin, and Clifford meets her in his wheelchair at the top of the drive, amid 'the wild, uncanny disturbance of an English spring'. 'Suddenly she struck him as lovely': she has now all the freshness and vitality of the season itself. She tells him she 'went fast asleep', 'in the keeper's hut, sitting in the sunshine'. Of course, it was not the hut where the pheasants are tended: it was the keeper's own cottage, where, in a tranquil, non-erotic scene, she has played the role of wife, as the destruction of the picture of Parkin and Bertha has suggested.

'And was the keeper there?' asked Clifford.

'Not at the hut,' she said. 'Why didn't you come and meet me? I kept expecting to hear the chair.'

'I didn't know where you'd gone,' he said. 'And on a day like this – especially an evening like this –' he looked up into the sky – 'I was by no means sure you would want me and my chair.'

'Why not?' she said quickly. 'I was thinking of you, as I came home, and wondering if you were out of doors, as you ought to be.'

But the only possible thought of Clifford has been contained in Parkin's warning: 'I won't come to th' gate with you, for fear there's somebody in th' park.'

'If there were any point in my being out of doors!' [Clifford] said, with a touch of bitterness. 'You look so lovely this evening, Connie! You want something different from me to come and meet you.'

She stopped, and looked at him.

'Why, Clifford?' she said.

'Why!' he answered ironically. 'A bath-chair, in the month of May! There goes the cuckoo, he's at it all day! I can't bear May.'

And again, as she tries to restrain his bitterness: 'The cuckoo only jeers at me, even the rooks. . . . Why doesn't somebody shoot me!' Though Clifford has earlier suggested that she ought to take a lover, if she must, the cry of the cuckoo can only intensify his 'nervous anger and misery' as he says, 'I ought to be shot, as a horse with broken legs is shot' (2LC, pp. 186–8).

This whole episode is removed in the third version, with the result that the subsequent episode where Clifford loses his temper with the balky motorised chair stands out starkly as an example of utterly outrageous behaviour. Lawrence has also taken steps to make Clifford even more unpleasant, for in the final version he has accentuated the anger by repeating the word 'snapped' and adding phrases like 'savage impatience' and 'rigid with anger' (3LC, pp. 172–4). Most important, however, is the removal of one significant aspect of the second version that adds a touch of humanity to the scene – and at the same time reminds us of the war. Connie has been sitting on a bank and watching the men work with the chair:

> But she was amused once more by the busy, interested free-masonry of men, as soon as it was a question of machinery. Then indeed class differences broke down a little. Parkin was no longer a gamekeeper: he was much freer and more active, perhaps as when he was in the war, and drove a lorry. And Clifford was the officer, a little impatient with the Tommy, a bit out of temper, but not at all the employer. (2LC, p. 209)

This takes a great deal of the sting out of the anger, and it follows naturally to hear that Clifford 'commanded' Parkin to let go of the machine, that 'the keeper dropped a pace into the rear', and that 'Parkin stepped smartly aside, like a soldier' (2LC, pp. 210–11). But in version three, 'commanded' is replaced by 'snarled', and the 'soldierly' phrases are gone (3LC, pp. 174–5). Finally, Clifford's effort at an apology comes through rather well in version two, with a little help from Connie:

> 'I'm afraid I rather lost my temper with the infernal thing!' said Clifford at last.

'It is annoying!' said Constance.

'Do you mind pushing me home, Parkin?' said Clifford. 'And excuse anything I said,' he added rather offhand.

'It's nothing to me, Sir Clifford!'   (*2LC*, p. 211)

But in version three, everything becomes stiff and haughty, on both sides:

'I expect she'll have to be pushed,' said Clifford at last, with an affectation of *sang froid*.

No answer. Mellors' abstracted face looked as if he had heard nothing. Connie glanced anxiously at him. Clifford too glanced round.

'Do you mind pushing her home, Mellors!' he said in a cold, superior tone. 'I hope I have said nothing to offend you,' he added, in a tone of dislike.

'Nothing at all, Sir Clifford! Do you want me to push that chair?'

'If you please.'   (*3LC*, pp. 174–5)

Thus Mellors has his revenge by forcing Clifford to ask him, in effect, three times, if he will push the chair. But then, we remember, Mellors was himself an officer in the army. This is almost a contest of equals; in the end, neither Clifford nor Mellors can win our sympathy here, whereas the power of the earlier version of this incident lies in the way in which Parkin and Clifford, as well as Connie, display subtle and complex human responses in their difficult relationship.

Even at the close of version two Lawrence manages to maintain something of the earlier view of Clifford as victim. When Connie returns to Wragby after her journey to the continent, as she has promised (and it is significant that in this version she has enough vestigial feeling for Clifford to keep this promise), Clifford goes into a total collapse after his effort to meet her at the station and demonstrate his new accomplishment at walking with crutches. Mrs Bolton explains his collapse in terms that link Clifford with his whole wounded generation of men:

'Was it too much for him?' asked Connie, fear-struck.

'Oh, I don't think so! But he suffers from these lapses of energy. You remember he always did. It seems as if men do suffer that way since the war, even men who were never touched, or never even in the war at all. But their energy collapses, without anything being wrong with them.' . . .

Connie was frightened. . . . Clifford seemed as if his very soul were paralysed; and he knew it, his eyes were haunted with fear and irritable horror. He hated Connie to see him like that. She had to leave him.   (*2LC*, p. 313)

The episode thus hovers ambiguously between the feelings of Connie and Clifford, as though some threads were still remaining of those old bonds. The whole scene forms the strongest possible contrast with the long scene of 'male hysteria' that we are forced to watch in version three, after Clifford receives the letter telling him that she will not return to Wragby because she is in love with another man (*3LC*, pp. 266–9).

Forced to watch: this phrase has perhaps unconsciously given my own impression of how one is likely to read the third version, after a careful reading of version two. The changes made in the third version may well come to seem almost acts of vandalism – the deliberate destruction of the bonds of sympathy that gradually weave version two into an impressive unity, in tune with the forces of nature. *The Second Lady Chatterley* develops a natural rhythm of growth and change, as the forces of nature work gradually to slough off, however painfully, the dying and useless remnants of the old consciousness. But in version three the old consciousness does not thus die away: it is violently rejected, by the authorial voice, as well as by the voices of Connie and Mellors.

The result is a pervasive withdrawal of sympathy, even in minor scenes, such as the visit that Connie pays to Mrs Flint at Marehay Farm. In version two this is a happy visit. Connie likes Mrs Flint, plays with the baby, finds 'the quiet female atmosphere . . . infinitely soothing'. 'And the two women enjoyed themselves, talking about the baby, and everything that came up' (*2LC*, p. 125). But in version three we learn that Connie at the outset 'suspected' Mrs Flint 'of being rather a false little thing', and the baby becomes 'a perky little thing' with 'cheeky pale-blue eyes', and the child is 'surrounded with rag dolls and other toys in modern excess' (*3LC*, pp. 118–19). Mrs Flint, described as a former schoolteacher in both versions, is at the close of version three made to put on schoolteacherly airs, with regard to her farmer-husband. In version two, as Connie is leaving, she sees the auriculas blooming in the front garden and exclaims simply, 'Oh, how pretty!' 'The recklesses?' Mrs Flint replies. 'Yes, aren't they a show!' But in version three Connie sees the flowers and remarks, 'Lovely auriculas'. '"Recklesses, as Luke calls them," laughed Mrs Flint.' In version two the local word passes unremarked in an atmosphere of sympathy and intimacy. The episode thus prepares the way for the domestic scene where Connie sleeps in Parkin's lap: she has in fact much in common with the farmer's wife.

More serious in its impact upon the novel is the hardening of attitude that occurs when Parkin is transformed into Mellors, with the difference that comes out near the close, when the gamekeeper, Connie and her sister Hilda meet in the keeper's cottage. In version two the conversation is tense, embarrassed, uncomfortable; everyone is making a great effort to keep the situation under control. Flashes of anger or resentment or worry leap out, but at the end:

> Suddenly Hilda leaned over the side of the car, holding out her hand.
> 'Good-night, Mr Parkin!' she said. He strode up, and took her hand.
> 'Good-night!' he said.
> 'If you feel you're right – ' she said, 'I suppose nobody has any business to interfere.' (*2LC*, p. 269)

In version three Mellors and Hilda quarrel violently, with Mellors lashing out at Hilda in a furious tirade that covers half a page (*3LC*, p. 226). After this, there can be no handshake at the end.

Such examples are symptoms of a hardening of attitude that is making its way through the entire body of version three. We sense the difference in the opening chapter of the final version, where the two-and-a-half-page prelude to life at Wragby has been expanded to eight pages, in which Connie and Hilda are introduced to sexual life in pre-war Germany, while most of the chapter is given over to a satirical account of how 'ridiculous' everything seemed in the pre-war years and even during the early years of the war itself – 'ridiculous' because of the superficiality and triviality of all emotions and relationships:

> And the authorities felt ridiculous, and behaved in a rather

ridiculous fashion, and it was all a mad hatter's tea-party for a while. Till things developed over there, and Lloyd George came to save the situation over here. And this surpassed even ridicule, the flippant young laughed no more.

In 1916 Herbert Chatterley [the elder brother] was killed, so Clifford became heir. He was terrified even of this.   (*3LC*, p. 11)

Lawrence saves his final touch of ridicule for the contemptuous final sentence of the chapter: 'But early in 1918 Clifford was shipped home smashed, and there was no child. And Sir Geoffrey [the father] died of chagrin.'

This acrid sense of the 'ridiculous' plays no part in the opening chapter of *The Second Lady Chatterley*. After two and a half pages of prelude, Lawrence takes the couple at once to Wragby, with these ominous words: 'But by the time the *Untergang des Abendlands* appeared, Clifford was a smashed man, and by the time Constance became mistress of Wragby, cold ash had begun to blanket the glow of the war fervour. It was the day after, the grey morrow for which no thought had been taken' (*2LC*, p. 3). The allusion to Spengler sets the theme: the war has set in motion, or rather, has accelerated, the decline of the West, and what lies before us is the story of human beings caught in that decline. Connie's deep unhappiness is gradually revealed by her decline in vitality, worrisome to her father, her sister and her aunt, and ultimately to Clifford, after her father has spoken to him about Connie's health.

The long opening movement of version two is brought to a climax in the powerful Chapter v, which begins with Connie's feeling of 'indefinable dread' at the approach of Christmas. 'But perhaps that was because Clifford had been wounded on Christmas day' (*2LC*, p. 52). It is a brief touch, but enough. Clifford is a victim, like his whole generation of men – as the conversations in this chapter will reveal, especially in the prophetic words of Tommy Dukes, the sensitive Brigadier General, who is 'fond of Clifford', has a sort of 'tenderness' for Lady Eva, and understands at once Connie's desire to be 'where a bit of life flowed'.

'You're quite right, Connie!' said Dukes, looking at her with his shrewd eyes. 'A flow of life, and contact! We've never had proper human contact – we've never been civilised enough.

We're not civilised enough even now, to be able to touch one another. We start away, like suspicious hairy animals. The next civilisation will be based on the inspiration of touch: believe me – But we shall never live to see it, so why talk about it?'

But when Connie reminds him that he never seems to want 'to touch anybody', Dukes looks at her in such a way that she is emotionally touched: 'He looked at her oddly, and her heart gave a queer lurch. This man might have been in love with her – if he'd had enough hope, if the weight of disillusion hadn't been too heavy.' Like the miners, Dukes has still some spark of life inside the covering ashes; and so he is given a speech that expresses the heart of Lawrence's evangelistic mission:

> there *will* be a new civilisation, the very antithesis of tabloids and aeroplanes: believe me! There will be a civilisation based on the mystery of touch, and all that that means; a field of consciousness which hasn't yet opened into existence. *We're* too much afraid of it – oh, stiff as wood, with fear! . . . Oh, there'll be a democracy – the democracy of touch. For the few who survive the fear of it.   (*2LC*, pp. 57–8)

Then, as the conversation turns upon one of Lawrence's favourite biblical texts, the *noli me tangere*, Connie says to Dukes, 'You mean you're not touchable, either', thus setting in flow a current of thought that lies at the heart of this version: 'I suppose that's what I do mean', Dukes answers. 'Don't touch me! for I am not yet ascended unto the Father! Perhaps that's about where we stand.'

The dance came to an end, and he left her. But vaguely in her consciousness the words of Jesus were moving: '*Noli me tangere!* Touch me not! for I am not yet ascended unto the Father!' What did they mean?

It meant they had died, these men. In the war, finally, they had died. And though they were still walking about in the flesh, and were still struggling for the life that should be theirs, after the resurrection, they had not yet got the body of the new life. . . .

How terrible the story of Jesus! It was the epitome of the story of all men. They had all been crucified, these men: all except Jack, who had balked it. But Clifford and Tommy Dukes and even Winterslow, they had all been killed, in some subtle way. And it was the strange, dim, grey era of the resurrection, with them, before the ascension into new life.

And perhaps they would never ascend really into life. They would remain the shadowy, almost incorporeal beings of the era between the rolling open of the tomb, and the ascending into the firmament of a new body. They lived and walked and spoke, but theirs was still the old, tortured body that could not be touched.   (2LC, pp. 61–2)

In version three all this apocalyptic talk is removed – and is replaced by empty conversation satirising the utter desiccation of the upper classes and the intellectuals, a fierce attack brought to a climax by the introduction of the playwright Michaelis and the nasty episode of Connie's 'affair' with him. A reading of Chapter v in version two along with Chapters iv and v in version three is in itself enough to show the immense difference between the two novels – yes, different novels, not truly versions, for they do not connect at heart. It is clear from the above passage that *The Second Lady Chatterley* is working from the heart of Lawrence's deepest hopes and beliefs: it leads inevitably into *The Man Who Died* and *Apocalypse*. *The Third Lady Chatterley* is, by comparison, a series of symbolic events, with commentary.

We have, then, essentially, two different novels, two different kinds of novel. Each defines its own nature in ways that indicate how clearly Lawrence knows his craft. The clue in *The Second Lady Chatterley* is given in the conversation, two-thirds of the way through the book, where Connie and Clifford discuss his liking for 'the ultra-modern, so-called futuristic writers, who grouped round Joyce or Proust', and Connie declares that *Ulysses* 'is a perverse activity of the will'. 'My dear Connie,' Clifford replies, 'I know your nature is evangelical.' The point is so important that Clifford repeats it three times here, saying that she speaks 'like an angel and an evangel', calling her 'my evangelical little wife' and 'an evangelist by profession' (2LC, pp. 217–18). It seems right, then, to see *The Second Lady Chatterley* as an 'evangelical' novel, a work that enters deeply into the woes of the human race, feels the inevitable forces of change at work, knows the agony of change, and yet foresees the possibility of a new, brighter, happier age ahead – however far in the future. Although this mode of writing will allow some measure of denunciation and bitterness (as in the gospels), the central tendency will be much gentler, in accord with the warning that Lawrence issues about a third of the way through: 'Whoever wants life must go softly towards life, softly as one would go towards a deer and a fawn that was nestling under a tree. One gesture of violence, one violent assertion of self-will, and life is gone' (*2LC*, p. 107).

In *The Third Lady Chatterley* Lawrence has chosen to compose a polemical, frequently satirical novel, in which all figures, except Connie, and to some extent Mellors, operate as types or symbols, with all the life concentrated in the now considerably extended sexual episodes. Again, Lawrence makes his method clear, in a little essay on the novel that comes about one-third of the way along, as Lawrence declares that 'even satire is a form of sympathy'.

> It is the way our sympathy flows and recoils that really determines our lives. And here lies the vast importance of the novel, properly handled. It can inform and lead into new places the flow of our sympathetic consciousness, and it can lead our sympathy away in recoil from things gone dead. Therefore, the novel, properly handled, can reveal the most secret places of life: for it is in the *passional* secret places of life, above all, that the tide of sensitive awareness needs to ebb and flow, cleansing and freshening. (*3LC*, p. 92)

This novel, then, is being constructed in episodes of flow and recoil, in an effort to move all sympathy towards Connie's torment and her rediscovery of life in the sexual episodes.

This procedure is revealed quite early in *The Third Lady Chatterley*, where Connie, though afflicted by a 'sense of deep physical injustice', goes on with her intimate tending of her husband's needs. But, we hear, 'The physical sense of injustice is a dangerous feeling, once it is awakened. It must have outlet, or it eats away the one in whom it is aroused. Poor Clifford, he was not to blame. His was the greater misfortune. It was all part of the general catastrophe' (*3LC*, p. 65). So far, this echoes the sympathetic approach of *The Second Lady Chatterley*. But now Lawrence deliberately turns the reader in another direction: 'And yet was he not in a way to blame? This lack of warmth, this lack of the simple, warm, physical contact, was he not to blame for that? He was never really warm, nor even kind, only thoughtful, considerate, in a wellbred, cold sort of way!' And then, as Connie's 'sense of rebellion' smoulders, the recoil moves into bitter denunciation and ridicule, her voice blending with the authorial voice:

> Even Clifford's cool and contactless assurance that he belonged to the ruling class didn't prevent his tongue lolling out of his mouth, as he panted after the bitch-goddess [success]. After all, Michaelis was really more dignified in the matter, and far, far more successful. Really, if you looked closely at Clifford, he was a buffoon, and a buffoon is more humiliating than a bounder.
>
> As between the two men, Michaelis really had far more use for her than Clifford had. He had even more need of her. Any good nurse can attend to crippled legs! And as for the heroic effort, Michaelis was a heroic rat, and Clifford was very much of a poodle showing off.   (*3LC*, p. 66)

It is important to note how all these changes, and especially the introduction of Michaelis, alter the 'evangelical' conception of Connie's character that runs throughout *The Second Lady Chatterley*: her basic innocence, her sensitive response to nature, her instinctive sympathy with other human beings, including Clifford, her longing for 'a God' to whom she could open her heart, and the epiphany of this possibility as she glimpses Parkin washing his body behind the cottage: 'And she felt again there was God on earth; or gods.' 'The sudden sense of pure beauty, beauty that was active and alive, had put worship in her heart again' (*2LC*, pp. 34, 44). It is her evangelical nature that makes it right for Lawrence to retain, as part of his conclusion, the visit of Connie to Parkin at the Tewsons' home in Sheffield, for the episode is essential in showing the effort to create a sympathy between the classes – and at the same time the impossibility of breaking through the barriers, right now. Finally, the pathetic meeting of the lovers at Hucknall is imbued with Connie's evangelical sadness ('Jesus wept'): 'They went into the dark church together. It was empty. And she looked at the little slab behind which rests the pinch of dust which was Byron's heart: in that thrice-dismal Hucknall Torkard. The sense of the greatness of human mistakes made her want to cry' (*2LC*, pp. 367–8). The image of Byron's withered heart sets the necessary sombre undertone. Despite their efforts to achieve a union, the time has not yet come, as Dukes has said.

In contrast with the nuances of this finale, we have the long, explicit closing letter from Mellors to Connie, with its contempt for 'the mass of people', and its view of love as a refuge from a doomed society:

> There's a bad time coming. There's a bad time coming, boys, there's a bad time coming! If things go on as they are, there's nothing lies in the future but death and destruction, for these industrial masses. I feel my inside turn to water sometimes, and there you are, going to have a child by me. But never mind. All the bad times that ever have been, haven't been able to blow the crocus out: not even the love of women. So they won't be able to blow out my wanting you, nor the little glow there is between you and me. We'll be together next year. (*3LC*, p. 328)

Probably so: after all, Mellors can pass for a gentleman.

NOTES

1. *The Collected Letters of D. H. Lawrence*, ed. Harry T. Moore, 2 vols (New York: Viking, 1962) II, pp. 1041–3, 1046, 1052–3.
2. Ibid., II, p. 1043.
3. Ibid., II, pp. 1046, 1052, 1060.
4. *Letters from D. H. Lawrence to Martin Secker, 1911–1930* (privately published by Martin Secker, Bridgefoot Iver, Bucks., 1970) p. 84; *Letters*, ed. Moore, II, p. 972. I follow Keith Sagar's dating in taking these allusions to refer to the second version, not the first: see Sagar, *D. H. Lawrence: a Calendar of his Works* (Manchester University Press, 1979) pp. 156–60.
5. D. H. Lawrence, *Le Tre 'Lady Chatterley'*, trans. Carlo Izzo and Giulio Monteleone (Milan: Mondadori, 1954), with important introduction by Piero Nardi.
6. Frieda Lawrence, *Not I, but the Wind* (New York: Viking, 1934) p. 220; *The Quest for Rananim: D. H. Lawrence's Letters to S. S. Koteliansky, 1914–1930*, ed. George J. Zytaruk (Montreal: McGill–Queen's University Press, 1970) p. 304.
7. *Letters*, ed. Moore, II, p. 933 (30 August 1926).
8. The phrase occurs in the opening sentence of all three versions.

9. D. H. Lawrence, *John Thomas and Lady Jane* (London: William Heinemann, 1972). All references to the second version are made to this edition; hereafter abbreviated to *2LC*.

10. D. H. Lawrence, *The First Lady Chatterley* (London: William Heinemann, 1972). All references to the first version are made to this edition; hereafter abbreviated to *1LC*.

11. D. H. Lawrence, *Lady Chatterley's Lover* (London: William Heinemann, 1960). All references to the third version are made to this edition; hereafter abbreviated to *3LC*.

I should like to call attention to an excellent study that appeared after this essay had been submitted in 1982: Michael Squires, *The Creation of Lady Chatterley's Lover* (Baltimore and London: Johns Hopkins University Press, 1983). The comparison of all three versions here is both illuminating and controversial, but I have made no changes in my essay as originally composed. Squires recognises many virtues in version two and sees a good many flaws in version three; he tends, however, to justify the trend of the changes in the final version, especially in regard to Mellors, as I would not.

8

Desire and Negation: the Dialectics of Passion in D. H. Lawrence

KINGSLEY WIDMER

After nearly a century, the presence of D. H. Lawrence as a mode of sensibility should be coming into greater definition. Now, any discussion of his writings that does not relate to his dialectics of 'passion' – his insistent concern (it is, indeed, his own *word*) and his ultimate value – can hardly be said to respond to the existential core of Lawrence. Should we say, then, as does one noted admirer, that 'he had a positive passion for life?' That does not tell us much, for Lawrence also had a passion for denial and death, an emphatic focus of so much of his writing. Other bland apologetics for a 'love ethic', 'a love of the natural world', or just 'love', also serve as reductive neutralisations of the peculiarity and extremity we experience with him.

Perhaps most simply, what a character says of his persona Birkin in *Women in Love* could well be said of Lawrence also: he was distinctive for 'his way of seeing some particular things vividly and feverishly, and his acting on this special sight'. Whether it be a flower or a phallus, a tremor of touch or a demand for apocalypse, he sought a total intensity. Obviously, he was often hard to take as a person, and that can also apply to his writing. But there is more to it than that since his 'polarity', as he called it, his love–hate fluctuations – more broadly, his desire–negation cycles – shape his passions, great and small. Lawrence often establishes his intense moments by contrasting 'wonder' and 'oblivion', 'heat' and 'nothingness', vividness and deadness, focus and chaos, 'flame' and 'darkness', 'desire' and 'negation', and frequently reversing them in the trembling flux of vital flow. An exacerbated sensibility, Lawrence's methods of heightening individual experiences – which is what he was largely aiming at in a modern world that he saw as otherwise empty of human values – move inseparably with the denial of those conditions which lessen responsiveness, and with radical awareness which intensifies and authenticates the passion.

The force of what Lawrence repeatedly calls 'the furious flame of passion' allows no simple moral and social affirmations – much must get burned – and, indeed, passional realisation often demands the amoral and antisocial, adultery and other violation, flight and other refusal. The overweening pursuit of extreme states of desire and negation also unbalances any lesser shaping in much of his writing. This is certainly true in his often awkward and askew novels; pursuit of the peculiarities of desire in a context of negation breaks conventional narrative, character and poetic order. It is true even with many of his shorter works of fiction, though some may be his most achieved art (as I argued a generation ago in my study of them, *The Art of Perversity*). The same unsettling intensity runs through many of his better poems (amidst his poetic jottings), his more than four volumes of vivid travel writings, and even the wild spate of essays and letters. The academic formalist piety of focusing the sense of Lawrence mostly on the novels has no doubt partly been a fallacy of misplaced concreteness, mistaking the conventional apparatus for the unusual quality. Other than in some novelistic passages, and in a minority of stories and poems, Lawrence's finest work may be in his 'incidental writing' (travel pieces, the 'Introduction' to the Magnus *Memoirs*, excursions on American literature, essays such as 'Insouciance', etc.). Most precisely, the vivid seeing and feeling, and the countering arguments, are *the* Lawrence mode.

Still, in spite of the burdens of ragged shapings and much bad writing, Lawrence's erratic longer works of fiction remain intriguing, and the focus of so much discussion that we may yet again consider some of the dialectics in them, even in those which are not so well ordered as *Sons and Lovers* and *Lady Chatterley's Lover*. To start at the appropriate end, in an often quoted passage in *Lady Chatterley's Lover* (Chapter IX), Lawrence editorially summarises his positive view of the nature of the novel. He says that it most essentially expresses the 'sympathetic consciousness' which really determines the living quality of human existence. In the pattern of that novel, this largely means intense eroticism, which counters the deadening by industrialism, money, class, and other false consciousness (specifically including traditional idealism, much modern art, and the mass media). The personal immediacy of fiction is more true because of its ability to explore 'the *passional* secret places of life' (Lawrence's italics, and obscene play).

In the immediate context of the statement, which is not usually noted, Lawrence was discussing Ivy Bolton – probably the best realised character in the novel – the nurse companion of impotent crippled Sir Clifford Chatterley, and the vivid power of her gossip. Intense gossip (which, after all, provides the subject of this novel – the conventionally outrageous adultery of the Lady with her servant) focuses the storyteller's special passionate sympathy. The storyteller within the story, Mrs Bolton, has this sympathy, Lawrence repeatedly notes, in spite of her manipulative 'perverse' relation to Clifford, for whom she becomes the obscene mothering muse of the emotional inadequacy which makes him a *'real* businessman'. For Ivy Bolton still retains some of the desire that she had for her long-dead miner-husband. That passion gives the power to her gossip. All true human response depends on such intense rooting in desire. Or, as Lawrence more reductively wrote in his poetic jottings: 'Sexless people transmit nothing.'

But this, too, should be put in dialectical perspective; after all, Bolton's gossip, her art, is only the reliving of desire, something for which her author did not have the highest regard. Unlike many of his contemporary modernists, Lawrence did not worship art. This novel almost obsessively scores anti-art points: in the mockery of Clifford's *success d'estime* as a writer of Bloomsbury-type, cleverly empty stories; in the contemptuous treatment of fawning Michaelis (with whom Constance has her first, and somewhat nasty, adulterous affair) and his explorative popular plays; in the sarcastic treatment of contemptible Duncan Forbes (pseudo-correspondent in the Lady's divorce case) and his abstractionist paintings of 'hats'; and even in criticism of Proust (in mockery of Clifford's admiration) and his mortuary labyrinth of eroticism. The exaltation of art and its artifacts apparently would be just another instance of what Lawrence's early spokesman in the novel (Tommy Dukes – inexplicably dropped) castigates as a 'mental-lifer' attitude. The thing-itself is the passional quality, and part of Lawrence's distinctive heroism among modernists – indeed, much of his special appeal – is to subordinate even art to the lived qualities of existence.

When gamekeeper Mellors describes the person he has most admired (his former commanding officer), he, of course, characterises him as 'a passionate man'. When Lawrence rather intrusively (as so often) editorialises on Constance's sexual rapture with Mellors, the crux is that she has achieved passion's state of impersonal transforming experience. But 'when passion is dead, or absent, then the magnificent throb of beauty is incomprehensible'. The passional thus provides the ultimate ethic and aesthetic.

Yet that state of being can be dialectically comprehended only with its antithesis. Clifford cannot have positive passion because he is sexually and emotionally absent – finally to Constance a 'celluloid soul' – with the nasty dedication to class, worldly success, power, and other false purposes. Most modern people cannot achieve the passional because 'the living intuitive quality was dead' from industrial-commercial society in which the 'Mammon' worship of the 'mechanical' overwhelms all human 'connection'. Other characters (Hilda, Duncan, *et al.*) fail because of their willed denial of the passional. But negation appears even more crucially in another way. Lawrence's advocacy of heightened 'touch' and intense responses depends on the apocalyptic vision that our 'civilised society is insane'; for the Western world, 'nothing lies in the future but death and destruction'; Lawrence–Mellors even foresees the 'extermination of the human species'. The awareness of utter negation, then, provides the essential context, need and polarity for the affirmation of immediate passion.

For Lawrence, the characteristic modern 'experience of the nothingness of life', with which the novel starts, also requires other negations. He twice rewrote his last novel, partly in order to increase the declassing of his protagonist (from Parkin to Seivers to Mellors) and present him as the outsider to the social order and most of its false values – a set of negations to counter the passional desire. (I have argued this issue in some detail in 'The Pertinence of Modern Pastoral: the Three Versions of *Lady Chatterley's Lover*', *Studies in the Novel*, v (Autumn 1973) pp. 298–313, which includes elaborate annotation.) In the rewriting Lawrence also more fully discovered, at the cost of some stridency, a further degree to which the passional regenerative consciousness requires the rejection of society and culture.

In a more complex way, passional change also requires some negation of the Lady, who discovers not only the crucial impersonality of erotic desire (as Lawrence's characters usually do) but also that she must lose her self-assertion – 'her will had left her . . . giving way . . . giving up', until she feels the man's 'slave'. No doubt part of this may be attributed to common male fantasy. But the impersonality of passion works both ways, and Constance, as a ravening 'Bacchante', also reduces the man to 'mere phallus-bearer'. However, Lawrence's male–female dialectics are not equal since Constance's 'new awakening' carries her beyond this to a submission which, paradoxically, we are to understand becomes her fulfilment as a person.

In another of the sexual scenes, Constance had to dare 'to let go everything, all herself, and be gone in the flood'. It should be noted that there is an obsessive slant, here and elsewhere, in which female-dominated Lawrence–Mellors rages against the 'self-will' of women, accusing them of being 'Lesbians' in their aggressive clitoral orgasms ('a beak tearing at me'), and demands sexual submission. Such vulnerability also provides part of the crux of the notorious (and critically somewhat over-debated) night of passion in Mellors' cottage in the woods, where the Lady must submit to a 'shameless sensuality', rather obviously including anal intercourse, in which she 'had to be a passive, consenting thing, like a slave, a physical slave'.

Lawrence had considerable empathy with women, and they are the central figures in a majority of his works of fiction, yet this should not obscure the demands he makes on them. As he makes even the tough Mrs Bolton acknowledge, the female must give in to the male on important demands. Lawrence wants to insist, as with Constance, that such submission creates women of fuller being, not only capable of intense desire but also able to negate class and other constrictions. Still, I suggest, the sexual submission scenes are rarely Lawrence's best because of an all too personally biased sexual need and insistence. With proper irony, the dramatisations of women negating men are better-written, be it Mrs Bolton manipulating Clifford, or Constance defying him and his modern schizophrenia of personal inadequacy combined with claims to power and authority (as in the woods when his motorised wheelchair, and other pretences of command, break down – see Chapter XIII, which is one of the best).

In *Lady Chatterley's Lover* as elsewhere, however much he claims to show 'tenderness', Lawrence gives far more strength to the negations than to the larger affirmations. The hope for true marriage remains rather uncertain with the ex-gamekeeper and the pregnant Lady separated and rather vaguely looking toward a new life in future exile – Lawrence's usual rather Pyrrhic ending. Uncertain, too, is Lawrence's major social deduction from the passional–pastoral logic, in the tradition of the Arcadian utopia: the fragments of a social vision to supersede the 'industrial epoch' where sensual males (dressed 'with legs close bright scarlet') would live by crafts in simple organic communities, and would practise Morris-dancing and the worship of Pan. The pagan–pastoral society has only the tones of a wistful yearning, though the negations of contemporary society are insistent and vehement. Almost always, Lawrence's art is in opposition, and should not be taken otherwise.

Let us also be clear that the affirmative passion in Lawrence is not what is usually taken as normative sexuality. By this I mean that not only are Lawrence's erotic situations rather variant (such as the anal, but not the oral) and include curious intertwinings of male narcissism and hostility, but that they also demand something else, another condition of being. As an obvious example, in his last novella, *The Man Who Died*, the young priestess of Isis turns disdainfully away as she observes a youth beat a young girl and then mount her in the 'frenzy of a boy's first passion'. That is merely the natural coitus of slaves. She searches rather for the mythical orgasms, the completion of and with an Osiris. For she is one of those 'rare women', a philosopher advised her, who waits 'for the re-born man'. In Lawrence's intentionally blasphemous transference of the Protestant conversion experience, and his outrageous punning on Christian sacramental language for eroticism, the virgin's lover can be no less than the scarred and sickly dark stranger, the post-crucifixion embittered Christ. Amoral sexual erection in place of spiritual resurrection is specifically based on his deceptively passing as the earlier dead-and-reborn deity. The eroticism may be summarised as piously slavish on the woman's part, anonymous, impersonal, religionist, overweening (images drawn from the ecstatic mystical tradition), a black-mass intercourse on an altar. Various violations seem required for being thus 'risen'. The man who died achieves not only the intense 'transcendence of desire' but a general revitalisation of the sense of 'touch' which reconnects him with the physical universe as well as exalted self-acceptance. Passion here is nothing less than the reformulation of being.

The 'dying' to reach that sexual conversion experience includes the termination of most social obligations. The ex-messianic malefactor–lover, now reinvigorated, takes a boat away from the slave youth (the one of merely natural sexuality), and defiantly flees in the night. His enemies are represented by the now pregnant priestess' Roman matriarch, who stands for 'property' and 'power'. The final metaphors turn him into a seasonal fertility demon – he returns 'sure as spring', and retains the magic of 'the gold and flowing serpent'. The vagabond, resexed Christ endlessly negates the 'lesser day' of the ordinary moral and social order.

Granted that last fable of the dying, and not-to-be-reborn, Lawrence suffers from its lushly redundant, obsessive, poetic-prose – far from his best style. But the dialectics remain more consistent than the manner. In his penultimate novella, *The Virgin and the Gipsy*, a more modest passional fairy tale combines with a harsh realism of social-moral negation. Lawrence dramatises Yvette, the lively young daughter of an anti-life idealising clergyman (Saywell), amid repressive genteel Christian middle-class surroundings. She recognised a man who deeply '*desired*' her, a sensitively crude gipsy 'outsider', older, married and amoral, but also a 'resurrected' man (in the same way as is Mellors, and like Lawrence's Christ). This is one of Lawrence's domestications of the demon lover.

Intellectual conspirator to the virgin's deflowering is a Lawrence spokesman, an older illicit lover, who advises her to follow the logic of passion rather than moral convention, since 'desire is the most wonderful thing in life'. The enemies are the life-hating Christian father, the 'fungoid' middle-class family deity, his mother, and the girl's own fears. Further fabulistic events, including a flood (caused by an old forgotten pagan tunnel), kill off the vicious matriarch and bring the gipsy to the girl's rescue. Yvette is warmed to life by the dark stranger in the rectory bed. The brief impersonal affair (she does not even know his name) with the demon lover is not salvational but does give her a new 'courage' of the body, and initiates her into the autonomy and truth of desire.

I recount this paradigmatic tale because its passional heroism of ordinary existence may reasonably be taken as a balanced centre of Lawrence's vision of eros. In it, 'desire' is explicitly affirmed but also distinguished from 'mere appetite'. In explication, we might well draw on a later Lawrence essay:

all that matters is that men and women shall do what they *really* want to do. Though here, as everywhere, we must remember that man has a double set of desires, the shallow and the profound, the personal, superficial, temporary desires, and the inner, impersonal, great desires that are fulfilled in long periods of time. The desires of the moment are easy to recognise, but the others, the deeper ones, are different.   (*Phoenix II*, p. 501)

The probing, and sometimes agonised, effort to find out what one truly desires, to reach the fullest responses that relate one to reality, to others and to the authentic self, provides the passional process. Even if this is taken as a vitalistic restatement of moral discrimination, it should be recognised as having a different emphasis. Where the traditional moralist believes in *goodness* which he achieves by *will*, and the Christian in *grace* which he achieves by the abnegation which becomes *faith*, the Lawrentian seeks *passion* which he finds through *desire*. Unlike the traditional moralist and Christian, he neither commands nor subdues subjectivity, but intensifies it. Where the classical ethical and religious imperatives require rejection of the imperfect and evil, which are frequently linked to desires, the Lawrentian must discover desires by negating the ideals, the will, the codes, the authorities, obscuring and denying the desires. Passion, too, has its serious casuistry.

Lawrence tried a variety of descriptive and metaphoric, 'realistic' and 'fabulistic', terms to present this serious awareness. Another argumentative statement: 'Living consists in doing what you really, vitally want to do: what the *life* in you wants to do, not what your ego imagines you want to do. And to find out *how* the life in you wants to be lived, and to live it, is terribly difficult' (*Phoenix II*, p. 438). Is 'life' here merely a synonym for 'spirit' in the more usual religious views? No, except for certain extreme heterodoxies (which did attract Lawrence), because it most emphatically includes the sensual body. It is, of course, an exalted demand, religious in that sense. Acting by desire is often more arduous that is acting by ethical rule. As with the mysticism of the antinomian Christian – or the *arété* of the classical hero, or the *satori* of the Zen Buddhist – fulfilment of deep desires carries one necessarily outside the ordinary ethos and order – beyond good and evil in the Nietzschean sense. The Lawrence vitalist must achieve a transcendent unity of self-affirmation, for 'a thing you truly believe in cannot be wrong'. The deepest feelings are autonomous and ultimate, 'desire itself being beyond criticism and moral judgment'. This is not true, of course, of its applications, for which it is the critical standard; there are true and false lovers, true and false sex.

Contrary to some rather ill-informed criticism, and to smug apologetics for more conventional moralisms, perhaps characteristics of a majority of Lawrence studies, this is not just the late Lawrence. The penultimate novella *The Virgin and the Gipsy*, as has been repeatedly noted, is partly a rewrite of an early work, *The Daughters of the Vicar*. There, another young virgin struggled for passional realisation against the genteel Christian ambience and its social-moral-vitalistic repression. In other versions, desire is less self-conscious, appropriately, as with his favoured Sleeping Beauty motif. (Perhaps the best known early version is 'The Horse-dealer's Daughter', originally entitled 'The Miracle'; for a male version, 'You Touched Me'.) The dark outsider in violation of the erotic norms, the demon lover, was also in the works of fiction from the beginning (cf. 'A Fragment of Stained Glass', c. 1907). Other parts of the passional dialectic, such as the desire–negation interchanges of love–hate and the death–rebirth obsessions were also present early (see, for example, not only the homoerotic 'The Prussian Officer' but also such fine underrecognised early stories as 'The White Stocking' and 'The Christening'). Lawrence changed, of course, but not all that drastically in his short life, and the desire–negation polarities and the passional intensification were present when he was young.

Many views of Lawrence as fictionist have patently been confused by focusing on the novels only, in chronological order, and with the emphasis on the middle period – all of which are quite misleading. Viewed chronologically, the novels show a slower development of Lawrence's dominant concerns with passion. While novels were not originally his best medium, there were external reasons for writing them (the hungering of a poor schoolteacher for conventional and commercial success; the need to appease his mother, then a lady friend, and then a mistress). Lawrence's slight first novel, *The White Peacock* (of which an advance copy was prepared for his mother on her death bed), mostly about the affections of proper provincial adolescents, appears trapped in moralisms (anti-drinking; sexual covertness; *petit bourgeois* social snobbery, synthetically upgraded one level) as well as a priggish schoolteacher's florid descriptions of nature and would-be fashionable artiness. While early bits of misogynistic rebellion against the woman-dominated order briefly appear with apocalyptic gamekeeper Annable (clear forerunner of Mellors in the final novel), and insistent but undeveloped homoeroticism (as when the touch of Cyril's and George's naked bodies produces 'indecipherable yearnings' and 'perfect' love), any passion has little place in this genteel exercise. Having a contract, Lawrence hastily wrote his second long novel, *The Trespasser* (an adaptation of Helen Corke's memoir), which is a fervidly murky and trite excursus on a sickly passion for guilt by an adulterous music teacher who futilely commits suicide. Essentially, the anti-passional women are to blame. Later, Lawrence's appropriate misogyny takes clear and emphatic shape in dozens of portraits of witches.

Sons and Lovers, his third novel, achieves a different magnitude, richly presenting familial and provincial lower-class life, and unpatronisingly so (as in his earlier stories, but rare in English fiction). The overall concern of the novel, I suggest, is less with the criticism-exaggerated Oedipal (though this is partly the natural insight, further encouraged by Freudian Frieda Weekley) than with the constricting provincial Protestant ethos. Protagonist Paul must reject Miriam because she personifies much of it: the anti-sensual (the graphic scenes with the swing and the pecking chickens, as well as the too-late 'sacrifice' sexuality), the naggingly moralistic 'fussy', the spiritual earnestness for 'higher things', the anti-spontaneous Christian 'martyr' psychology, the puritan wilful 'proud humility'. Also, for the first time in a novel, though it had appeared in the shorter fictions, there is the crucial antithesis, the 'baptism of fire in passion', the sexual realisation of 'impersonal desire'. Paul and Clara's intercourse, for example, in a field at night, is not mere coitus but transformation. It 'included in their meeting . . . the cry of the peewit, the wheel of the stars', in a generally heightened immanent sense of being. Thus 'having known the immensity of passion', they also 'know their own nothingness', which is the desire–negation recognition of the true ultimate flow of life. While the dark nothingness of the 'Derelict' conclusion to the novel (more represented than caused by the dead mother) shows little of the countering erotic polarity dramatised earlier, it negatively confirms the effects of the constricting and defeating order so essential to the texture and the issue of *Sons and Lovers*.

The next three novels show increased consciousness of erotic intensification. Perhaps because of that, *The Rainbow* has been discussed more positively than this suggestive but ragged saga of the Brangwens – the passional history of three generations of nineteenth-century provincials – deserves. Much of the writing is portentously inflated, redundant and confused. Passion is intermittently given larger terms, as with Tom's 'desire to find in a woman the embodiment of all his inarticulate, powerful religious impulses', but remains dramatically inarticulate. Lawrence strains and churns with obsessive metaphors for the sacralisation of erotic torment. Passion now appears as 'eternal knowledge' as well as the 'highest intensity' of response. Some of the 'deep-hidden rage of unsatisfied men against women' is revealed in the otherwise positive and tradition-bound marriage of farmer Tom to Polish-exile widow Lydia. (The foreignness, as in so much of Lawrence's fiction as well as in his life, exotically transmutes Oedipal fears and conflictfully heightens the relation.) In the next generation, with daughter Anna and religious craftsman Will, the 'passion' continues the 'unknown battle' between male and female, with considerable defeat as each 'relinquished the adventure into the unknown'. But partial victory is Anna's in her submergence in compulsive childbearing and consequent subordination of the male. Will's defeated 'longing for the infinite' by way of erotic passion continues in the third generation with daughter Ursula, and approximately half the novel becomes the story of her passional perplexity, now more fully conscious.

Ursula's history to her early twenties (and into the start of this century) includes the novel's more tangible scenes, such as her brutally negative role in doing the 'collective, inhuman thing' of compulsory schoolteaching. Her lesbian affair with teacher Winifred (who ends, perversely, by marrying 'putrescent' industrialist Tom, Jr) and her inchoate yearnings for individual self-realisation (which makes her fail in the 'commercial shrine' of a university) are little dramatised. Much of her love-affair with her socially conventional army officer cousin, Anton, seems perplexing. While he seems to provide erotic heightening – Ursula 'entered the dark fields of immortality' – she in part becomes a male-predatory 'harpy' (like Mellors' first wife) after 'her sexual life flamed into a kind of disease'. But apparently Lawrence's committed view that the 'passion' self is alien to the establishment 'social self' must banish 'will broken' Anton to a stock marriage in the colonies, leaving a pregnant Ursula outcast and miscarrying as she enters the world of modern alienation, though still longing for a man 'from the Infinite'. She still 'grasped and groped to find the creation of the living God, instead of the old, hard barren forms of bygone living'. The devolving generations have fractured male–female continuities and organic forms, and so the concluding rainbow promises little but perverse passional yearnings in Lawrence's desperate effort to separate good sexual desire from a badly negative society.

In fact, the Ursula of *Women in Love* (which followed, though little related and far more thoroughly wrought) does make a marriage to Birkin, the Lawrence persona, but in an alienated individualist way into barren self-exile rather than in any organic 'form'. Rootless bohemia, of course, had become the only class and country of most of the characters as well as of Lawrence. Consequently, *Women in Love* is less a novel, in many traditional senses, than intensely metaphoric – partly dramatised, partly argued – dialectics about the 'passionate struggle into conscious being' (as Lawrence wrote in the Foreword) of marginal characters shaped by 'the bitterness of the war'. Hence much is sheer negation.

Some of this (as with witch-Hermione) is a personal and class 'consummation of hatred'. But Lawrence's Great War rage also becomes fully misanthropic (as evident from his first novel onwards): 'mankind is a dead tree'; 'Man is a mistake; he must go'; 'man is not the criterion' of life and meaning. As Lawrence even notes of his synthetic upper-class surrogate, his 'dislike of mankind . . . amounted almost to a disease'. The negations are often acutely focused elsewhere as well: against the new instrumental rationalisation of the industrial order – 'pure organic disintegration and pure mechanical organisation' (partly represented by Gerald); against the related dehumanising modernist art (Gudrun and Loerke); against the vestigial upper class (the Crichs and the people at Breadalby), the unrebellious sensation-seeking lower classes (the colliers' Saturday night), the nastily futile bohemians – indeed, just about everyone and everything that can be viewed as 'disintegrative'. It should also be admitted that the paeans to death – 'how grand and perfect death was, how good to look forward to' (here and in 'The Reality of Peace', 'England, My England', the later *Kangaroo*, etc.), and the longing for death as the 'great consummation' – go beyond any thematic and dramatic coherence. An essential part of Lawrence's imagination is utterly extreme in revulsive negation.

More dialectical, and sometimes charming, is Lawrence's partial negation of women, to him repositories of controlling 'will'. This is aimed not only at the destructive man-manipulators (Hermione and Pussum and Gudrun) but more generally: 'woman was always so horrible and clutching, she had such a lust for possession, a greed of self-importance in love. She wanted to have, to own, to control, to be dominant.' Inverting his earlier maternal fixation, Lawrence attacks the 'Great Mother of everything', as when Birkin furiously stones the reflections of the female moon and curses Cybele and others ('Moony'). This antifeminism may be linked to the homosexuality avowed in the deleted 'Prologue': 'It was the man's physique which held the passion and the mystery to him', and for which 'he felt the hot, flushing, roused attraction'. In the novel proper, this leads to the attempted Birkin–Gerald 'conjunction between two men' and the *Bludbruderschaft* ritualisation of it, including the rather self-consciously forced scene of naked wrestling ('Gladiatorial'). The male-on-male passion provides the concluding motif to the novel. Says supposedly superlatively-married Birkin, 'I wanted eternal union with a man too'. His wife concludes that it is a 'perversity'.

The destructive perversity of Gudrun drives Gerald to his suicidal end, terminating the male love affair. Just why and how, sexually and otherwise, Gudrun engaged in the 'mystic frictional activities of diabolic reducing down, disintegrating the vital organic body of life' in her insistence on dominating Gerald, other than through pure female wilfulness, seems unclear. It is declared that the will to industrial control by Gerald destroys organic connections, and hence desire. Both figures serve Lawrence's dialectical polarity. The attack on 'will' balances the meaning of 'desire'. 'Desire, in any shape or form, is primal, whereas the will is secondary, derived. The will can destroy but it cannot create.' So for the male–female battle. (This 'Prologue' summary may seem contrary to the Nietzschean Will to Power, but Lawrence's repeated use of the Last Metaphysician is actually an affirmation of it.)

In his wilful arguing of the doctrine, Birkin–Lawrence engages Ursula–Frieda in a 'fine passion of opposition', in some delightful scenes. This adversarial eroticism may be rather more persuasive than are the avowed 'mystic conjunctions'. As Ursula says, much of his version of the erotic argument is masculine 'bullying'. Still, it may be distinctly Lawrence himself positing a 'stark and impersonal' passion, 'not meeting and mingling . . . but an equilibrium of two single beings . . . as the stars balance each other'. Whether heroic individualism or a terrible fear of female domination, 'I don't want love', says Lawrence's spokesman, 'I want to be gone out of myself, and you to be lost to yourself'. Such passion also seeks the obliteration of mere social roles, guilts and self-consciousness, in the yearning to achieve an unanxious 'dark involuntary being'. The arguments for passion really serve a holistic ontology.

This is but another version of Lawrence's polemical claims for the notorious 'blood knowledge', 'instinct', 'intuitive life', 'animal nature', and other 'dark' states. Yet, we might well note, this is often treated with the critical intelligence which makes Lawrence something other than a mere fundamentalist of his erotic imagination. His Birkin, for just one example, shrewdly attacks the very Lawrence doctrine archly spouted by Hermione: 'What is it but the worst and last form of intellectualism, this love of yours for passion and the animal instincts?' Lawrence here provides the line of major attack on himself. The complex strategies of the intellectual anti-intellectualism should also be recognised as part of the post-enlightenment 'crisis' ideology of modernism.

Whatever the erotic dialectic sometimes claims, the crucial applications continue to demand female submission. As Birkin demands of Ursula, he wants her to abnegate her 'assertive *will*' and so achieve 'the surrender of her spirit'. The female threat (which we see also with the Crich girl dragging her lover to his death in Willey Water, Hermione smashing Birkin's head, Gudrun driving Gerald to suicide, etc.) requires that she be his 'humble slave' (more genially phrased as his 'patient Griselda' in the parallel ragged comedy *The Captain's Doll*). Ursula's erotic submission, like Constance Chatterley's, includes pleasuring 'the darkest poles of the body' to be reached 'at the back of the base of the loins'. Further specifications of the anal gratification are not given, though perhaps linked with the homosexual longings, and with the 'dark passion' violations of genteel 'adoration love' (the later characteristic of villainous idealists, such as Clifford Chatterley, and Boris in the murky-demonic *Ladybird*, as well as most of the women). But, after all, Birkin (like Tom Brangwen,

Mellors, the risen Christ, *et al.*) is making a religious demand via sexuality, for 'his resurrection and his life'.

Lawrence's other erotic novel in the Great War period, *The Lost Girl*, though archly rough in form and sloppy in writing (and ignored in trite criticism), interestingly suggests a somewhat perverse feminism in its liberation of small-town midlands spinster Alvina from shabbily repressive lower-middle class life. She seeks 'not mere marriage' but 'a profound and dangerous interrelationship', as well as escape from domination by the 'mechanical' and 'mediocre'. So she chooses passional domination by a wandering Italian vaudeville performer (producing some very silly scenes) with his 'dark flicker of ascendency', a characteristic of Lawrence's usual alien lover. While merging with him made 'her his slave', Lawrence paradoxically insists that this also provides a kind of completion of the woman, a 'perfected' self. She becomes 'bewitched' in a 'sleep-like submission to his being', even feeling at times like 'a sacred prostitute'. The 'desperate passion that was in him sent her completely unconscious' of her egotism and social role. Yet though completely yielding in the 'acquiescent passion' of the primordial female, the loss of self remains incomplete – failure or victory?

Having given up nursing (and possible comfortable marriage to a middle-aged doctor) to marry her lover and return to his primitive family farm in the Abruzzi, Alvina's passion certainly leads her to extremity, and Lawrence to some of his strong 'travel' writing. The 'spirit of place', as often in his fiction, becomes part of the passional dialectic. These 'potent negative centres' are 'places which resist us, which have the power to overthrow our psychic being' with their aegis of savage pagan gods. Lawrence lends little romance or sentiment to the Italian countryside with his emphasis on its particular discomforts, hardness, and even 'malevolence'. But there is a negative exaltation which becomes a passional affirmation.

Whatever else happens, the ironically liberated heroine is unlikely to become a repetition of her mother, who withdrew into invalidism, or of the devastated spinsters (Miss Frost and Miss Pinnegar), the 'Dead Sea fruit' of the repression and emotional 'mediocrity' of puritanic lower-middle class provincial life. Lawrence saw, probably rightly, that it takes drastic assaults on the psyche to transform petit bourgeois sensibility. Again, a 'lost girl' ends by being isolated, pregnant, with husband conscripted in the Great War, and unfulfilled. Yet she has adventured into the realms of passional being, however wedded to the negative, and thus into fuller experience and meaning. And that is much of what is at issue in Lawrence's terribly insistent demands for 'more vivid life!'

There is little convincing loving, sexual or otherwise, in Lawrence's next long narratives, leaving aside the covert homoeroticism (Aaron and Lilly in *Aaron's Rod*, Somers and Kangaroo in *Kangaroo*). Love in a wider sense is around only in Lawrence's polemical savaging of the 'putrid, stinking', Christian derived 'ideal of love' (*Aaron's Rod*) and the 'dead' ethic of Western 'Love, Self-sacrifice, Humanity united in love' (*Kangaroo*). The Nietzschean ideologising aims for an uncertain hero-worship of passionately exceptional men in these crude, carelessly crafted and heavily tendentious stories.

The tendencies to doctrinally reify passion may be seen to culminate in Lawrence's worst novel, *The Plumed Serpent*, though most of the religiosity there is not directly erotic. Returning to a female central figure, middle-aged Englishwoman Kate Leslie in Mexico, Lawrence orders a conversion experience: 'Ye must be born again. Out of the fight with the octopus of life, one must win the soft bloom of being'. (This hectoring and muddled mixture of the archaic and abstract fairly represents much of the style.) The jaded middle-class lady hungers 'to be merged in desire beyond desire', to 'be gone in the body beyond the individualism' by becoming a 'morning star' female goddess, subordinate to the dark sun of generic man. More literally, she self-hatingly accepts a diabolic 'male power', the reactionary Indian conspirator of a syncretistic Aztec methodism, General Cipriano Viedma, in 'submission absolute'. Representing for Lawrence the negation of despised Western bourgeois consciousness, this abnegation not only includes intelligence and decency but also usual sexual gratification (the by now notorious 'Aphrodite of the foam' passage, which clearly rejects direct female orgasm). Kate becomes the General's servile sexual and religious mistress, subordinate partner in the authoritarian revivalist cult's military takeover of chaotic modern Mexico. *The Plumed Serpent* might be partly salvaged for intelligent interest by treating it as a failed 'thought experiment' or a symptomatic document of sickness, but even so, the main passion in the fantasy may be (to quote it against itself) 'a fathomless lust of resentment, a demonish hatred of life itself', pretending to be a new communion. It may also have utility in reminding the reader that new religions are largely old illnesses.

It is surprising that Lawrence could, in the same period, write *St Mawr*, one of his more suggestive short novels, with wit and verve. The quest of young Lou Witt, the returning Anglicised American, for 'positive living' of course requires the invigoration of passional awareness, first represented by the demonic defiance of the eponymous stallion, that is dropped midway. (This is often the case with other totemic images of passional qualities – moles, a fox, birds, etc. – since the human intensity, not any symbolisation, is the reality.) The story shifts from London social satire, such as of the invert upper-class husband who wants to castrate the justifiably rebellious horse, to the metapsychology of the American South-west in the search for the nontheistic religious state Lawrence calls, again, 'wonder' and usually links with erotic desire. Along the way, not only the passional horse who raised the consciousness, but also the for once comically treated wilful matriarch, the nastily tight English society, the possibility of sexual submission to the primitive (the Indian groom Phoenix), and much else, are negated by Lou. As often in Lawrence's work, there are intrusive declarations, such as an early apocalyptic warning against over-population, over-mechanisation, and conseqeunt authoritarian ideologies, and a later one for vitalist cultural evolution. Paradoxically (though common for Lawrence), vehement negation is most central to the search for positive living.

Curiously, *St Mawr* never becomes directly erotic. The vitalistic metaphors transfer from the horse (and the parallel English and American grooms) to Lawrence's New Mexican ranch. Its history also emphasises a non-sexual demonic passion, the *'ne plus ultra'* of the harshly beautiful enlivening, a godless 'absolute'. (*'Jesus and a God of Love'* and any other claim to 'Universal love' are *'nonsense'*.) Only by defiance of a sordid civilisation and its dead ideals, and identification with this splendid negation, can his heroine, an odd sort of godless saint of the immediate, find 'life, intense bristling life'.

St Mawr provides an interesting and pivotal place to end this commentary on the novels, for what may be viewed as Lawrence's essentially erotic dialectic nonetheless sometimes re-reified 'desire'. Having gone beyond the phallic, the heroic woman is again left in isolation but has achieved through nihilistic vitalism a regeneratively intense awareness. Lawrence naturally returned to the erotic in his last novel and novellas (discussed first, as is proper, above), but we might conclude that a state of intense passional *consciousness*, however fully based in bodily responses, is much of what is at issue in the unending psychomachia of extreme desire and negation.

From this perspective, how righteously quaint of the late F. R. Leavis in his three books on Lawrence to turn such erratic writing into perfected art and such passional extremity into normative moralisms. And how even more irrelevant are the many sentimentalist critics. (I am willing to assume that, say, Mark Spilka has outgrown his 'love ethic' and its obvious misreadings, though the sentimentalist contemners, such as Eliseo Vivas and Frank Kermode, probably cannot.) As Lawrence delightfully warned: sentimentality 'covers viciousness as inevitably as greenness covers a bog'. To take a different and more recent example, how irrelevant of Michel Foucault (in the conclusion to *The History of Sexuality*, vol. 1) to quote several unmeshing passages from late Lawrence as confirmation of normative sexual discourse and our modern episteme of control, when Lawrence so fully violates those. The minimal centenary gesture would be to return to Lawrence some of his peculiarity.

Let me conclude with several qualifications of my inevitably summary treatment. Granted, this has considerably emphasised the passionally positive in Lawrence. Some of his most insightfully perfected art is rather more purely negative, such as that fine anti-middle class fable 'The Rocking-Horse Winner' and the devastatingly acute mockery of the destructiveness in idealism, 'The Man Who Loved Islands'. Not always as well crafted, but including some apt writing and perceptions, were his almost endless fictions attacking wilful women and their social order – 'None of That', 'The Princess', 'Mother and Daughter', 'The Blue Moccasins', 'The Lovely Lady', and so on – a considerable literature of hatred. But perhaps this point needs no more elaboration. Lawrence, the positive prophet of vital life, was one of the most thrustingly negative writers of his time. I have argued that there is intimate intercourse between the two.

Autobiographically, the concern of the sickly Lawrence may have expressed itself as preoccupation with both annihilation and heightened immanence. So, too, with his social role. Self-consciously of lower-class origins, he spent most of his adult life in bohemian circles and deracinated self-exile. He employs the dialectics of passion to attack the dominant patterns of Anglo-American personality, social connection and response – the 'passionless' middle class, high and low – for *How beastly the bourgeoisie is.* To read his work properly is to see him negatively countering that enemy, which has also been his audience, excoriated with puritan seriousness. Lawrence angrily fled his provincial Protestant background, yet continued it in everything from his puritan domestic work habits through his sexual moralising to his key psychology of 'conversion' and 'rebirth' experiences. To suggest yet one more context, Lawrence exacerbatedly responded to the 'crisis in consciousness' of the twentieth century – metaphorically, the Great War – which he, too, saw as the death of God, organic community, traditional ideals, affirmative social order, and heroic persons. No wonder, then, that he sought a regenerative passion inseparable from nihilism. Everything must be intensified in this destructive civilisation and emptied universe, from flowers to phalluses, from individual touch to the cataclysm of *homo sapiens*. The passion for desire and negation is finally all the meaning there is. Lawrence, at times, dallied with other hopes and sentiments, but never for long. For the vitally negative dialectics usually carried a desire for truth. Typically: 'let it be a great passion and then death, rather than a false or faked purpose'. There remains a heroism to such dialectics.

9

The Philosophy of D. H. Lawrence

P. N. FURBANK

In the early months of 1915, simultaneously with the completion of *The Rainbow*, D. H. Lawrence began to set down on paper his 'philosophy'. He did so to put into order the insights of the novel, and also those of his chaotic *Gai Savaire* or 'Study of Thomas Hardy' which had been his first *riposte* to the War. In his own self-image he was a messiah, newly risen after five months in the tomb. Nevertheless, 'philosophy' was always the term he used of what he now wrote, and I am interested in justifying the word. Evidently Lawrence had also a creed, just as he had 'views', but neither a 'creed' nor 'views' is the same as a philosophy.

When a novelist or playwright has a philosophy, it tends to be begrudged him by critics. This has notoriously been the case with Thomas Hardy; and maybe there the critics were in the right. Bernard Shaw also had a philosophy, but it was not of much help to him: it was a poor little thing compared with his scintillating 'views'. Hemmed in by 'philosophies', the 'modernist' writers in the Edwardian period cultivated a strong distrust of all 'ideas'; and much of the effort and genius of Henry James, who came of a philosophical family, went into *not* having a philosophy.

For these reasons, it is not surprising that critics have rather turned their faces against Lawrence's 'philosophy'. They acknowledged, of course, that he possessed a creed – for how otherwise could he have acquired a throng of disciples? But apart from this, the standard procedure has been to hold up the 'art' as a rebuke to the 'thinker' – his own 'Do not trust the teller, trust the tale' coming in very handily for this purpose. Frank Kermode, in his *Lawrence* (1971) says:

> But 'art speech is the only speech', as Lawrence observed, and
> he spoke fully only when speaking it. His mind needed

strenuous engagement with art, with a text, or at least with recollected experience, before it could achieve the complex expression it needed; we have already seen him engage his own and others' art in this way. That is why *The Sea and Sardinia*, written immediately before the *Fantasia* in 1921, is so much more satisfying than the purer flight of 'metaphysic'.[1]

As a general principle, this sounds as if it ought to be true. Actually, though, I think it involves a fallacy. For if we consider the long essay *The Crown*, which Lawrence was writing in March and April 1915, what stands out is that it *is* 'art-speech', and 'art-speech' of a magnificent kind.

I do not deny that there is a problem in studying Lawrence's thought. One always seems on the point of grasping his thought as a whole, then this goal recedes bafflingly. The problem is related to repetition, or repetition-with-a-difference; his work seems to be encumbered with the ashes of past Phoenixes. All the more reason, then, to pay attention on this occasion when he seems to want to be 'grasped' and to grasp himself. Hence, I wish to focus here entirely on *The Crown* and on one closely-related piece, the brief essay 'Him With his Tail in his Mouth'.

Philip Hobsbaum, in his *Reader's Guide to D. H. Lawrence* (1981), complains of *The Crown* as being 'curiously contextless' and as incomprehensible without a knowledge of *The Rainbow*. Here again I detect a stock reaction. At a first reading, *Also Sprach Zarathustra* can seem 'contextless' too, but it is really only a matter of unfamiliarity. It is because Nietzsche's writing is unique, as is *The Crown*, and if you are patient and allow them to work upon you, they reveal all the self-sufficiency of high art. Just to recall some of the phrases and epigrams in *The Crown* helps to convince us of the force of mind at work: 'Our universe is not much more than a mannerism with us now';[2] 'Everything must be "universal" to the conquering worm';[3] 'Thus are we, then, rounded upon a void, a hollow want';[4] 'In the name of love, what horrors men perpetrate, and are applauded!'[5]

Again, the tone is so beautifully controlled and varied; at one moment he is engaged, with delicate care, upon concept-making; at another he grows fervent, until we think he is ranting – and then, with a sudden drop, he is tweaking us avuncularly and reminding us of common sense. With what resourcefulness and even rigour, combined with gaiety, does he explore, in the first section, the symbolism of the Lion and the Unicorn in heraldry and nursery-rhyme. You might, for a second, mistake it for bumbling sermon-talk ('Dear friends, I was thinking only the other day about the symbolism of the royal coat of arms . . .'), and this is an example of the sort of risks that Lawrence, as philosopher, was ready to take.

Even larger risks attend his use of systems of symbolism and of the esoteric generally. He labours some set of symbols, or some metaphor, for pages at a time, and then, dizzyingly, he has swerved away into another, or into half a dozen others. At the time of *The Crown*, he was in love with traditional or 'Italian-primitive' Christian symbolism, and he makes most beautiful use of it:

> Here are the opposing hosts of angels, the ruddy choirs, upright, rushing flames, the lofty Cherubim that palpitate about the Presence, the Source; and the tall, still angels soft and pearly as mist, who await round the Goal, the attendants that hover on the edge of the last Assumption.[6]

What matters most, however, is not his use of this or a dozen other symbolic repertoires, but the terms upon which he has dealings with them. I have heard complaints that, in this period, each new book that Lawrence read appeared to him the revelation of ultimate truth. This seems entirely wrong: it evokes an uneducated seeker after truth, whereas Lawrence was by now a very knowing, even *blasé*, connoisseur of unorthodox books – occultist, theosophical, apocalyptic, or whatever. That he was intellectually impatient and opportunistic is of course true, but another matter. What is also true is that he was totally without intellectual snobbery. It is quite natural for him to tell a friend that he has been reading 'a little half-crown vol. in the *Little Books on Art* series by Methuen' and likes it very much, 'because it puts me more into order'.[7]

Obviously, there is a place for discussion of Lawrence's 'sources', yet – and one feels this especially with the two books by Emile Delavenay[8] – to do it at any length seems bound to be misleading. Delavenay wrote a whole book about the influence of Edward Carpenter on Lawrence; and the problem with this is not that Lawrence may have never read Carpenter (for, on the other hand, he may have done so); rather, it lies in the notion that he held 'ideas' in the same manner as did Carpenter, and therefore could be 'influenced' by him. Life is unfair, for it might be said that Carpenter lived his theories more visibly than Lawrence ever did: he really pursued the Simple Life that he preached, made sandals, and laboured daily in the fields. Nevertheless, in a more important sense, his 'ideas', whether Hindu, occultist or Tolstoyan, belong only to the lecture-hall and have no power to command our minds and feelings.

Lawrence, as it happened, had a novelist colleague who also possesed a vital and viable philosophy: E. M. Forster. Indeed, there were, as both sensed, some close affinities between their philosophies. Forster may be helpful to us in this discussion. Philosophically as well as humanly speaking, he attached supreme significance to relationships, and could imagine that human relationships were the sole true material of history. For him, people mattered only relatively, being as they were in a condition of ceaseless flux and dissolution; what, for him, seemed to offer more reality and permanence were achieved relationships. (It is the symptom of Mrs Moore's sickness, in *A Passage to India*, that she begins to imagine – 'vision or nightmare'? – the opposite, namely that 'though people are important the relations between them are not'.[9])

Now, strip Forster's 'relationships', for a moment, of their humanistic associations, and you find that something will survive this stripping-away: 'relationship', a philosophical concept (not to say a mathematical or chemical one) in a technical and formal sense. The same is true of Lawrence. Relationship is quite central to his system, according to which God or 'the absolute' is revealed only in a relationship.

> Behind me there is time stretching back for ever, on to the unthinkable beginnings, infinitely. And this is eternity. Ahead of me, where I do not know, there is time stretching on infinitely, to eternity. These are the two eternities.
>
> We cannot say, they are one and the same. They are two and utterly different . . .
>
> They are only *one* in their mutual relation, which relation is timeless and absolute.[10]

More immediately to my purpose, though, are that brilliant page or two about the Lion, the Unicorn and the Crown. What is the true nature of the relationship between these three, he asks? The logic, or you might say the grammar, of their relationship is explored by him with much formal rigour, and is shown to be subtle and not at all what the lazy mind would anticipate.

> The lion and the unicorn are not fighting for the Crown. They are fighting beneath it. And the Crown is upon their fight. If they made friends and lay down side by side, the Crown would fall on them both and kill them. If the lion really beat the unicorn, then the Crown pressing on the head of the king of beasts alone would destroy him. Which it has done and is doing.[11]

One might think of this as theology, like some doctrine regarding the Trinity, but I would prefer to consider it as epistemology. The point I am working towards is that this is the area of philosophy in which these novelists are likely to shine. For, as a matter of professional practice, are they not continually concerned with 'point of view'; with the status of any given report on a human situation; with the paradoxes and problems of 'angle' (certain objects being visible from any given angle, and others concealed); with the formal relationship, and the rights and wrongs of this relationship, of author to privileged narrator and narrator to what is related? Thus, when Lawrence writes in *The Crown*, 'Analysis presupposes a corpse', he is stating amongst other things a theory of *literature*. And he is doing so, equally, when he writes in 'Him With his Tail in his Mouth':

> Of course, if you stay outside the fourth dimension, and try to measure creation in length, breadth and height, you've set yourself the difficult task of measuring up the Monad, the Mundane Egg. Which is a game, like any other. The solution is, of course (let me whisper): *put his tail in his mouth!*
> Once you realise that, willy nilly, you're *inside* the Monad, you give it up. You're inside it and you always will be. Therefore, Jonah, sit still in the whale's belly, and have a look round. For you'll *never* measure the whale, since you're inside him.[12]

It is a visible affinity between Lawrence and Forster that, in the vision of both, the *self* is robbed of its privileges. This is achieved by a manoeuvre in regard to death, one which takes the form of assigning a mystical as well as a literal significance to the terms 'life' and 'death'. (It is with almost the same voice that the two novelists pity the pale unsatisfied ones who never achieve their 'life', their 'crown'.) Once one's own physical death can be reassigned to the natural order of things and genuinely felt not to be a violation of one's privileges, many other things in the universe seem to rearrange themselves. It becomes possible to take a complete look at the universe, rather than having partial vision from a privileged angle. Lawrence found the method of *The Crown* especially adapted to this complete view, writing to Gordon Campbell (20 December 1914):

> I think there is the dual way of looking at things: our way, which is to say '*I* am all. All things are but radiations out from me.' – The other way is to try to conceive the Whole, to build up a Whole by means of symbolism, because symbolism avoids the I and puts aside the egotist; and, in the Whole, to take our decent place. This was how man built the Cathedral.

Now, these are novelists' preoccupations. The programme of Flaubertian Realism prescribes turning life into a spectacle, at enormous cost both to the thing seen and to the seer. The speculations of Lawrence and Forster seem designed to extricate the novelist from this dilemma, to heal the breach between art and life. The enemy, according to Lawrence, is egoism. (He was, I would say, a genuinely unegoistic man, though an excessively wilful one.) Egoism prevents acceptance of physical death and the attaining of a 'crown'. Egoism is a perverse effort to hold life in a state of arrest – one which turns out, given the nature of existence, to be an effort to dissolve and undo life and reduce it to its elements.

> From top to bottom, in the whole nation, we are engaged, fundamentally engaged in the process of reduction and dissolution. Our reward is sensational gratification in the flesh, or sensational gratification within the mind, the utter gratification we experience when we can pull apart the whole into its factors. This is the reward in scientific and introspective knowledge, this is the reward in the pleasure of cheap sensuality.
> In each case, the experience remains as it were absolute. It is

the statement of what is, or what was. And a statement of what *is*, is the absolute footstep in the progress backward towards the starting place, it is the *undoing* of a complete unit into the factors which previously went to making its oneness.[13]

The link between 'a statement of what *is*' and Realism in literature is obvious and direct, and of course it becomes explicit in his literary criticism.

I want to argue that Lawrence is very acute on epistemological questions, i.e. as to what you can know of the universe, and how you can know it. I find the same philosophical expertise in 'Him With his Tail in his Mouth'. This essay is in a somewhat different tone from *The Crown*, more breezy, pi-jawing and manifesto-like, but it strikes me as being equally brilliant. Under a guise of fooling, the essay offers a very rigorous critique of 'cyclical' cosmologies. 'Him' in the title is in the accusative, implying a missing antecedent, for the same reason, no doubt, that in Joyce's *Finnegan's Wake* the first sentence of the book is the continuation of the last. The technique at work is similar to that applied to the Lion and the Unicorn: Lawrence is subtly teasing out the meanings bound up in a common symbol – here the serpent swallowing its own tail – the purpose being, this time, to discredit the symbol. We could not look for a better proof that Lawrence is not the slave of the esoteric systems from which he borrows, nor is credulous towards their ridiculous pentagrams and gyres. He is indulgent towards them, as his essay makes clear, only because they bring out into the open an error which lies more concealed in 'respectable' philosophies and religions, like Christianity and Buddhism. The error, according to him, runs thus. To measure the whale or the 'Mundane Egg', you must pretend you are outside it; and from that vantage point, all that will seem interesting to you are beginnings and ends, origins and goals, the primitive or the utopian. These are topics apt to awe the unlettered, and all the more so if the ends and the beginnings can be made to join up; but in fact it is all not much more than a game, a game known as 'putting his tail in his mouth'. 'Bunk of beginnings and ends, and heads and tails', writes Lawrence, with fine zest and scorn. 'Why does man always want to know so damned much? Or rather, so damned little? If he can't draw a ring round creation, and fasten the serpent's tail into its mouth with the padlock of one final clinching idea, then creation can go to hell, so far as man is concerned.'[14] Lawrence's theme here, it seems to me, is original and profound, and he handles it with splendid comedy and cleverness.

Jehovah creates man in his Own Image, according to His Own Will. If man behaves according to the ready-made Will of God, formulated in a bunch of somewhat unsavoury commandments, then lucky man will be received into the bosom of Jehovah.

Man isn't very keen. And that is Sin, original and perpetual.

Then Plato discovers how lovely the intellectual idea is: in fact, the only perfection is ideal.

But the old dragon of creation, who fathered us all, didn't have an idea in his head.

Plato was prepared. He popped the Logos into the mouth of the dragon, and the serpent of eternity was rounded off. The old dragon, ugly and venomous, wore yet the precious jewel of the Platonic idea in his head. Unable to find the dragon wholesale, modern philosophy sets up a retail shop. You can't lay salt on the old scoundrel's tail, because, of course, he's got it in his mouth, according to postulate. He doesn't seem to be sprawling in his old lair, across the heavens. In fact, he appears to have vamoosed.[15]

None of this, in Lawrence's part, is in fact a denial of 'eternal recurrence'. His conception is set forth in the last section of *The Crown*, entitled 'To Be and to Be Different'. It runs somewhat thus: we cannot know God, we can know only the revelation of God in the physical universe. And 'the revelation of God is God', but 'it vanishes as the rainbow'; it cannot be held on to even by memory, which is a mere 'persistence'. Thus, for Lawrence, there is recurrence, but precisely shorn of the repetitiousness and regularity dear to theosophy. 'God is gone, until next time. But next time will come. And then again we shall *see* God, and once more, it will be different. It is always different.'[16] It is the same conception of recurrence as he evokes earlier in *The Crown* when he says (very finely) of the Earth going round the Sun, that 'it goes round as the blood goes round my body, absolutely mysteriously, with the rapidity and hesitation of life'.[17]

In support of my thesis that Lawrence had something to give to philosophy, I would point finally to his concept of the ideal or 'absolute'. He denies absolutes, only to assert them after all. 'The eternities are temporal and relative. But their relation is constant, absolute without mitigation.'[18] According to him, we may have *all* the great experiences and visions, on condition that we do not try to cling on to them. There are implications here for art. Lawrence allows to art a relative permanence.

> On the slow wave of matter and spirit, on marble or bronze or colour or air, and on the consciousness, we imprint a perfect revelation, and this is art . . . Because the revelation is imprinted on stone or granite, on the slow, last-receding wave, therefore it remains with us for a long, long time, like the sculptures of Egypt. But it is all the time slowly passing away, unhindered, in its own time.
>
> It passes away, but is not in any sense lost.[19]

His language is not at its most lucid here, but it will be seen how, again, he is circumventing all ideas of conflict between art and life. His is a concept very unlike the 'eternising' or *aere perennius* of the Roman or Elizabethan poets; and also we cannot help contrasting Lawrence with James Joyce, a man possessed with so furious a desire to create – artificer-like – hard and 'imperishable' shapes. We are perhaps moving out of philosophy here, for we shall not get far by asking ourselves which attitude is 'right', but a couple of quotations from Lawrence's letters will at least help to complete his train of argument, a very coherent and philosophically plausible one.

The first is to Bertrand Russell (24 February 1915): 'the ultimate passion of every man is to be within himself the whole of mankind'; and the second is to Gordon Campbell (3[?] March 1915): 'It is not that I care about *other people*: I know that *I* am the English nation – that *I* am the European race . . . L'Etat c'est moi. It is a great saying, and should be true of every man.' Granting this assertion, which after all is a very reasonable one, then we can also grant to Lawrence that each man is capable of *all* the great experiences and visions. And we reflect that by this large and simple gesture he is arriving directly and easily (perhaps too easily) at the truth which Flaubert attained only with much heroism and pain, namely that 'Mme Bovary, c'est moi'.

NOTES

1. F. Kermode, *Lawrence* (Fontana, 1971) p. 91.
2. D. H. Lawrence, *The Crown*, in *Phoenix II*, ed. Warren Roberts and Harry T. Moore (London, 1968) p. 415.
3. Ibid.
4. Ibid., p. 366.
5. Ibid., p. 394.
6. Ibid., p. 383.
7. Letter to Gordon Campbell, 20 December 1914.
8. Emile Delavenay, *D. H. Lawrence and Edward Carpenter* (1963) and Emile Delavenay, *D. H. Lawrence: the Man and his Work* (1972).
9. E. M. Forster, *A Passage to India*, ch. 14.
10. Lawrence, *The Crown*, pp. 409–10.
11. Ibid., p. 371.
12. D. H. Lawrence, 'Him with his Tail in his Mouth', in *Phoenix II*, ed. Roberts and Moore, p. 431.
13. Lawrence, *The Crown*, p. 393.
14. Lawrence, 'Him with his Tail in his Mouth', p. 428.
15. Ibid., p. 427.
16. Lawrence, *The Crown*, p. 414.
17. Ibid., p. 397.
18. Ibid., p. 410.
19. Ibid., p. 412.

10

Lawrence and Forster: their Vision of a 'Living Religion'

G. K. DAS

It is curious that one should get a sense of living religion from the Red Indians, having failed to get it from Hindu or Sicilian Catholics or Cingalese.

(Lawrence, 'New Mexico')[1]

Religion is a living force to the Hindus . . .

(Forster, *A Passage to India*)[2]

Among the celebrated writers of this markedly secular age of ours, D. H. Lawrence will be remembered best for his criticism of secularism and for his originality, power and complexity as a religious writer. It was a characteristic mark of that complexity that he should have written to E. M. Forster in 1916 telling him not to go to India, for 'All religion is bad',[3] and that yet he should have come under a profoundly religious spell, when some six years later he travelled to New Mexico and the 'vast and pure religion'[4] of the Red Indians came to him as a 'revelation'. Like Forster, Lawrence had 'got over' the Christian dogma in his early youth,[5] and in the year of publication of *A Passage to India*, he wrote: 'If I had lived in the year 400, pray God, I should have been a true and passionate Christian. The adventurer. But now I live in 1924, and the Christian venture is done. The adventure is gone out of Christianity. We must start a new venture towards God'.[6] He was soon to publish *The Plumed Serpent*, a novel which presents his controversial religious theme and is remarkably similar in this respect to Forster's book. In studying the religious visions of the two authors which throw light on their significance to each other, we note that while for Forster his religious achievement was embodied rather uniquely in his Indian novel – 'the religious atmosphere of Dewas', he says, 'certainly helped to establish the spiritual sequence I was seeking'[7] – with Lawrence the religious passion found expression in almost every major work, and reached a point of culmination in the Mexican experience, which was chiefly embodied in *The Plumed Serpent*.

In their religious aspects, the two novels, which won compliments from each author to the other, make rewarding study in relation to one another.[8] Forster considered *The Plumed Serpent* to be Lawrence's 'finest novel',[9] and Lawrence too thought it was 'nearer my heart than any other work of mine'.[10] Undoubtedly, the main strength of the novel, despite its obvious artistic weaknesses,[11] lies in its spirit of mystery and wonder, which both Lawrence and Forster regarded as the essence of life and of a living religion. 'The general effect has been superb', says Forster; 'we have assisted at a great mystical ceremony, and all the Mexican landscape has come alive'.[12] And as Lawrence speaks through Don Ramón – 'The earth is alive and the sky is alive, and between them we live'[13] – the book prompts us to wake to the living mystery of our existence and to what Kate Leslie calls 'the greater mystery beyond'.[14]

In *A Passage to India*, similarly, the elements of mystery and wonder play a key role. The British depicted in the novel, with the significant exception of Mrs Moore, have a generally mundane, matter-of-fact consciousness – 'I do so hate mysteries', says Adela, to which Fielding adds: 'We English do'[15] – but their Indian experience awakens in them the impulse to make room for the mystery and wonder of the unseen. As Fielding tells Adela at a later stage in the novel: 'It is difficult as we get on in life, to resist the supernatural. I've felt it coming on me myself';[16] and subsequently it is he, 'a black, frank atheist', who tells Dr Aziz: 'There is something in religion that may not be true, but has not yet been sung . . . Something that the Hindus have perhaps found'.[17] The quest of mystery and wonder is, of course, at its most intense in the story of Mrs Moore. Her deepest desire is 'to be one with the universe',[18] and we notice that India brings her a fulfilment of that desire.

Mrs Moore, whom the club had stupefied, woke up outside. She watched the moon, whose radiance stained with primrose the purple of the surrounding sky. In England the moon had seemed dead and alien; here she was caught in the shawl of night together with earth and all the other stars. A sudden sense of unity, of kinship with the heavenly bodies, passed into the old woman.[19]

In its deepest layers Mrs Moore's experience in India is religious, in the profoundly Lawrentian sense, as is Kate Leslie's experience in Mexico. 'The root meaning of religion', writes Lawrence in 'New Mexico', is the 'direct contact with the elemental life of the cosmos',[20] which both Mrs Moore and Kate achieve. Like Mrs Moore, who realises that God 'had been constantly in her thoughts since she entered India',[21] Kate finds her 'instinct to believe' aroused in Mexico: 'We must take up the old, broken impulse that will connect us with the mystery of the cosmos again',[22] she says to herself, living by the lake Sayula, and like Mrs Moore, she feels the mysterious life of the cosmos around her, in the brilliant sun, the bluish dark earth, and the shadowy water of the lake under the stars in the 'night, timeless, hourless night'.[23] We also note that Kate's roused religious consciousness is marked by feelings of tenderness and reverence for life, even the life of a scorpion, as she thinks one night of scorpions on the floor of her room; the small detail is significantly reminiscent of Mrs Moore's tenderness for the wasp inside her room in *A Passage to India*. The symbolic presence of the scorpion in the religious evolution of Kate, like the equally meaningful presence of the wasp in the story of Mrs Moore, underlines the element of religious wonder that Lawrence saw in all forms of consciousness, including what he calls 'insect consciousness':

Plant consciousness, insect consciousness, fish consciousness, all are related by one permanent element, which we may call the religious element inherent in all life, even in a flea: the sense of wonder. That is our sixth sense. And it is the *natural* religious sense.[24]

The distinctiveness of the religious consciousness that is at the centre of both *A Passage to India* and *The Plumed Serpent* is that it is non-Christian and universal. Institutional Christianity, as well as a consciousness that is conditioned by its doctrines, is repudiated in both the novels. The church, the clergy, their beliefs and their preachings are all shown in them as meaningless. 'Poor little talkative Christianity' is pushed to the 'edge' of Mrs Moore's mind, and she realises that 'all its divine words from "Let there be light" to "It is finished" only amounted to "boum" '.[25] This is similar to Kate's experience as she goes through a liberation of her consciousness outside the boundaries of Christianity. At forty, 'she no longer wanted love, excitement, or something to fill her life',[26] but her eyes widen in amazement and she is overwhelmed to hear the young Mirabal talk of a new religious awakening to come in place of Christianity, which is dead:

> Think of *Jehovah*! *Jehovah*! Think of *Jesus Christ*! How thin and poor they sound! Or *Jesus Cristo*! They are dead names, all the life withered out of them. Ah, it is time now for Jesus to go back to the place of the death of the gods, and take the long bath of being made young again.[27]

The universal, cosmic aspect of religion as against its humanistic aspect is seen by both Lawrence and Forster as an inexhaustible force. Its living presence and power are conveyed by them through the use of cosmic symbolism in *The Plumed Serpent* and in *A Passage to India*. The most central and potent symbol in both the novels is that of the sun. 'It is so easy to understand', says Lawrence, 'that the Aztecs gave hearts of men to the sun. For the sun is not merely hot or scorching . . . It is of a brilliant and unchallengeable purity and haughty serenity which would make one sacrifice the heart to it. Ah, yes, in New Mexico the heart is sacrificed to the sun and the human being is left stark, heartless, but undauntedly religious.'[28] We observe that Kate's experience in *The Plumed Serpent* is a fictional portrayal of such a religious belief. Kate wanted to turn her back on the mechanical 'cog-wheel world', and while in Mexico she willingly submits herself to the pervasive mystery and life-giving power of the sun: 'To shut doors of iron against the mechanical world. But to let the sunwise world steal across to her, and add its motion to her, the motion of the stress of life, with the big sun and the stars like a tree holding its leaves.'[29]

Kate's religious progress culminates in her marriage to Cipriano, which symbolically represents her willing submission to the sun, for Cipriano is 'of the Red Huitzilopochtli and the power from behind the sun'.[30] In marrying him Kate undergoes a transformation of her individual self into the eternal life of the god of the sun.

She trembled, and her limbs seemed to fuse like metal melting down. She fused into a sudden unconsciousness, her will, her very self gone, leaving her lying in molten life, like a lake of still fire, unconscious of everything save the eternality of the fire, which has no death. Only the fire can leave *us*, and we can die.

And, Cipriano, the master of fire. The Living Huitzilopochtli, he called himself. The living firemaster. The god in the flame; the salamander.

One cannot have one's own way, and the way of the gods. It has to be one or the other.[31]

The sun symbolism in *A Passage to India* is equally full of religious overtones. In the beginning of the novel, the sun is presented as the supreme source of life and power. Describing the great sky over the city of Chandrapore – 'The sky settles everything – not only climates and seasons but when the earth shall be beautiful . . . when the sky chooses, glory can rain into the Chandrapore bazaars or a benediction pass from horizon to horizon. The sky can do this because it is so strong and so enormous' – the author goes on to add, significantly, that 'Strength comes from the *sun* [my emphasis], infused in it daily, size from the prostrate earth'.[32] As we proceed to the centre of the novel, we observe that symbolically the catastrophe associated with the Marabar caves happens as the sun with all its power is ignored by humanity, who fail to comprehend its mystery and retreat from its presence.

> All over the city and over much of India the same retreat on the part of humanity was beginning, into cellars, up hills, under trees. April, herald of horrors, is at hand. The sun was returning to his kingdom with power but without beauty – that was the sinister feature. If only there had been beauty! His cruelty would have been tolerable then. Through excess of light, he failed to triumph, he also; in his yellow-white overflow not only matter, but brightness itself lay drowned. He was not the unattainable friend, either of men or birds or other suns, he was not the eternal promise, the never-withdrawn suggestion that haunts our consciousness; he was merely a creature, like the rest, so debarred from glory.[33]

The failure of the British in India, in general, to see the larger, universal dimensions of life is a failure on the religious plane, and it is represented symbolically in their inability to face the Indian sun. We note that at the moment of Mrs Moore's departure from the country, as her steamer rounds Colaba and 'the cliff of the Ghats melted into the haze of the tropic sea', Lady Mellanby, the Lieutenant-Governor's wife, who is also sailing for England, advises her not to stand in the heat of the sun: 'We are safely out of the frying-pan', she says, 'it will never do to fall into the fire'.[34]

Mrs Moore dies during the voyage, presumably of heat.[35] Her death thus could be interpreted as a sacrifice to the sun, and in the Lawrentian context the symbolism, like that of Kate's self-submission to the sun through her marriage to Cipriano, is striking. It is also worth remarking that, like Kate 'dying' in her own self and achieving union with an eternal one, and owning Mexico permanently, Mrs Moore lives in India spiritually even after she is dead. She becomes an immortal legend with the Indians, almost like a Hindu goddess, and it is especially significant that she is spiritually present at the Hindu ceremony, in the last section of the novel: in Godbole's loving remembrance of her during his dance before Krishna, as well as through the visit of her children Ralph and Stella, who attend the celebrations like her spiritual heirs.

Against a background of religion in its cosmic aspect, as reflected in the human longing for the sun, there is a concentration of interest both in A Passage to India and in The Plumed Serpent upon questions concerning a personalised manifestation of the eternal mystery or godhead. Krishna and Quetzalcoatl are equally important. 'Do you know anything about this Krishna business?'[36] asks Fielding of Dr Aziz; 'Does one need gods?' asks Kate, and Don Ramón says: 'Why, yes. One needs manifestations, it seems to me.'[37] In Hinduism as well as in the old religion of the Aztecs the idea of manifestations or incarnations of the godhead is important as they alone give shape and form to a vision of the infinite and the inconceivable. Forster rightly interprets the various manifestations of Hindu gods as 'steps towards the eternal':[38] they are divine as well as human, have attributes purporting good as well as evil, and represent infinite mystery in body and spirit. At Krishna's birth ceremony in A Passage to India, the assembly of people can directly feel the presence of the Lord of the Universe: 'seeing him in this or that organ of the body or manifestation of the sky'.[39] Like Krishna, Quetzalcoatl, the god of The Plumed Serpent, is also a supreme manifestation of the eternal god-stuff:

'the god-stuff roars eternally, like the sea', says Kate for Lawrence; 'Even the gods must be born again.'[40] The manifestation of Quetzalcoatl is the triumphant theme of the novel (as is Krishna's manifestation in *A Passage to India*), for he is a more complete embodiment according to Lawrence: the god of the earth and the sky, the body and the soul – 'lord of two ways' ('Thou wert lord of the one way', Quetzalcoatl says to Christ).[41]

Lawrence's demolition of Christianity is accomplished with the simultaneous debunking of the supremacy of the 'soulless' white man in *The Plumed Serpent*. As Kate repeatedly says to herself: 'The white men had had a soul, and lost it'; 'The white men brought no salvation to Mexico. On the contrary, they find themselves at last shut in the tomb along with their dead god and the conquered race'; 'Perhaps the white man has finally betrayed his own leadership',[42] etc. The betrayal, according to Lawrence, was essentially on the plane of religion. When he read *A Passage to India* – he was then working on *The Plumed Serpent* – he discovered that Forster's book confirmed his own views relating to the failure of the white man and his religion. Admiring the novel, he wrote to Middleton Murry in a letter which is otherwise rather critical of Forster: 'But the *Passage to India* interested me very much. At least the repudiation of our white bunk is genuine, sincere, and pretty thorough, it seems to me. Negative, yes. But King Charles *must* have his head off. Homage to the headsman.'[43]

NOTES

1. *Phoenix: the Posthumous Papers of D. H. Lawrence*, ed. Edward D. McDonald (London: Heinemann, 1961) p. 144.
2. Chapter 36, p. 294; the pagination is that of the Abinger edition of E. M. Forster, *A Passage to India*, ed. Oliver Stallybrass (London: Edward Arnold, 1978).
3. I am thankful to the Provost and Scholars of King's College, Cambridge, for permission to consult the Forster–Lawrence correspondence. The letter referred to was written by Lawrence on 30 May 1916, when Forster was working as a Red Cross volunteer in Alexandria, feeling Egypt to be 'unmysterious and godless', and had received an invitation from the Maharaja of Dewas to come to India as his Private Secretary (see P. N. Furbank, *E. M. Forster: a life*, ii (London: Secker & Warburg, 1978) pp. 22–9).
4. See 'New Mexico', in *Phoenix*, ed. McDonald, p. 147.
5. 'By the time I was sixteen', says Lawrence, 'I had criticised and got over the Christian dogma'. See 'Hymns in a Man's Life', in *Phoenix II*, ed.

Warren Roberts and Harry T. Moore (London: Heinemann, 1968) p. 599.

6. 'Books', in *Phoenix*, ed. McDonald, p. 734.

7. 'Three Countries', in *The Hill of Devi and Other Indian Writings*, ed. Elizabeth Heine (London: Edward Arnold, Abinger edn, 1983) p. 298.

8. A meaningful inter-connection between *A Passage to India* and *The Plumed Serpent* is suggested by Carl Baron in his essay 'Forster on Lawrence', in *E. M. Forster: a Human Exploration*, ed. G. K. Das and J. Beer (London: Macmillan Press, 1979); there is also a detailed critical account of Lawrence's appreciation of Forster by John Beer in his essay '"The Last Englishman": Lawrence's Appreciation of Forster', in the same book.

9. 'E. M. Forster on Lawrence's Art and Ideas', *The Listener*, 30 April 1980, pp. 753–4; reprinted in *D. H. Lawrence: the Critical Heritage*, ed. R. P. Draper (London: Routledge, 1970).

10. See letter to G. R. G. Conway, 10 June 1925, in *The Collected Letters of D. H. Lawrence*, ed. Harry T. Moore (London: William Heinemann, 1962) ii, pp. 843–4.

11. In their criticism of *The Plumed Serpent*, F. R. Leavis (*D. H. Lawrence: Novelist*, London: Chatto and Windus, 1955) and Eliseo Vivas (*D. H. Lawrence: the Failure and the Triumph of Art*, Evanston, Ill.: Northwestern University Press, 1960) consider the novel as one of Lawrence's failures. It is described by Kingsley Widmer in his essay 'Desire and Negation . . .' in the present volume as 'Lawrence's worst novel'.

12. *The Listener*, 30 April 1930.

13. D. H. Lawrence, *The Plumed Serpent*, ch. 10, 'The First Rain', p. 196; the pagination is that of the William Heinemann edition (London, 1962).

14. Ibid., ch. 17, 'Fourth Hymn and the Bishop', p. 247.

15. Forster, *A Passage to India*, ch. 7, p. 62.

16. Ibid., ch. 26, p. 229.

17. Ibid., ch. 31, p. 265.

18. Ibid., ch. 23, p. 198.

19. Ibid., ch. 3, p. 24.

20. *Phoenix*, ed. McDonald, p. 147.

21. Forster, *A Passage to India*, ch. 5, p. 45.

22. Lawrence, *The Plumed Serpent*, ch. 8, 'Night in the House', pp. 133–4.

23. Ibid., ch. 7, 'The Plaza', p. 128.

24. 'Hymns in a Man's Life', in *Phoenix II*, ed. Roberts and Moore, pp. 598–9.

25. Forster, *A Passage to India*, ch. 14, p. 141.

26. Lawrence, *The Plumed Serpent*, ch. 3, 'Fortieth Birthday', p. 54.

27. Ibid., p. 57.

28. *Phoenix*, ed. McDonald, p. 143.

29. Lawrence, *The Plumed Serpent*, ch. 6, 'The Move Down the Lake', p. 100.

30. Ibid., ch. 22, The Living Huitzilopochtli', p. 364.

31. Ibid., ch. 20, 'Marriage by Quetzalcoatl', p. 317.

32. Forster, *A Passage to India*, ch. 1, pp. 3–4.

33. Ibid., ch. 10, p. 106.

34. Ibid., ch. 23, p. 200.
35. See ibid., ch 26, pp. 234–5.
36. Ibid., ch. 37, p. 309.
37. Lawrence, *The Plumed Serpent*, ch. 19, 'The 'Attack on Jamiltepec', p. 288.
38. See E. M. Forster, 'The Gods of India', *The New Weekly*, 30 May 1914, p. 338.
39. Forster, *A Passage to India*, ch. 36, p. 304.
40. Lawrence, *The Plumed Serpent*, ch. 3, pp. 53–4.
41. Ibid., ch. 15, 'The Written Hymns of Quetzalcoatl', p. 225.
42. Ibid., ch. 4, 'To Stay or not to Stay', p. 73; ch. 8, 'Night in the House', p. 132; ch. 9, 'Casa De Las Cuentas', p. 144.
43. *Collected Letters*, ed. Moore, II, p. 811.

11

D. H. Lawrence and the Fantasias of Consciousness

JOHN B. VICKERY

It is unlikely that D. H. Lawrence's reputation as a major author will ever come to depend on anything other than his achievement as a writer of prose fiction. Yet that reputation cannot but be enhanced by the recognition of his significant and often original accomplishments in other genres as well. Elsewhere, I have suggested that the cardinal virtue of his poetry is its delicate mediation between, say, *The Waste Land* and *Paterson*, and its sanely balanced sense of the realities of matter and the potentialities of myth. Here, however, I wish to examine a facet of Lawrence's work which has received little sustained consideration, and to suggest a way of approaching it which may draw it more firmly and centrally into the corpus. I refer to his principal writings on psychology and religion, namely *Psychoanalysis and the Unconscious*, *Fantasia of the Unconscious* and *Apocalypse*. Though they obviously have significant and subtle connections with his fiction and poetry, as well as with material in such volumes as *Assorted Articles*, *Phoenix I* and *Phoenix II*, they will, by themselves, more than suffice for the space at my command.

A valuable study, but one which I shall not carry out, would be a rigorous, scholarly examination of the provenance and validity of the ideas Lawrence advances in these three works together with an assessment of the relationships, asserted and actual, between them and the views of those he draws on, such as Frazer, Jane Harrison, Burnet and Carter, or questions, such as Freud, Jung, Einstein and Archdeacon Charles. What I have in mind, however, is something perhaps less dissolvent of those texts because rooted in the great central fact about Lawrence. He is pre-eminently and constantly a creative writer, that is, a writer for whom the imagination is the primary structuring power of whatever it is that he sees, feels and thinks. To embark on a scholarly examination of such a writer will certainly help to cleanse our perceptions as to the demonstrable legitimacy and efficacy of his ideas as arguable propositions about, say, education, psychology, physiology and anatomy, and religion or religious history. But it is unlikely to enable us to comprehend how the ideas and works articulate a poetic cosmology which emerges from at the same time as it informs the more obviously imaginative works. In short, I am suggesting that Lawrence's *Fantasia* and similar volumes are generically related to Yeats' *A Vision*, Graves' *The White Goddess* and Auden's *The Enchafèd Flood* as they are not to his own *Movements of European History*, Graves' *Good-bye to All That*, or MacLeish's *A Time to Speak*. The former fall into a recognisable but unnamed category, class or family which, with Lawrence's own deprecating irony, we might call ' "pollyanalytics" '. Or better, taking our cue from Northrop Frye, it might be labelled the canonical code by which we would be suggesting that though not 'the great code', it is nevertheless the individual artist's functional displacement of that code (the Bible) which Frye sees as central to English literature. For Lawrence, the connection between the canonical code and Frye's great code is most explicit in *Apocalypse*, though it exists at least implicitly in the other two works as well. And if one wonders why modern creative artists should appear more prone than were earlier writers to develop an explicit statement of their code, part of the answer would lie in the decline of the great code's impact and authorial familiarity with it together with the writer's resultant effort to define or clarify for himself exactly what the components, structure and animating principles of his imaginative universe are.

Lawrence's sense of the ontological relation and of his own historical situation is neatly captured when he remarks in the Foreword to the *Fantasia*:

it seems to me that even art is utterly dependent on philosophy: or if you prefer it, on a metaphysic. The metaphysic or philosophy may not be anywhere very accurately stated and may be quite unconscious, in the artist, yet it is a metaphysic that governs men at the time, and is by all men more or less comprehended, and lived. Men live and see according to some gradually developing and gradually withering vision. This vision exists also as a dynamic idea or metaphysics – exists first as such. Then it is unfolded into life and art. Our vision, our belief, our metaphysic is wearing woefully thin, and the art is wearing absolutely threadbare.[1]

Thus, his starting point is a deep conviction of historical and cultural crisis, a conviction which in large measure occasions the three principal features of his work on psychology and religion. I refer to the recurring note of apocalyptic urgency surging through the texts; the didactic, often hectoring, tone which periodically surfaces with more than a touch of stridency; and the election of what, following Lawrence himself, we might call fantasia or free form.

The logic underlying these three quasi-formal features is of the following order. Firstly, the conviction of imminent disaster and bankruptcy in which 'we have no future; neither for our hopes nor our aims nor our art. It has all gone grey and opaque.'[2] Actually, Lawrence oscillates (a response I shall return to as integral to his cosmology) between the inevitability of man's demise and the consequent nullity of effort of any kind, and the convulsive conviction that self-destruction may yet be avoided if only the right course can be found. And because he does so oscillate, Lawrence instructs us as to our methodological course of action:

> We've got to rip the old veil of a vision across, and find what the heart really believes in, after all: and what the heart really wants, for the next future. And we've got to put it down in terms of belief and of knowledge. And then go forward again, to the fulfilment in life and art.[3]

The actual volumes themselves are, at least in part, instructional manuals on the realities of self and society, man and cosmos, which detail the terms of the present, existent individual's realignment with those realities. Lawrence, like Nietzsche, sees his instructional role as nothing less than the transvaluation of values and the radical restructuring of the human consciousness in despite of the weight of mores, habit and received knowledge. Hence his tone often becomes hectoring and strident, sometimes deliberately as a pedagogical strategy but more often out of a frustration borne of his audience's obdurate or blithe refusal to recognise the urgency he senses.

Yet it is important to see that these texts are not merely indices of Lawrence's irascibility quotient. Taken as a group, they are also instances of the fantasia form in which the governing principle is the free play of the author's mind over his subject. And the reason Lawrence opts for such a form in these works is a function of the logic of his cultural situation: imminent disaster and the need to do or discover something coupled with profound intellectual and ideological uncertainty as to what that 'something' may be. Hence the mind is encouraged to play with usually ignored, or dimly if at all comprehended, or purely fanciful and speculative notions, in the hopes that something vital, meaningful and sustaining will turn up. Such an approach avoids, for Lawrence, a mindless Micawberish confidence in a benign or providential fate by the brooding presence of catastrophe compounded of apocalypse and 'gotterdammerung' which hovers over the historical moment and the human mind. And it does so not only because of these factors but because the fantasia form is itself the creative artist turning back on and drawing from his own creative process. Lawrence, in short, does what any artist does when confronted with a challenge to his own role and identity. He plays with the elements or contents of his consciousness (here taken to encompass the unconscious whether Freudian or Lawrentian) in order to generate a vision that is both an action and a text.

The result of this play appears in both content and form, matter and mode. The central materials on which Lawrence's mind plays throughout the works mentioned are the human being, the family, and their creations within the categories of space and time which prove to be the cosmos and history repectively. In 'New Directions from Old', Northrop Frye sketched some of the chief differences between traditional and Romantic cosmologies. When one looks at the constituent elements and patterns in Lawrence's cosmology, one is struck by the unique manner in which he draws from or parallels aspects of antecedent structures of both imagery and action. Thus, he regards the sun and moon positively as sources of force or energy but does not see them as part of an upper, divine or paradisal world; indeed, his vision of the meeting-point of such a world and the ordinary physical one is distinctly ironic, as we shall see in his account of Pisgah and its denizens. At the same time, he shares the Romantic view that 'the only place left for any *locus amoenus* is the buried original form of society'[4] now existing in the subjective unconscious – the lumbar ganglion and the solar plexus – which provides the first 'polarized duality, psychical and physical, of the human being' and 'is always the original fount and home of the first and supreme knowledge that *I am I*'.[5]

What is perhaps most distinctive about Lawrence's cosmology is the primacy he gives to the individual human being over the external world, and the steadfastness with which he refuses to frame a myth of origins, or to frame such a myth in anything other than the terms of a comic fairy tale.[6] For him the universe is dependent on the individual, not the other way around: 'Out of living creatures the material cosmos was made. . . . Where you got the living creature from, that first one, don't ask me. He was just there.'[7] Such a dismissal of originary matters is either the logical consequence of or reason for his indifference to causal as distinct from synchronic explanations.[8] Underlying all his elaborations of conceptual synchronicity is his first cosmological principle, namely, that of polarities, which range from the internal anatomical and psychological structure of the individual to the external astronomical relations of sun and moon.

Viewed as causal, empirical, predictive explanations, Lawrence's account of sympathetic and voluntary, positive and negative, plexuses and ganglia, sun and moon, fire and water, light and dark polarities in man and cosmos may engender amusement or anger, depending on the degree of seriousness with which they are entertained. But seen as synchronic linkages, as a sustained series of connections enabling everything to fit together coherently so that *post facto* explanations (the only kind the poet is really interested in) are both possible and internally plausible, this intricate network of polarities assumes an imaginative power directly commensurate with its factual unlikelihood. Indeed, Lawrence's invoking of the 'authority' of Anaximander in *Apocalypse* as embodying 'the first "scientific" duality which the pagans found in the universe'[9] testifies both to his awareness of the persistence of the tradition of polarities and to his embattled sense of the precise nature of that authority to which he appeals, the authority, as Frye reminds us, which derives from the fact that 'cosmology is a literary form, not a religious or scientific one'.[10]

A second distinguishing characteristic of Lawrence's cosmology, one which enables him to avoid the static dualism of classical ontology, is his total reliance on the principle of dynamism or psychic and cosmic energy. For him, such a principle functions reciprocally, moving beings, bodies, minds and entities into union and identity or into separation and differentiation, the two ultimate modes of which would appear to be sex and death. Crucial also to the operation of this principle is his detachedly balanced relativity of attitude toward the energy's directional flow. Lawrence is at pains to emphasise that in the fundamental or perfectly functioning integrated circuitry of being which he charts, the balance of action and reaction must be exquisitely and organically, not quantitatively and mechanically, adjusted. This emphasis informs not only his comments on human and cosmic relations but also his attitudes and expressions concerning these and other subjects. Such, surely, is the basis for the authorial voice which can declare at one point that 'I would rather listen now to a negro witch-doctor than to Science'[11] and at another jocularly insist that 'I'm writing a good sound science book, which there's no gainsaying'.[12] For Lawrence, these texts themselves are poles of energy in constant vital flux. Rather than dialectically poised linguistic or ontological entities, they are complex *dispositions* of mind, psyche and soul which taken together make up, Lawrence seems to say,[13] the individual or whole self.

As a result, one sees that the third and final key principle animating Lawrence's cosmology is that of linguistic oscillation or attitudinal contradiction both of oneself and of others. If the former is clearly exemplified in the subject of science, then the latter, it may be argued, is equally sharply rendered with regard to religion and, less markedly, psychoanalysis. In jibing, in the opening of *Psychoanalysis and the Unconscious*, at 'the *ex cathedra* Jung' and 'Freud on the brink of . . .a *Menschanschauung*', Lawrence sardonically argues that 'it is time the white garb of the therapeutic cant was stripped off the psychoanalyst'.[14] Yet the opening of *Fantasia of the Unconscious* begins with 'a little apology to Psychoanalysis' which quickly modulates into full-blown expository judiciousness: 'We are thankful that Freud pulled us somewhat to earth, out of all our clouds of superfineness. What Freud says is always partly true. And half a loaf is better than no bread.'[15] And in *Apocalypse*, the same ambivalence and oscillation is shown over Archdeacon Robert Charles, who virtually simultaneously is hailed as 'a true scholar and authority in Apocalypse, a far-reaching student of his subject' and a hopelessly orthodox critic warped by 'his terrific prejudice' against allowing any pagan thought, image or belief to intrude on the Bible or Christian thought.[16]

The strongest instance of Lawrence's embracing of the principle of contradiction occurs in the battle that he wages throughout the whole of *Apocalypse* to accept or reject the Book of Revelation. This struggle sets the young child Lawrence against the mature reader of 'comparative religion and the history of religion'.[17] More importantly for the cosmology, it sets Lawrence the savage satirist of the jeremiad against Lawrence the celebratory visionary. The former decries the stultifying vulgarity and arbitrary meaning that the thoughtful modern reader finds in the Bible; the latter is drawn with exploratory wonder and fascination to the pagan core that still exists in it, though all but obliterated by the deliberate corruption of textual alteration, rewriting and misunderstanding, and which is one of the earliest and oldest forms of that myth of the cosmos which Lawrence himself is struggling to articulate.

Yet Lawrence ultimately works a final reversal or contradiction on his furious struggle to disentangle the vital from the sterile and dead in Revelation. In the final analysis, he finds such an act of engagement to be of the same order as the earlier Christian transformations of the pagan myth, that is, a perversion of the nature of textual being. Thus, he acknowledges and accepts the ultimate contradiction of self against other and others, of the dynamic polarity existing between his cosmological myth and that actually present in the Book of Revelation as it stands:

> The Apocalypse shows us what we are resisting, unnaturally. We are unnaturally resisting our connection with the cosmos, with the world, with mankind, with the nation, with the family.
> . . .
> But the Apocalypse shows, by its very resistance, the things that the human heart secretly yearns after.[18]

In short, Lawrence dramatises in the full finality of imaginative open-endedness his cosmological principles of dynamic polarity surging and receding in the oscillatory rhythms of full consciousness when he satirically turns his back on the false vision of Revelation after having laboured to reveal and resuscitate the immemorial power of its symbols – horse, dragon, woman, sun – which his own vision claims as the ultimate link to the original cosmology.

So far as the play of form, which is our other main interest here, is concerned, it too focuses on three major facets, though complicated by their appearance under four related but distinct rubrics. These, perhaps, can best be rendered initially in the following tabular diagram:

Rhetorical mode	Genre	Type	Purpose or Function
celebratory	rhapsode	myth	vision
declaratory	essay	manual	instruction
hortatory	satire or invective	jeremiad	abusive direct address

In each instance, there is (in terms of the diagram) an upward progression in the teleology of Lawrence's attitude and imagination. That is, his initial thrust is to exhort his audience to attend to a pressing cultural and individual threat by addressing them directly and by excoriating their actions and attitudes as not only wrong and harmful but absurd and ridiculous. This yields to or rather is incorporated into a declaratory mode which sets forth informally and incompletely an expository 'how to' manual of child-rearing, education and human relations. Yet because Lawrence places the individual at the centre of his cosmology and because he is a creative writer – that is, one for whom statement, argument and invective figure less significantly than do image, metaphor and symbol – he is impelled on to a vision of organic harmony which transcends the existing abstractions governing mankind while immanent in the realities of human existence. Such a vision, for Lawrence, is a cosmological myth of creation and rebirth which proceeds by a radical metaphorising of fact and concept and a purging of primordial symbols' historical and cultural accretions.

Though all three facets operate in each of the works, individually they do possess distinctive major chords, as it were. *Psychoanalysis and the Unconscious* disintegrates or deconstructs the psychoanalytic unconscious as a misleading and destructive alternative to the world crisis, brought on by idealism whose twin masks are science and Christianity. As a result, it stresses the expository vein of argument and analysis. In *Fantasia of the Unconscious*, Lawrence, despite a declarative surface, brings image and metaphor into the core of his writing in order to construct a cosmology of what he calls child-consciousness and the individual self which represents the reality of existence from a structural if not historical perspective.

And finally, *Apocalypse* merges jeremiad and vision in a sustained act of symbol interpretation (rather than symbol-making) designed to disengage the vital from the dead (the pagan from the Judaeo–Christian) in the historical forms taken in the upper consciousness by the old myth.[19]

A thorough exploration of Lawrence's handling of the fantasia form obviously would demand a detailed rhetorical and stylistic analysis of the three works in question. The best that can be offered here, however, is a series of illustrative suggestions as to how one might go about such an examination. As a satirist, Lawrence here has two chief goals: to dispel rival existing cosmologies or conceptual patterns, and to disconcert his reader into active response rather than the customary passive receptivity. The first he does by, among other things, travestying prominent ideological trends of his time and thereby producing a brief burlesque of modern intellectual history:

> They say that way lies the New Jerusalem of universal love: and over there the happy valley of indulgent Pragmatism: and there, quite near, is the chirpy land of the Vitalists: and in those dark groves the home of successful Analysis, surnamed Psycho: and over those blue hills the Supermen are prancing about, though you can't see them. And there is Besantheim, and there is Eddyhowe, and there, on that queer little tableland, is Wilsonia, and just around the corner is Rabindranathopolis.[20]

But in keeping with the free play of the fantasia, Lawrence immediately undercuts the possible response that this is mere burlesque by introducing a narrator who, in an ironic reversal of the Swiftian projector, from his presumed vantage point 'on top of Pisgah', nevertheless declares: 'But Lord, I can't see anything. Help me, heaven, to a telescope, for I see blank nothing' because, we are meant to infer, there is nothing to see.[21]

In his Foreword, Lawrence has already registered his indifference to his readers and his acceptance of their right to their indifference to him. But once into the books, he turns to direct address on a number of occasions as a means of asserting both the centrality of the individual to his cosmology and the irreducible gap between writer and reader or individuals in general. Thus he declares flatly:

There is no straight path between you and me, dear reader, so
don't blame me if my words fly like dust into your eyes and grit
between your teeth, instead of like music into your ears. . . .
Don't get alarmed if *I* say things. It isn't your sacred mouth
which is opening and shutting. As for the profanation of your
sacred ears, just apply a little theory of relativity, and realise
that what I say is not what you hear, but something uttered in
the midst of my isolation, and arriving strangely changed and
travel-worn down the long curve of your own individual
circumambient atmosphere. . . .

So I hope now I have put you in your place, dear reader. Sit
you like Watts' Hope on your own little blue globe, and I'll sit
on mine, and we won't bump into one another if we can help
it. You can twang your old hopeful lyre. It may be music to
you, so I don't blame you. It is a terrible wowing in my ears.
. . .

Now I am going to launch words into space, so mind your
cosmic eye.[22]

The nervy dissonance of this sort of language is clearly designed
to galvanise the reader not only into a state of alert attention and
active involvement but also into a process of individual
thoughtfulness rather than the customary thinking based on habit
and learned conceptual responses. At first sight, it appears to be
the antithesis of the rhetoric of persuasion, but on closer inspection
it does carry its own kind of persuasiveness. Its emancipation
declaration on behalf of the reader's response and its jocular
readiness to admit its own individuality and relativity engenders
in the reader a disposition to regard the writer as an honest,
candid exponent of personal beliefs, a kind of Kent of cosmology,
as it were.

In effect, this recurring use of direct address and reader
involvement establishes what might be called a truncated dialogic
form in which Lawrence challenges the reader to assume his own
individualistic stance. On occasion, as if to emphasise this play of
what in a different context has been called the dialogue
imagination, Lawrence even vents his exasperation with his own
ideas while projecting himself into the sensibilities of his readers,
as when he declares:

Oh, damn the miserable baby with its complicated ping-pong

table of an unconscious. I'm sure, dear reader, you'd rather have to listen to the brat howling in its crib than to me expounding its plexuses. As for 'mixing those babies up', I'd mix him up like a shot if I'd anything to mix him with. Unfortunately, he's my own anatomical specimen of a pickled rabbit, so there's nothing to be done with the bits.

But he gets on my nerves.[23]

By this tactic of directing his invective or 'splenetics' at himself also, Lawrence effectively reminds us that he is using a literary mode, not merely venting personal abuse. At the same time, he dramatises what elsewhere he declares expositorily, namely, that individuals should reject not only repression but also suppression of their deepest and most authentic feelings in order to 'fight their way out of their self-consciousness'.[24] In short, those qualities of direct address, jeremiad and invective pervading the works are formal exemplifications of Lawrence's cosmological principles of dynamic energy, oscillatory consciousness and logical and verbal contradiction.

In a number of places, these qualities permeate the exposition as well, but in its purest form the declaratory mode is squarely in the vein of the informational manual and the educational essay. For lucid exposition of a personal or individual point of view, the following could scarcely be bettered, regardless of what one may think of the ideas themselves:

Consciousness develops on successive planes. On each plane there is the dual polarity, positive and negative, of the sympathetic and voluntary nerve centres. The first plane is established between the poles of the sympathetic solar plexus and the voluntary lumbar ganglion. This is the active plane of the subjective unconscious, from which the whole of consciousness arises.[25]

Several things about this sort of writing in Lawrence's cosmology stand out. Firstly, it makes such a distinct contrast with both the incitive language I have already looked at and the mythic, visionary, rhapsodic level I shall consider shortly. The juxtaposing, counterpointing and free intermingling of these radically dissimilar levels of language function not only as disintegrative of habitual reader expectations concerning modal and generic uniformity and typological simplicity, but also as profoundly integrative of linguistic functions and purposes. For Lawrence, invective or direct verbal assault by itself would become little more than profanity and a profanation of language since neither vision nor instruction would be attained. Similarly, instruction whether in textbook or essay form left unalloyed must, for him, inevitably disintegrate into a mechanical, and therefore sterile, manual of task-mastery devoid of ultimate purpose because lacking a cosmological context. The result would be a perverted exercise in authorial will as a Gradgrind schoolmaster figure bullyingly compels assent from a literal non-entity in an existential vacuum. And finally, vision, myth and the rhapsodic left wholly to their own devices would etherealise into the abstract, ungrounded mysticism which Lawrence hated. This is a form of what he calls 'idealism', meaning 'the motivising of the great affective sources by means of ideas mentally derived', to which he attributes in its final stages the mechanical formulation of the incest motive by the human reason.[26] By refusing to compartmentalise and restrict these language modes and uses, Lawrence heeds his own injunction concerning the integration of the several planes and poles of human consciousness: 'To stress any one mode, any one interchange, is to hinder all, and to cause corruption in the end.'[27]

Another distinctive and significant trait of Lawrence's expository mode is that there should be so much of it in works marked by nervous volatility over the contemporary scene, and rapt imaginative communing with an almost originary past. This suggests that whatever else may be true about Lawrence's cosmological works, they are extended communicative statements of transferable attitude, belief and action. Though he inveighs mightily against 'the Moses of Science and the Aaron of Idealism', that is largely because of their opting for the single modality outlook.[28] His conviction that 'the true goal of education' is 'the full and harmonious development of the four primary modes of consciousness' makes it imperative that the language of propositional assertion as well as those of expletive and symbol be utilised.[29]

Thus, Lawrence seriously envisages the possibility of a 'scientific, comprehensive psychology' which will follow from his view of consciousness as a matter of 'dynamic poles, . . . dynamic-vital flow' and 'resultant physical-organic development and activity'.[30] In setting forth the rationale and the procedure for such a psychology, he makes clear by both statement and style that analytic examination of its subject matter in a step-by-step manner is perfectly congruent with his own unprofessional, exploratory beginnings by which, as he says, 'we merely wish intelligibly to open a way'.[31] The equable, measured tone and the simple nobility of the announced goal signal that Lawrence casts his cosmology in the fantasia form not so much to ignore or reject factual realisation as to fully realise free imaginative aspiration:

> Education can never become a serious science until the human psyche is properly understood. And the human psyche cannot begin to be understood until we enter the dark continent of the unconscious. Having begun to explore the unconscious, we find we must go from centre to centre, chakra to chakra, to use an old esoteric word. We must patiently determine the psychic manifestation at each centre, and moreover, as we go, we must discover the psychic results of the interaction, the polarised interaction between the dynamic centres both within and without the individual.
>
> Here is a real job for the scientist, a job which eternity will never see finished though even tomorrow may see it well begun. It is a job which will at last free us from the most hateful of all shackles, the shackles of ideas and ideals. It is a great task of the liberators, those who work for ever for the liberation of the free *spontaneous* psyche, the effective soul.[32]

Such a free spontaneous psyche is the quintessence of dynamic polarity, demanding as it does both isolation and togetherness, silence and violent speech, serenity and emotional combat.[33] Yet this bipolar dispositional action ultimately issues in the psyche's gaining a sense of the primordial cosmos through 'the old pagan process of rotary image-movement'.[34] The central feature of this last is that 'the old human consciousness process has to *see something happen*, every time. Everything is concrete, there are no abstractions.'[35] So long as the perception is an individual, isolate complex realised by a single being, it can be rendered with startling vividness through the phenomenology of the verbal image, as much of Lawrence's writing, particularly the travel books, demonstrates. But when the image is powerful enough to affect more than the surface of consciousness, as sun, dragon and woman do for him, then several things occur.

Firstly, the person experiencing the image or event becomes aware that his encounter is not so much unique as extremely durable, as persisting throughout time rather than occurring once in space. Hence, he is drawn to envisaging others encountering the same situation and to contemplating his own sense of their awareness of the strangeness and awesomeness of the natural world of the cosmos. It is the momentousness of this vision, standing apart from, though not at odds with, argument and exposition, which Lawrence registers almost in his own despite in, among other places, Chapter 4 of *Fantasia*. Suddenly, he is pulled away from his ostensible subject of child-consciousness by the distracting trees of the Black Forest where he is composing the book itself whose action is a function of this very distraction. The tree intrudes on his consciousness so powerfully and with such a wealth of detail that he comes to see it as a distinct, animate being, both like and unlike man:

> This marvellous vast individual without a face, without lips or eyes or heart. This towering creature that never had a face. . . . he thrusts himself tremendously down to the middle earth, where dead men sink in darkness, in the damp, dense undersoil; and he turns himself about in high air; whereas we have eyes on one side of our head only, and only grow upwards. . . .
> A huge, plunging, tremendous soul. I would like to be a tree for a while. The great lust of roots. Root-lust. And no mind at all.[36]

From this sense of profound personal intimacy, which transforms the trees from 'huge primeval enemies' to Lawrence's 'only shelter and strength',[37] he then rhapsodically articulates his own legend of their impact on Roman legionnaires, on anonymous and ancient others:

> They met the faceless silence of the Black Forest. This huge, huge wood did not answer when they called. Its silence was too crude and massive. And the soldiers shrank: shrank before the trees that had no faces, and no answer. A vast array of non-human life, darkly self-sufficient, and bristling with indomitable energy. The Hercynian wood, not to be fathomed. The enormous power of these collective trees, stronger in their sombre life even than Rome.[38]

Here Lawrence renders not simply the process of nature but the power of it throughout time. What is created thereby is a narrative of nature rather than a foregrounded image focused on the perceiver and the present. Though, as he makes clear, this account is a digression (a technique or element essential to both the fantasia form and his cosmology), it is apparent that at least in embryo it is also one version or a part of his myth of the origin of myth as well as his myth of nature.

Central to this myth of nature is its personal quality, which, Lawrence claims, distinguishes the modern relation to the cosmos from that of the pagan: 'Landscape and the sky, these are to us the delicious background of our personal life, and no more.'[39] But beyond this myth is the greater one of the cosmos in which man stands in a vital relationship to all the other elements of the universe, particularly the sun and moon, a relationship identical with that obtaining between the polarities of his own individual being. This cosmic myth in Lawrence's version not only celebrates something greater than himself, as did the pagan, but also, like the Christian tradition, makes a central point of the loss of a vital relationship: 'We have lost the cosmos, by coming out of responsive connection with it, and this is our chief tragedy.'[40]

Out of this joint sense of an original 'magnificent reality' and its loss, there emerges an overwhelming imaginative thrust to regain what has been lost.[41] It is this drive that makes Lawrence utilise all three facets of the fantasia form while presenting his mythic vision of man and cosmos. A vision ignored and disbelieved, a myth abandoned and viewed as 'Urdummheit',[42] will necessarily be articulated by the myth-maker not in its pristine form but in a manner giving expression both to argument in order to persuade and to invective in order to overwhelm. Thus, when Lawrence renders the centrality of the moon he does so by an amalgam of all three modes:

And we have lost the moon, the cool, bright, ever-varying moon. It is she who would caress our nerves, smooth them with the silky hand of her glowing, soothe them into serenity again with her cool presence. For the moon is the mistress and mother of our watery bodies, the pale body of our nervous consciousness and our moist flesh. . . . But we have lost her, in our stupidity we ignore her, and angry she stares down on us

and whips us with nervous whips. Oh, beware of the angry
Artemis of the night heavens . . .

Now this may sound nonsense, but that is merely because
we are fools. . . . If we get out of contact and harmony with the
sun and moon, then both turn into great dragons of destruction.
. . .

Now all this is *literally* true, as men knew in the great past,
and as they will know again.[43]

Such a combination of sensuous image, allusion, peremptory
assertion, metaphor and insistent exposition advances not so
much received myth as myth embattled and struggling to reassert
itself and to regain its status as the content of worship. As such, it
is essential that the genuine be differentiated from the spurious,
which is what Lawrence recurrently is at pains to effect even
while advancing his cosmic vision:

What we lack is cosmic life, the sun in us and the moon in us.
We can't get the sun in us by lying naked like pigs on a beach.
The very sun that is bronzing us is inwardly disintegrating us –
as we know later. Process of katabolism. We can only get the
sun by a sort of worship: and the same with the moon. By *going
forth* to worship the sun, worship that is felt in the blood. Tricks
and postures only make matters worse.[44]

It is this same concern with the differentiation of the genuine
which shapes his primary approach in *Apocalypse*. There he seeks
to separate out the compelling pagan core compounded of 'the
myth of the birth of a new sun-god from a great sun-goddess, and
her pursuit by the great red dragon' from the 'many Jewish and
Jewish-Christian overlays'.[45] At the critical point in Revelation
when the seventh seal has been opened, Lawrence's ongoing
effort 'to sense its structure vertically, as well as horizontally', to
feel it as 'a section through time' and 'the work of no one man,
and even of no one century' assumes an added dimension, one
that represents his modulation of the ancient consciousness's
concentration on seeing something happen.[46] Here, differentiation
yields to transformation or substitution. A redaction of ancient
pagan custom is also as close as Lawrence can come to a ritual
celebration of the initiation myth by which contemporary man can
regain his integral harmony with the cosmos and himself:

Here we can see, in spite of the apocalyptist, the pagan initiate, perhaps in a temple of Cybele, suddenly brought forth from the underdark of the temple into the grand blaze of light in front of the pillars. Dazzled, reborn, he wears white robes and carries the palm-branch, and the flutes sound their rapture round him, and dancing women lift their garlands over him.[47]

With this Lawrence moves from the structure of man's consciousness to the structure of the action of coming to full consciousness. From myth to ritual. Yet where his cosmological myth is highly individual and marked by the contemporaneity of the timeless, the ritual is derivative and firmly anchored in a largely forgotten and no longer viable past. Of the authenticity and legitimacy of that myth Lawrence has, as we have seen, no doubt whatsoever. But by placing the ritual in the past, he tacitly admits that communal or societal celebratory acceptance of the myth is unlikely in the present. Yet in so doing, he preserves the imaginative validity of his cosmology by limning in the uncertainties of that enterprise as dogma while underscoring both its potentialities as poetry and the necessarily problematic character of those potentialities.

NOTES

1. D. H. Lawrence, *'Fantasia of the Unconscious' and 'Psychoanalysis and the Unconscious'* (London: William Heinemann, 1961) Phoenix Edition, pp. 9–10.
2. Ibid., p. 10.
3. Ibid.
4. Northrop Frye, 'New Directions from Old', in *Myth and Mythmaking*, ed. Henry A. Murray (New York: Braziller, 1960) p. 130; punctuation has been altered slightly to accommodate syntax, but the sense is intact.
5. Lawrence, *Fantasia*, pp. 32, 30; author's italics.
6. See ibid., pp. 15–16.
7. Ibid., p. 16.
8. Ibid., p. 14.
9. D. H. Lawrence, *Apocalypse* (New York: Viking, 1966) p. 56.
10. Frye, 'New Directions', p. 115.
11. Lawrence, *Fantasia*, p. 148.
12. Ibid., p. 22.
13. Ibid., pp. 130–1.
14. Ibid., pp. 197–8.

15. Ibid., p. 11.
16. Lawrence, *Apocalypse*, p. 69; see also pp. 58, 61–2; cf. the *Dictionary of National Biography* entry.
17. Lawrence, *Apocalypse*, p. 15.
18. Ibid., pp. 198–9.
19. See ibid., p. 126.
20. Lawrence, *Fantasia*, p. 15.
21. Ibid., p. 21.
22. Ibid., pp. 19–20; author's italics; see also pp. 21–2.
23. Ibid., p. 37.
24. Ibid., p. 187.
25. Ibid., p. 232.
26. Ibid., p. 206.
27. Ibid., p. 240.
28. Ibid., p. 15; see also pp. 212–13.
29. Ibid., p. 64.
30. Ibid., p. 233.
31. Ibid., p. 234.
32. Ibid., p. 233; author's italics.
33. See ibid., pp. 134, 188.
34. Lawrence, *Apocalypse*, p. 83.
35. Ibid.; author's italics.
36. Lawrence, *Fantasia*, p. 39.
37. Ibid.
38. Ibid., p. 40.
39. Lawrence, *Apocalypse*, p. 41.
40. Ibid., p. 42.
41. Ibid., p. 41.
42. Ibid., p. 69.
43. Ibid., pp. 43–5.
44. Ibid., p. 47; author's italics.
45. Ibid., p. 134.
46. Ibid., p. 62.
47. Ibid., pp. 108–9.

12

Bay: the Noncombatant as War Poet

KEITH CUSHMAN

Bay, the small book of poems which D. H. Lawrence published in 1919, is one of the least-known of all his works. *Bay* is a product of Lawrence's hard times during the First World War, circumstances that have been ably documented by Paul Delany in *D. H. Lawrence's Nightmare*.[1] Lawrence and Frieda Weekley, having been evicted from Cornwall, were living hand-to-mouth during the last stages of the war, often depending on the generosity of friends. Lawrence was practically *persona non grata* in England. *The Rainbow* was banned, *Women in Love* was unsaleable, and every shilling that could be earned from his writing was a shilling to the good.

   Bay has been almost totally ignored by critics. Sandra Gilbert's *Acts of Attention* and Tom Marshall's *The Psychic Mariner*, full-scale studies of Lawrence's poetry, each devotes but a short paragraph to *Bay*. Gail Porter Mandell's *The Phoenix Paradox* is concerned only with Lawrence's revision and rearrangement of the *Bay* poems for incorporation in the *Collected Poems* of 1928. Indeed, anyone who wants to read *Bay* is apt to have a difficult time, for there are only about 175 copies in existence. All the *Bay* poems can be found in the *Collected Poems* of 1928 and in the several variants of the *Complete Poems*, but they are not identified as *Bay*, they do not appear together or in the same order, and many are in revised versions.

   In this essay I shall attempt to rescue *Bay* for the Lawrence canon. The book is noteworthy in several respects. Lawrence's tribulations in getting the book published are interesting and amusing. *Bay* is his first press book, and it is part of an important series of twentieth-century press books. Most significantly, Lawrence wrote *Bay* during a richly creative period in his career. He described the poems as 'in their own way the rarest things I've done' (*L*, p. 494).[2] The *Bay* poems form a true sequence, and their subject is one of Lawrence's most important: the First World War. Surely these poems merit critical examination. In this essay I shall address each of the following interrelated topics: the writing and publication of *Bay*, *Bay* as a press book, and *Bay* as a book of poetry.

Cyril Beaumont was a bookseller and small publisher who had established the Beaumont Press in 1917 with the idea of publishing, in a fine format, new works by contemporary writers. He had noticed that finely printed books 'were invariably limited to classic authors, and being deeply interested in the literature of our own time, it seemed to me a pity that modern writers should not be afforded an opportunity of having their works published in a choice form during their lifetime' (CB, p. 1).[3] New literature in a fine format was appealing to lovers of literature, collectors, and writers, and Beaumont was to make a success of his idea. The first twenty books of the Beaumont Press include not only *Bay* but also books of poetry by de la Mare, Blunden, Aldington, Herbert Read and W. H. Davies, Conrad's short play *One Day More*, letters from Wilde to Robert Ross, and essays by Arthur Symons. On the whole, the series had a Georgian flavour.

Lawrence was one of the writers whom Beaumont considered for his first volume in 1917, but instead he published some poetry by John Drinkwater. Early in the next year, Lawrence and Lady Cynthia Asquith devised a plan in which Beaumont would publish *Women in Love*, but this plan failed, partly because Beaumont feared legal action. Beaumont believed that parts of the novel 'had merit – but it was worse than *The Rainbow*'.[4]

In March 1918, Lawrence offered Beaumont a book of poems about the war, to be called *All of Us*. Beaumont turned these poems down, and the next year *Poetry* published twelve of them under the title 'War Films'.[5] Meanwhile Lawrence, undaunted, offered Beaumont *Bay*: 'I have now got a little book of 18 poems – à propos of the war – called *Bay*. Let me know if you are still alive and still publishing and still wanting the MS. – and I'll send it along' (L, p. 233). The agreement, signed on 21 May 1918, gave Lawrence only £10 for the rights, but it stipulated that after six months he could sell any of the poems to magazines, where, ultimately, he was able to place about half of them.[6]

In his introductory note to the *Collected Poems*, Lawrence says that the *Bay* poems 'were written mostly in 1917 and 1918, after I left Cornwall perforce'.[7] There is meaning in the word 'mostly', for five of the eighteen poems are reworkings of unpublished poems that date back to his schoolmaster days. But even the revised poems, as we shall see, are carefully integrated into the unified whole that is *Bay*.

Lawrence was a shrewd businessman, but as a deeply creative artist and a son of the working class, he had his doubts about press books and book collectors. 'A book that is a book flowers once, and seeds, and is gone', he wrote. 'First editions or forty-first are only the husks of it.'[8] Any project involving Lawrence and Beaumont, temperamentally so different, was almost doomed to be unstable. It is hard to imagine Lawrence getting on with this 'very fair, flaxen, fresh-complexioned, quite boyish-looking man', devoted to the art of fine books. It is also recorded that when Beaumont first met Lawrence, he was 'full of amazement at him'.[9] The Lawrence–Beaumont episode reads rather like a story by D. H. Lawrence, and an essentially comic story at that.

The Beaumont Press was a very small operation, with Beaumont doing much of the work himself. When the contract was signed in the spring of 1918, Beaumont was busy with other projects and did not even begin work on *Bay* until early in 1919 – that is, until after the Armistice had robbed the book of its topicality. Despite Lawrence's protestations, it took Beaumont eighteen months to publish the eighteen poems; he also made a number of mistakes in the book's format.

Lawrence's letters to and about Beaumont and *Bay* are masterpieces of sarcasm and invective. For example, Beaumont asked the American expatriate Anne Estelle Rice, a close friend of Katherine Mansfield who had been associated with her in the *Rhythm* circle, to do the illustrations, prints from zinc blocks. Beaumont records that Rice decorated the poems 'finely' (CB, p. 35). Lawrence felt these illustrations were 'almost comic', 'absurd and unsuitable' (*L*, pp. 360, 362).

In September 1918, Lawrence was already complaining about the 'poems: that miserable little Beaumont is waiting for some opportunity or other: they *will* come, certainly: and I expect before Christmas'. One year later, Lawrence was hopeful that the book would be ready for Christmas 1919, and 'that miserable little Beaumont' had become 'dear, foetid little Beaumont'. There was nothing Lawrence could do, as the publisher 'slowly filters through the poems', and by now there was no mollifying him. Lawrence said the signed edition was printed 'on Japanese vellum-rubbish', and Beaumont was 'a bewildered chicken' (L, pp. 287, 395, 462, 494).

One must make allowances for Lawrence's mental equilibrium at this time, but he had reason to be exasperated. His letter to Catherine Carswell of 5 February 1920, after he had at last received a copy of *Bay*, rings all too true: 'But he's *non compos*. You should see his letters. He hasn't done a thing I want him. He's left out poems, he left out the inscriptions, he left out everything. To my violent expostulations he writes inane imbecilities – the man is hopeless' (L, p. 469).

In his own defence, Beaumont blamed some of the delay on Lawrence's departure for Italy, though Lawrence did not leave until November 1919, sixteen months after the contract was signed. It is also characteristic of Beaumont's odd obliviousness that he publishes Lawrence's observation that the illustration for 'Last Hours' is printed upside-down, which indeed it is – and then offers no explanation, regret, or even comment on this blunder.

Anne Rice was to design the cover as well as execute the illustrations, and in fact she is credited in the colophon with the cover design. But Beaumont disliked the design she submitted, and decided to do one himself. He discovered though that he was uncertain of what Lawrence was trying to communicate in the book. 'Was it a tribute to the victorious conclusion of the War or was it an expression of defiance?' He realised that he 'ought to have asked Lawrence' (CB, p. 36), but ask he did not. Instead, he decided that *Bay* celebrates the end of the First World War, not a very intelligent decision considering that the book was contracted for six months before the war ended (and at a time when the outcome was in doubt). Beaumont based his cover design on this false assumption. Lawrence acknowledged that the design was 'awfully pretty', but he also asked, with some incredulity, 'isn't it rather like spring?' (L, p. 465).

Worst of all, Beaumont omitted the dedication which had been promised to Lady Cynthia Asquith. She was rather dubious about being honoured with these poems 'with very little rhyme or rhythm about them', though at least they were 'mainly (thank Heaven)! *not* erotic'.[10] Lawrence expresses his frustration over the missing dedication almost plaintively: 'But now, *why* did you forget to inscribe it to Cynthia Asquith? I promised it to her, and I *know* she's looking forward to it. Can't you do anything about it?

Please print it in, if you can. Just put – "To Cynthia Asquith." I reminded you so often' (*L*, p. 465). Beaumont did supply the dedication 'by printing the requisite number of single leaves on the three papers of the edition and pasting them in' (CB, p. 39), but he did it less than perfectly. My own copy of the version on cartridge paper has a dedication page of a lighter-weight stock.

The best joke of all is that five years later, in spite of everything, Beaumont asked Lawrence to write an introduction to the fifteenth volume in his series. For once Lawrence was discreet and said he was 'very busy on some other work' (CB, p. 66).

The Beaumont Press published *Bay* in an edition of 200 copies in three different variants. The first thirty copies are printed on Japanese vellum and signed by the author and artist. There were to be fifty copies printed on cartridge paper, but only about twenty-five of these survive – much to the delight of collectors who own one. Beaumont had placed the printed sheets to dry on shelves fixed to the wall of his workroom. Workmen were doing some sort of repairs on the other side of the wall, and one of them drove a long nail through the wall and through many of the cartridge paper sheets. Beaumont had already distributed the type and could not bring himself to reset it. The third variant consists of 120 copies on hand-made paper.

Bay is essentially a pleasing little book, though it is not without its crudities. Visual awkwardness results from several of the typographical choices, including the decisions to capitalise all the letters in the titles and place the titles flush with the left-hand margin of the poems, and also to include running titles for the poems that are longer than a page. The type is dirty and the printing uneven. Lawrence did like the 'beautiful paper and print' (*L*, p. 469), and he told Beaumont that 'the essential format is . . . quite beautiful' (*L*, p. 465). He was probably just being petulant when he called *Bay* 'a silly-looking little book' (*L*, p. 469).

The illustrations create a special problem. Lawrence complained about the 'silly little wood cuts, so out of keeping with the poems' (*L*, p. 469) and he has a good point. The designs are bold and striking, but they march to a different drummer from the one heard by the poet. There are ten illustrations for the eighteen poems, and there is almost no evidence that Anne Rice noticed that *Bay* is about the First World War. Only the illustration to 'Winter-Lull' has anything to do with battle, and the cypress trees and rather Byzantine-looking church steeple in the background are purely the unlikely inventions of Anne Rice. Where in 'Town' Lawrence depicts wartime London, 'Original, wolf-wrapped/In pelts of wolves, all her luminous/Garments gone' (*Bay*, p. 17),[11] Rice offers an utterly placid Thames scene with civilised, modern-looking buildings on the far bank. Rarely do the illustrations reinforce Lawrence's poems, and often they are at cross-purposes.

'Guards!' – the first poem in *Bay* – presents a powerfully threatening impression of a review of soldiers in Hyde Park in 1913, thus prefiguring the horror to come. Rice's picture depicts not the soldiers but the trees in the distance, which seems to suggest that she did not read beyond the first phrase. Also unnerving is her decision in three of the ten pictures to illustrate not the poem but a metaphor from the poem. This does work rather effectively in 'War-Baby', where Lawrence compares the newborn baby to 'mustard-seed' (*Bay*, p. 39) and Rice depicts the plant rather than the infant. But in the illustration for 'After the Opera', we see no beautiful girls on the opera stairs but a multicoloured, large-plumed bird. The illustration for 'Obsequial Ode', a poem that meditates on the passage from life to death, picks up a sailing image from the second and third stanzas, and somehow makes the ship a Spanish galleon. The artist has either no understanding of or no respect for the integrity of the poems. The illustrations are local in feeling, and they fragment what Lawrence is trying to unify.

I have one final criticism. The illustrations are hand-coloured in the vellum and cartridge paper copies. The colours are strong and bright, demonstrating that Anne Rice learned a good deal from Matisse in his Fauve period. But in a book of such a small format, the rather garishly coloured illustrations tend to overwhelm the text. The comparative restraint of the uncoloured illustrations in the hand-made paper copies is aesthetically more successful.

It must not be forgotten that the Beaumont Press, in its ambition to produce contemporary works of literature 'in a choice form', was implementing an idea that 'had something of novelty' (CB, p. 1). Beaumont was very much a pioneer, which is hard for us to realise at a time when press books in signed, limited editions by almost every writer of repute pour out at a nearly daily rate. (Like limited edition plates and porcelain figurines, these books are now known as 'collectibles'.) Beaumont had taught himself bookmaking almost from scratch, and *Bay* is only the fourth book that the Beaumont Press printed by hand. It is fair to say that in the history of modern fine bookmaking Beaumont is finally more important for what he did than the way that he did it. He remains a publisher of high standards and great dedication. It is also true that Lawrence was especially hard to please during these years.

In *Bay* Lawrence became a war poet. In doing so, he was writing about something in which everyone was deeply interested and had a personal stake. It also allowed him to confront the overriding question of the day, the destruction of European civilisation. Lawrence had another motive, closer to home, for writing about the war. A generation of Englishmen was being tested and laid waste in the agony of the Western Front. As much as Lawrence loathed the war and the reasons behind it, he had complex personal feelings about not participating, especially considering the traditional notion of 'manhood' that was so important to him. At some level it was young Bert Lawrence all over again, playing with the girls because he was too delicate for the rough games with the boys. His private feelings about not fighting help explain the hysteria of his reaction to undergoing the army's physical examinations. These feelings are also part of the shrillness of the 'Nightmare' chapter in *Kangaroo*. In writing the *Bay* poems, he was participating imaginatively in the decisive experience of his generation. As Harry Moore has said, 'Lawrence was vicariously living through things that his health did not permit nor his inclination approve of'.[12] The noncombatant became a war poet without setting foot in France.

Bay is not, however, a model of military verisimilitude. Indeed, there is not a trench in sight in *Bay*, though about half the poems are set on the Western Front. Poems like 'Bombardment' and 'Ruination' even suggest that Lawrence believed that the war in France and Belgium was mainly fought in towns. (Similarly, in 'England, My England' he seems confused about exactly what a machine-gun is.)

One of the obstacles to understanding *Bay* is its enigmatic title. Perhaps the primary association is the bay laurel with which the poet is traditionally crowned and honoured. But any poet who is part of the society that produced the Great War can invoke the laurel wreath only ironically. Instead he finds himself embattled, baying at his enemies who in turn hold him at bay. The poet now counts for nothing; no one pays any attention to him. Yet the poet must remain true to his vision and calling. He must create his poems even if they go unheeded and unregarded. The vocation remains sacred even if there is no one to award him the bay wreath.

The poems of *Bay* are written in Lawrence's early style, making use of traditional rhyme, metre and stanza in a flexible and often awkward manner. The poems are not well known: 'After the Opera' appears in both the Rexroth and Sagar *Selected Poems*, but no other *Bay* poem can be found in either. Though some of the poems surely deserve to be better known, I do not intend to argue that the book is filled with neglected masterpieces. The achievement of *Bay* is in its wholeness and in its imagistic and intellectual integrity; it is much more than the sum of its parts.

The structure of the book is essentially but not perfectly or purely narrative in nature. What is involved is more than the thematic, verbal and imagistic patterning of Yeats' monographs but less than the displaced short novel that is Meredith's *Modern Love*. In 1917 Lawrence published his more famous sequence, *Look! We Have Come Through!* which presents 'an essential story, or history', the poems 'unfolding one from the other in organic development'.[13] The *Bay* sequence is less personal and less grand in conception, but a carefully worked out sequence it is nonetheless.

The central figure is a young man from the provinces who is caught up in the Great War. He seems representative of the millions of men whose lives were altered, and, all too often, ended. The sequence begins with the young man at a review of the Scots Guards in Hyde Park in 1913. Then comes the war: two poems depict his regret and anxiety about leaving the security of home, two more show us London in wartime. The next eight connected poems are the heart of *Bay*. These are the battle pieces proper, beginning with 'Going Back', which shows the soldier returning to his regiment, and culminating climactically with his death in battle and with a poem he speaks from the other side of the boundary of life. The dead soldier is in turn addressed in two poems by the living, who question and mourn.

'Ruination' and 'Rondeau' are a connected pair, the one a poem in which a soldier on the Western Front expresses his fear of death, the other in which a conscientious objector in England speaks of the uselessness of his life. The last three poems provide a formal conclusion. In 'Tommies in the Train', Lawrence supplies a broader perspective on the process of disintegration embodied in the war. Then in the last pair of poems, 'War-Baby' looks to the future, 'Nostalgia' to the past.

Bay is also bound together by the images which Lawrence wove throughout the poems. The images are rich and open-ended, and have an incremental effect. The ghosts and shadows in the last poem in *Bay* are all the more powerful because so many ghosts and shadows have preceded them. Furthermore, these images provide one of the main vehicles for Lawrence's visionary interests – for even as a war poet, Lawrence remains very much a visionary poet. I have space to speak of only a few of these images in any detail. Images of darkness and light (and of black and white) are associated with the shadows. There are also key images clustered around trees, flowers and birds, the sun and the moon. Travelling by train, marching and sleeping also recur, along with much colour imagery.

'Guards!' is the prelude to *Bay*, just as it is the prelude to the Great War. In *Bay*, the review of the Scots Guards in Hyde Park is dated 1913, one year before the war. The date in the *Collected Poems*, 1910, is probably the date of the actual experience. 'Guards!' is one of four *Bay* poems that originated in the 'little college notebook' Lawrence kept while a student at University College, Nottingham, the notebook he called 'the foundation of the poetic me'.[14]

'Guards!' is divided into two sections, 'The Crowd Watches' and the clumsily-titled 'Evolutions of Soldiers'. In 'The Crowd Watches', 'a still line of soldiers, red motionless range of guards/Smouldering with darkened busbies beneath the bayonets' slant rain', is at rest. A general gives the command, and in 'Evolutions of Soldiers' the soldiers begin their irresistible forward motion, 'emerging as blood emerges from inward shades of our night/Encroaching towards a crisis, a meeting, a spasm and throb of delight'. The five- or six-beat, mostly unrhyming, lines of 'The Crowd Watches' yield to swinging, Swinburnesque rhymed seven-beat lines in 'Evolutions of Soldiers', as Lawrence attempts to capture the frightening relentlessness of the marching Guards. The 'wave of soldiers' is regimented, but its irresistible forward flow is organic and threatening. The language is primarily that of sexual crisis, and afterwards comes the 'ebb-tide' when the soldiers have passed by, 'the red-swift waves of the sweet/Fire horizontal declining and ebbing' (*Bay*, pp. 9–11). This suggestion of detumescence carries with it a feeling of the deep satisfaction that comes from killing, a satisfaction which these Guards will shortly be able to enjoy. The control of diction and metre is too awkward for 'Guards!' to be fully convincing, though the poem does strive for unusual effects.

In 'The Little Town at Evening' we see the poet back at home listening to 'The chime of the bells' of the church clock and 'the babel of children still playing in the hay'. The 'houses fall asleep', and the 'church moves, anxious to keep/Their sleeping, cover them soft unseen' (*Bay*, p. 12). The little town is secure, but the poet is not: 'I wish the church had covered me up with the rest/In the home-place. Why is it she should exclude/Me so distinctly from sleeping the sleep I'd love best?' (*Bay*, p. 13). The poet feels excluded because his thoughts are already on the war and the army he will be part of.

'The Little Town at Evening' was originally a schoolmaster poem also found in the early notebook. In the original conception, the poet feels incipient exile only because he has accepted a teaching job in Croydon and must leave the town in the provinces that he loves so much. It was easy enough to adapt the poem to the circumstances of the war.

The same is true of 'Last Hours', another schoolmaster poem based on a draft in the college notebook. We find the poet lying under an oak whose shade

> Falls on me as I lie in deep grass
> Which rushes upward, blade beyond blade,
> While higher the darting grass-flowers pass
> Piercing the blue with their crocket spires.   (*Bay*, p. 14)

This 'green, brave town/Vegetable, new in renown' – a town whose inspiration is clearly *Leaves of Grass* – is dukedom large enough for the poet. 'How lovely it is to be at home/Like an insect in the grass/Letting life pass', he reflects. The first three stanzas – eight or six lines long – go on in this vein, but the title, 'Last Hours', has already put the experience into melancholy perspective. The poet is desperate to lose himself in his 'green, brave town' (*Bay*, pp. 14–15) for a reason that the final stanza, just four lines long, makes evident:

> Down the valley roars a townward train.
> I hear it through the grass
> Dragging the links of my shortening chain
> Southwards, alas!   (*Bay*, p. 15)

The alterations of stanza and metre for dramatic effect is reminiscent of Hardy's 'The Voice'. Originally, 'Last Hours' was a poem about being evicted from the Eden of one's childhood to take up adult responsibilities in the suburbs of London. In *Bay*, that eviction has become much ruder, for it is the army that beckons.

The sequence then moves from the happy valley of 'The Little Town at Evening' to 'Town', a depiction of London in wartime, and what a long journey it is from one town to the other. Modern London 'Used to wear her lights splendidly,/Flinging her shawl-fringe over the River', but now 'There are no gleams on the River' and 'No lamp-fringed frock'. The metropolis has reverted to 'London, with hair/Like a forest darkness, like a marsh/Of rushes, ere the Romans/Broke in her lair'. In the atmosphere of wartime, the ancient, primitive town has re-emerged. This discovery does not seem dreadful to the poet who was last seen lying in the grass and dreading the townward train. He proclaims that 'It is well/That London . . ./Has broken her spell' (*Bay*, pp. 16–17). *Bay* is never simply anti-war in its attitudes.

London is depicted as a woman in 'Town', thus connecting the poem with the vision of beautiful women on the opera stairs in 'After the Opera'. These women in their finery do not seem to realise that London is once again like a woman 'with hair/Like a forest darkness' (*Bay*, p. 17). 'After the Opera' is another revamped early poem, though it cannot be found in the early college notebook. We know that Lawrence tried to arrange the first volume of the *Collected Poems* in the order in which he wrote the poems.[15] Fourteen of the *Bay* poems are grouped together there, though in a different sequence from that of *Bay*. The poems he separated out and moved to the early pages of Volume I are 'The Little Town at Evening', 'Last Hours', 'Guards!' and 'After the Opera'.

Indeed, the theme of 'After the Opera' identifies it as the work of the young Lawrence, just come down form Eastwood. The poem is built on the distinction between the girls 'with their large eyes wide with tragedy' on the opera stairs and the barman with 'reddened, aching eyes' and 'thin arms'. The barman makes the poet 'glad to go back to where I came from', back to his own working-class, provincial people. 'After the Opera' is another adaptation of earlier material to fit the context of *Bay*. The meaning of the poem seems changed, for the 'tragedy' which the beautiful young girls 'take . . . so becomingly' (*Bay*, pp. 18–19) was originally intended as the operatic tragedy which they have just witnessed. In *Bay*, this tragedy seems to have become the tragedy of a generation of doomed Englishmen, which the girls manage to put aside.

Paul Fussell has commented on the 'ridiculous proximity of the trenches to home'.[16] The world of gentlemen's clubs, opera, ballet and music-hall continued in full-swing just across the English Channel from the trenches. This incongruity, a commonplace of English literature of the Great War, is the central point of 'After the Opera', and this is also one of the best poems in *Bay*. Lawrence captures the post-opera atmosphere and skilfully evokes the 'Ladies/Stepping like birds with their bright and pointed feet' who 'Peer anxiously forth, as if for a boat to carry them out of the wreckage' (*Bay*, p. 18). What clinches the poem, however, is the poet's injection of his own presence, first standing and smiling detachedly at the girls and then drinking at a pub, looking at the barman, glad to be back among his own kind (and away from women).

We have not seen the poet at the Front, but in the next poem he is 'Going Back' to his regiment there. In 'Last Hours' he had dreaded the 'townward train' (*Bay*, p. 15). Now he is on another train, 'outward bound' as 'The night turns slowly round', going in the direction of the 'Voices of men/Sound of artillery, aeroplanes, presences' his 'spirit hears'. 'Going Back' is the first of the battle poems in *Bay*, and it introduces the central theme of the struggle between life and death. Like 'Tommies in the Train', a later train poem in the sequence, 'Going Back' is visionary, for as the poet-soldier returns to the Front, he is also returning in time to the still point of the turning world where 'There, at the pivot/Time sleeps again'. At this point of timelessness there is no past or future, 'only the perfected/Silence of men'. This concluding couplet is ominous, for the silence of men is perfected only in death. The pun contained in the 'dead-sure silence' and 'dead certainty' (*Bay*, pp. 20–1) is self-explanatory. The poem effectively blends its present moment with the soldier's solemn vision of timelessness.

Immediately afterwards, the soldier is 'On the March' in a poem with rhyming quatrains and a non-stop marching rhythm that is built on iambic tetrameter and the trick of ending each quatrain with a kind of refrain on the pattern of 'onward the long road goes'. The marching itself threatens the identity, which seems swallowed up by the relentless beat. This loss of self is expressed above all by the metre and rhythm. 'Pale shadows' flee from them, 'Pale, sleepy phantoms are tossed about': all too soon the soldiers may become shadows and phantoms themselves. They march, knowing full well that the end of the road may be 'oblivion'. Lawrence uses one of the main images of annihilation from *Women in Love* when the speaker imagines himself and his comrades 'gone/Down the endless slope where the last road goes' (*Bay*, pp. 22–3).

The next poem brings us to the third town of *Bay*, and this one is under 'Bombardment'. The poet is far from the peace and security of his little town in England, and the 'insouciant flowers' (*Bay*, p. 15) that he lay among are cruelly remembered in the image of the bombarded town as a 'sinister flower', a 'flat red lily with a million petals', that has 'opened to the sun' (*Bay*, p. 24). The descent of the mortar shell is also registered in mock-pastoral terms: 'A dark bird falls from the sun./It curves in a rush to the heart of the vast/Flower: the day has begun' (*Bay*, p. 24). Just another day on the Western Front. This excellent, brightly imagistic twelve-line poem is written in three-line stanzas, and the first and third lines of each stanza rhyme on 'sun'. The entire vignette is depicted in terms of sexual congress between the sun and the town. In the world gone mad, the life-giving sun has become a destroyer. (The mortar shell as 'dark bird' can also be found in 'England, My England'.)

The noise of 'Bombardment' yields to the sinister silence of 'Winter-Lull': 'Uninterrupted silence swings/Invisibly, inaudibly/To and fro in our misgivings' (*Bay*, p. 25). This silence calls to mind the 'perfected silence' (*Bay*, p. 21) of dead men in 'Going Back', and, as in 'On the March', the experience obliterates the soldiers' identities: 'We are folded together, men and the snowy ground/Into nullity'. There is no peace, for they know how the silence will be broken. They wait, 'disastrously silence-bound!' (*Bay*, pp. 25–6). 'Winter-Lull' achieves some persuasive atmospheric effects, but it pales in comparison with Wilfred Owen's 'Exposure', which depicts the same situation. Owen had the advantage of horrible first-hand experience, and he uses more original and compelling poetic means to convey that experience.

The silence of 'Winter-Lull' is broken all too inevitably in the tenth and climactic poem of *Bay*, 'The Attack'. As happens so often in the sequence, the experience, this time of battle, is rendered in visionary terms. When the soldiers come out of the woods, 'The night uprisen stood/In white' (*Bay*, p. 27). The whiteness of the night is insisted on, over and over. Lawrence seems to be describing the moment of the soldier's death when the speaker says, rather clumsily: 'A pale stroke smote/The pulse through the whole bland being/Which was This and me' (*Bay*, p. 27). Notice, though, how a oneness has been achieved between the outer world of experience and the inner world of the self, between 'This and me'. At his death, 'In ecstatic reverie' (*Bay*, pp. 27–8), with the black trees blossoming, the soldier is granted ultimate vision:

> I saw the transfiguration
> And the present Host.
> Transubstantiation
> Of the Luminous Ghost.   (*Bay*, p. 28)

In this moment of heightened religious revelation, the soldier is able to see a Ghost – but he has been living with 'sleepy phantoms' (*Bay*, p. 22) all along, and on the Western Front, men were transformed into ghosts at a record rate. Lawrence seems to undercut the religious vision even as he presents it.

'The Attack' is reminiscent of Lawrence's war story 'England, My England', in which the protagonist Egbert is killed in battle at the end. Lawrence was fascinated by the individual life-and-death struggles in France and Belgium, and indeed the central poems of *Bay* explore not simply death in battle but rather the relationship between life and death and the nature of the mysterious boundary between.

'The Attack' is followed by three poems that establish a dialogue across the dividing line between life and death. The speakers in 'Obsequial Ode' and 'Bread upon the Waters' address the dead soldier: 'But what of us who are living/And fearful yet of believing/In your pitiless legions' (*Bay*, p. 31). The female speaker in 'Bread upon the Waters' mourns her loss. Between these two poems is 'Shades', the only interesting piece of the three, in which the dead soldier explains what dying and death are like. The speaker describes a visionary situation in which there is no real separation between living and dead. Instead both are part of a single oneness. The wholeness achieved at the moment of death continues:

> And so I seem
> To have you still the same
> In one world with me.
>
> In the flicker of a flower,
> In a worm that is blind, yet strives,
> In a mouse that pauses to listen
>
> Glimmers our
> Shadow; yet it deprives
> Them none of their glisten.   (*Bay*, p. 32)

The main image of this oneness is the shadow, a condition partaking of both dark and light, death and life, 'As if it were part and parcel, One shadow' (*Bay*, p. 32). The church stood in shadow in 'The Little Town at Evening', the poet lay in the 'oak's unchequered shade' (*Bay*, p. 14) in 'Last Hours', the soldiers encountered 'pale shadows' (*Bay*, p. 22) while on the march. Now in 'Shades' the image has at last found its true meaning. The unifying shadow imagery calls to mind *Twilight in Italy*, where Lawrence makes crucial use of images of darkness, light and shadow in his search for transcendence.

The next two poems of *Bay* are more loosely integrated into the sequence, for after following one soldier from his home town into battle and then to death and beyond, we are back at the Front with another soldier who awaits his 'Ruination'. This is a short poem made up of two quatrains. At sunrise with the sun 'bleeding . . . its fires upon the mist', a soldier observes the steady advance of 'tall angels/Of darkness'. This is a poem about living in perpetual fear of imminent death. 'Ruination' is paired with the 'Rondeau' of a conscientious objector, engaged in land work back in England, that follows. The metaphorical 'drear grey sea' (*Bay*, p. 34) of 'Ruination' is echoed by the 'dull grey heap' (*Bay*, p. 35) of sand that the conscientious objector is piling up, and the 'misty waste-lands' (*Bay*, p. 34) of the Front are matched by the 'waste lands' (*Bay*, p. 35) that the conscientious objector plods through. An image of 'street-ends' like 'cliffs abutting in shadow' (*Bay*, p. 34) in 'Ruination' is answered in 'Rondeau' by 'a star' that 'commands/Shadows to cover our stricken manhood' (*Bay*, p. 36).

'Rondeau' is an ironic title, for the conscientious objector is weary of his work and the 'dull hours' of his daily routine. Even worse is the shame he feels because of his 'stricken manhood' (*Bay*, pp. 35–6). Lawrence tries for a rondeau-like effect by using only two end-rhymes (on 'sands' and 'west') in the five quatrains of the poem. The reiteration of those two sounds also reinforces the feeling of imprisonment. The main significance of the poem, however, is in the way it plays off 'Ruination' and the earlier experience of death and transfiguration in battle. There are worse fates than 'Ruination'. (Interestingly, 'Rondeau' is also drawn from an early poem in the college notebook; obviously it was readily adaptable.)

The visionary 'Tommies in the Train' is one of the best poems in *Bay*. It is also a summarising poem: Lawrence draws back to provide perspective on England's experience of the Great War. As the soldier rides in the train with his comrades, the sun is shining happily, and the 'steeple/In purple elms', the daffodils, the 'luminous hills/Beyond' are beautiful – beautiful because there are 'no people' visible. The image of flowers along the railway banks that 'Shine like flat coin which Jove in thanks/Straws each side the lines' (*Bay*, p. 37) carries the suggestion that materialism may be one of the root causes of the war.

The soldier-protagonist wonders 'What are we/Clay-coloured, who roll in fatigue/As the train falls league by league/From our destiny?' (*Bay*, p. 37). As so often happens in *Bay*, the soldier experiences an obliteration of self, this time caused by the motion of the train. The train seems to be falling through space, and as it falls, taking the soldiers from their destiny: the war has deflected them – and England – from the lives they should have lived. They are all headed for catastrophe. The soldier covers his face with his hand and peeps between his fingers 'To watch the world that lingers/Behind, yet keeps pace' as the train 'falls like a meteorite'. The final image is one of massive disintegration as 'we fall apart/Endlessly, in one motion depart/From each other' (*Bay*, pp. 37–8).

Lawrence ends *Bay* with 'War-Baby' and 'Nostalgia', one a vision of the future that has been cursed, the other a vision of the past that has been lost forever. 'War-Baby' is a short poem that Lawrence wrote with the birth of John Carswell, the son of his friends Catherine and Donald Carswell, in mind. Even in the midst of death there is life: 'Look, it has taken root!/See how it flourisheth./See how it rises with magical, rosy sap! (*Bay*, p. 39). The child is 'like mustard-seed' (*Bay*, p. 39), and Jesus preached that 'If ye have faith as a grain of mustard seed, ye shall say unto this mountain, Remove hence to yonder place; and it shall remove' (Matthew xvii.20). But 'our faith' also started from a 'little, hasty seed' (*Bay*, p. 39), and that faith has led only to the slaughter in France and the deadly mustard gas that killed and injured countless thousands. The child's birth is blighted. The sharply sardonic little poem ends with a mockingly bitter song: 'Sing, it is all we need./Sing, for the little weed/Will flourish its branches in heaven when we slumber beneath' (*Bay*, p. 40).

Nor at the end of *Bay* is there any returning home. A soldier attempts to go home in 'Nostalgia', but the 'shadowy house below/Is out of bounds' since his father died; it now belongs to 'strangers'. The soldier is left in the darkness, 'and only the old ghosts know/I have come' (*Bay*, p. 42). The returned soldier yearns for the past, kisses the stones, kisses the moss on the wall. But the final note offers not solace but apocalypse: 'I wish I could take it all in a last embrace./I wish with my breast I here could annihilate it all' (*Bay*, p. 43). The past is lost, and even worse, the war experience has invalidated it, along with the faith that was its foundation. The final message of 'Nostalgia' – and of *Bay* – is sombre indeed. After such knowledge, what forgiveness?

In *The First Score*, Cyril Beaumont quotes a review of *Bay* which opines that 'this volume with its vigorous and charming decorations by Anne Estelle Rice and its chintz-like cover is altogether charming' (CB, p. 39). Lawrence must have cringed or laughed if he saw this review, for if the decorations and chintz-like cover are charming, there is nothing at all charming about the poems. Lawrence judged accurately when he said that some of these poems are 'really beautiful and rare' (*L*, p. 469). His opinion of *Bay* must have fallen subsequently, since he broke up the book in the *Collected Poems*. I hope this essay has taken the first step in restoring *Bay* to the collected works of D. H. Lawrence. *Bay* is not merely something like a lost work, it is also a work of genuine achievement.

NOTES

1. Paul Delany, *D. H. Lawrence's Nightmare: the Writer and his Circle in the Years of the Great War* (New York, 1978).
2. This abbreviation (*L*) cites *The Letters of D. H. Lawrence*, vol. III, ed. James T. Boulton and Andrew Robertson (Cambridge, 1984).
3. This abbreviation (CB) cites Cyril Beaumont's *The First Score* (London, 1927), his account of the first twenty books published by the Beaumont Press. Much of my information about the making of *Bay* is taken from this book.
4. Lady Cynthia Asquith, *Diaries 1915–1918*, ed. E. M. Horsley (New York, 1969) p. 419.
5. Keith Sagar, *D. H. Lawrence: a Calendar of his Works* (Austin, 1979) p. 76.
6. Delany, *Nightmare*, p. 354.
7. Introductory note to *The Collected Poems of D. H. Lawrence*, I (London, 1928) p. 6.
8. D. H. Lawrence, 'This Bad Side of Books', Foreword to Edward D. McDonald, *A Bibliography of the Writings of D. H. Lawrence* (Philadelphia, 1925) p. 14.
9. Asquith, *Diaries*, p. 419.
10. Ibid.
11. This citation refers to number 49 of the Beaumont Press edition of *Bay* (London, 1919).
12. Harry T. Moore, *D. H. Lawrence: His Life and Works* (New York, 1964) p. 162.
13. D. H. Lawrence, *Look! We Have Come Through!* (London, 1917) p. 5.
14. D. H. Lawrence, Foreword to the *Collected Poems*, in *The Complete Poems of D. H. Lawrence*, ed. Vivian de Sola Pinto and F. Warren Roberts (New York, 1971) p. 849.
15. Introductory note to the *Collected Poems*, I, p. 5.
16. Paul Fussell, *The Great War and Modern Memory* (New York, 1975) p. 64.

13

'Strange, torn edges': Reading the *Collected Poems* of D. H. Lawrence

HOLLY A. LAIRD

The common reader of D. H. Lawrence approaches his poetry through the *Collected Poems* (1928), which comprises approximately half of the *Complete Poems* (1971), edited by Vivian de Sola Pinto and F. Warren Roberts, and which will continue to form the basis for his collected poetry in the forthcoming Cambridge edition, compiled by F. Warren Roberts and Carole Ferrier. After publishing the collection, Lawrence designed two further volumes, *Pansies* and *Nettles*, which he considered books of 'doggerel', while his late poems on death were edited posthumously by Richard Aldington. Of Lawrence's nine individual books of poems (including the six incorporated into *Collected Poems: Love Poems and Others, Amores, New Poems, Bay, Look! We Have Come Through!* and *Birds, Beasts and Flowers*), only three are now in print.[1] The *Collected Poems* represents Lawrence's final and most complete testament to the order of his poetic works – his harmonium. Unlike the poetry of Stevens or of Yeats, this opus coheres not into a melodic or unified image, but into a deliberately cracked organ.

In his 'Note' to the *Collected Poems*, Lawrence advises us that he has placed his poems in 'chronological order' to form an 'emotional and inner biography' because, he explains,

It seems to me that no poetry, not even the best, should be judged as if it existed in the absolute, in the vacuum of the absolute. Even the best poetry, when it is at all personal, needs the penumbra of its own time and place and circumstance to make it full and whole. If we knew a little more of Shakespeare's self and circumstance how much more complete the Sonnets

199

would be to us, how their strange, torn edges would be softened and merged into a whole body!²

This apology invites the reader to transcend the effects of fragmentation in this collection of poems, even to find a healing power in the cohesion of fragments into a single body. The book of poems is a self 'Torn, to become whole again, after long seeking for what is lost' ('Tortoise Shout', p. 367).

But this comment on biography is as irritating to a reader as it is inviting, if only because it plays upon the anxiety the reader feels when faced with construing poems with 'their strange, torn edges'. Lawrence's most notable detractor, R. P. Blackmur, expressed this typical reaction: 'As for Shakespeare's Sonnets, if we did know more about Shakespeare's self, we should only know a little more clearly where he failed as a poet; the Sonnets themselves would be not a whit improved'.³ Lawrence's comments were meant for just such a reader as Blackmur, whose conception of what poetry should be was antithetical to that of Lawrence; and yet like Blackmur, Lawrence was striving to revise the role of biography in understanding poetry. No critic has thought to examine the autobiographical design behind *Collected Poems*. The 'Note' should be taken not as a literal biographical gloss on the poems, but as a rhetorical preface, instructing us how to read his book.⁴

Lawrence blasted the orthodox reader for his fear of confession and for concealing himself behind the veils of conventional wisdom. Andrew Lang's *Selected Poems of Robert Burns* offers an example of Lawrence's target for attack. This book fuelled one of Lawrence's favourite debates, and he may well have had it in mind when he wrote his 'Note'. Burns's controversial life intrigued him and became one of his models, but Lang believed,

> His character, his career, are themes from which one is tempted to shrink in terror, so perilous are they. Once I ventured to say – Principal Shairp had said it before – that I wished we knew no more of Burns's life than of Shakespeare's. It was a vain thing to wish; we cannot keep his poetry, with its frequent confessions, and be ignorant of his life. But I meant no more than a natural desire to be spared sermons, scandal, tattle about a poet.⁵

Lawrence, too, wished to be spared 'sermons, scandal, tattle about a poet', but only because he saw these as cheap and shallow responses, an attempt to fend off the 'demonic' power of poetry. He overturned such tattle by revitalising the nether parts of poetry – by scandalising the critics. He conscientiously retained with 'his poetry, with its frequent confessions' an outline of the circumstances of his life, to assure himself that the confessions of his poetry would be heard. He provided the poetry with a biographical context not, as Blackmur argued, to 'improve' upon the craft of the poet, but to sensitise the reader to the poet's 'new knowledge'.

Lawrence prescribed a radically rhetorical function for art. In one of his major statements on poetry, found in an 'Introduction' to *Chariot of the Sun* by the minor poet Harry Crosby, and which Lawrence wrote just after arranging his collection of poems, he argued that genuine art must break through repressive, socially conditioned conventions to 'fertilise' the reader. To renew vision, man's senses must be revitalised, and this could be accomplished by overthrowing his sense of the norm, throwing his senses into chaos. 'Chaos' was a key term for Lawrence, which he defined as the illimitable, unknown, vital world within – the life of the unconscious with its 'surging' emotional drives. Man fears yet desires chaos and, according to Lawrence, must be induced to face this fear: poets 'reveal the inward desire of mankind'.[6] Lawrence recalled comments such as Lang's only to reverse their tenor, turning Lang's 'terror' and 'desire' upside down into a description of poetry. The poem is not a privileged or protected spot-of-time, from which either author or reader derives simple pleasure or insight. The visionary poet destroys and revolutionises the vision of the reader.

Lawrence asked of his readers no less than he asked of himself, to submit to a process of continual self-revision. This demand informs all his self-portraits including, for example, the portrait of himself as a younger poet with which he begins his 'Note':

The first poems I ever wrote, if poems they were, was when I was nineteen: now twenty-three years ago. I remember perfectly the Sunday afternoon when I perpetrated those first two pieces: 'To Guelder-Roses' and 'To Campions'; in springtime, of course, and, as I say, in my twentieth year. Any young lady might have written them and been pleased with them; as I was pleased with them. But it was after that, when I was twenty, that my real demon would now and then get hold of me and shake more real poems out of me, making me uneasy.   (p. 27)

Lawrence portrays himself here as an earnest poetaster who, despite himself, produces 'real' poems. This is a mocking self-portrait, in which he deliberately diminishes himself in order to project the figure of an intense demonic self beyond him. And by mocking himself, he mocks us, his readers: he teases and diminishes our sense of civility, challenging us to overturn our conventional notions of the good and the known, to yield to a deeper knowledge.

Lawrence's self-portrait in the 'Note' holds the key to reading the *Collected Poems* as a whole. The 'Note' records an early experience of emotional crisis in which the poet is overwhelmed by a demonic inner self, and this experience is given the fictional form of a battle in which the demon momentarily triumphs over the poet's more timid everyday nature. The reader is placed in the role of this timid self, whom the mature narrator diligently challenges. Lawrence's autobiography thus performs at least three functions: to express experiences of personal crisis, to fictionalise these as stories of self-transcendence, and to 'shake' the reader, rhetorically challenging and reforming a reader's conventional views. Lawrence gives us neither accurate biography, nor practical philosophy. He creates instead an art in which he redefines himself not to convert, but to awaken the reader's instinct for conflict. The statements in this 'Note' and in the poems and, I believe, the order itself of the *Collected Poems*, must be read as reflections of Lawrence's argument with himself and with the reader.

Lawrence's life has often been used to gloss his art, but it might just as easily be argued that he lived life as if it were material for a novel. Like his Romantic predecessors, he saw his life as an exemplary form and considered it his mission, as he said in *Sons and Lovers*, to 'sift the vital fact' from experience.[7] This vital fact was for Lawrence that of eruptive change. His life was characterised by a continual struggle to remake his circumstances, by a deep restlessness to have done with one situation and begin the next. Paradoxical though this might seem, change afforded a rule for living, a rule according to which man never settles into a conventional mould, but exists in a state of flux.

So too in his books, Lawrence found in crisis a rule for ordering experience. He altered the actual circumstances of his life to reconstruct them in accordance with this rule of change, frequently modelling his books of poems to create optimistic myths of self-revolution. With the exception of his first book, *Love Poems and Others* (1913), which he did not order himself, each of the poetic books (like the novels) is a fictionalised account of experience. Lawrence described even *Collected Poems* as if it were an autobiographical novel with changes in scene, characters and a full history of crises and climaxes (pp. 27–8), yet *Collected Poems* is no more a strict chronicle of the life than is Lawrence's figure of the possessed young poet a scrupulous portrait of the young man. He organised the poems in this collection just as he shaped his self-portrait, to give his autobiography in verse a significant, symbolic form.

Lawrence first conceived of his poetry as comprising a significant form in 1916, when he selected material for his second book, *Amores*, which, he explained, makes a 'sort of inner-story of my life, from 20 to 26',[8] and soon after compiling *Amores* he began work on *Look! We Have Come Through!* (1917), which he called an 'essential story' from the 'sixth lustre of a man's life' (p. 191). The poems in both these books were revised and collected several years after the recorded events took place, and they conform to a story of struggle through the crisis of his mother's death in *Amores* and marriage in *Look! We Have Come Through!*

Lawrence's designation of the book as an 'essential story, or history, or confession' was influenced by *The Story of my Heart* by Richard Jefferies, which had already encouraged Lawrence's development of a lyrical form for his novels. Jefferies undertook an unusual experiment with the confessional mode, exploring his personal thoughts, allowing them to unfold of themselves, to discover 'new ideas'. Jefferies analysed *The Story of my Heart* as a 'confession' in which

the Author describes the successive stages of emotion and thought through which he passed, till he arrived at the conclusions which are set forth in the latter part of the volume. He claims to have erased from his mind the traditions and learning of the past ages, and to stand face to face with nature and with the unknown.[9]

The philosophical aims and design of *The Story of my Heart* fully anticipate the mythic and formal methods of Lawrence's art, his intention to supplant previous traditions and, by an instinctive movement from one moment to the next, to discover a new vital existence.

With each successive book, Lawrence wrote and rewrote his autobiography, recurrently deriving still another 'new story' to accommodate his changing experiences. Even his short wartime books were written and organised as personal chronicles of apocalyptic change in the world, whether prophesying destruction in *Bay* (1919) or that mythic moment in *New Poems* (1918) when cities and people are 'coming awake'. After the war, he explained in *Fantasia of the Unconscious* (1922) that still another 'new story' must begin, that of men who 'wish to make the world new',[10] and this informs *Birds, Beasts and Flowers* (1923) where, as Lawrence expresses it in 'The Red Wolf',

> Since I trotted at the tail of the sun as far
>   as ever the creature went west,
> And lost him here,
> I'm going to sit down on my tail right here
> And wait for him to come back with a new story. (p. 405)

When in 1927 Lawrence arranged his six books into the two-volume *Collected Poems*, he divided his career into two phases. The first volume, 'Rhyming Poems', recounts the story of the poet as a young man, while the second volume, 'Unrhyming Poems', tells the story of the poet as a mature, married man. In letters of 1927, Lawrence refers frequently to the work he invested in revising his poems, proudly 'sweating' over them. He worked steadily on the verse for four months, the length of time it took him to write, for example, his long novel *Kangaroo*. But in addition to revising individual poems, he rearranged the sequences within each book to create the 'chronological order' of *Collected Poems*. Lawrence may indeed have recalled and recreated portions of the original sequence in which he wrote his poems, though it is impossible to prove this since he assigned no dates to the early verse. The manuscripts are of little help in deciding this issue because the poems do not appear there in a strictly chronological order; their arrangement does not correspond to the known events of his life. The order of the *Collected Poems*, while apparently in closer correspondence, is also suspect.[11] Lawrence did not only shuffle previous sequences; he also altered the sequence in which his books had originally appeared. In this last act of revision, he consciously ignored the actual chronology of his poems, in order to reshape his career.

Of the four books collected in Volume I of *Collected Poems – Love Poems and Others* (1913), *Amores* (1916), *New Poems* (1918) and *Bay* (1919) – *Amores* alone was already organised in a roughly chronological sequence. The others were thematically ordered collections, establishing the character of the poet in *Love Poems and Others*, or reflecting the turbulence of wartime England in *Bay*, an atmosphere still present in *New Poems*. Lawrence did preserve long sequences of the elegies from *Amores* at the centre of Volume I, which he describes in the 'Note' as a cycle of 'death-experience', issuing from the poet's struggles as a child, and culminating with the 'long haunting of death in life' (p. 28). Moreover, his reorganisatoin of the chronological sequence of published books transformed what was a history of repeated, continually expanding struggles with himself and the world into a single movement through change: from old-world English experience in Volume I, recorded in Lawrence's early love poems, elegies and war poems, into new-world experience (not restricted to any single geographical location, but travelling through the world) in Volume II, recorded in *Look! We Have Come Through!* (1917) and *Birds, Beasts and Flowers* (1923).

Even Lawrence's choice of titles for the two volumes, 'Rhyming Poems' and 'Unrhyming Poems', reflects a symbolic, rather than real change in writing. The opposition in titles suggests a radical break in career from the poetry of Volume I to that of Volume II, as if at a single critical juncture he had cast off conventional habits of writing verse. In fact, he never opposed rhyme altogether. He despised a mechanical rhyme scheme and a poetaster's theory which insists on rhyme for its own sake.[12] Nor do the titles refer strictly to actual rhyming procedures in those volumes. In many of the 'Rhyming Poems', Lawrence uses rhyme inconsistently, while in Volume II he often employs a consistent rhyme structure. Lawrence's titles function primarily to announce his determination to undo outmoded habits, especially those habits which he himself had outgrown.

The story of *Collected Poems* represents a deliberate fictionalisation not only of Lawrence's poetic development, but also of his life at the time of collecting his poetry. In 1925 he almost died in Mexico of tuberculosis, and after returning to Europe, this experience resurfaced in tales of personal resurrection as, for example, in the novella *The Man Who Died*. His letters testify to his struggle to endure the 'change of life' which, according to Frieda Ravagli, took the form, traumatic for Lawrence, of sexual impotence.[13] But Lawrence described maturity as a process of resurgent phallic power, and in *Lady Chatterley's Lover*, which he finished shortly before *Collected Poems*, as well as in his poetry, he fictionalised his experience to create a myth of phallic resurrection.

Lawrence's revisions of poems for his collection supply several well-known examples of this myth.[14] In an early version of 'Virgin Youth', he alluded only indirectly to the phallus, and his sudden excitement ended in a vain embrace: 'my docile, fluent arms/Knotting themselves with wild strength/To clasp – what they have never clasped' (p. 896). In the 1928 revision of 'Virgin Youth', Lawrence no longer beat around the bush:

> My soft, slumbering belly,
> Quivering awake with one impulse and one will,
> Then willy nilly
> A lower me gets up and greets me;
> Homunculus stirs from his roots, and strives until,
> Risen up, he beats me.   (p. 39)

The poet-persona of the revised poem cheerfully surrenders to the power of his revived Homunculus.

So too in the 'Note' Lawrence advises us to read Volume I as a cycle of English experience, but within this condition the iconoclastic life of a young man in Volume II breaks through, giving the demon a 'new run for his money' (p. 851). Volume I as a whole is an extended anecdote of the poet's 'change of life': the poet-persona continually battles to release his youthful powers. The poet is a 'war-baby' who surges with emotional power and who will mature when 'Dawns my insurgent day' into a fully 'procreant groom'. 'Rhyming Poems' is filled with prophecies of this final phallic breakthrough, though it ends still awaiting a change. Volume I closes with a perpetuation of the struggle for renewed power: 'wake and be free/From this nightmare we writhe in,/Break out of this foul has-been' ('Autumn Sunshine', p. 177).[15]

But neither does he triumph – or he triumphs only momentarily –

in 'Unrhyming Poems'. *Look! We Have Come Through!* and *Birds, Beasts and Flowers* are, despite many forecasts and a few instants of celebration, endless series of repeated struggle. Lawrence asserted in the 'Note' that 'what was uttered in the cruel spring of 1917 should not be dislocated and heard as if sounding out of the void' (p. 28), yet he broke the chronological sequence of his war poems, separating those in *Bay* from those which end *Look! We Have Come Through!*, so that both 'Rhyming Poems' and *Look! We Have Come Through!* end with poems written during the war, creating in each volume poignantly inconclusive endings in which the poet yearns for a final release. *Birds, Beasts and Flowers* ends, with even richer irony, picturing a puzzled eagle wondering whether or not he should be reborn.

The division itself of *Collected Poems* into two volumes effectively reinforces Lawrence's description of the collection as a history of the poet's transformation from a conventional young man into a demonic, free man, but the suggestion that a single crisis splits the career overly simplifies these two volumes.[16] Volume I tells of the poet's loss of youth and re-entry into the world, while the two books in Volume II tell first the story of his struggle to steal with Frieda out of the past, then of the self-renewing world they have entered. Furthermore, crises are embedded in numerous groups of poems, and in a sense every poem enacts its individual crisis. The divided collection merely reproduces on a larger scale the rule of order which governs every episode in the poet's life and work.

Lawrence was powerfully drawn to confessional stories of progress made along a fragmented path, and he intended the arguments of his own books to proceed, strangely, by breaking into pieces. He compared the Book of Job, for example, to a 'story of your own soul'[17] which closely resembles that of the poetry: a man who has lost both material and spiritual goods must struggle with himself and society, to gain a higher bodily and spiritual wealth. This argument possesses only an implied beginning and end, and actually consists in a perpetually repeated series of struggles. Rather than limiting the shape of the book to a distinct or necessary set of narrative events (with an Aristotelian beginning, middle and end), an argument presupposes for Lawrence the coexistence of at least two potential plots of tragic loss and comic recovery which are, nonetheless, only implied in a sequence of perpetual, existential conflict. At the heart of this argument is the

Heraclitean paradox: that the basis for order is an a-causal, anti-evolutionary, indeed non-systematic, yet spontaneous flux in life, transpiring through naked conflict between antithetical elements: 'white-hot lava, never at peace/Till it burst forth blinding, withering the earth;/To set again into rock' ('Peace', p. 294).

While instructing us how to read his books, either by creating clearly bounded sequences or by providing prefaces with arguments for the poems, Lawrence does not dictate our progress. On the contrary, he complicates the reading process for us, compelling us to find our own way. And while Lawrence's prefaces occasionally provide us with guidelines, they also alert us to the argument that he has with us. He provokes us into active relationship with the poetry, forcing us to become part of his argument as we trace our pilgrim's progress through his books.

The 'Note' to *Collected Poems* briefly and persuasively outlines the argument for the collection, with special attention to the first volume of 'early poetry' since the books in Volume II, *Look! We Have Come Through!* and *Birds, Beasts and Flowers*, already possessed prefaces and well-developed structures which Lawrence wished to leave essentially intact.[18] Without explicit guidelines to these volumes, we would easily overlook their designs, missing, for example, in 'Rhyming Poems', the scene changes, the three women in his life (there could be many women here or only two), and even the crisis of the volume, which passes quickly in three brief poems, 'The End', 'The Bride' and 'The Virgin Mother'. When we turn from examination of the ways in which Lawrence organised his collection as a whole, to a closer look at the final order for 'Rhyming Poems', we find a series of groups of poems which deepen the fragmentary, self-embattled character of this volume. In the original editions of *Collected Poems*, a table of contents was printed in the back of each volume, and each poem appeared on a separate page. (Although no table of contents is included in *The Complete Poems*, one will appear in the forthcoming Cambridge edition of the poetry.) This format made it easy to locate any single poem within the collection, while creating for each poem a separate space. Aside from the fact that Lawrence clearly wished each poem to be read as an individual piece, 'Rhyming Poems' particularly benefited from a format in which short poems do not run into each other, but at the same time can be easily pieced into the rest of the volume.

Looking at a table of contents of 'Rhyming Poems', we can begin to trace Lawrence's shifting argument through the poetry. The argument winds through a series of grouped poems, beginning with an early cluster from his childhood, from 'The Wild Common' to 'Last Hours'. Even these poems, however, from the Beulah-like 'laddishness' of Lawrence's earliest years, are full of emotional conflict, 'discord', 'confusion' and 'fatigue'. The volume begins with a child's double experience of nurture and loss. With a change in scene in 'Flat Suburbs, S.W., in the Morning', the volume enters into Lawrence's city and school poems, in which the city is both a centre of decay and an 'inner continent' full of the 'transformations' of a rural landscape. These first two groups set the scene for a volume of antinomies, where urban decay becomes a locus for pastoral renewal.

Lawrence's love affairs appear sporadically up to this point. The theme deepens and takes hold with 'A Winter's Tale', a poem in which the poet separates from a lover: 'Why does she come so promptly, when she must know/She's only the nearer to the inevitable farewell?/The hill is steep, on the snow my steps are slow –' (p. 85). This broken-love theme rapidly gains intensity and, as suddenly, shifts into the elegies with the poem 'Suspense'. In the long sequence of elegies, the poet suffers his mother's death, dying with her, then experiencing rebirth through her death. A second group of love poems, from 'Excursion Train' to 'Under the Oak', presents a series of frenzied efforts to make and, as quickly, break engagements with women. The poet then returns to a small group of mystical elegies, from 'Brother and Sister' to 'Blueness', in which he dies a second time, to be reborn as a slight 'flame' in the wilderness. From one group to the next, there is never a pause in the speaker's vacillation between love and its loss.

Following this series of broken and mending relationships there is a second group of city poems and reminiscences which look forward ambivalently to 'the outcasts' of wartime England and nostalgically backward to experiences of the past – regaining yet regretting its tender scenes in poems like 'Piano' and 'Twenty Years Ago'. With 'Noise of Battle', the volume enters a final group of war poems in which London and the British land crack painfully with birth pangs, culminating in a vision of mass revolution in 'Dreams Nascent' and in two elegies in which the poet swears to rise again from death-born England. It would be a mistake to suppose that this sequence of groups refers with any accuracy to the events in Lawrence's life. He reproduced the main drift of his life in a progression which emphasises not the continuities in his experience, but its oscillations from landscape to city, from lover to mother, from death scenes to scenes of surging, cosmic power.

As 'Rhyming Poems' proceeds from one group to the next in this extended anecdote of struggle, the individual poem takes on the character of a small rite of passage, which does not, however, proceed in a simple forward direction. True to Lawrence's style of self-redefinition, the individual poem moves forward in a retrogressive direction. The poet-persona breaks 'through' inertia by breaking down. The poems dramatise a sudden slide back into childhood or childlike pathos. The protagonist breaks down in the middle of a kiss or in the midst of any simple activity, lying in a field or listening to a piano. He sees himself as a child again as in 'Piano', or falls into despondency as in 'Dog-Tired', or suddenly sees his lover as a pallid ghost as in 'Lightning'. The protagonist's sense of sight, of hearing, of touch, even of smell instantaneously breaks down into a demonic or pathetic vision of experience: 'The acrid scents of autumn,/Reminiscent of slinking beasts, make me fear/Everything' ('Dolour of Autumn', p. 107).

At the same time, the protagonist learns that the passion felt in these moments is a source of new power, that he should take his ghostly lover through fire as in 'Last Words to Miriam', or that he must move through weariness and grief into rekindled life as in 'The Shadow of Death' and 'Blueness'. Lawrence discovers his demonic powers by regressing into pure emotionalism. The poem 'Piano', for example, dramatises in miniature the dilemma of his double, strife-ridden self. This poem turns his self-portrait as presented in the 'Note' inside out, so that the mature narrator, listening to a woman singing 'in the dusk' is 'mastered' by the song until he sinks emotionally back into a scene from his childhood – a Sunday evening in a cosy parlour. No longer a conventional young man 'shaken' by his demon, he is a man 'cast down' by 'the glamour of childish days'. The doubled irony of this poem seizes the reader through value-laden words, for example, in 'betrayal': In spite of myself, the insidious mastery of song/Betrays me back'. It is not a passion for the woman which is betrayed. Rather the passion of her song betrays his childhood passion: he is doubly trapped, doubly revealed, as a man with a deep range of sentimentality, as a boy enchanted passionately by a woman: 'The glamour/Of childish days is upon me, my manhood is cast/Down in the flood of remembrance, I weep like a child for the past' (p. 148).

I. A. Richards featured 'Piano' in his *Practical Criticism* to reveal the unskilled practices of students, who were alternately touched and appalled by the 'sentimentality' of this poem. 'Sentimentality', he points out, arises from an excessive response to an object, on the part of readers as well as authors. But Richards suggests that 'Piano' is a study, not an indulgence, of emotionalism.[19] Such a poem, he believed, deserves close, skilled reading. Reread in context, 'Piano' is found to be even more than a controlled ironic study of emotionalism. Placed in a volume which re-enacts the poet's 'change of life', this poem reveals the source of Lawrence's power ('song,/Betrays me') in the antagonistic and generative conflict between a maturing narrator and the eternal child.

NOTES

1. *Birds, Beasts and Flowers, Last Poems* and *New Poems* are listed in *Books in Print, 1983–4* (New York: R. R. Bowker, 1983), *Authors*, II.
2. D. H. Lawrence, 'Note' to *Collected Poems: The Complete Poems*, ed. Vivian de Sola Pinto and F. Warren Roberts (New York: Viking, 1971) p. 27. Extracts from *The Complete Poems* will hereafter be cited by page reference in the text.
3. R. P. Blackmur, *Form and Value in Modern Poetry* (New York: Doubleday, 1952) p. 255.
4. Even Lawrence's champions neglect the rhetorical stress of his art. Harold Bloom, Vivian de Sola Pinto and Sandra Gilbert restore Lawrence to his place in the Romantic tradition by describing his poetic practice, respectively, as mythopoeic, organic and epistemological in nature. The special idiom of his poetry, however, derives from his complex aim to write as Whitman had written, productively autobiographical and rhetorical verse. See Harold Bloom, 'Lawrence, Blackmur, Eliot and the Tortoise', in *A D. H. Lawrence Miscellany*, ed. Harry T. Moore (Carbondale: Southern Illinois Press, 1959) p. 368; Vivian de Sola Pinto, 'Introduction', in *The Complete Poems*, pp. 1–10; and Sandra Gilbert, *Acts of Attention* (Ithaca: Cornell University Press, 1972) pp. 21–4.
   Publication of a book on the *Collected Poems* occurred too late for me to include it in my argument; while this concerns the narrative design of the *Collected Poems* (especially as reflected in revisions of individual

poems), I examine the structural rearrangement of Lawrence's previous
sequences of poems and the reconstruction of his career: see Gail Porter
Mandell, *The Phoenix Paradox: a Study of Renewal through Change in the
Collected Poems and Last Poems of D. H. Lawrence* (Carbondale: Southern
Illinois Press, 1984).

5. Andrew Lang, 'Introduction', in *Selected Poems of Robert Burns* (London:
Kegan Paul, Trench, Trubner, 1892) pp. xx–xxi. See also *The Letters of
D. H. Lawrence*, ed. James T. Boulton (Cambridge University Press,
1979) I, pp. 487–9, 504–5.

6. *Phoenix: the Posthumous Papers of D. H. Lawrence*, ed. Edward D.
McDonald (New York: Penguin, 1978) pp. 255–7.

7. *Sons and Lovers* (New York: Penguin, 1977) p. 148.

8. 'To Lady Ottoline Morrell', in *The Collected Letters of D. H. Lawrence*, ed.
Harry T. Moore (New York: Viking, 1962) I, p. 419.

9. Richard Jefferies, 'Preface', in *The Story of my Heart* (London: Longmans,
Green, 1898) p. ix. See also *Letters*, ed. Boulton, I, pp. 137, 337, 339, 353;
and W. J. Keith, *Richard Jefferies: a Critical Study* (Toronto: University of
Toronto Press, 1965).

10. D. H. Lawrence, *'Fantasia of the Unconscious' and 'Psychoanalysis and the
Unconscious'* (London: Penguin, 1977) p. 108.

11. To compare the order of poems in early manuscripts with that in
'Rhyming Poems', see Carole Ferrier, 'D. H. Lawrence's Pre-1920
Poetry: a Descriptive Bibliography of Manuscripts, Typescripts and
Proofs', *The D. H. Lawrence Review*, 6 (1973) 333–59. For alternative
views on whether the poems in an early notebook appear in a
chronological order, see Carole Ferrier and Egon Tiedje, 'D. H.
Lawrence's Pre-1920 Poetry: the Textual Approach: an Exchange', *The
D. H. Lawrence Review*, 5 (1972) 149–57. For further textual history of the
poetry, see Carole Ferrier, 'D. H. Lawrence's Poetry, 1920–1928: a
Descriptive Bibliography of Manuscripts, Typescripts and Proofs', *The
D. H. Lawrence Review*, 12 (1979) 289–304.

12. 'To Edward Marsh', 19 November 1913, in *Collected Letters*, ed. Moore, I,
pp. 243–4.

13. Harry T. Moore, *The Intelligent Heart: the Story of D. H. Lawrence* (New
York: Grove Press, 1962) p. 477; 'To E. H. Brewster', 27 February 1927,
in *Collected Letters*, ed. Moore, II, p. 967.

14. For an early study of Lawrence's revisions, see Phyllis Bartlett,
'Lawrence's *Collected Poems*: the Demon Takes Over', *PMLA*, 66
(September 1951) 583–93.

15. Note that the editors of *The Complete Poems* added three poems,
'Song-Day in Autumn', 'Disagreeable Advice' and 'Restlessness', to the
end of Volume I, which originally concluded with 'Autumn Sunshine'.

16. On 17 January 1928, Lawrence finished the 'first half' of what was then
to be a one-volume edition, and agreed shortly afterwards to publish
two volumes as a set; see *Letters from D. H. Lawrence to Martin Secker,
1911–1930*, ed. Martin Secker (privately published, 1970) pp. 98–100.

17. *Collected Letters*, ed. Moore, I, p. 301.

18. Lawrence added introductory notes to the individual sections of *Birds,
Beasts and Flowers* later in 1929 for the illustrated Cresset edition. See

Keith Sagar, *D. H. Lawrence: a Calendar of his Works* (Austin: University of Texas Press, 1979) p. 189.
19. I. A. Richards, *Practical Criticism* (New York: Harcourt, Brace & World, 1929) pp. 99–112, 241–54.

14

The Retreat from Reason or a Raid on the Inarticulate

R. N. PARKINSON

> these plays show us that we have lost half a century. For
> what Lawrence was then trying to do, and what hardly
> anyone knew that he had done, is what for the last ten
> or fifteen years a generation of writers has again been
> attempting.
>
> (Raymond Williams, Introduction to
> *D. H. Lawrence Three Plays*
> (Harmondsworth: Penguin, 1969) p. 14)

A centenary tribute to D. H. Lawrence is the right place to
emphasise what Raymond Williams makes so plain in the words
of the above epigraph – that it has now become a commonplace of
Lawrence criticism to recognise that his plays (at least the early
plays) were, like his novels, years ahead of their time. At the
beginning of this century, Lawrence's novels challenged the
supposed dominance of reason in individual behaviour and in
society at large, and this challenge was recognised during
Lawrence's lifetime as one of the heralds of a new age in fiction. It
might, perhaps, be said that the challenge had not turned into
orthodoxy until the *Lady Chatterley* trial in the 1960s. If this were
so, then there had been a long period of softening up as a prelude
to recognition. It took much longer for the British public to
recognise that Lawrence had written plays which embodied the
same sort of fundamentally subversive propositions as those in
the novels, for, while the novels created their own climate of
opinion, the plays fell stillborn from the press, and their rare and
obscure performances aroused little interest.

It was not the message of the plays which prevented
performance. The late nineteenth century and the early twentieth
were full of romantic rebels. 'I hate reasonable people. The activity

of their brains sucks up all the blood out of their hearts.' This might be the later Lawrence speaking, but in fact it is the early Yeats, writing, appropriately enough, about the novels of George Eliot, with all the energy of an enthusiastic iconoclast who hates other people's idols simply because they are other people's. Respect for reason seemed to be the enemy: we can imagine the later Lawrence adding, as Yeats himself does: 'I was once afraid of turning out reasonable myself.'[1] What is more to the purpose of this essay is to note how well in accord with the spirit of much modern English drama are Yeats' remarks. Unreason seems to predominate. It is the stage Author in N. F. Simpson's play *A Resounding Tinkle* who declares: 'The retreat from reason means precious little to anyone who has never caught up with reason in the first place.'[2] By the mid-1950s, reason appeared to be in full retreat, even in drama. The typical hero of that decade is a monster of unreason who cannot understand the causes of his own fury and therefore blames others for it – and wishes to hurt them as some sort of compensation for his own sense of hurt. By ignoring Lawrence's achievement for nearly two generations, English drama had to start the post-war period by making some of his discoveries anew. My main purpose is to remind us of how sensitively and how powerfully Lawrence had embodied such feelings in his own plays, while examining the causes of these feelings with sympathetic but not self-indulgent understanding.

In attempting to put Lawrence's dramatic achievement into perspective, we must remember that his plays were acted hardly at all during his lifetime. (It was 1926 before *The Widowing of Mrs Holroyd* was produced on the London stage, and Lawrence was not there to see it.) The first London season of Lawrence plays was that directed by Peter Gill at the Royal Court in 1967 and 1968, more than ten years after Osborne's *Look Back in Anger*, the play which is taken by general agreement to mark the beginning of the new drama in Great Britain. Forty years after Lawrence had pioneered a revolution in drama, the revolution took place without him. Ten years of the new plays, in the late 1950s and early 1960s, prepared the public to listen sympathetically – even enthusiastically – to Lawrence on the stage. In this respect, history continually repeats itself: the artist is at least a generation in advance of his day. As Pound rightly put it: 'Artists are the antennae of the race.' Consider that in the later 1960s Büchner's *Woyzeck* was intriguing provincial audiences in Great Britain.

Who, in the nineteenth century, would have dared to predict that the experimental plays of Büchner (if he had known them) would find popular audiences in the twentieth century? The same historical irony operated for Lawrence as for Büchner: twentieth-century playgoers were prepared for appreciating the more radical innovators of the past by the successes of our contemporaries, of Beckett and Pinter, of Osborne and Wesker, and of a host of others who began to make their names in the 1950s and early 1960s. Büchner was interesting to the disciples of the new wave of post-war drama because he appeared to them to anticipate, for example, the experimental socialisation of the drama by Brecht or the abandonment of reasonableness by Beckett. Lawrence's new and growing reputation as a dramatist owes much to a similar change in public opinion.

When the first plays of the new wave were published in the 1950s and 1960s, editors and critics acclaimed their newness without recalling Lawrence by name, but their praises were frequently cast in a mode which was preparing readers for recognition of Lawrence's plays. When Penguin published the first volume of their New English Dramatists series in 1959, E. Martin Browne declared in his preface

> The British theatre has for too long been stuck in a rut, dug partly by those who insisted on everyone adhering to the commercially saleable, because familiar, form of the realistic three-act play, and more deeply by those who banned a considerable amount of what goes on in real life from being shown in the theatre.[3]

It is surprising to recall that he was writing of three plays which now seem unremarkable: Doris Lessing's *Each His Own Wilderness*, Bernard Kops' *The Hamlet of Stepney Green* and Arnold Wesker's *Chicken Soup with Barley*. But the reasons behind Browne's commendation of these as 'real life' plays are suggested in Alan Pryce-Jones' praises of the three plays to be published in the next volume of the Penguin series. It was their inventiveness and variety which attracted him: the high theme of Wesker's *The Kitchen*; the air of lightning improvisation in N. F. Simpson's *A Resounding Tinkle*; and the sympathy and perception with which, in *Epitaph for George Dillon*, John Osborne and Anthony Creighton caught 'the tone, the colour and the feeling of a middle class household'.[4] Much of the real life in the six plays is, however, lower class; and for this reason the plays' auditors certainly felt them to strike new notes in the exploration of human situations.

As these new plays reached first the experimental and then the West End stage, they found an audience which was, like E. Martin Browne, ready for something – perhaps for anything – new. What is surprising is that few playgoers and few critics seem to have found any echoes from the earlier realism of the twentieth century. While the critics of the 1950s admired forthrightness, inventiveness, humour and serious attempts to render the feelings of the working classes (because, they thought, there had been no previous attempts in drama to take the working classes seriously), it would seem that they had never heard of Lawrence's plays, or of Harold Brighouse, Alan Monkhouse, Stanley Houghton, Miss Horniman or the Gaiety Theatre in Manchester. Mention of these will remind us that there had been the beginnings of a vernacular and a working-class drama in Lawrence's own day, before the First World War, but that this had gained little recognition outside the provinces. The most obvious thing that Lawrence's plays had in common with this earlier movement was the attempt to give a recognisable, individual voice to the working classes of a particular district – Nottingham and the mining country.[5] Bernard Shaw, having seen a production of *Mrs Holroyd*, praised the 'torrent of profuse yet vividly effective dialogue', and, according to Rolf Gardiner, said that the dialogue was the most magnificent he had ever heard, and his own stuff was *The Barber of Fleet Street* in comparison.[6]

The success of Lawrence's early attempts lay, however, not primarily in providing a vernacular drama, and not in the use of dialect, but in the voicing and enacting of the feelings of the most sensitive amongst the miners and artisans of pre-First World War England. Lawrence was beginning to articulate for the inarticulate the feelings which so often possessed them: this he could do because so many of them were his own feelings. It was twenty years later that he declared 'What really torments civilised people is that they are full of feelings that they know nothing about',[7] but in 1910 he was already partly conscious of this important truth; and he sought in the plays to articulate some of the feelings which were tormenting him and his contemporaries. Of *Sons and Lovers*, Lawrence was to write: 'It is the tragedy of thousands of young men in England.'[8] He felt the predicament of Paul Morel to be a representative as well as individual one. What is as remarkable in the plays as it is in the novels is the nature and degree of Lawrence's articulacy about the predicament. The feelings of his characters are so intense as to amount to the 'torment' which he later voiced in his essay 'The State of Funk', where he claimed that men are at the mercy of feelings which they have not identified because 'they can't realise them, they can't fulfil them, they can't *live* them'. Such inarticulacy has frightful consequences: 'and so they are tortured. It is like having energy you can't use – it destroys you.'[9]

In his three earliest plays, Lawrence shows the torments of working-class people who suffer from powerful feelings which they cannot understand or identify. His characters suffer because of their inarticulacy, and they make discoveries about themselves only as their feelings drive them to desperate self-expression. In some cases that expression takes the form of action or failure to act; in others the characters are urged into speech which astonishes the speakers, by giving them a true awareness of character and situation. The plays embody the emotional stresses of their protagonists through the enactment of the emotions: the character sees the real truth about himself only when the experiences of the play and the words of the other characters drive him to such self-realisation. A good example is that of Mrs Holroyd: she is pushed into a new self-awareness by the gradual action of ordinary causes significantly telescoped within the structure of a three-act play. Her young daughter says 'wistfully' to her (of the drunken and disagreeable father and husband): ''Appen if you said something nice to him mother, he'd happen go to bed and not shout'; while her mother-in-law points out 'a man 'as been shut up i' th' pit all day. . . . He must have a bit of relaxation', and 'I was always sorry my youngest married a clever woman. He only wanted a bit of coaxing and managing and you clever women won't do it.'[10] And so Mrs Holroyd is forced to acknowledge, little by little, that her husband had stayed down the pit after the others on the crucial evening of his death because he was still resentful at her treatment of him; and she is driven to admit to herself: 'He'd have come up with the others, if he hadn't felt – felt me murdering him.'[11] The depth of her feeling for him is revealed by the dramatic language (which is all the more forceful as coming from a woman who has held herself in tight restraint): she is facing up to what she had previously been unable to recognise about her scornful and spiteful treatment of her husband – and the realisation is a tragic one.

Lawrence wrote of his aims as a novelist: 'My field is to know the feelings inside a man and to make new feelings conscious.'[12] It is just such a bringing of hidden feelings to consciousness that characterises much modern drama, whose marked change in methods and aims was needed in order to obtain recognition for Lawrence's plays. Time and again in the 1950s and 1960s, dramatists recognised that what they were attempting was to articulate for their lower-class characters the feelings which tormented them. Such articulation, such realisation, could bring a measure of release from the torment – and sometimes the possibility of action to remove it. When Ann Jellicoe explains

> I write this way because – the image everybody has of the rational, intellectual and intelligent man – I don't believe it's true. I think people are driven by their emotions, and by their fears and insecurities[13]

she is making for herself and for her contemporaries a discovery which Lawrence had embodied in his plays nearly two generations before. What she has to say about the action of her own play, *The Sport of My Mad Mother*, makes her sound very much like Lawrence: 'my play is about incoherent people – people who have no power of expression, of analysing their emotions'.[14] Where her people do not achieve articulate speech, she tries to present them in action which will speak for them, though it is doubtful whether her success in doing this is as great as Lawrence's – merely because even his least ordinarily articulate people have their climactic moment of verbal self-expression whereas hers do not. If Ann Jellicoe's characters rarely reach the degree of articulacy to which she aspires on their behalf, working-class characters in the dramas of other modern playwrights do find a voice of their own. One of the most remarkable pieces of dramatic self-discovery in the plays of the 1950s is the discovery of Wesker's Beattie Bryant in *Roots* that, after all her dependence upon Ronnie for education, she has somehow lifted herself up by her bootstraps to the point where she has views of her own and can speak for herself; at the end of *Roots* she says in bemused wonderment: 'I'm talking. . . . I'm not quoting no more. . . . It does work, it's happening to me. I can feel it's happened, I'm beginning, on my own two feet – I'm beginning.'[15] It is almost as though the new generation had taken as their text one of Lawrence's pronouncements: 'The struggle for verbal consciousness should not be left out in art. It is a very great part of life. It is not superimposition of a theory. It is the passionate struggle into conscious being.'[16]

It is something of this 'passionate struggle into conscious being' that is so well enacted in Lawrence's plays. In the earlier three he embodies the struggles of the lower-class characters who, as they begin to realise something of what they are, begin to develop into the middle-class characters of the later plays. The struggle into consciousness, of necessity, pushes the inarticulate into a different way of life, when they begin to be able to think about their own feelings.

It is natural, when we turn to Lawrence's plays, to think of them in two groups: those of the Nottingham mining country – *A Collier's Friday Night*, *The Widowing of Mrs Holroyd* and *The Daughter-in-Law* – and those which either leave the miner's life or look at it from the outside – *The Married Man*, *The Fight for Barbara*, *Touch and Go* and *The Merry-go-Round*. (*David* and the Noah fragment are in a different category.) It is easy enough to see that the two main groups represent two stages in Lawrence's processes of self-discovery, and to find interesting parallels between the substance and manner of the plays and novels which treat similar episodes in Lawrence's life. The first three plays barely reach beyond the material of *Sons and Lovers*. Particular episodes, like the burning of the loaves in *A Collier's Friday Night*, are virtually dramatisations of the same 'real-life' situations that we find in *Sons and Lovers*, and they carry similar thematic and symbolic significances. It is the same Beatrice in both versions who works the mischief for which Ernest/Paul's preoccupation with Maggie/Miriam is blamed; and the spoiling of the mother's work and the destruction of the daily bread, which the mother makes for the family and entrusts to her son, carries similar emotional and symbolic overtones.

The very stage directions are taken over from the novel – or perhaps we should say that they are attempts to enable the actors to capture the family tensions which can be treated at so much greater length in *Sons and Lovers*: when the father returns home in *A Collier's Friday Night*, 'No one speaks. . . . There is a general silence as if the three listeners were shrugging their shoulders in contempt and anger.' Nellie, his daughter, speaks to him 'with a cold contempt'. No wonder Lambert considers that the mother 'eggs 'em on against me', and 'stares at her dumbly, between anger and shame and sorrow, of which an undignified rage is predominant'.[17] If indeed the dramatic version is earlier than the fictional, it is easy to see that the greater length permitted by the narrative may have appealed to Lawrence as a way of controlling more precisely the reader's response to the father: it certainly did allow him more episodes with which to build up a rather more ambiguous picture of family tensions than is given by the clear cut lines of the play.

Some of the stage directions put an almost impossible burden upon actor and audience alike, as when the last stage direction of the play tries to indicate how much should be expressed by the tones of the final goodnight between mother and son: 'There is in their tones a dangerous gentleness – so much gentleness that the safe reserve of their souls is broken.' What is important in such directions is their attempt to go beyond the realistic, beyond what Raymond Williams in his preface calls 'high naturalism', to create in the auditor the character's awareness of an emotional pressure which he has not yet learnt to put into words.

This emotional pressure is revealed again and again in the stage directions. One may well ask how the actress is to interpret the direction that Maggie shall glance 'splendidly' at Ernest or 'laugh up at him a moment, splendidly'. Is she happy, proud, expectant, joyful, conscious of power over him? – or all of these? We are more at home in the commentaries upon the relationships between Ernest and his mother, as when, after an embrace which conveys their passion for one another, Lawrence brings them back to a more mundane tone with the explanation: 'There are, in each of their voices, traces of the recent anguish, which makes their speech utterly insignificant. Nevertheless, in thus speaking, each reassures the other that the moment of abnormal emotion and proximity has passed, and the usual position of careless intimacy is resumed.'

It is one of the successes of *The Daughter-in-Law* that Lawrence no longer feels the necessity of such careful explanation in his stage directions. The changing emotions of Luther and Minnie are more subtly embodied in action and dialogue. To compare the endings of these two early plays is to see how much Lawrence had learnt about the craft of the dramatist in the three years or so which lie between the earliest versions. After all the quarrels and misunderstandings between Luther and Minnie, the new awareness of each other and the recognition of the real love between them is very simply and movingly embodied in the natural impulse of Minnie to help her emotionally exhausted and physically injured husband to take off his boots:

> LUTHER: Minnie – I want thee to ma'e what tha can o' me. [He sounds almost sleepy.]
>
> MINNIE [crying]: My love – my love!
>
> LUTHER: I know what tha says is true.
>
> MINNIE: No, my love – it isn't – it isn't.
>
> LUTHER: But if ter'lt ma'e what ter can o' me – an' then if ter has a childt – tha'lt happen ha'e enow.
>
> MINNIE: No – no – it's you. It's you I want. It's you.
>
> LUTHER: But tha's allers had me.
>
> MINNIE: No, never – and it hurt so.
>
> LUTHER: I thowt tha despised me.
>
> MINNIE: Ah – my love!
>
> LUTHER: Dunna say I'm mean, to me – an' got no go.
>
> MINNIE: I only said it because you wouldn't let me love you.
>
> LUTHER: Tha didna love me.
>
> MINNIE: Ha! – it was you.
>
> LUTHER: Yi. [He looses himself and sits down heavily.] I'll ta'e my boots off. [He bends forward.]
>
> MINNIE: Let me do them. [He sits up again.]
>
> LUTHER: It's started bleedin'. I'll do 'em i' ha'ef a minute.
>
> MINNIE: No – trust me – trust yourself to me. Let me have you now for my own. [She begins to undo his boots.]
>
> LUTHER: Dost want me?
>
> MINNIE: [she kisses his hands]: Oh, my love! [She takes him in her arms.] [He suddenly begins to cry.]

In that last brief stage direction we can *see*, on stage, that Luther at last feels safe enough to break down in front of his wife. He no longer fears her and we are confident that, *now*, he will find comfort in her love and understanding. The situation as well as the dialogue has articulated this reconciliation.

In such a scene, Lawrence conveys a greater wealth of pent-up emotion than we find in all the dialogues of Pinter. We must, of course, admit that it is a very different kind of emotional tension from that, say, of the two hired toughs in *The Dumb Waiter*, or of Ruth and Teddy as they insist indirectly upon the significance of bed in the opening scene of *The Homecoming*. What is more surprising, in view of the universal praise of Pinter's realism, is that Lawrence's characters command more of our fundamental sympathies: they are in themselves worthier, more admirable and attractive as human beings. Such an impression has little to do with our capacity for sentimentalising over the past – for seeing more in Lawrence's plays than is actually there, or for pretending to emotions that we have not really experienced – the impression is really created by the quality of Lawrence's dialogue and, oddly enough, by the effect of the detailed stage directions.

There is indeed a lot of detail and the detail matters, whether it is the set, the dialect words, or just what a working girl thinks of as a treat in 1910. *A Collier's Friday Night* opens with Lawrence's first lengthy Shavian stage direction, and it demands the impossible of audience and producer alike. Nevertheless, it is illuminating and vital, historic and informative. Who, now, would remember that individual bookshelves were covered with 'green serge, with woollen ball fringe' (though table covers and chenille curtains of this green fringed and bobbled kind survived almost into our own day)? And what was a *quiver* clothes horse (evocative certainly of the sheer hard labour of a hand-wash-day with its tub and posser and rubbing board, and maybe a creel drawn up to the kitchen ceiling to rescue what could be dried out for the attentions of a flat-iron heated on the kitchen stove)? Perhaps Reeves' water-colours still stand for quality, and certainly all the individually-named books and authors show an aspiration to culture beyond that of an average miner's home, like the 'pleasing' prints on the walls whose provenance ('Stead's Christmas Numbers') and whose quality ('satisfactory enough') are so carefully vouched for. There is a touching earnestness in these self-conscious details, as there is in the 'woman in the rocking chair [who] is dressed in black, and wears a black sateen apron'. The last touch, 'She wears spectacles, and is reading The New Age', is almost pure Osbert Lancaster,[18] though we are not meant so to see it. We must rather remark the unusually intellectual note struck by the mention of Orage's publication, which even then contained Ezra Pound's notes on contemporary music and the arts. There is a deliberately marked unconventionality and 'modernness' about the plainness of Nellie Lambert's clothes, the preoccupation with books and prints, and the farewell to some kinds of Victorian and Edwardian fussiness. Perhaps also there is an uneasy pretentiousness, of which the author was not himself perfectly aware, in Lawrence's attempts to show or to share Ernest's culture. It is not only an uneasiness about cultural identity which makes Ernest address his mother variously as *Mater*, *Mütter*, *Matouschka* and *Mütterchen*: it is also his desire to show a change in his relationship to her. These foreign variations are in deliberate contrast to the dialect words which come so naturally from the mouths of all the characters: it needs a Nottinghamshire education and not just a northern one to make sense of a list which includes *gaby*, *swarfed*, *jinking*, *slikey* and *'ormin'*, *slivin'* and *Sorry* (for Mister).

Matching the dialect are the stage directions for the homecomings of father and children: Lambert's clothes and snap-bag are those of Morel in *Sons and Lovers*; Nellie's liking for tinned apricots, the burnished steel fender and the gas tap in the cellar are part of a way of life solidly realised and vividly recalled. In such a society, heavily conscious of the necessity for hard labour among men and women, in mine or home, it is no wonder that Ernest feels the need of his 'gift of coloured words' or that, when he exercises it, he is a little impatient with a Maggie who does not share his enthusiasm – except by imitating it. His rendering of the effect of the poetry of Baudelaire is persuasive proof of his intelligence and unusual sensibility:

> It's so heavy and full and voluptuous: like oranges falling and rolling a little way along a dark blue carpet; like twilight outside when the lamp's lighted; you get a sense of rich, heavy things, as if you smelt them, and felt them about you in the dusk.[19]

What we feel at work in this earliest of Lawrence's plays is a combination of gifts which produces a peculiar and characteristic depth and intensity of feeling. *A Collier's Friday Night* is intended to have as rich a texture of feeling as has *Sons and Lovers*: given the detail of the stage directions both in terms of physical surroundings and of the actions of the characters, it becomes possible for the actors to convey some of the emotional intensities which are aimed at by the more abstract and intense stage directions which we noted earlier. What we also experience are the emotions of people who take themselves more seriously than we take ourselves.

It is this fundamental seriousness and sincerity which turn

Lawrence's first three plays into deeply-moving experiences for their audiences, rather than into pieces of social history or of *avant-garde* experiment. The same cannot be said with such confidence for the plays which followed. What is remarkable about them, in the 'most complete' versions published in 1965, is the sudden enlargement of range, and the extrapolation of some themes from the miner's home into several different worlds outside it. They show Lawrence in the first stages of feeling about the world of *Women in Love*, intent upon the wider problems of the marriage relationship, and ready to leave Bestwood behind. What is most striking about them is the constant attempt to see through pretence and to reveal the real feelings of the principal characters whether in the situation of the individual marriage or in the context of a world which imposes pretences – damaging pretences – upon everyone.

> I think a man ought to be fair. He ought to offer her love for just what it is – the love of a man married to another woman – and so on. And, if there is any strain, he ought to tell his wife – 'I love this other woman.'[20]

Thus the new sincerity of the emancipated Elsa Smith in *The Married Man*; but it does not prevent the married man of the title from returning, when called upon to do so, to the wife whom he had deserted. Like the characters of *The Merry-go-Round*, those of this play attempt to practise an often laboured sincerity, which sometimes has a comic extravagance of effect. Lawrence puts upon his audience, if not upon his characters, demands which tax sympathy and credulity. If in *The Married Man* he tries to give a picture of the discovery of real feeling in the class immediately above that of the colliers in *The Merry-go-Round*, he comes very near to farce. It is not only the introduction of a real live goose which sets problems of production: it is also the presence of characters and situations so near to farce: a comic German Baron is an unlikely incumbent for the church in an English village, and his Baroness is even less credible. The tone of the whole, for all its realistic moments, is a cross between that of pantomime and that of farce. It is only with difficulty that Lawrence tidies up the endings of the play by reference – in the best tradition of comedy – both to Shakespeare and to Restoration drama, by pairing off all

the most probable lovers with perfunctory humour and justice
with a reference to *As You Like It*:

> DR FOULES: Nurse, will you be asked in church with me next
> Sunday?
> BAKER: Susy, will you be asked in church with me next Sunday?
> HARRY: Rachel, shall you be axed in church with me next
> Sunday?

The last words of the play convey a view of marriage to be
repeated often, in a great variety of ways.

> DR FOULES: It's 'As You Like It'.
> BAKER: It's 'As You *Lump* It'.[21]

For his village characters of every class, Lawrence insists upon the
unsatisfactory nature of ordinary human relationships and
ordinary social institutions: at the very best, his three married
couples have arrived – after achieving some degree of self-
knowledge – at a series of compromises which may or may not
succeed. What is clearly apparent is that none of them is capable
of such depths of feeling as are the principal characters of the first
three plays.

When it comes to *The Fight for Barbara* and *Touch and Go*,
Lawrence has moved into his own new world – a world which
does much more than reflect upon the reasons for the feelings
which it has discovered. If the situation and some of the language
of *Barbara* reminds us of earlier plays, it lacks much of their
warmth because its realities are no longer those of the miner's life.
The setting, for all the protests about the warmth of Italian
peasants ('I like him as he stands there – he looks like a wild
young bull or something, peering out of his hood'), is less solid.
Neither Wesson nor Barbara feels the compulsion of a particular
pattern of daily living, and each of them appears the less real for
this lack. From the beginning, Barbara has the distinguishing
marks of the bright young things whom Lawrence was to render
so effectively in *St Mawr* – far too many words in italics, and a
nervous intensity which feeds upon itself. Wesson, the young
miner's son with whom Barbara has run off to Italy is Jim,
Giacomo, Giacometti, Gia – any creation of her fancy but his real
self. Has Wesson persuaded her to run off with him, or has she
fallen for a new amusement? She is a doctor's wife and the

daughter of a baronet. They have come to Italy to live cheaply, and seem to be enjoying a perpetual wrangle about the sincerity of their loves for one another. We hear the protests from Barbara which have a modern ring as she claims that Wesson wants to 'humble me, and make me nothing – and then swallow me. And it's *wrong*. It's *wrong* for you to want to swallow me. I am myself – and you ought to leave me free',[22] and Wesson's jealous intensity of feeling as he accuses her of coquetting with the young Italian butcher or finds himself unable to convince Barbara of the reality of his own love for her. Their dialogues are a perpetual argument, and it is only when Barbara is confronted by the weakness of Tressider, her husband, that she begins to feel Wesson to be the man with whom she can live. But the final dialogue with which Wesson is supposed to establish her renunciation of Tressider (whom she says she only pities) has little of the dramatic power of the last scenes of the first three plays: it argues rather than enacts.

Touch and Go, the last play of the second group, is unique in having been written wholly after the First World War, possibly in response to a request for a play for the People's Theatre Society. Lawrence's Preface to the play (republished in *Phoenix II*) is curiously unenlightening, with its suggestion that he had written a play about the quarrel between Labour and Capital. Certainly, one of its obvious purposes is to show industrial conflict as both a personal and a class struggle. It also resumes the attack upon false Christianity which had been mounted first in *Women in Love*. Its greatest success lies in the way it suggests and demonstrates that bad industrial relations are rooted in ill-managed and ill-understood personal relations. There is more of an attempt in this play than in most of Lawrence's work to dramatise the public consequences of private inadequacy. If it is dramatically less satisfying than the earliest plays, it is attempting to do far more. It continues the process of experimentation by showing the personal struggles of some middle-class characters into self-awareness, within the context of a wider society. The social determinism suggested in the comedy of *The Married Man* and *The Merry-go-Round* is here taken seriously.

Men and masters are caught up in a continuing economic conflict because they have not thought sufficiently about the basic sources of satisfaction in human life. It is implicit in the earlier plays that self-discovery and personal sincerity are the first necessities for any kind of satisfaction or of happiness in life. This play insists, far more than any of its predecessors, that there is a relationship between the quality of the individual private life and the form of the larger society. Self-evidently, Lawrence is not working from a particular political or philosophical position which is to be exemplified in the play: typically, he is feeling his own way forward to articulation, by experimenting with the lives of his characters. He expects to arrive at discovery through action and reaction – the plays provide an emotional analogy to dialectical process. If, at the end of the play, we are not sure what the action has *meant*, no more is Lawrence. This is a sort of living through drama which has many modern analogies: Arden is an obvious practitioner of similar methods.

In *Touch and Go* three obvious major themes emerge. The first is stated in the opening scene: to show industrial conflict as both a personal and a class struggle. At this level Gerald Barlow, the mine-owner, hates Job Arthur Freer the union leader because he is an unworthy leader, but Gerald makes little or no effort to examine the justice of the men's claims. He says merely that he will not be bullied by Job or by the men. The second theme is the inadequacy of the old Christian attitudes to deal with mass meetings and large-scale industrial relations. Lawrence does not totally reject these attitudes. Old Mr Barlow is meant to be a totally inadequate figure with his regrets about the older days of smaller-scale working and better personal understanding between masters and men which is based upon Christianity. Nevertheless, his idealism is not ridiculous. The working-class leader of real feeling and human potential, Willie Houghton, speaks naturally in terms of Scriptural analogies and illustrations which have some effect on the men, though his viewpoint is rejected.

The third theme is the most important: the need to understand and cleanse the self, before any helpful change in life-patterns can be discovered or worked out. All the characters appear to have different objectives. Willie looks for an idea of freedom; Winifred knows that if she has a life-work she can be happy; Anabel recognises that a living thing has 'inexpressible poise' and feels the lack of this in her own earlier life with Gerald. All the characters are hoping, in their different ways, to find a sense of freedom, a life-work which will embody or allow it and the creative satisfaction which is indicated by Anabel's phrase. None of these things is to be achieved simply by willing it. Anabel has discovered already that sexual relations – which she has thought

to be potentially the most rewarding of human relationships –
may turn out to be the very reverse of rewarding. She says to
Oliver: 'You don't realise how awful passion can be, when it
never resolves, when it never becomes anything else. It is hate,
really.'[23] As so often in Lawrence, the hate may be destructive,
but it may also be a learning experience. Gerald claims to hate
everything, and we are made to see that the hatred is his way of
expressing his fundamental dissatisfaction with himself and with
his own way of life – successful as it has appeared to be in every
material sense. As he says, in anticipation of the angry generation,

> I'm angry with the colliers, with Labour for its low-down
> impudence – and I'm angry with Father for being so ill – and
> I'm angry with Mother for looking such a hopeless thing . . .
> I'm angry with myself for being myself – I always was that. I
> was always a curse to myself.[24]

It is as though we are hearing Jimmy Porter in the 1920s. The fact
that it is Gerald who is speaking, underlines the truth that
dissatisfaction and anger are not the prerogative of a particular
class or generation. Gerald's anger is almost totally self-
destructive – almost, for even Gerald entertains some expectation
of good from it:

GERALD: Nobody is more weary of hate than I am – and yet we
    can't fix our own hour, when we shall leave off hating and
    fighting. It has to work itself out in us.
ANABEL: But I don't *want* to hate and fight with you any more. I
    don't *believe* in it – not any more.
GERALD: It's a cleansing process – like Aristotle's Katharsis. We
    shall hate ourselves clean at last, I suppose.[25]

Anger and hate and conflict are, then, necessary elements in the
process of self-discovery – and in the process of social reform.
Gerald asks for strife in his mining business, and he kicks Job
Arthur Freer to the ground with such savage violence that it
seems as if he meant to kill him. His mother dwells with almost
insane insistence upon the need for strife in order to keep a part
of oneself free for oneself. Finally, the strikers tear Gerald from
his car and, in resentment of his refusal to account for his hatred
of them, throw him to his knees and bait him before attempting to

lynch him. At this point, Anabel, who is now his wife, appeals to the men to recognise that he is a man as they are. Emotions have risen to so dangerous a pitch that Anabel has to scream above the noise of the crowd to be heard and to prevent the lynching. There is about the whole public process a violence which matches (and is greater than) the violence of the emotions which the characters have expressed in private life. Then, just as Anabel has met Gerald's violence of repudiation by entering upon a marriage in which there may well be anger and fighting, Gerald has to meet the men in the acknowledgement that he, too, wants a new way of life, though he cannot describe it better than by saying 'I think we ought to be able to alter the whole system – but not by bullying'. Such a way of life is to be discovered only by struggle. The play ends with the recognition of the need for a common purpose, but it is clear from Gerald's last remarks that there will be no easy agreement upon its nature or upon the road to finding it: 'Now then, step out of my way.'

This is, virtually, a dramatisation of the feelings expressed by Birkin at Breadalby in *Women in Love*:

> I want every man to have his share of the world's goods, so that I am rid of his importunity, so that I can tell him: 'Now you've got your fair share of the world's gear. Now you one-mouthed fool, mind yourself and don't obstruct me.'[26]

These feelings are repeated at some length in the essay on 'Democracy'. Here Lawrence faces the central paradox of romantic idealism, and refuses to offer any recipe for resolving it:

> The only thing man has to trust to in coming to himself is his desire and his impulse. But both desire and impulse tend to fall into mechanical automatism: to fall from spontaneous reality into dead or material reality. All our education should be a guarding against this fall.[27]

The oddity is that the self has to be educated into spontaneity. *Touch and Go*, in its title and in its action, attempts to show this process of education at work in a particular society: it is not a recipe or an example, but an individual instance of possibility.

In providing such instance, *Touch and Go* differs from many of its more pessimistic successors. It holds out a hope for the individual. Gerald can be saved from self-destruction by his wife's confidence that their relationship has meaning. He is saved from the infuriated mob by her insistence that 'He is a man as you are' – that the individual life has value. With some reluctance, Gerald concedes that the mob consists of individuals who can command his sympathy, when he says: 'Look here! I'm quite as tired of my way of life as you are of yours. If you make me believe that you want something better, then I assure you I do: I want what you want.'[28] This longing for a better life is at the heart of all Lawrence's work, but, as Birkin in *Women in Love* and Gerald, here, point out, it is not primarily a bigger share in the world's goods that will bring satisfaction. The real search is the search into the individual nature and into the purpose of human relationships.

> And so each venture
> Is a new beginning, a raid on the inarticulate
> With shabby equipment always deteriorating
> In the general mess of imprecision of feeling,
> Undisciplined squads of emotion.[29]

Odd though it may seem, Eliot's lines perfectly express the aims and progression of Lawrence's plays, and they pinpoint the similarities of the plays to the drama of today, as well as pointing to a fundamental difference from most contemporary drama. Lawrence's characters are so often at the mercy of emotions which they cannot understand: when they begin to understand them, to bring the reasons for the emotions out into the open and to examine them, this process of articulation is painful. It is the beginning of healing and understanding: a new beginning, through recognition of where we are, from which we can make further progress. Lawrence is not a philosophical thinker or a political revolutionary, but his view of human nature is promotive of both thinking and revolution. For all its fierce courage of repudiation of the ways of life around him, Lawrence's drama has roots in them. This high valuation of individual man is one of the relics in Lawrence of that Christian principle which he so often seems to reject because he rejects its uninspired misapplication. His plays make us *feel* that the individual matters, and they assert human dignity. His retreat from reason in order to proclaim the primacy of feelings drives him back again and again to articulate feeling in order to gain control over it. The plays provided an important means for such articulation and control. No less than the novels, they proclaim and enact two apparently opposing truths – the truth that there is no final retreat from reason, and the truth that reason alone is not enough. Emotion cannot merely be indulged and enjoyed, and yet an entirely rational control of conduct may be destructive of the vital powers of the emotions. What Lawrence embodies in his plays is a series of instances or examples of intelligence and intuition working together to prevent either the rational or the emotional from assuming complete control: each hero attains his own dynamic balance or dangerous equilibrium with difficulty, and his life-work is to maintain the balance as he walks the tightrope of experience – a process in which 'There is only the fight to recover what has been lost/And found and lost again and again'.

NOTES

1. W. B. Yeats, *The Letters of W. B. Yeats*, ed. Allan Wade (London: Rupert Hart Davis, 1954) p. 31.
2. N. F. Simpson, *A Resounding Tinkle*, in *New English Dramatists 2*, three plays introduced by Alan Pryce-Jones and edited by Tim Maschler (Harmondsworth: Penguin, 1960) p. 140. The play was first published in 1958.
3. *New English Dramatists 1*, three plays introduced and edited by E. Martin Browne (Harmondsworth: Penguin, 1959) p. 7.
4. Alan Pryce-Jones, in *New English Dramatists 2*, p. 9.
5. 'Nottingham and the Mining Country' is the title of an essay by Lawrence published in 1929.
6. The first remark is from a contribution of Shaw's to *Time and Tide*, 6 August 1932, and the Rolf Gardiner letter is published in *D. H. Lawrence: a Composite Biography*, ed. Edward Nehls (Madison: University of Wisconsin Press, 1957–9) 3 vols; vol. 3, p. 121. I am indebted for both references to *The Life of D. H. Lawrence*, Keith Sagar (London: Eyre Methuen, 1980) p. 214.
7. 'The State of Funk', in *Selected Essays of D. H. Lawrence* (Harmondsworth: Penguin, 1950) p. 99.
8. Letter to Edward Garnett, 14 November 1912 in *Selected Letters of D. H. Lawrence* (Harmondsworth: Penguin, 1950) p. 48.
9. Lawrence, 'The State of Funk'.
10. *The Widowing of Mrs Holroyd*, in *Three Plays by D. H. Lawrence*, with an introduction by Raymond Williams (Harmondsworth: Penguin, 1969) pp. 183, 186, 188.
11. Ibid., p. 197.

12. Lawrence, 'The State of Funk', pp. 98–9.
13. Ann Jellicoe, in an interview in the *New Theatre Magazine*, published by members of the drama faculty of the University of Bristol and cited in John Russell Taylor, *Anger and After* (Pelican, 1963) pp. 69–70.
14. Ibid., p. 67.
15. Arnold Wesker, *Roots*, with introduction by Bernard Levin (Harmondsworth: Penguin, 1959) p. 77.
16. Foreword to *Women in Love*, in *Phoenix II*, ed. F. Warren Roberts and Harry T. Moore (London, 1968) p. 276.
17. Lawrence, *Mrs Holroyd*, pp. 23 ff.
18. See 'Ordinary Cottage', in Osbert Lancaster, *Homes Sweet Homes* (London: John Murray, 1939) and 'Reconstruction', in Osbert Lancaster, *Facades and Faces* (London: John Murray, 1950).
19. Lawrence, *A Collier's Friday Night*, in *Three Plays*.
20. Lawrence, *The Married Man*, in *The Complete Plays of D. H. Lawrence* (London: William Heinemann, 1965) p. 98.
21. Lawrence, *The Merry-go-Round*, in ibid., pp. 468, 469.
22. Lawrence, *The Fight for Barbara*, in *Complete Plays*, p. 280.
23. Lawrence, *Touch and Go*, p. 336.
24. Ibid., p. 352.
25. Ibid., p. 368.
26. Lawrence, *Women in Love* (London: Heinemann, 1921) p. 107.
27. Lawrence, 'Democracy', in *Selected Essays*, p. 91.
28. Lawrence, *Touch and Go*, p. 385.
29. 'East Coker', in T. S. Eliot, *Four Quartets* (London: Faber, 1944) sect. v, p. 22.

15

Lawrence as Historian

GĀMINI SALGĀDO

It is not, perhaps, surprising that *Movements in European History* should be the most neglected of all Lawrence's writings. Yet there are many reasons why anyone interested in Lawrence the novelist, poet or thinker would find his unique venture into the field of school textbooks rewarding reading. Not the least of these is that most of the 300-odd pages of *Movements* are compulsively readable in a sense of that threadbare word which does not exclude mental alertness on either the writer's or the reader's part.

The circumstances of the book's composition and publication are recounted in detail in James Boulton's careful introduction to the 1971 reprint (from which all quotations are taken). They will be referred to here only in order to emphasise certain matters relevant to a just appraisal of Lawrence's effort and achievement. The first point worth making is that although Lawrence wrote the book on a specific commission (at a time when he was very poor and had little or no profitable work to hand), his preoccupations at the time chimed in perfectly well with the task in hand. It was not until sometime in July 1918 that Lawrence received his commission from Oxford University Press (through his friend Vere G. Collins who worked in the OUP London office) to produce a European history text 'for junior forms in grammar or upper forms in primary schools'.[1] But three months earlier he had begun reading Gibbon and the German 'anthropologist' Frobenius. 'I am reading Gibbon', he wrote to Cecil Gray on 18 April 1918. 'I am quite happy with those old Roman emperors – they were out-and-out, they just did as they liked, and *vogue la galère*, till they were strangled. I can do with them.'[2] Ten days later he told Mark Gertler that he 'found great satisfaction' in reading *The Decline and Fall*, but lamented the fact that he had only one of the seven world's Classics volumes by him.[3] It was probably during the walk in the hills with Vere Collins, mentioned in the letter to Edith Eder dated 21 May 1918,[4] that the idea of a history textbook was first mooted. At any rate, the beginning of July finds Lawrence 'in a historical mood', being very near the end of Gibbon, a mood which he elaborates in his letter to Cecil Gray:

> The chief feeling is that men were always alike, and always will be, and one must view the species with contempt first and foremost, and find a few individuals if possible . . . and ultimately, if the impossible were possible, to *rule* the species. It is proper ruling that they need, and always have needed. But it is impossible because they can only be ruled as they are willing to be ruled: and that is swinishly or hypocritically.[5]

The essentialism embodied in the opening remarks was by no means a constant feature of Lawrence's outlook, any more than the low view of humanity that goes with it. Both he and Frieda were influenced by the impact of the harassment which they had suffered since the outbreak of the First World War and by the progress of the war generally. Less than two months earlier, Lawrence had confessed to feeling 'such profound hatred myself, of the human race, I almost know what it is to be a Jew'[6] (apropos Gibbon's remark that 'the Jews are the great *haters* of the human race').

It was not however, a vague and generalised 'historical mood' brought on by reading Gibbon that made the prospect of taking an overall view of European history congenial to Lawrence. The other writings with which he was engaged during the period when he was at work on *Movements* (July 1918 to February 1919) were all concerned with problems of authority and leadership, the individual and the mass, the nature and sources of power in the public world. Chief among these other works were *Aaron's Rod*, begun in September 1918 (not autumn 1917 as Boulton says), *Studies in Classic American Literature* (first completed in June 1918 but revised in August of that year) and four essays on Education, originally intended for the *Times Educational Supplement* but never published there. Many passages in the textbook recall similar ones in both *Aaron's Rod* and the later *Plumed Serpent*, and the Epilogue, commissioned for a 1924 reprint of the book but not published until 1971, is especially illuminating as a commentary on Lawrence's preoccupations in the 'political' novels. Since Lawrence brought to whatever he wrote the energy and temperament of 'the whole man' alive, it is not surprising that *Movements* should also recall, in a simplified form, some of the themes of earlier novels such as *Women in Love* (completed in 1916 but not published until 1920).

Boulton finds a discrepancy between what is promised at the outset by Lawrence, a portrayal of 'the great surging movements which rose in the hearts of men in Europe', and what is actually found in the book, which he calls 'conventional'.[7] However, this contention seems to be based largely on the admittedly conventional-sounding chapter headings – 'The Popes and the Emperors', 'The End of the Age of Faith', 'The Renaissance', and the like, which, according to Boulton, 'prove' that 'the framework for [Lawrence's] historical vision was conventional'. This contrasts oddly with the view expressed immediately afterwards that 'judgments of unusual percipience jostle with bizarre statements' and, together with the allusion to 'a Carlylean approach to the European past',[8] it certainly does more justice to the nature of Lawrence's approach. It would be absurd to claim for Lawrence, on the basis of *Movements*, the status of an original historiographer. He was content to borrow from Gibbon not only most of the information about the history of the ancient world, but even some of the vivid particular detail which lights up an episode or character with memorable brilliance, as in the account of the death of Attila with his bride 'crouching trembling in a corner beside the bed' (p. 81). Gibbon's tone of lofty detachment, with a dash of Carlylean spleen, also appealed to Lawrence's mood in the last months of the war. As for the later period, his chief sources appear to have been G. W. Kitchin's *A History of France*[9] and G. G. Coulton's *From St Francis to Dante*, a book which Lawrence had read in 1916 and which, as L. D. Clark persuasively suggests, was a key influence on Lawrence's view of historical progression, a point to which we shall return later.[10] It is also characteristic that while he was actually writing the book, Lawrence asked friends not so much for weighty works of historical scholarship, but for such books as *Legends of Charlemagne* and Scheffel's *Ekkehard* ('I began him once and never had a chance to finish him', he wrote to S. S. Koteliansky).[11]

But neither the conventional nature of the chapter headings nor a catalogue of influences gives us the fine flavour of Lawrence's engagement with history in this book. The fact that the intended audience was one of schoolchildren (the book was published by the Juvenile and Elementary Schools Department of OUP) naturally sets it apart from the rest of Lawrence's work, but in no way belittles the importance of *Movements* as the author's longest sustained analytical work. His original brief had been 'not . . . to write a formal, connected textbook, but a series of vivid sketches of movements and people',[12] and the very title of the work suggests the fluid and dynamic quality of Lawrence's approach to history, though it is not clear whether it was Lawrence himself or Vere Collins who first proposed it.[13] This also suggests why Lawrence may have been less interested in chapter headings than in the ebb and flow of the work as a whole. Writing to Nancy Henry, to whom he was sending chapters of the book as he completed them, Lawrence makes a clear distinction between the necessary compartmentalisation without which no systematic progress in writing was possible, and the 'clue of developing meaning' which he constantly sought:

> I am going on with the history. I have only one more chapter. Every chapter, I suffer before I can begin, because *I do loathe the broken pots of historical facts*. But once I can get hold of the thread of developing significance, then I am happy, and get ahead. I shall need to revise rather carefully. But you'll see, when you get these 4 last chapters, the book does expand nicely and naturally. I am rather pleased with it. *There is a clue of developing meaning running through it*: that makes it real to me.[14]

This distinction informs the forthright Introduction in which Lawrence identifies three kinds of history. Firstly, there is 'the old bad history' which 'consisted of a register of facts. It drew up a chart of human events, as one might draw up a chart of the currants in a plum-pudding, merely because they happen promiscuously to be there. No more of this' (p. xxv). Only a little less misleading than this is 'graphic history' which consists of 'stories about men and women who appear in the old records, stories as vivid and as personal as may be' (p. xxv). These may be satisfactory for young children, but even for them the personal element, if over-emphasised, would tend to obscure the mystery and otherness of the past by assimilating it too closely to the present for 'personality is local and temporal', whereas true historical writing should confront rather than exclude 'the strange, vast, terrifying reality of the past' (p. xxv). Here Lawrence has a head-on collision with what he calls 'the scientific school' whose business is 'the forging of a great chain of logically sequential events, cause and effect demonstrated down the whole range of time' (p. xxvi). As Lawrence very properly remarks, the only objection to this procedure is the danger of forgetting that the logical sequence which we have established is an abstraction, not something we are discovering but something we are constructing – 'and then it exists as a new piece of furniture of the human mind' (p. xxvi).

None of these approaches corresponds to what Lawrence has in mind, though the collection and arrangement of 'broken pots of historical facts' is an inescapable chore. The essentialist nature of Lawrence's conception of history emerges clearly when he speaks of his task as an attempt 'to give some impression of the great, surging movements which rose in the hearts of men in Europe' (p. xxvi), and explicitly denies that these movements have any ascertainable cause – rather, they are the groundwork of causality:

> Inside the hearts, or souls, of men in Europe there has happened at times some strange surging, some welling-up of unknown powers. These powers that well up inside the hearts of men, these are the fountains and origins of human history. And the welling-up has no ascribable cause. It is naked cause itself. (p. xxvii)

As Lawrence was clearly aware, there is a constant tension between the need for sequential arrangement in some sort of quasi-causal pattern and the charting of the 'strange surging, [the] welling-up of unknown powers'. But the reader of *Movements* is sufficiently conscious of the latter to cast doubt on Boulton's assertion that the framework of Lawrence's historical vision was conventional.

An instance of Lawrence's devotion to 'the clue of developing meaning' may be found in his approach to the question of the great man in history. Sidney Hook, in *The Hero in History*,[15] makes a useful distinction between the eventful hero, who embodies in himself and stands at the head of certain crucial tendencies of his time, and the *event-making* hero, who gives a decisive new direction or emphasis. In these terms, Lawrence's heroes are eventful rather than event-making. Indeed, this would seem to be a necessary consequence of the view of history as the attempt to capture the 'great motions from within the soul of mankind' (p. xxvii) which are, in Lawrentian terms, strictly inexplicable. As he explains at the outset, personality is local and temporal, not only in the sense that 'each age has its own' but also because 'each age proceeds to interpret every other age in terms of the current personality', as Shakespeare and Shaw interpret Caesar as respectively Elizabethan and Victorian (p. xxv). The 'eternal impersonal Caesar whom we *can* know, historically' is the figure who incorporates into himself 'the great surging movements' of his time which are 'greater than any one man, though in individual men the power is at its greatest' (p. xxviii). And since, by definition, these movements are ultimately embodied within individuals, the great man is in some sense a representative of the will of the people, however undemocratic or unconstitutional the steps by which he had attained power. This view of the hero emerges clearly in Lawrence's remarks on Napoleon:

> Napoleon became an almost absolute sovereign, much as Louis XIV had been. But Napoleon ruled in the name of the people, according to the agreement of the people. Though he was supreme, he was supreme because the people willed it, not because he had been appointed by God. Louis XIV claimed to be king by divine right: the people had nothing to do with it. Napoleon was emperor by the will of the people, although, for form's sake, he crowned himself in presence of the Pope. (p. 251)

In the account of the Gallic chieftains and their power and influence, the same notion is present: 'It was a glitter of arrogance and bravery, and a humbling of all people for their glorification in one man. Of course it was the people who chose this' (pp. 86–7). Even such an unpromising figure as Attila is pressed into service as a man of the people: 'Attila is perhaps the greatest barbarian conqueror that ever lived. His people loved him, worshipped him as a great magician. "Attila, my Attila" sang the warriors' (p. 76). The great periods of history, in Lawrence's view, are characterised by the appearance of heroes who truly incarnate within themselves the passion that, in milder measure, animates their people.

The preoccupations that were to find their culmination in *The Plumed Serpent* (begun in 1923), and the novel's enquiry into the possibility and implications of one man embodying and transcending the general will, are clearly anticipated here. They are not finally abandoned until, two years before his death, Lawrence writes to Witter Bynner that 'The hero is obsolete, and

the leader of men is a back number . . . the leader-cum-follower
relationship is a bore'.[16]

True to his vision that consciousness determines social existence
and that the decisive shifts of consciousness in history are not
'caused' but are 'naked cause itself', Lawrence does not hesitate
to chart such shifts as unambiguously mysterious. Remarks such
as 'some men were weary to death of fighting . . . they wanted
peace and the stillness of the soul above all things' (p. 97) and 'All
over Europe began a great ferment in the souls of men' (p. 172)
occur throughout the book. Even the 'simple-minded shorthand',
in Boulton's dismissive phrase, of comments such as 'After the
Age of Faith dawned the Age of Reason' (p. 170) may be the
result of a deliberate intention to emphasise 'the impersonal,
terrific element, the sense of the unknown' (p. xxvi) in history, for

> All that real history can do is to note with wonder and reverence
> the tides which have surged out from the innermost heart of
> man, watch the incalculable flood and ebb of such tides.
> Afterwards, there is a deducible sequence. Beforehand there is
> none.   (p. xxviii)

But if the central shifts of consciousness are strictly inexplicable,
developments within them are amenable to exposition in terms of
'a deducible sequence'. Thus we are offered explanations which
are undeniably historical in the ordinary sense, whether we find
them convincing or otherwise, as for instance that 'the spirit of
Germanic independence and individual liberty had combined
with the old Roman ideal of social unity, and the first signs of real
European life appeared' (p. 106). Similarly, Lawrence's
account of Christianity is both coherent and plausible. It owes a
good deal to Gibbon and even achieves a quasi-Gibbonian urbanity
in its account of the odd behaviour of the Jews towards towards
the pagan gods. It combines a Nietzschean view of Christianity's
appeal to slaves with a playful description of pagan worship,
Keats without the time-hauntedness; and its exposition of Christian
inability to participate in much of Roman social life because it was
so permeated with religion is both succinct and sensible.

The misanthropy and crude essentialism expressed in the letter
to Cecil Gray ('men were always alike and always will be, and one
must view the species with contempt') is clearly a product of
Lawrence's experiences in the war years. It is by no means a

pervasive feature of the book which is characterised at its best by the sense of wonder and reverence that Lawrence proposed to himself as an ideal. Nor are 'the great surging movements which rose in the hearts of men in Europe' entirely without pattern or significance. Lawrence's historical vision is a curious amalgam of the cyclical, the apocalyptic and what we called, clumsily, mystical whiggery. To take the last first, there is a reading of European history as falling into three phases: up to the Renaissance history is the story of man's appetite for military glory and conquest, while from the Renaissance to the eighteenth century men 'live in the joy of producing, the joy of making things' (p. 197). This is followed by the period which European history is presently in, 'when the leaders of industry, the rich men of the middle class really rule' (p. 293). The mysticism appears when Lawrence looks to the future and sees the commercial and industrial ruling class at last giving way to 'the last reign of wisdom, of pure understanding, the reign which we have never seen in the world, but which we must see' (p. 198). Looking back from the perspective offered here, it is clear, as L. D. Clark points out in *The Minoan Distance*, that the ultimate source for Lawrence's tripartite view of history is the apocalyptic vision of the twelfth-century theologian Joachim of Flora, which Lawrence would have come across in his reading of Coulton's *From St Francis to Dante*. The Joachite view of history sees it as divided into three phases: the first is the period of the dispensation of the Father, when Law and Faith are dominant. This lasts until the coming of Christ, when it is succeeded by the gospel of Love under the dispensation of the Son. The last age, whose advent Joachim puts at *c*. 1260, is the age of wisdom under the dispensation of the Holy Ghost. In this last age, the Holy Ghost would work directly through the hearts of men, using as instruments great and good men outside the clergy.

Lawrence is understandably vague about 'the last reign of wisdom'. The words come in the chapter on the Renaissance, where they form the conclusion of a paragraph and are not directly referred to again in the body of the book. But in the Epilogue, he returns to the idea by way of variations on one of his favourite metaphors, that of the tree of life or of man.

The Epilogue was commissioned by Oxford University Press in order to bring the history up to date when a reprint was planned in 1924. In the event, it was not used and remained unpublished until 1971. Charles Williams, the poet and novelist, and C. R. L. Fletcher, a Fellow of All Souls (the writer of *The Making of Modern Europe* and co-author, with Rudyard Kipling, of *A School History of England* (1911)), reported for the Press on the Epilogue. Williams was generally in favour, though he could find little more in the Epilogue than 'general advice to "be good" ', and confessed to having lost interest in Lawrence since he 'got religion'. Fletcher, however, was unequivocally hostile. Among much else, he found fault with Lawrence's grammar (' "Like a tree" is not a sentence'), with Lawrence's remarks on Lloyd George and the bracketing of the latter with the wartime swindler Horatio Bottomley, and with 'the doctrine that the war was either the cause or the effect of the sudden death of humanity' (p. xv). Nevertheless, the Epilogue remains a key document for the understanding of Lawrence's views on European history, past and present.

The tree metaphor appears in the second sentence, together with the essentialism that figures throughout the book: 'Mankind is like a huge old tree: there are deep roots that go down to the earth's centre, and there is the massive stem of primitive culture, where all men are very much alike' (p. 307). While 'in its root and trunk, Mankind is one' (p. 308), its branches are the different races, each with its own 'growing tip' (a phrase whose repetition in the Epilogue brought Fletcher, by his own account, to near-hysteria). This notion of each race having its own distinctive rhythm and direction of development combines uneasily with the idea that 'the whole tree of Man has one supreme travelling apex, one culminating growing tip' (p. 309). During the past millenium that growing tip has been Europe. But the European spirit progressively decayed until the First World War finally disintegrated it – 'Now we are directionless' (p. 310).

The motive forces of progress and free competition, and the associated ideals of liberty, equality and fraternity, have been shown up for the dead wood they are by the storm of the war. But the alternatives that face post-war Europe, Socialism or Fascism, are equally unappealing. Though Lawrence categorically declares: 'Myself, personally, I believe that a good form of Socialism, if it could be brought about, would be the best form of government' (p. 315), both Fascism and Socialism become forms of bullying when power is divorced from responsibility. The most sinister and pervasive example in the modern world of irresponsible power is the force of Finance: 'A few hundred men on the face of the earth, with huge sums of money behind them, exert their wills and minds in order that money shall and must go on producing money, no matter what lives or loss of honour it may cost' (p. 319). Not surprisingly, the central question facing the modern world becomes that of incorporating responsible power in appropriate political institutions. Democratic election by itself can no more guarantee this than can Socialism or Fascism, for the masses have been conditioned to desire short-term material objects only, nor is there anything to be expected from Monarchy or the traditional Aristocracy. The only hope lies in each man recognising in himself the spark of true *noblesse oblige* (Lawrence's term) and acting from it, rather than from his materialistic impulses, in order to bring to power those individuals who have the strength and the will to act in the public arena from similar impulses. The 'great historical change' becomes a change of heart, when each man or woman recognises 'the spark of nobelesse' within and determines 'to follow only the leader who is the star of the new, *natural noblesse*' (p. 321; Lawrence's italics).

Perhaps Charles Williams was right in remarking that the Epilogue came to no more than Tennyson's 'we needs must love the highest'. Leavis once remarked that we would not go to Lawrence for advice on political action. Nevertheless, the Epilogue does demonstrate clearly that Lawrence's refusal to engage in a specific political programme was not due to what Eliot in a notorious phrase called 'an incapacity for what we ordinarily call thinking'. Given his view that a change of consciousness must precede a change in social institutions, Lawrence addresses himself to the question of where such a change must originate, and locates it in the 'better self, which is quiet, and slow, and which is most of the time puzzled' (p. 312), which each man has and which is distinguished from the 'herd-self, which is vulgar, common, ugly'. To put the point in language which may be more acceptable though no clearer, political action must spring from true consciousness rather than from the false consciousness which results from the internalisation of the dominant ideology. All truly human action, when it is not determined by habit or fear, springs from this self, which is closely identified with the Lawrentian (as opposed to the Freudian) notion of the unconscious which is 'the well-head, the fountain of real motivity' as

Lawrence calls it in *Psychoanalysis and the Unconscious*. It is from this source that 'the last reign of wisdom, of pure understanding' must come, if it is to come at all.

It remains to note briefly some points of contact between *Movements* and some of Lawrence's other writings. As already mentioned, Lawrence was at work on the book from early in July 1918 to the end of April in the following year. During this period he was also engaged in writing and reviewing *Studies in Classic American Literature* (completed May–June 1918, revised August 1918), and *Aaron's Rod* (begun September 1918, completed April 1921). The apocalyptic vein of the Melville essay in the former (Doom of our white day) is faintly echoed in the textbook ('So Europe moves from oneness to oneness . . . from the beginning to the end' (p. 306)) and there is a parallel between the idea of the modern American as the product of a fusion between the European and the native Indian, and of the modern European as the outcome of a similar fusion between the races of the icy North and the warm South. But the latter notion has important consequences for the polarities dramatised in, for instance, *Women in Love*, and it is worth pausing at Lawrence's formulation of it in *Movements*:

> The Romans of Latium were short, dark men of the wine-loving lands. Their great strength lay in their courage, and in their power of faithfulness, their intelligent, disciplined acting together for one united purpose. . . .
> The great Teutonic race seemed the indomitable opposite of the Romans. These short, energetic dark-eyed men looked with astonishment at the huge naked fair limbs of the men from the northern forests, at fresh, fierce faces with their blue eyes, and at the yellow hair – or the hair dyed bright red. These almost naked, big, white-skinned men lay and lounged about in an abandoned indolence, when no warfare was at hand: whereas the Romans were always spruce and aware of their conduct.   (pp. 43–4)

Lawrence explains the failure of the Romans to conquer decisively the Teutonic north as being due to the fact that in pursuing them to the gloomy forests of the north, the Romans 'felt they had gone beyond their natural limits' (p. 44) and his further description of the Nordic type irresistibly recalls the descriptive imagery associated with Gerald Crich:

> It is as if the white-skinned men of the Germanic races were born from the northern sea, the heavy waves, the white snow, the yellow wintry sun, the perfect beautiful blue of ice. They had the fierceness and strength of the northern oceans, the keenness of ice. (p. 45)

It is interesting to note though, that in portraying Gerald in these terms, Lawrence seems to have transposed to him some of the attributes of the Roman type, such as intelligence, discipline and efficiency, and invested Birkin with something of the insouciance of the Teutons' 'minds utterly indifferent and negligent'.

The reader of Lawrence's novels could hardly fail to recognise the tremendous stress placed in *Movements* on changes of consciousness as the motive force of historical change, though not its trigger mechanism. Just as the narrative rhythm of *Women in Love* is based on changing states of feeling in the principal characters, which impel them to act and respond to others in certain ways, so it is the 'welling-up of unknown powers' as they are amplified into 'the great, surging movements which rose in the hearts of men in Europe' which the history avowedly attempts to trace. This goes a long way to counteract the mechanical dividing of the book into chapters, and contributes as much to the feeling that it often 'reads like a novel' as do the occasional brilliant descriptions which recall Lawrence at his best – 'the plain of Salices white with the big bones of the Goths, the smaller, finer bones of the Romans' (p. 60). Also very Lawrentian is the manner in which concrete images are developed in *Movements*. There are, inevitably, a certain number of set pieces ranging from the memorable to the perfunctory, the former category including Constantine's vision of his new city (pp. 14–15) and parts of the chapter on the Crusades. But, in the main, Lawrence's historical thinking develops in images rather than scenes, and this is related to the Lawrentian intuition of the individual's essential thinking being historical, in the sense that history is not so much where you are as what you want. This element of libidinal investment is characteristic of Lawrence's presentation of the great men in history, and serves to distinguish it from the Carlylean approach to the hero. The central figures in Lawrence's history are those who are more sharply and fully aware than others of what they want, and the images of their desire animate Lawrence's writing throughout. From this point of view, Gerald Crich may be seen as a 'failed' great character, and figures such as Rawdon Lilly, Somers in *Kangaroo* and Don Ramón in *The Plumed Serpent* as great characters in the making, coming into full awareness of their desires while at the same time mysteriously gathering into themselves the will of the people. Rawdon Lilly's words could very easily have been part of the Epilogue to *Movements*.

> All men say, they want a leader. Then let them in, their souls *submit* to some greater soul than theirs. At present when they say they want a leader, they mean they want an instrument, like Lloyd George. A mere instrument for their use. But it's more than that. It's the reverse. It's the deep, fathomless submission to the heroic soul in a greater man.[17]

The difference between a leader and an instrument is precisely one of desire, sharpened and self-aware.

Movements in European History cannot, perhaps, be regarded as one of Lawrence's major writings. The constraints under which it was written, in particular the necessity to address itself to adolescent readers and to rely largely on secondary source material, make it less than completely Lawrentian. Yet it is not so far away from characteristically Lawrentian concerns and modes of expression as to justify its current neglect. In Lawrence's own words it attempts, very often successfully, to 'introduce the deep, philosophic note into education: deep, philosophic reverence'.

NOTES

1. *D. H. Lawrence: a Composite Biography*, ed. E. Nehls (Madison: University of Wisconsin Press, 1957–9) I, p. 471.
2. *The Collected Letters of D. H. Lawrence*, ed. Harry T. Moore (London: Heinemann, 1962) I, p. 550.
3. Ibid., p. 551.
4. Ibid., p. 553.
5. Ibid., p. 561.

6. Ibid., p. 553.
7. D. H. Lawrence, *Movements in European History*, with an Introduction by James T. Boulton (Oxford: Oxford University Press, 1971) p. xviii. All subsequent references are to this edition.
8. Ibid., p. xix.
9. See the article on the ill-fated Irish edition of *Movements* by P. Crumpton in *D. H. Lawrence Review*, xiii, no. 2 (Summer 1980).
10. L. D. Clark, *The Minoan Distance* (Tucson: University of Arizona Press, 1980).
11. *Collected Letters*, ed. Moore, i, p. 573.
12. *Biography*, ed. Nehls, i, p. 471.
13. See 'Mark Tellar' (Vere Collins), *A Young Man's Passage* (London, 1952) and Lawrence's letter of 3 February 1919 to Nancy Henry, in *Letters*, ed. A. Huxley (London: Heinemann, 1932) p. 467.
14. Ibid., p. 466; my italics.
15. Sidney Hook, *The Hero in History* (London, 1945) pp. 107–27.
16. *Collected Letters*, ed. Moore, ii, p. 1045.
17. D. H. Lawrence, *Aaron's Rod* (Harmondsworth: Penguin, 1950) p. 347.

16

D. H. Lawrence: the Hero-Poet as Letter Writer

GEORGE A. PANICHAS

'But the great are near; we know them at sight'.
(Ralph Waldo Emerson)

I

Of D. H. Lawrence's letters it can be said, as Lionel Trilling once said of John Keats' letters, that they give a picture of a certain kind of man: a hero. There are, of course, different kinds of heroes and different gradations of heroism. In Keats, according to Trilling, we discern a heroic vision of the tragic life and the tragic salvation, 'the soul accepting the fate that defines it'.[1] Lawrence's conception of heroism is far more passional than tragic, or, as he himself wrote in the Preface to his play *Touch and Go* (1922): 'Tragedy is the working out of some immediate passional problem within the soul of man.'[2] In his Introduction to Giovanni Verga's *Mastro-don Gesualdo*, Lawrence laments the absence of heroic awareness, and hope, and insists on the primacy of heroic effort, 'that instinctive fighting for more life to come into being'. For Lawrence, modern man's tendency to make the hero self-conscious and introspective reduces the possibility of splendour and self-enhancement. 'Life', he declares, 'without the heroic effort, and without *belief* in the subtle, life-long validity of the heroic impulse, is just stale, flat and unprofitable'.[3] In his own life, heroic effort characterised Lawrence's struggle 'for more life to come into being'. Even when one reads his death-poems, written at the end of his life, it is the heroic impulse that remains evident. This heroism, at once personal and critical, is at the heart of Lawrence's letter indicting Aldous Huxley's *Point Counter Point* (1928):

I have read *Point Counter Point* with a heart sinking through my boot-soles and a rising admiration. I do think you've shown the truth, perhaps the last truth, about you and your generation, with really fine courage. It seems to me it would take ten times the courage to write *P. Counter P.* that it took to write *Lady C.*: and if the public knew *what* it was reading, it would throw a hundred stones at you, to one at me. I do think that art has to reveal the palpitating moment or the state of man as it is. And I think you do that, terribly. But what a moment! and what a state! if you can only palpitate to murder, suicide, and rape, in their various degrees – and you state plainly that it is so – caro, however are we going to live through the days? Preparing still another murder, suicide, and rape? But it becomes of a phantasmal boredom and produces ultimately inertia, inertia, inertia and final atrophy of the feelings. Till, I suppose, comes a final super-war, and murder, suicide, rape sweeps away the vast bulk of mankind. It is as you say – intellectual appreciation does not amount to so much, it's what you thrill to. And if murder, suicide, rape is what you thrill to, and nothing else, then it's your destiny – you can't change it *mentally*. You live by what you thrill to, and there's the end of it. Still for all that it's a perverse courage which makes the man accept the slow suicide of inertia and sterility: the perverseness of a perverse child.[4]

We see crystallised in this passage Lawrence's heroic impulse, personal and prophetic as well as literary and cultural, or what F. R. Leavis sums up as 'the life-courage in the product of his creativity'. Lawrence's heroism, as it expresses and defines itself in his letters with astonishing consistency and sincerity, and as such expresses and defines his deepest self, is not to be seen on a grand scale or in some majestic framework, for in this aspect, too, he maintained strong and direct control: that of a controlling intelligence always in touch with reality. Any careful rereading of Lawrence's indictment of *Point Counter Point* should confirm an interweaving critical intelligence and a humanistic concern that give his words their tone and authority, their integrity – their humility. Lawrence's heroism does not produce ecstatic flight, it does not fall into illusion, it does not induce reverie; it is neither a martial heroism nor a romantic heroism, but rather substantive, active and humane heroism, sensitive to limits and respectful of the differences between appearance and reality. It is, in short, a living and discriminating heroism. In its critical honesty, too, there reside its sympathy and generosity. Its openness – the attempt of the writer to give of himself as authentically as he can, without any attitudinising or moralising, without the sham of mechanical or politic pieties – is exactly that openness which Lawrence, in a letter to Catherine Carswell, associates with the writing of poetry itself (in a passage later praised by T. S. Eliot): 'The essence of poetry with us in this age of stark and unlovely actualities is a stark directness, without a shadow of a lie, or a shadow of deflection anywhere. Everything can go, but this stark, bare, rocky directness of statement, this alone makes poetry today.'[5] Lawrence as a letter writer speaks that language of honesty and courage which he demands not only of poetry but also of one's spiritual being. In the face of the persistent attempts of critical revisionists to submerge Lawrence in the 'river of dissolution', it needs to be insisted that his letters underscore an innately religious vision and search, conveyed and conducted with that endemic moral strength that Lawrence discloses in this sentence; 'For me, it is better to die than to do something which is utterly a violation to my soul.'[6]

One ultimately reads Lawrence's letters, in their totality and spiritual unity, as *explications de héroïsme*. An unfailing and undoubting consistency informs the letters from beginning to end. No matter what the degree of adversity or the pull of despair, his letters accentuate a note of final affirmation: 'Life *can* be great – quite godlike. It *can* be so.'[7] Early on in his letters, Lawrence casts the heroic element in the form of rebirth. Writing to A. W. McLeod, he declares: 'I hate England and its hopelessness. I hate [Arnold] Bennett's resignation. Tragedy ought really to be a great kick at misery. But *Anna of the Five Towns* seems like an acceptance – so does all the modern stuff since Flaubert. I hate it. I want to wash again quickly, wash off England, the oldness and grubbiness and despair.'[8] Shortly after, this time in a letter to Joseph Conrad's (and Lawrence's) generous friend and helper, Edward Garnett, he has this to say on the great novelist: 'But why this giving in before you start, that pervades all Conrad and such folks – the Writers among the Ruins. I can't forgive Conrad for being so sad and for giving in.'[9] Lawrence's decision to be his own man as an artist was nothing less than heroic: 'They want me to have form: that means, they want me to have *their* pernicious ossiferous skin-and-grief form, and I won't.'[10] A mixture of confidence and arrogance often characterises his statements: 'Read my novel [*Sons and Lovers*]', he advises Garnett. 'It's a great novel. If *you* can't see the development – which is slow, like growth – I can.'[11] His faith in his genius, and in his destiny as a man and his mission as an artist, have an impelling resoluteness of purpose. 'I shall change the world for the next thousand years', he declares. It is as a catechumen that Lawrence speaks in this extraordinary passage in an early letter to Ernest Collings: 'I often think one ought to be able to pray, before one works – and then leave it to the Lord. Isn't it hard, hard work to come to real grips with one's imagination – throw everything overboard? I always feel as if I stood naked for the fire of Almighty God to go through me – and it's rather an awful feeling. One has to be so terribly religious, to be an artist.'[12]

These words remind us of a presiding reverence in Lawrence's life and art. Reverence embodies a disciplined fusion of passion and principle, the two most active energies that, for Lawrence, create a delicate equilibrium and that belong to and embody the life of virtue and the idea of value. The possession of this quality of reverence is for Lawrence a precondition to the religious search for meaning and to one's need to attain a fuller relationship between one's self and the universe and between one's self and one's fellow men and women. 'We have to know how to go out and meet one another, upon the third ground, the holy ground', we find Lawrence writing to Rolf Gardiner in 1926, his words containing the biblical pulsebeat that one hears in some of his most inspired prose fiction.[13] Spiritual heroism, in the context of 'the courage to be', radiates in Lawrence's letters. A metaphysic of virtue and value, however, remains dangerously one-dimensional, incomplete and unconsummated without due attention to what Lawrence called 'the phallic consciousness'. His adjectival emphasis here undoubtedly troubled even some of his most ardent supporters as his experiment with the language of emotions became increasingly radical, to judge especially by late writings like *Lady Chatterley's Lover* (1928) and *The Man Who Died* (1931). But critical irritability should not be allowed to distort Lawrence's heroic vision, anchored as it is in concern and commitment. His art is his heroic vision insofar as Lawrence also creates there, *inter alia*, his phallic conception of heroism and embodies heroic qualities appropriate to the modern age. Lawrence's is a heroism of possibility; eventually it is even an apocalyptic heroism, to be viewed against the background of the great crisis of civilisation that announced itself with the Great War of 1914–18. If Lawrence was aware of the need for virtue and value in relation to what Simone Weil terms 'the need for roots', he was also aware of a need for returning to 'the source of all real beauty, and all real gentleness': 'And those are the two things, tenderness and beauty, which will save us from horrors'.[14]

What impresses one when reading Lawrence's letters is the religious tone of his language, particularly when he discourses on his literary aesthetic. A numinous quality is pervasive, disclosed in a reverent awareness of the idea of the holy, which reminds us of Lawrence's contention that the imagination is, at its maximum, religious. What perhaps best distinguishes Lawrence's letters, when they are read and judged in their collective thrust and meaning, is the element of transcendence that informs and defines, giving distinction and recognition to, his burden of vision, his view of himself as a novelist-poet. That self-view is heroic in precisely that spiritual sense that Jacob Burckhardt identifies with 'greatness of soul', which gives the poet 'the power to forego benefits in the name of morality, in voluntary self-denial, not merely from motives of prudence but from goodness of heart'.[15] Strength and greatness of soul, at their depths heroic in the full sense of the word, are at the heart of Lawrence's vision. For what else better identifies what Lawrence terms the 'heroic effort' that must be exerted before enacting the kind of self-searching, and self-humility, that appears in this passage of a letter to Edward Garnett: 'But primarily I am a passionately religious man, and my novels must be written from the depth of my religious experience. . . . But you should see the religious, earnest, suffering man in me first, and then the flippant or common things after.'[16]

Thomas Carlyle recalls for us the great worth of the 'Hero-Poet' in whom we hear the voice of genius, 'to be heard of all men and times'.[17] In Lawrence's letters that voice never wearies; his seriousness of purpose and commitment and his honesty are undeviating and uncompromising. Lawrence's transparency is one of the most exceptional qualities of his heart and mind and soul, in their triadic harmony of relationship. The letters, as an extension of and commentary on his art, possess an equivalent honesty, the language of which, in its thought and expression, discloses a constant attempt to communicate 'a complete truth of feeling'. Lawrence's letters dramatise his innate concern with providing a language of integrity, enabling him to confront himself in relation to another without recrimination or guilt. His quest is always that of transcending, by defeating and excising, any attitudinal or false language that impedes the emotional and linguistic approximation of a deeper and a purer truth as it emerges from one's tensions of consciousness. Lawrence's letters, in their spontaneity of expression, bring one into contact with an inviolable, innocent self; and that contact is Lawrence's attained version of virtue as a diffracted form of moral life. 'A true virtue', Romano Guardini tells us, 'signifies an ability to penetrate with a glance the whole existence of man'.[18] In his art, Lawrence's 'glance' acquires its consummate and universal scope. In his letters, however, it is Lawrence's interior 'glance' that stirs one most. Self-examination, *de rigueur*, is the process encountered here, especially in the pre-1918 letters. What Lawrence writes about his second novel, *The Trespasser* (1912), tells us something also about his epistolary process, in its own inner struggle and demands: 'But this is a work one can't regard easily – I mean, at one's ease. It is so much oneself, one's naked self. I give myself away so much, and write what is my most palpitant, sensitive self, that I loathe the book, because it will betray me to a parcel of fools.'[19]

In the letters prior to the Great War, one sees Lawrence the aspiring poet-novelist, unalterably loyal to his commitment to his art. A kind of electrical energy infuses his literary effort to understand and clarify and define his vision; and invariably his letters attest to the seriousness of his purposes as an artist. Moral courage is at the centre of his attempt to come to grips with his imaginative genius; fearless exploration of his sensibility brings from him self-revelation of profound significance: 'But one sheds one's sicknesses in books – repeats and presents again one's emotions, to be master of them'.[20] 'I have always tried to get an emotion out in its own course, without altering it. It needs the finest instinct imaginable, much finer than the skill of the craftsmen.'[21] 'I don't care about physiology of matter – but somehow – that which is physic – non-human, in humanity, is more interesting to me than the old-fashioned human element – which causes one to conceive a character in a certain moral scheme and make him consistent.'[22] The early letters abound with statements like these, filled as they are with faith and courage and with enthusiasm and confidence. Lawrence's concern with literary criteria, as these bring him closer to a realisation of his genius, shows a tough and persevering critical intelligence. If that concern is self-critical, it is also selfless in the context of Lawrence's total involvement in mastering his creative impulse. 'It needs a certain purity of spirit to be an artist, of any sort', he was to write in a 1929 essay, 'Making Pictures'.[23]

II

The Great War was undoubtedly a dire threat to Lawrence's belief in heroic impulse and effort, and posed the kind of danger to Lawrence's 'societal instinct' ('Myself, I suffer badly from being so cut off') that, analogously, his mother's death in 1910 caused to his personal life. These twin disasters did not, in the end, defeat Lawrence's heroic apprehension of life, though they did sharpen his sense of the immense difficulties impinging on the possibilities of existence. We find progressively in Lawrence, after 1914, heroic endurance in the face of loss and desolation. We are now in connection with a man who sees himself in a world falling apart and in which possibility gives way to death. 'I've got again into one of those horrible sleeps from which I can't wake', we find him writing to Lady Ottoline Morrell. 'I can't brush it aside to wake up. You know those horrible sleeps when one is struggling to wake up, and can't.'[24] The struggle to awake from 'those horrible sleeps' remained his fate until his death in 1930. It is not hard to make a connection between Lawrence's nightmare of war and the conditions that he deplores in his indictment of *Point Counter Point*. Huxley's novel is a verification of Lawrence's prophetic witness and testimony. His suffering during the war years, and its aftermath, was in its unique way prophetic: 'The persistent nothingness of the war makes me feel like a paralytic convulsed with rage.'[25] But these words of negation are repeatedly assuaged by Lawrence's heroic determination not to surrender to the Negative: 'One must speak for life and growth, amid all this mass of destruction and disintegration.'[26] Lawrence never abandoned his faith in the redemptive theme, 'Look! We have come through!' Paul Tillich's words help us to fathom the condition of Lawrence's interior self and the essence of his heroic outlook: 'Courage is the self-affirmation of being in spite of the fact of nonbeing.'[27]

The letters of this period are a graph of those sharp tensions of consciousness, of being versus nonbeing, that Lawrence confronted in the years after 1914. Externally, of course, this was a time of perils to humanism, for the war embodied a total crisis of civilisation, when 'the past, the great past', as Lawrence wrote, was 'crumbling down, breaking down . . . the past, the past, the falling, perishing, crumbling past, so great, so magnificent'.[28] 'Hopelessness', 'decomposition', 'decline', 'nothingness', 'blasphemy': these words form a leitmotiv in Lawrence's language of nonbeing in relation to his feelings about the teleology of 'the outer world'. At the same time, Lawrence's inner being had to face even greater menaces, these often becoming, in the process, painful 'wounds to the soul, to the deep emotional self', as his creative genius, with its 'heaps of vitality', wrestles with an outer world of nullity; as the power of being, to paraphrase Tillich, struggles to transcend nonbeing with its anxiety of emptiness, meaninglessness, guilt and condemnation. Lawrence invokes a deeper form of courage, religious and spiritual in its roots: an ascetic heroism that brings St Paul to mind (and prefigures Tillich's paradigms of 'the courage to be') when one considers this passage from one of Lawrence's letters of 1916: 'One must forget, only forget, turn one's eyes from the world: that is all. One must live quite apart, forgetting, having another world, a world as yet uncreated. Everything lies in *being*, although the whole world is one colossal madness, falsity, a stupendous assertion of not-being.'[29] Lawrence's frantic search for 'another country', for a 'new life' to be found there in 'the unreal world' and in the 'inner soul', now commences and continues until the end, when he finally sails away on his 'ship of death' ('for you must take/the longest journey to oblivion./And die the death, the long and painful death/that lies between the old self and the new'). A ceaseless interior debate rages between the Lawrence of nonbeing and the Lawrence of being; between the Lawrence who cries out, 'for I am no more a man, but a walking phenomenon of suspended fury',[30] and the Lawrence who affirms, 'Only the living heart and the creative spirit matters – *nothing else*'.[31] In addressing himself to the perennial debate between *pro and contra*, Lawrence expresses a power of self-affirmation rooted in courage and transcendence; he expresses, in effect, a heroism of great spiritual magnitude when viewed in those defining contexts of which Tillich writes: 'The faith which makes the courage of despair possible is the acceptance of the power of being, even in the grip of nonbeing.'[32]

Yet Lawrence's faith should not be approached as a theology of heroism, for it is too closely shaped by what Huxley once spoke of as his friend's 'mystical materialism'. That is, Lawrence's heroism, like his art, was the product of his *daemon*, ultimately manifested as a *numen*. Lawrence renders that heroism concretely rather than abstractly. Belonging to the realm of creative thought, it is a heroism of striving and possibility rather than of revelation and grace. 'It is necessary to get the germ of a new development *towards the highest*, not a reduction to the lowest', he stresses.[33] Lawrence is not a hero-saint but rather a hero-poet whose articles of faith, in the form of 'the living intuitive faculty', give substance to what Dr Leavis terms 'the living principle'. 'Let us be easy and impersonal', Lawrence writes to Katherine Mansfield, 'not for ever fingering over our souls, and the souls of our acquaintances, but trying to create a new life from the roots that are within us. . . . [W]e must grow from out deepest underground roots, out of the *unconsciousness*, not from the conscious concepts which we falsely call ourselves.'[34] In the war, Lawrence saw the substitution of pseudo-heroism for the integral heroism that is needed to create 'a perfectly new *body* of purpose'. 'But we are not compelled to live', Lawrence wrote in an essay, 'The Reality' (1917). 'We are only compelled to die. . . . We must *choose* life, for life will never compel us.'[35] If, before the war, Lawrence was seeking to find the best means of presenting the courage of his genius ('write what is my most palpitant, sensitive self') and to discipline and refine his vision, without violating that 'certain purity of spirit' that he deemed indispensable for an artist, during and after the war he discerned his main task to be one that sought for the survival, and the resurgence, of 'the great creative process'. 'War cannot be thought of, for me, without the utmost repulsion and desecration of one's being', he wrote to Lady Cynthia Asquith.[36] The need of survival no doubt presented serious problems for the Lawrence who suffered the full extent of his 'deaths in belief'. In his war letters, as they might be called, Lawrence was often to show an ability to withdraw from a 'foul world' and to maintain 'a separate isolated fate': 'Believe me, I am infinitely hurt by being thus torn off from the body of mankind, but so it is, and it is right'.[37]

At times, in his furious protestations against the war, Lawrence discloses an independent lyrical note and his language becomes infused with tragic grandiloquence, as well as excessively self-righteous pleas and feelings. On these occasions the role of the preacher in Lawrence gets the better of him as missionary zeal and a pontifical style colour his reactions: 'I think I am almost ready to set out preaching also, now: not only cessation of war, but the beginning of a new world.'[38] But these occasions are essentially abbreviated and transitional, another phase in 'the voyage of discovery towards the real and eternal and unknown land'. In the letters that record these occasions, it is Lawrence the moralist rhetor who is speaking, simultaneously revealing the art of reasoning and teaching by similitudes and analogies, as found in this excerpt from a letter to Lady Cynthia Asquith:

> Oh, and *do not think* I blame the Government or howl at it. The fools who howl at the Government make my blood boil. I respect the Prime Minister [Herbert Henry Asquith] because I believe in his real decency and I think Lloyd George, etc., are toads. I must here assert again that the war is and continues because of the lust for hate and war, chiefly hate of each other – 'hate thy neighbour as thyself' – not hate of Germany at all which is in the hearts of people; and their worship of Ares and Aphrodite – ('But a bitter goddess was born of blood and the salt sea foam') – both gods of destruction and burning down. But in many hearts, now, I fully believe that Ares and Aphrodite have ceased to be gods. We want something else: it is fulfilled in us, this Ares–Aphrodite business: let us have something else, let us *make* something else out of our own hearts. Germany, peace terms, etc., don't matter. It is a question of the living heart – that only.[39]

Whatever the rhetorical flourishes in this passage, it is a heroic critical insightfulness that also appears, stamped by the experience and the truth of history when 'we were all drowned in shame'. Lawrence did not fight in the Great War, but no doubt he felt some deep inner need to disclose a commensurate heroism. That is, he was to disclose a critical rather than a martial heroism; a prophetic heroism that digs beneath surface experience and meaning. His letters portray a concomitant humanistic concern as Lawrence confronts the creative needs in himself and the social needs outside and around him. Though repeatedly speaking of the need to transform human society, especially after the war, he never fails to acknowledge a humane awareness. His phallic radicalism is invariably moderated by his passional humanism, that is to say, by his inherent reverence for the 'living heart'. That innate humanism not only saves Lawrence from his phallic extrapolations but also constitutes an inner check that tempers his sometimes exacerbated urgings for the attainment of what he calls 'spontaneous-creative fullness of being'. Indeed, Lawrence's humanistic sympathy explains his appreciation of the ancient Greek historian Thucydides, whose *History of the Peloponnesian War* Lawrence was reading in 1916. 'He is a very splendid and noble writer', Lawrence writes of Thucydides, 'with the simplicity and the directness of the most complete culture and the widest consciousness. I salute him. More and more I admire the true classic dignity and self-responsibility.'[40] In Thucydides' 'widest consciousness', Lawrence views precisely those humanistic virtues that he believed were being murdered on the Western Front. Indeed, is it not the destruction of the humanistic world that Lawrence bemoans in his indictment of the world of *Point Counter Point*?

III

After 1918 one detects in Lawrence's letters a more reflective, subdued, and even at times nostalgic tone. The slaughter of innocence generally associated with the consequences of the First World War was for Lawrence and the 1914 generation, 'our broken, fragmentary generation', as he describes it, an irreversible fact. No wonder, then, that he was willing to change the title of his war novel, *Women in Love*, to *Day of Wrath*! The 'insouciance' that Lawrence always hankered for was hardly obtainable after 1919, a year which was to see the beginning of Lawrence's 'savage pilgrimage'. In the letters of the post-war years, Lawrence saw disenchantment everywhere: 'The "world" has no life to offer. Seeing things doesn't amount to much.' A desperate courage identifies his epistolary observations in the early 1920s, those years when the survivors were slowly starting to grasp what had gone wrong and what had been lost, even as the map and psyche of European man were irreversibly transformed by epochal events, or as Virginia Woolf observed: 'Disorder, sordidity and corruption surround us.' It is a dream-like yearning, yet intuitively cognisant of the infinite pain of change and of death itself – the death of humane civilisation – that Lawrence reveals in a letter to Ernest Collings: 'I wish there could be a new spring of hope and reality in mankind: I do wish a few people could change, and stand for a fresh and happier world. I suppose it will come, and we shall live through. That is our business, at any rate. We must live through, for the hope of the new summer of the world.'[41] Not the 'courage to be' but the courage to forbear shapes Lawrence's view of the world during and immediately following the hostilities. Writing to Thomas Seltzer, his publisher, Lawrence has this to say about the life-emptiness of the post-war world and about the terrors that would come again after 'the long week-end': 'But one feels, the old order has gone – Hohenzollern & Nietzsche & all. And the era of love & peace & democracy with it. There will be an era of war ahead: some sort of warfare, one knows not what. But Mars is the god before us: the real Mars, not Jesus in arms.'[42]

Clearly, the early 1920s were for Lawrence a period of trouble and darkness. Any hope that he ever entertained about men meeting one another, 'upon the third ground, the holy ground', was now arrested. Lawrence's heroic vision, in so far as it shaped his attitude and thought, was during these years to comprehend the malaise that afflicted the whole of life. The war and its aftermath were to crystallise his estrangement and to intimidate his inherent affirmation of what he called man's 'thought-adventure'. A severe questioning of the very purposes and possibilities of existence racked Lawrence in the early 1920s: 'Will the bird perish,/Shall the bird rise?'[43] This cruel question underlines Lawrence's existential predicament, when his heroism necessarily passes through a stage of dread and despair that come with the 'end of the modern world'. Lawrence is to be viewed at this point as a 'pilgrim of the apocalypse', when he can be neither a 'hero of God' nor a 'hero of civilisation'. He exists in the brackets of nonbeing, abstracted from existence, as seen in the repeated references in the letters regarding his need to flee from the responsibilities of historical being. Unconsolable alienation was to constrict Lawrence in these years: 'I feel a stranger everywhere and nowhere.'[44] He found himself forced to summon all his resources of courage to combat the meaninglessness of an age in which the reifying process accelerated in all spheres of existence. A spiritual homelessness was to signalise his wanderings. The pressures that Lawrence felt so intensely in Europe were equally inescapable in the East, as these words in a letter written from

Ceylon show: 'Well, here we've been for a fortnight – rather lovely to look at, the place – but very hot – and I don't feel at all myself. Don't think I care for the East.'[45] Conditions in America were no less oppressive, to judge by these observations in another letter:

> Everything in America goes by *will*. A great negative *will* seems to be turned against all spontaneous life – there seems to be no *feeling* at all – no genuine bowels of compassion and sympathy. . . . America is neither free nor brave, but a land of tight, iron-clanking little *wills*, everybody trying to put it over everybody else, and a land of men absolutely devoid of the real courage of trust, trust in life's sacred spontaneity. They can't trust life until they can *control* it.[46]

The five or six years preceding Lawrence's death in 1930 disclose a metaphysical heroism as Lawrence increasingly contemplates not only the disarray in the world but also the disruption in his soul. This final stage of Lawrence's heroism reveals a deepening spiritual perception of his own and of the human condition. 'People who inherit despair', he insisted, 'may at last turn it into a greater heroism'. A contemplative vision marks his last years. The obsessive anger and disgust of the years directly following the war, though not eradicated, are reduced in intensity, as Lawrence confronts both the world in himself and himself in the world. How does one grapple with the problem of disorientation as it grips man in society? That, for Lawrence, constitutes a major question. The tone of the last letters, like that of the 'last poems', is reflective, invocatory, controlled, transcendent, as Lawrence appeals for the re-emergence of 'human tender reverence'. 'What we want is life and *trust*', Lawrence pleads with one correspondent; 'men trusting men, and making living a free thing, not a thing to be *earned*. But if men trusted men, we could soon have a new world, and send this one to the devil.'[47] In some of his last letters, Lawrence offers specific spiritual guidance, the voice of the moralist preacher in him remaining inextinguishable to the end: 'The chief thing is to be one's own real self, and to be at peace with oneself. Then life comes easily again. While one is in conflict with oneself, life holds back and is difficult all the time.'[48] Religious questions also arouse a more responsive and resonant chord as he considers the eternal clash between the sacred and the profane. For Lawrence, the 'journey through dread' must finally reach 'the new unknown'. The widespread moral nihilism of the late 1920s and early 1930s does not overcome him. As one who probed and rendered the possibilities of existence, even when these were under fire, Lawrence instinctively rejected the limit-situation of the Existentialists. The confirmation of possibility was Lawrence's answer to the Heideggerian 'possibility of impossibility'. 'I know there has to be a return to the older vision of life', he writes in a letter dated 4 July 1924. 'But not for the sake of unison. And not done from the *will*. It needs some welling up of religious sources that have been shut down in us: a great *yielding*, rather than an act of will: a yielding to the darker, older unknown, and a reconciliation.'[49]

Heroism, especially since the Great War, has lacked those archetypal qualities that one usually associates with the heroic prototype and attitude. Heroism has been increasingly technicalised or collectivised as uniformity and standardisation have taken toll of those opportunities that validate the heroic temper and *praxis*. A devalued and desanctified heroism, lacking promise of greatness and assimilating common and pluralistic habits of mind, fabricates modern forms of the heroic. Heroism has also been robbed of its intrinsically divine element, for the recrudescence of which Lawrence is asking when he writes to an American correspondent, the psychologist Dr Trigant Burrow: 'There is a *principle* in the universe, towards which man turns religiously – a *life* of the universe itself. And the hero is he who touches and transmits the life of the universe.'[50] Lawrence's words also remind us that it is a moral heroism, rooted in individual heroic effort, that he is invoking. His letters depict a life of perpetual striving in the face of those dehumanising conditions that debase the 'heroic impulse'. To see Lawrence as does Eric Bentley, as merely in the tradition of Heroic Vitalism, with its emphasis on the implementation of power (that for too long led Bertrand Russell and others to connect Lawrence with protofascism), is to oversimplify Lawrence's understanding of a heroism that he believes must be centred in what he terms the 'God-knowing human consciousness'.

More than ever the theme of Lawrence's letters in his last years is adumbrated by his credal statement, his '*eroica*', as it were: '*My single constancy is love of life!*'[51] His letters preach a loyalty to this article of faith, and his firmness in adhering to and defending it underlines his heroic capacity. 'I shall live just as blithely', he declares, 'unbought and unsold'. In the world in which he lived and created, Lawrence saw a heroism reduced in stature, vitality, dignity; a devalued heroism in accord with an age of demystification in which a pernicious process of 'living death' triumphed. With 'the subordination of every organic unit to the great mechanical purpose', modern civilisation had reached a point of stasis. 'The hero is obsolete', writes Lawrence to Witter Bynner, 'and the leader of men is a back number. After all, at the back of the hero is the militant ideal: and the militant ideal, or the ideal militant, seems to me also a cold egg. We're sort of sick of all forms of militarism and militantism, and *Miles* is a name no more, for a man.'[52] Human experience had been so much altered since 1914, Lawrence believed, that the leader-cum-follower relationship of earlier times was now inoperative. Life in an age in which, as Joseph Campbell has reminded us, the old mysteries have lost their force, and in which, therefore, their symbols no longer interest the psyche,[53] requires a new and intuitive heroism, possessing a 'curious close intimacy' and 'an instinct of beauty', as Lawrence would have it. In his letters Lawrence never ceases to call for an epiphanic heroism, as it might well be described: 'And the new relationship will be some sort of tenderness, sensitive, between men and men and men and women, and not the one up one down, lead on I follow, *ich dien* sort of business.'[54]

For Lawrence, a hero must be a 'great-souled man', a man of honour and integrity, fearless and persistent. Heroism needs to be passional and instinctive, expressed individually as well as collectively. In the Mexican people, for example, Lawrence finds his standards of heroism satisfied for the reasons he gives in this extract from one of his letters: 'But there is a sort of *basic* childishness about these people, that for me is the only manliness. When I say childishness, I only mean they don't superimpose ideas & ideals, but follow the stream of the blood. A certain innocence, even if sometimes evil. And a certain childlike patience & stoicism. – I like it really, our tough, dry, papier-mâché world recedes.'[55] The sacred and the heroic are, in Lawrence's contexts, qualitative equivalences in so far as they emerge from a common spiritual centre, or noumenon. In a sense, Lawrence's concepts of heroism are both ancient and modern: in his reverence for the idea of the holy, as it moulds the heroic impulse, he clearly reveals an understanding of biblical and sacramental rhythms as these preserve, in the recesses of the human consciousness, a religious value of permanent worth. His increasing respect for Roman Catholicism shows an interesting facet of his religious attitude in the last years of his life: 'I think too the Roman Catholic Church, as an institution, granted of course some new adjustments to life, might once more be invaluable for saving Europe: but not as a mere political power.'[56] True heroism for Lawrence is essentially an inner heroism that influences conscience and character, and fortifies mind and soul. Sanctity and candour are direct expressions of this process at its highest point of development. It is not the definition but the immanent expression of the heroic that Lawrence advocates. There is nothing schematic about his approach to heroism; its remobilisation is his main goal. An intrinsically moral form of that heroism appears in this paragraph from one of Lawrence's letters: 'I tried Casanova, but he smells. One can be immoral if one likes, but one must not be a creeping, itching, fingering, inferior being, led on chiefly by a dirty sniffing kind of curiosity, without pride or clearness of soul. For me, a man must have pride, good natural inward pride. Without that, cleverness only stinks.'[57]

As a hero-poet, Lawrence illuminates in his letters the traits of 'an aristocrat of life': 'greater being', 'a purer manhood', 'a more vivid livingness'. His heroism, however, defies absolute categories precisely because, as André Malraux has observed, 'Lawrence has no wish to be either happy or great, he is only concerned with being'. His is a life-heroism of character, robust and responsible, earthy, and natural, resistant to the abstract gestures that he linked with 'disintegrated lifelessness of soul'. The brave man, he believed, is one who, in 'the democratic age of cheap clap-trap', seeks for 'a new revelation' and 'a living relation in sacredness'. 'Never yield before the barren', Lawrence stresses, his words here epitomising a heroism of *living* and *being*, at the same time adverting to a philosophy of heroism. But that philosophy must not be confused with, say, a Nietzschean non-morality of the purely natural Will to Power. Lawrence's devotion to the necessity of tenderness and of 'the old blood-warmth of oneness and togetherness' saves him from surrendering to the *Uebermensch*. Nietzsche's heroism of despair – 'Oh eternal everywhere, oh eternal nowhere, oh eternal – in-vain!' – is filled with the vacuity and fatality that negate any possibility of redemption. 'Those who cannot bear the sentence, "There is no redemption", *ought* to perish', Nietzsche said. For Lawrence, too, the crisis of modern life was desperate, and he wondered whether there would be 'a new wave of generosity or a new wave of death'. But as his letters show, he never lacked creative faith, creative understanding or creative responsibility. He cared about man, as his credal statement clearly shows: 'One writes out of one's moral sense for the race, as it were'. And he cared about his life's work: 'I care about my books – I want them to stand four-square *there*, even if they don't sell many.'[58] In caring about things that really matter, Lawrence affirms a restorative heroism, the constituents of which he sees in this ascending order of redemption: 'Patience, tenacity, the long fight, the long hope, the inevitable victory – that's it.'[59]

NOTES

1. See *The Selected Letters of John Keats*, ed. Lionel Trilling (New York, 1951) pp. 3, 40, 41.
2. *Phoenix II: Uncollected, Unpublished and Other Prose Works by D. H. Lawrence*, ed. Warren Roberts and Harry T. Moore (New York, 1970) p. 291.
3. Ibid., p. 282.
4. *The Letters of D. H. Lawrence*, ed. Aldous Huxley (New York, 1932) p. 765.
5. Ibid., p. 312.
6. Ibid., pp. 382–3.
7. Ibid., p. 43.
8. Ibid., pp. 66–7.
9. Ibid., p. 68.
10. Ibid., p. 89.
11. Ibid., p. 79.
12. Ibid., pp. 110–11.
13. Ibid., p. 679.
14. Ibid., p. 716.
15. Jacob Burckhardt, in *Force and Freedom: Reflections on History*, ed. James Hastings Nichols (New York, 1943) p. 331.
16. *Letters*, ed. Huxley, p. 192.
17. See Thomas Carlyle, 'The Hero as Poet. Dante; Shakespeare', in *On Heroes, Hero-Worship and the Heroic in History* (London, 1897).
18. Romano Guardini, *The Virtues: On Forms of Moral Life*, trans. Stella Lange (Chicago, 1967) p. 2.
19. *Letters*, ed. Huxley, p. 23.
20. Ibid., p. 152.
21. Ibid., p. 137.
22. Ibid., pp. 199–200.
23. *Phoenix II*, ed. Roberts and Moore, p. 604.

24. *Letters*, ed. Huxley, p. 233.
25. Ibid., p. 255.
26. Ibid., p. 260.
27. Paul Tillich, *The Courage To Be* (New Haven, 1952) p. 155.
28. *Letters*, ed. Huxley, pp. 275–6.
29. Ibid., p. 348.
30. Ibid., p. 444.
31. Ibid., p. 386.
32. Tillich, *The Courage To Be*, p. 176.
33. *Letters*, ed. Huxley, p. 304.
34. Ibid., p. 294.
35. *Phoenix: The Posthumous Papers of D. H. Lawrence*, ed. Edward D. McDonald (London, 1936) p. 673.
36. *Letters*, ed. Huxley, p. 383.
37. Ibid.
38. Ibid., p. 407.
39. Ibid., pp. 385–6.
40. Ibid., p. 347.
41. Ibid., p. 404.
42. *Letters to Thomas and Adele Seltzer*, ed. Gerald M. Lacy (Santa Barbara, 1976) p. 20.
43. *Letters*, ed. Huxley, p. 598.
44. Ibid., p. 523.
45. Ibid., p. 547.
46. *The Collected Letters of D. H. Lawrence*, ed. Harry T. Moore (New York, 1962) II, pp. 721–2.
47. *Letters*, ed. Huxley, p. 779.
48. Ibid., p. 844.
49. Ibid., p. 613.
50. Ibid., p. 696.
51. Ibid., p. 657.
52. Ibid., p. 719.
53. Joseph Campbell, *The Hero with a Thousand Faces* (Princeton, 1949) p. 390.
54. *Letters*, ed. Huxley, p. 719.
55. *Letters to Thomas and Adele Seltzer*, ed. Lacy, p. 118.
56. *Letters*, ed. Huxley, p. 549.
57. Ibid., p. 529.
58. *Letters to Thomas and Adele Seltzer*, ed. Lacy, p. 155.
59. Ibid., p. 142.

17

Rananim: D. H. Lawrence's Failed Utopia

GEORGE J. ZYTARUK

The earliest manifestation of Lawrence's desire for an ideal society can be found in a statement attributed to him by one or both of the Chambers sisters (Jessie and May) and was apparently uttered in his seventeenth or eighteenth year. Jessie, who was 'the threshing floor' for most of his early beliefs, reports: 'When he was 17 or 18 he said to me how fine it would be if some day he could take a house, say one of the big houses in Nottingham Park, and he and all the people he liked could live together.'[1] This general idea is fleshed out in an account supposedly written by May Chambers which not only supplies the setting for the extended family circle, but also draws attention to the advantages of communal living. Bert, as the young Lawrence was familiarly known, asks:

> 'Don't you think it would be possible, if we were rich, to have a large house, really big, you know, and all the people one likes best live together? All in the one house? Oh, plenty of room inside and out, of course, but a sort of centre where one could always find those one wanted, a place all of us could come to as a home. I think it would be heaps nicer than to be all scattered and apart. Besides, there'd always be someone one liked near at hand. I know I should love something of the sort. Haven't you often felt sad at the thought of the gradual breakup of families or groups of friends like ours? I have – and it could be avoided, if we had the means. I should like to be rich and try it, shouldn't you?'[2]

It is perhaps significant that Lawrence's ability to function within the proposed communal group is questioned even at this early stage. 'I was dubious', recalls Jessie Chambers, 'and suggested that his friends might not agree if they all lived

266

together',[3] and in the expanded version, the narrator also voices her misgivings: 'Besides, he found fault with those who were very kind to him like my mother, so I had no faith in his success as head of a house full of friends. He would criticize them as he criticized us, which I felt, in our house, eating our food, was unfair.'[4]

One more preliminary observation should be added – the prominence that Lawrence gives to his mother. Jessie Chambers specifically recalls Lawrence's statement: 'Perhaps I shall be something one day, I mean a bit more than ordinary. If ever I am, I should like to have a big house – you know there are some lovely old houses in the Park with gardens and terraces. Wouldn't it be fine if we could live in one of those houses, mother and all the people we like together? Wouldn't it be fine!'[5]

The foregoing pronouncements were, of course, youthful aspirations such as any idealistic young man might utter, but in Lawrence's case it is important to note that even before he was twenty, he was already concerned about shaping the world around him to satisfy his personal needs. He threw over his career as a schoolteacher to become a full-time writer, and he eventually eloped with Frieda Weekley, the wife of a former professor. Both actions should be regarded as definite logical steps towards achieving a life of individual fulfilment, a life which once he had secured it for himself, he would very soon decide must be embraced by all his friends.

It is not surprising that in Fiascherino, where he had settled with Frieda in September 1913, and where he appears to be extremely happy in his work and his marriage, we find him yearning for others to join him in his idyllic retreat. To cite only a few examples from his letters:[6] to Edward Garnett: 'Now you will come and see us – and so will Constanza Davidovna' (L. II, p. 78); to Edward Marsh: 'Tell [W. A.] Davies he ought to come before Spring' (L. II, p. 85); to Arthur McLeod: 'You must come in the Spring' (L. II, p. 86); to Lady Cynthia Asquith: 'I wish you could try it too' (L. II, p. 88); to John Middleton Murry and Katherine Mansfield: 'We could get you, I believe, a jolly nice apartment in a big garden, in a house alone for 80 Lire a month' (L. II, p. 112); and, finally, to William Hopkin: 'And now, after all this [i.e. Lawrence's descriptions of life in Fiascherino], you must come – you and Mrs Hopkin at least – and Enid if she can' (L. II, p. 123).

It is characteristic of Lawrence that no matter how happy he was, he always seemed to need to involve other people in his particular circumstances; it is also characteristic of him as a writer that his creative efforts did not appear to be sufficient in themselves. Living in Fiascherino, with Frieda, in a relationship which he described as having at last fulfilled all his expectations – 'But now, thank God, Frieda and I are together, and the work is of me and her, and it is beautiful, I think' (*L.* ii, p. 161) – Lawrence nevertheless seemed impelled to enlist others in creating a world according to his vision of what that world should be. At the heart of that world is, naturally, the perfected relationship between man and woman; but, in addition, he wants some sort of concerted effort with other men. Thus, writing to Henry Savage on 2 June 1914, he gives expression to this second dimension of a vital life: 'I *should* like to see a few decent men enlist themselves just as fighters, to bring down this old regime of dirty, dead ideas and make a living revolution' (*L.* ii, p. 179). While the context in which this remark was uttered may be viewed as highly theoretical, the idea of 'a living revolution', as we shall see, became much more than a mere passing thought in Lawrence's scheme of things.

If we try to identify the one event or circumstance which appears to have forced Lawrence to grapple with the utopian element in his make-up and which precipitated him into trying to formulate in a systematic way his vision of an ideal society, that event is surely the outbreak of the First World War. He and Frieda were married on 13 July 1914, and in slightly more than two weeks, the world he had hoped to create for them both (and for his fellow human beings as well) was in imminent danger of collapsing. Until then, Lawrence had managed legitimately to earn his living by writing, meagre though that living was; he was shortly to become economically dependent upon the generosity of his friends and upon the impersonal support of the Royal Literary Fund. The war, which burst upon Europe while Lawrence and his friends roamed the Westmorland hills, had very suddenly altered the whole frame of the writer's existence.

When he returned from Barrow-in-Furness, Lawrence wrote to Koteliansky, who had accompanied him on the walk in Westmorland: 'I am very miserable about the war' (*L* ii, p. 205). For a week or so, he was uncertain about his next move, but it was clear that he could not go back to Italy as matters stood; he wrote to J. B. Pinker: 'I think I shall try to get a tiny cottage somewhere, put a little bit of furniture in it, and live as cheaply as possible' (*L.* II, p. 207). He decided on Chesham, Buckinghamshire, and by 16 August 1914, he and Frieda were 'living the ultra-simple life' (*L.* II, p. 208), as he phrased it. What a contrast this must have been, after the picturesque setting of Fiascherino! From reading the letters of this summer, we see very clearly how desperately Lawrence tried to rationalise his new circumstances. Whitewashing the rooms of the cottage, picking blackberries, urging friends to visit, he despairs 'war is just hell', and confesses 'I can't get away from it for a minute: live in a sort of coma, like one of those nightmares when you can't move, I hate it – everything' (*L.* II, p. 211). The last phrase is significant, for Lawrence's hatred of the war is already spreading to affect other parts of his life. Nor can the love between Frieda and him compensate for the misery of the war: 'I can't say we're happy, because we're not, Frieda and I: what with this war, and one thing and another' (*L.* II, p. 212). One can almost hear the rising desperation in his voice as he utters: 'What a miserable world. What colossal idiocy, this war' (*L.* II, p. 212).

It is little wonder, then, that Lawrence began the 'little book on Hardy', as he put it, 'Out of sheer rage' (*L.* II, p. 212). The writing of this book took much longer than did any other of his creative efforts, and, ironically enough, the work was not published in his lifetime. The reason for the difficulty in writing is obvious; the book which started as a critical analysis of Hardy's novels became a vehicle for working out a statement of his most fundamental philosophical beliefs. For a writer of Lawrence's stature, to try to set down his deepest convictions would be a difficult enough task under any circumstances; to try to do so in the period under discussion was nothing short of impossible. Even a brief history of this work, at this point, can show little of the immensity of the task that Lawrence set for himself, and only a reading of the existing correspondence, until the letter dated 30 August 1917 when he finally sends the complete manuscript entitled 'At the Gates' to J. B. Pinker, can truly convey how much of Lawrence's effort went into grappling with what he came to call his 'philosophy'. Although the war seriously affected his material life, Lawrence continued to assert that 'The war doesn't alter my beliefs or visions' (*L.* II, p. 218). At the centre of that vision, as we shall see, is the absolute necessity for a vital man–woman relationship, the need to 'get our sex right' (*L.* II, p. 218). Beyond that, Lawrence is less certain: 'the vision we're after, I don't know what it is – but it is something that contains awe and dread and submission, not pride or sensuous egotism' (*L*. II, p. 218).

It is regrettable that the only surviving version of Lawrence's 'philosophy' was first published under the misleading and inaccurate rubric 'Study of Thomas Hardy',[7] for as Lawrence himself was aware, the book 'which is supposed to be about Thomas Hardy – seems to be about anything else in the world but that' (*L*. II, p. 220). Since the surviving typescript clearly gives Lawrence's title for the work as 'Le Gai Savaire', it is more appropriate that this title should be used to refer to his 'philosophy'. We should note in passing, as the correspondence reveals, that Lawrence struggled very hard to find another suitable title, at various times having considered the following: 'The Signal', 'Morgenrot', 'Confessio Fide' and 'Goats and Compasses'; he finally decided on 'At the Gates', when the last version was completed on 30 August 1917.[8] No version bearing the latter title has yet been found. It is, however, clear that some of his basic philosophical ideas eventually found their way into such essays as 'The Crown' (October–November 1915), 'The Reality of Peace' (March 1917) and 'Education of the People' (November 1918). His remark made many years later in *Fantasia of the Unconscious* (1923), that a writer's metaphysic 'is deduced from the novels and poems, not the reverse',[9] may help to explain why he appears to have been unable to complete the writing of his 'philosophy' until after the full creation of the two novels *The Rainbow* and *Women in Love*. The book on Hardy forced Lawrence to confront the fundamental questions about the nature and purpose of life, to formulate what he called his 'metaphysic', and it is essential to understand this 'metaphysic' before we can examine his vision of utopia.

It is apparent that sometime during the course of writing 'Le Gai Savaire', Lawrence began thinking about a new society. What was it that, in the midst of his struggle with *The Rainbow* (he sent Pinker 'the first hundred or so pages' (*L*. II, p. 240) on 5 December 1914), made him contemplate starting his own ideal community? Was it, perhaps, that as he thought through the history of the three generations of Brangwens and began to realise that the society in which his heroine Ursula would have to achieve her own fulfilment, her own flowering, so to speak, Lawrence concluded that the existing social order was somehow inadequate? Or was he pondering his own circumstances, his recent marriage to Frieda, the war which had begun in earnest, their confinement in England, the meagre out-of-the-way cottage in Chesham, where he seemed condemned to eke out his future existence in isolation from the rest of his fellow human beings, his already dismal economic prospects (he was forced to apply to the Royal Literary Fund for assistance in 1914) – had he concluded that, as matters stood, there was little hope in England for a fair share of human happiness? Since the social context in which he and Frieda must now attempt to achieve their individualities had changed so radically, it is understandable why, in the words of H. G. Wells, whose work *A Modern Utopia* (1905) was no doubt familiar to him, Lawrence began to yearn for 'Utopia, where men and women are happy and laws are wise, and where all that is tangled and confused in human affairs has been unravelled and made right'.[10]

Whatever the combination of circumstances – personal, social and political – and we shall return to some of these as our discussion proceeds, the chronologically crucial event in Lawrence's progress towards attempting to establish his own utopia was a party which he organised at the Chesham cottage for Christmas 1914. Writing to Amy Lowell, in anticipation of that memorable celebration, Lawrence proclaimed: 'We shall have a great time, boiling ham and roasting chickens, and drinking Chianti in memory of Italy' (*L.* II, p. 243). And so it was, the party including the Murrys (Katherine Mansfield and John Middleton Murry, as yet unmarried), Gordon and Beatrice Campbell, who had lent Lawrence their flat in Kensington during the preceding summer, Mark Gertler, a young painter, and Koteliansky. Frieda has recorded: 'We had a gay feast' (*L.* II, p. 252). But it was much more, although none of those present seems to have left an account of the pertinent details – or it may be that just then, Lawrence kept to himself the vision of the utopia he had glimpsed. There is no doubt, however, that 'Rananim' was conceived that memorable Christmas in 1914, even if its formal proclamation in writing was still a few days hence. That some talk at Christmas had taken place is surely apparent from Lawrence's enthusiastic announcement to Koteliansky on 3 January 1915: 'What about Rananim? Oh, but, we are going. We are going to found an Order of the Knights of Rananim' (*L.* II, p. 252). The writer appears to take for granted that Koteliansky will have no difficulty understanding the meaning of the apparently esoteric name; we may even assume that there is a shared understanding of the

'Order', as well, for Lawrence obviously sees no need to explain that term. And we see clearly how Lawrence's mind is already working, how his artistic imagination projects his thought symbolically (for the details of organisation have yet to be developed); the pressing need is to symbolise the new vision. The name of the utopia has been chosen, and 'Rananim' shall henceforth join the company of those other imaginary societies, among whose names we find *Aristopia* (1895), *Ionia* (1898), *Solaris Farm* (1900), *Neustria* (1901), *Liminora, the Island of Progress* (1903), *Geyserland* (1908), *Newaera* (1910), *Athonia* (1910) and *Kalomera* (1911), to cite only a few of the more exotic sounding nomenclatures.[11] Besides a name, there is also a 'motto' for the new society, namely 'Fier' or the Latin equivalent 'Superbus'; this is to be not a society of the meek, but a utopia of the proud and the strong. And, because for Lawrence symbolism is always paramount, 'Rananim' must have a 'flag' like that on a pirate ship, a 'blazing, ten-pointed star, scarlet on a black background' (*L.* II, p. 253). Finally, there is what Lawrence calls the 'badge', in other words, 'a device or token, especially, of membership in a society or group', drawn by the author in his letter and embodying, as it were, the form and substance of his proclaimed utopia: 'The badge is So: an eagle, or phoenix argent, rising from a flaming nest of scarlet, on a black background' (*L.* II, pp. 252–3). Although, at this point, Lawrence appears to suggest that the symbolic bird might be either an 'eagle' or a 'phoenix', his later adoption of the 'phoenix' as a personal symbol indicates his early preference; and the bird drawn by him is unmistakably a phoenix, rising from its flaming nest. Whether or not he had already written the passage about the phoenix in his 'little book on Hardy'[12] by the time he drew the illustration has not been established – the probability is that he had, for he was certainly by then familiar with Mrs Henry Jenner's explanation of the mythical bird's symbolic value: 'its [that of the phoenix] special meaning was the resurrection of the dead and its triumph over death' and, further, 'the Phoenix in itself was a recognised emblem of the Resurrection of Christ'.[13] Whatever multiplicity of meanings may be inherent in the symbol of the phoenix, the notion that from the dead world a new world can rise is obviously what Lawrence intends to communicate here as he envisions his 'Rananim'.

What precisely Lawrence had in mind when he wrote about founding 'an Order of the Knights of Rananim' (*L.* II, p. 252) was never fully developed. Indeed, as the subsequent history will show, Lawrence's utopia was constantly changing. In the beginning (January 1915), the plan appears to have taken the somewhat conventional form of settling on a remote island where a new society would be established. We know this much, because Katherine Mansfield, who was an active participant in the discussion during those early days, records in her journal for 2 January 1915: 'Dined at the Lawrences' and talked the Island.'[14] That Lawrence was thinking about an island utopia is confirmed further by one of his own remarks written on 24 February 1915 to Mary Cannan, who seems also to have known about the early plan. Lawrence writes: 'We have changed our island scheme. After all it was a sort of running away from the problem' (*L.* II, p. 292). Earlier, however, on 18 January 1915, he had laid down some of the main guidelines for his new community, his 'pet scheme' as he then phrased it:

> I want to gather together about twenty souls and sail away [apparently to some island] from this world of war and squalor and found a little colony where there shall be no money but a sort of communism as far as necessaries of life go, and some real decency. It is to be a colony built up on the real decency which is in each member of the Community – a community which is established upon the assumption of goodness in the members, instead of the assumption of . . . badness. (*L.* II, p. 259)

Although he was just moving to Greatham, Pulborough, Sussex, and only a few days earlier had made the artistically historic decision to split 'The Sisters' into two volumes – had, indeed, dispatched on 20 January 1915 to his agent J. B. Pinker a portion of the 'Rainbow' manuscript – Lawrence appeared at this time to be very much committed to the establishment of his new society.

Shortly after settling in Sussex, he voices to E. M. Forster what must be regarded as a fundamentally deep and earnest desire: 'I want somebody to come and make a league with me' (*L.* II, p. 262); a desire that continued to assert itself even in the blackest days of the war. When he writes to Forster on 28 January 1915 about the question of class, he states his conviction that in the ideal state (although he does not put it this way directly), the social structure should enable each individual to live 'to one's end' (*L.* II, p. 265). No class, neither aristocratic nor that of the common people, can automatically guarantee such an end – the ideal is 'the naked, intrinsic, class-less individual' (*L.* II, p. 265). 'I am tired of class, and humanity, and personal salvation' (*L.* II, p. 266), Lawrence exclaims. He goes on to describe the social structure which he envisioned for his utopia:

> In my Island, I wanted [had he already realised that his hope was futile?] people to come without class or money, sacrificing nothing, but each coming with all his desires, yet knowing that his life is but a tiny section of a Whole: so that he shall fulfil his life in relation to the Whole. I wanted a real community, not built out of abstinence or equality, but out of many fulfilled individualities seeking greater fulfilment.   (*L.* II, p. 266)

The problem is to find people who are willing to make a commitment to such an ideal. Lawrence confesses that among his 'friends' there are none such: 'They seem so childish and greedy, always the immediate desire, always the particular outlook, no conception of the whole horizon wheeling round' (*L.* II, p. 266). When he analyses the particular shortcomings of his friends, those to whom he has obviously broached his conception of an ideal society, we can almost certainly identify the individuals whom he has in mind: 'he wants love of a woman, and can't get it complete' (*L.* II, p. 266) obviously fits J. Middleton Murry; 'he wants to influence his fellow man (for their good of course)' (*L.* II, p. 262) applies to Bertrand Russell; and 'he wants to satisfy his own soul with regard to his position in eternity' (*L.* II, p. 266) must refer to Gordon Campbell. How could Lawrence hope to unite such a disparate group to join in 'seeking greater fulfilment'! For the moment, he despairs of being able to make any progress; 'I feel frightfully like weeping in a corner' (*L.* II, p. 267), he groans. Prophets, perhaps, should be made of sterner stuff.

It is not known when Lawrence wrote out a long draft of a proposed constitution for 'Rananim', which he gave to Gordon Campbell. I assume that it must have been done sometime after the move to Greatham, in Sussex. Since there seems to be substantial correspondence with the Campbells between January and March 1915, it is likely that the historic document was produced during this latter period. According to Beatrice Campbell, 'the document, which consisted of several sheets of paper covered with Lawrence's own beautifully careful writing . . . were never found and their disappearance remains a mystery'.[15] It may be recalled that Lawrence wrote down, for Bertrand Russell in July 1915, 'Herakleitos, on tablets of bronze' (*L.* II, p. 364), as he phrased it, recalling his reading of Burnet's *Early Greek Philosophy*, and the constitution for 'Rananim' might have been written in a similar format, but this is a mere speculation. Still, if I may borrow a phrase that Lawrence used in an entirely different context, one 'would give a good deal' to be able to read the lost 'pages', the whereabouts of which are still 'a mystery'. Of course, as a teacher of history and, later, the author of the textbook *Movements in European History*, Lawrence would have been conversant with various political constitutions and, therefore, would have had little difficulty in adapting an appropriate constitutional framework for his own concept of the ideal state. What might he have put down as the first 'article' in such a constitution? Would he, like the eighteenth-century French utopist, Graschus Babeuf, who envisioned 'A Society of Equals', begin with some basic principle such as 'Nature has given to each individual an equal right to the enjoyment of all the goods of life'?[16]

If we look at Lawrence's methods of writing about various philosophical matters, there are reasonable grounds for speculating that the former schoolmaster might have enumerated the several articles of his constitution in Babeuf's manner. Take, for example, Lawrence's 'Reflections on the Death of a Porcupine', the essay in which he spells out what he terms 'the inexorable law of life' in five categorical statements, as follows (I quote only the first sentence in each case):

1. Any creature that attains to its own fulness of being, its own *living* self, becomes unique, a nonpareil.
2. At the same time, every creature exists in time and space.
3. The force which we call *vitality*, and which is the determining factor in the struggle for existence, is, however, derived also from the fourth dimension.
4. The primary way, in our existence, to get vitality, is to absorb it from living creatures lower than ourselves.
5. No creature is fully itself till it is, like the dandelion, opened in the bloom of pure relationship to the sun, the entire living cosmos.[17]

Speculation as to what would likely have been Lawrence's first and overriding principle for 'Rananim' must be postponed in order to consider several more references to the ideal society in the letters of this period. Following Lady Ottoline Morrell's visit to Greatham on 1 February 1915, Lawrence writes after she has 'just gone' and expresses again his desire for a 'new community'. Although he says 'I want you [Lady Ottoline] to form the nucleus of a new community which shall start a new life amongst us' (*L.* II, p. 271), it is Lawrence himself who sets out the basis for a new society. In the same letter he restates his own messianic mission, when he says: 'I hold this the most sacred duty – the gathering together of a number of people who shall so agree to live by the *best* they know, that they shall be *free* to live by the best they know. The ideal, the religion, must now be *lived*, *practised* [Lawrence's italics]' (*L.* II, p. 272). This letter to Lady Ottoline is similar to that which he had addressed to William Hopkin on 18 January 1915, since the utopia projected here is also basically communistic: 'It is a communism based, not on poverty, but on riches, not on humility, but on pride, not on sacrifice but upon complete fulfilment in the flesh of all strong desire, not on forfeiture but upon inheritance, not on heaven but on earth' (*L.* II, p. 273). That at least one aim of the new society is to alleviate economic poverty is evident from Lawrence's statement: 'And this shall be the new hope: that there shall be a life wherein the struggle shall not be for money or for power, but for individual freedom and common effort towards good' (*L.* II, p. 272). It is Lawrence's fervent wish that those who join in the new effort shall be able to work collectively 'towards goodness', for that purpose as far as he is concerned 'is surely the richest thing to have now' (*L.* II, p. 272). And he is hopeful that all of the members of the new society will be able to put aside their private interests and strive for common endeavours: 'I do hope that we shall all of us be able to agree, that we have a common way, a common interest, not a private way and a private interest only' (*L.* II, p. 273). There is a realistic admission that it may not be possible to achieve a wholesale transformation of society along the lines just described, but Lawrence seems to have been willing to compromise if they could 'at least set it into life, bring it forth new-born on the earth' (*L.* II, p. 273).

It was during Lady Ottoline's visit that Lawrence was urged by his guest that he must meet Bertrand Russell, 'the Philosophic-

Mathematics man' (*L.* II, p. 273), as Lawrence styled him. Lady Ottoline volunteered to bring Russell to Greatham, and Lawrence, in a gesture of gratitude, sealed the pact by sending a box painted especially for her, which bore a 'phoenix on the bottom' (*L.* II, p. 275), his own 'badge and sign' (*L.* II, p. 275). The new society would rise from the ashes of the old. As he informed Koteliansky, when the date of the visit from Ottoline and Russell was fixed, they were 'going to struggle with my Island idea – Rananim' (*L.* II, p. 277). He would tell Koteliansky about it later, but one significant modification in the plan has already been made: 'the island shall be England' and the founders 'shall start [their] new community in the midst of this old one, as a seed falls among the roots of the parent' (*L.* II, p. 277).

It is important to note that even as Lawrence continued to revise *The Rainbow* (on 2 February 1915 he wrote to Gordon Campbell asking whether the character Skrebensky, who was 'a subaltern in the Engineers' (*L.* II, p. 274), should be more appropriately described as being in the 'Royal Engineers'), his belief had already shifted to the view that it was no good merely talking or writing about an ideal society, because 'the religion, must now be *lived, practised*' (*L.* II, p. 272). He is convinced, as he explains to Lady Ottoline, 'that there are enough decent people to make a new start with' (*L.* II, p. 272). His call to action is, therefore: 'Let us get the people' (*L.* II, p. 272). For this reason, he must have welcomed the opportunity to meet Bertrand Russell, for the latter would obviously have been one of the 'decent people' who might be enlisted in the new venture. Yet something of diplomacy was surely lacking, since Forster, who was equally a good prospect for 'Rananim', is unceremoniously accused by Lawrence of reaching 'the limit of splitness' (*L.* II, p. 275), and criticised that in his last books, he is 'intentional and perverse and not vitally interesting' (*L.* II, p. 276), neither of which opinions would likely have encouraged Forster to set aside his own concerns and join Lawrence 'to make a start' at a new society. Lawrence was not known for tempering his criticism, no matter what the circumstances, and the kind of assault that he makes on Forster was to be repeated in his dealings with Russell just a few months later.

In any case, following Russell's visit to Greatham – and it is unfortunate that neither Lady Ottoline nor Russell has left any details of that first meeting and the discussions that took place –

the letter dated 12 February 1915 (which is Lawrence's first to Russell) launches squarely into the plans for 'Rananim'. That Russell appears to have forced Lawrence to consider the importance of the economic factor is clear from the following statement: 'There must be a revolution in the state. It shall begin by the nationalising of all . . . industries and means of communication, and of the land – in one fell blow. Then a man shall have his wages whether he is sick or well or old – if anything prevents his working, he shall have his wages just the same' (*L.* II, p. 282). There is no doubt that Lawrence's personal economic circumstances, brought about by the war, figure in his view of the economic changes that would be essential in a new society. When he says, further, that 'no man amongst us, and no woman, shall have any fear of the wolf at the door' (*L.* II, p. 282), he is thinking of Frieda's and his own situation. The image he uses is repeated in a letter to J. B. Pinker, written on 24 February 1915, when he says: 'Do be getting me some money, will you? I heard the wolf scratch the door today' (*L.* II, p. 293). It is clear that his theory of the ideal state requires him to 'provide another standard than the pecuniary standard, to measure *all* daily life by' (*L.* II, p. 282), but it is equally clear that Lawrence has to face up to and try to solve his own bleak economic prospects. That he tries to accomplish the latter through an imaginary leap of gigantic proportions, that is, by envisioning a wholesale restructuring of the economic system, reveals how impracticable his scheme was. To try to nationalise even a single area of economic life would pose immense political difficulties in any state; to try to do so in England at this particular time in history must be regarded as an extreme form of daydreaming. In this respect, certainly, Lawrence's economic programme for utopia could have had very little chance for success. Lawrence may argue that we 'must be free of the economic question' (*L.* II, p. 282), that 'Economic life must be the means to actual life' (*L.* II, p. 282), but he obviously has no understanding of the practical difficulties inherent in any political or social attempt to try to 'make it so at once' (*L.* II, p. 282). For him, 'nationalising' everything which relates to the 'economic question', in his words, 'practically solves the whole economic question for the present' (*L.* II, p. 282), but for any utopist who would seriously attempt to cope with this complex issue, the problem has not even been adequately defined.

Why was Lawrence so impractical? How does one explain his

political naivety? In formulating an answer, it may be instructive to reread the entire letter of 12 February 1915, in which he addresses the 'economic question'. Of the nearly five pages which comprise this letter to Russell, only three short paragraphs deal with the 'question' – the rest of the letter is devoted to a description of 'a free soul' versus 'a resigned soul'. There is a long metaphorical analysis (in terms of the myth of Prometheus of E. M. Forster's psychological problem, which Lawrence diagnoses as an inability to act because Forster cannot 'Take a woman and fight clear to his own basic, primal being' (*L.* II, p. 283)); there is a lengthy digression on sodomy; and only after these expostulations does Lawrence address the 'economic question' and 'the frame' that must be smashed. 'The land, the industries, the means of communication and the public amusements shall all be nationalised' (*L.* II, p. 286) – note the slight change in the order here and the significant addition of 'public amusements' – to which Lawrence tacks on a reference to the appropriate role for woman, namely 'whether she work or not, so long as she works when she is fit – keeps her house or rears her children' (*L.* II, p. 286). He implores Russell (and we as readers should perhaps heed the plea) to 'have patience with [him] and understand [him] when [his] language is not clear' (*L.* II, p. 286), but it is difficult to be patient at this point. It is the other conditions that are of paramount importance to Lawrence, not the means of achieving the final aim. Only when the 'economic question' is out of the way, he seems to suggest, would he be prepared to 'examine marriage and love and all' (*L.* II, p. 286). The evidence, however, indicates that for Lawrence, there are other matters which are of primary importance, and he is not interested enough in the practical questions of economics to bother with analysing them systematically. As the letter to Russell shows, Lawrence is much more concerned with what should happen in the individual soul, and parallel with that, in what must happen in the fundamental relation between man and woman. His statement 'Any man who takes a woman is up against the unknown' (*L.* II, p. 285) is a much more important basic concept for him in establishing the ideal society than are any consequences of nationalisation. It harkens back to his belief that there is no use trying to do anything before 'we get our sex right', a belief that was to occupy his artistic energy for most of his life. His momentary digression into the economic question is probably only a symptom of the influence that Russell and Lady Ottoline were exerting on his thinking at the time. If we are really to try to grasp the outlines of Lawrence's vision of 'Rananim', we must seek them in his exploration of personal relationships.

Further discussions of the 'Revolution' apparently took place at Koteliansky's house in Acacia Road on 15 February 1915, following which Lawrence continued to be optimistic that 'in spite of everything' (presumably disagreements on the practical economic matters), the revolution in the lives of those who were prepared to commit themselves to 'a bigger cause' would come about. Lady Ottoline was certainly one such: 'you are one with us in a bigger hope' (*L.* II, p. 288), Lawrence writes. He appeared confident, almost buoyant in the hope of a better society – 'my soul feels as fixed as a star in its orbit' (*L.* II, p. 288) is the imagery in which he expresses his feelings of the moment.

It was at this time that, almost as if by design, Murry turned up at Greatham and was immediately enlisted in the programme for 'Rananim'. Notwithstanding Murry's unsettled relationship with Katherine Mansfield, Lawrence proclaimed him as 'one of the men of the future' (*L.* II, p. 291) and one with him 'for the Revolution'. Indeed, Lawrence states unequivocally: 'At present he [Murry] is my partner – the only man who quite simply is with me' (*L.* II, p. 291). In the light of Lawrence's confidence in Murry, it is perhaps ironic that the latter did not recall anything specific about this particular period and the current plans for 'Rananim'. In his *Autobiography*, Murry refers only to the earlier discussions at Chesham, where one of his 'chief solaces', as he describes his 'various miseries', had been 'daydreaming with Lawrence of the island, Rananim, to which we were all to escape'.[18] For his part, Lawrence was full of commitment. He continued to urge Forster that he must 'stick to the idea of a social revolution, which shall throw down artificial barriers between men, and make life freer and fuller' (*L.* II, p. 292). Lawrence himself remained firmly convinced that: 'Any big vision of life must contain a revolutionised society, and one must fulfil one's visions, or perish' (*L.* II, p. 292). When he wrote to Mary Cannan on 24 February 1915, he admitted that 'we [presumably Murry, Lady Ottoline, Forster, Russell] have changed our island scheme. After all it was a sort of running away from the problem' (*L.* II, p. 292). But he repeated his belief in 'a social revolution' and sketched for his correspondent and for her husband Gilbert Cannan the basic principles of nationalising the chief industries and the provisions for social security which he had described earlier in his letter to Bertrand Russell. He indicated also that the time had come to 'form a revolutionary party' (*L.* II, p. 292), which he planned to 'go into . . . more thoroughly' (*L.* II, p. 292) during his forthcoming visit to Russell at Cambridge. There was also a plan to issue a revolutionary publication, based on Lawrence's 'philosophicalish' book which was 'slightly about Hardy'. This would now be rewritten and published in 'pamphlets', which would serve to 'create an idea of a new, freer life, where men and women can really meet on natural terms, instead of being barred within so many barriers' (*L.* II, p. 293). There was urgency to take action, too: 'Something must be done, and we must begin soon' (*L.* II, p. 293). He invited Gilbert and Mary Cannan to Greatham: 'Come and see us and let us talk about it' (*L.* II, p. 293).

On the same day that he wrote to the Cannans, Lawrence answered one of Russell's letters, one which unfortunately has not been preserved. Whatever Russell said, Lawrence seems to have found it necessary to state again his own conviction that 'a vision of a better life must include a revolution of society' (*L.* II, p. 294), and he also found it necessary to reiterate that 'the great living experience for every man is his adventure into the woman' (*L.* II, p. 294). His concern is still the same: what is needed first is a change in the male and female relationship. He was willing to talk about the other things, the economic questions, but the 'campaign for this freer life' (*L.* II, p. 295) was going to be a concerted effort first to 'get our sex right'. That was the essence of 'Le Gai Savaire', 'a book about those things' as Lawrence described his work; but that must now be rewritten, made 'as good as' it can be made, and published 'in pamphlets, weekly or fortnightly' (*L.* II, p. 295), to bring about a new understanding of human relationships. The visit to Cambridge, Lawrence hoped, would give him an opportunity 'to talk about it' with Russell.

The failure of that much anticipated visit is well known, but only recently more details about it have become available. There is no doubt that Lawrence went to Cambridge to try to enlist at least some of Russell's friends in the cause of the social revolution in the state, but his failure to do so and thereby to initiate 'the great and happy revolution' (*L.* II, p. 299), as he says in a letter to Viola Meynell on 2 March 1915, was to leave him devastated. He had, however, completed *The Rainbow*, 'bended it and set it firm' (*L.* II, p. 299) before he went to Cambridge; and he was ready 'to begin

a book about Life' (*L.* II, p. 299) which would be a more direct
appeal to the public and which, in his own words, would be his
'revolutionary utterance' (*L.* II, p. 300). Even as he wrote these
words, he apparently realised that what he wanted was 'not a
political revolution' – and this must be stressed – rather, what he
hoped to achieve was in the nature of a new 'great, collective
vision' (*L.* II, p. 301), in other words, an 'instant social revolution
from indignation with what *is*' (*L.* II, p. 301). The means towards
this end have changed little from the initial dream of an 'order of
the Knights of Rananim'. He tells Gordon Campbell: 'I want us to
form a league – you and Murry and me and perhaps Forster – and
our women' (*L.* II, p. 302). Although he omits Koteliansky, Russell
and Lady Ottoline from the list, they would presumably have
been welcome and numbered among 'any one who will be added
on to us – so long as we are centred around a core of reality, and
carried on one impulse' (*L.* II, p. 302). Even if Lawrence could
write 'the finest lyric poetry or prose' (*L.* II, p. 302), he would still
consider expressing his utopian vision the more important task,
because what is needed is 'the utterance of the great racial or
human consciousness' (*L.* II, p. 302). He admits that he is not
really sure how to give expression to this vision, but he must
content himself with struggling, no matter how 'clumsily to put
into art the new Great Law of God and Mankind' (*L.* II, p. 302).
Nevertheless, he hazards all he has on this artistic venture: 'and if
I botch out a little of this utterance, so that other people are made
alert and active, I don't care whether I am great or small, or rich
or poor, or remembered or forgotten' (*L.* II, p. 302). In his own
mind, the direction that he will take is clear, as he assesses the
relative importance of the various activities that he must perform:
'I can see nothing to begin on, but a social revolution. For I write
my novels, and I write my book of philosophy, and I must also
see the social revolution set going' (*L.* II, p. 303).

It was certainly in this frame of mind that Lawrence went to
Cambridge, but following that visit there is virtually nothing in
the correspondence to indicate how that visit affected his hopes
for gaining additional support in his quest for 'Rananim'. In a
letter to Barbara Low, written on 10 March 1915, he coldly states:
'I went to Cambridge and hated it beyond expression' (*L.* II,
p. 305), and, finally, when he does write to Russell, on what is
almost certainly 15 March 1915, he omits any direct reference to
the 'social revolution'. Instead, he concentrates on the problem

which he has with writing his 'philosophy', and somewhat despairingly expresses himself in images of 'darkness', 'chaos', 'the grave' and the 'womb'. He still hopes that Russell will 'be with [him] – in the underworld – or at any rate to wait for [him]' (*L.* II, p. 307), both rather vague and tenuous requests; and the desire for some sort of a league is still there, for he says: 'I wish you would swear a sort of allegiance with me' (*L.* II, p. 307). Something, however, seems to have happened to his enthusiasm for a new order, as if his confidence in his vision of that order were seriously undermined, and he retreats into his own subconscious, grappling with the forces of good and evil or, to use his own terms, 'God and the devil – particularly the devil – and . . . immortality' (*L.* II, p. 307).

The visit to Cambridge is an important turning point in Lawrence's vision of a utopia, or to put the matter in another way, his experience at Cambridge appears to have put an end to his plan for the kind of new society that he thought could realistically be established in England. His thinking about 'Rananim' periodically surfaces after Cambridge, but there is never again the kind of wholesale commitment to founding a new order as we have witnessed prior to the Cambridge episode. It would be oversimplifying to regard the hopelessness of the war as dashing Lawrence's optimism, although it is true that an attempt to revolutionise a whole nation's social outlook would be particularly problematical during a period of war, when the majority of the population is preoccupied with a military struggle. I wish, however, to draw attention to what seems to me to be an abandoning of the utopian vision by Lawrence, and to show how that change in his outlook grew out of his acceptance of Russell's invitation to Cambridge. I have already stated that Lawrence went to Cambridge at the height of his enthusiasm for a social revolution and that he must have seen the entrée to Cambridge as an opportunity to broaden his base of support, to enlarge the rather limited circle of possible recruits for spearheading a fundamental change in society. A recently published detailed analysis of the Cambridge visit substantiates that 'what he talked about was Socialism', and that at least one of his listeners 'was specially struck by Lawrence's eloquence'.[19]

In view of what we have already seen as the essential principles of Lawrence's plan for utopia, 'socialism', or 'nationalisation' of industries, land, communications and amusements lay at the heart of his proposed revolution. Yet it would be a mistake to conclude that because Lawrence gained little support at Cambridge for the version of 'socialism' which would form the economic basis of his new society, it was for that reason that he came away discouraged and retreated to struggle once more with his philosophy. We know, from surviving correspondence, that Russell was still prepared to support Lawrence in 'his socialist revolution'. In Russell's own words: 'I couldn't dream of discouraging his socialist revolution. He has real faith in it, and it absorbs his vital force – he must go through with it'; and Russell adds, significantly: 'He talks so well about it that he *almost* makes me believe in it'.[20] Russell has also recorded that John Maynard Keynes, who attended the dinner for Lawrence at Cambridge, was 'hard, intellectual, insincere' in his conversation with Lawrence. This is not surprising, since Keynes' views of economics and those which Lawrence put forth in his advocacy of 'socialism' could hardly be compatible.

It is my view, however, that it was not the disagreement on economic matters that finally shattered Lawrence's belief in making a new start for a better life, important though that disagreement was. As S. P. Rosenbaum has demonstrated so clearly, it was 'Keynes's homosexuality more than anything else that repulsed Lawrence'.[21] But it is only when we place this repulsion within the context of Lawrence's basic framework for 'Rananim' that we can begin to appreciate why the Cambridge experience was so devastating. Until then, Lawrence was absolutely certain that at the centre of the social revolution lay the inviolable principle of revitalised relationships between men and women, and all his vision for a new society was built on this foundation. Now his confrontation with Keynes at Cambridge which, in Lawrence's own words 'was one of the crises in [his] life' (*L.* II, p. 321), appears to have shaken his belief in the sacredness of the male–female relationship. 'Lawrence's intense and complex reaction to homosexuality',[22] as Rosenbaum points out, cannot be explained very easily and, certainly, no explanation will satisfy all students of Lawrence; and it is not my purpose here to attempt yet another explanation of that 'intense and complex reaction'. There can be no doubt, however, that the nature of the relation between the sexes has been and must be a major consideration for any utopist, and Lawrence is no exception. He often outlined how the male–female relation is paramount, and his hope for utopia is grounded in the belief that when this relationship is put right, all other things needful will follow: 'And upon what is this new era established? On the perfect circuit of flow between human beings. First the great sexless normal relation between individuals, simple sexless friendships, unison in family, and clan, and nation, and group. Next, the powerful sex relation between man and woman, culminating in the external orbit of marriage. And, finally, the sheer friendship, the love of comrades, the manly love which alone can create a new era of life.'[23]

Lawrence's first recorded reference to the effect of the Cambridge visit, as we have seen, leaves no doubt about the impression that he received: 'I went to Cambridge and hated it beyond expression' (*L.* II, p. 305). So profound was his revulsion that Lawrence seems to have retreated to making his decorative boxes, and he commissioned Koteliansky to send him various painting supplies for this activity. When he wrote to Russell afterwards, he still tried to convince the latter to 'keep somewhere, in the darkness of reality, a connection with [him]' (*L.* II, p. 307), but the enthusiasm for founding a new order is gone. The 'smell of rottenness, marsh-stagnancy' (*L.* II, p. 309) made him feel 'very black and down' (*L.* II, p. 309), and he now raised the question with Russell: 'How can so sick people rise up? They must die first' (*L.* II, p. 309). Russell paid a visit to Greatham, and they seem to have got on well – 'really been people living together' (*L.* II, p. 312), he writes to Lady Ottoline, and as if trying to reassure himself, he adds: 'I know Russell is with me, really, now' (*L.* II, p. 312.

Despite such protestations, however, nothing more definite with respect to the 'social revolution' emerged. Lawrence continued to struggle with his 'philosophy', and even found a new name for it, 'Morgenrot', but this version was never completed. Correspondence with Russell, who seems to have been his main hope for establishing an alliance for reform, lapsed, and when he finally writes again, on 29 April 1915, the subject of the letter is Lawrence's divorce costs and his intention to become 'a bankrupt' (*L.* II, p. 327). As for transforming England into a new society, Lawrence expresses 'hatred of the whole establishment' (*L.* II, p. 328), and vows 'to lay a mine under their foundation' (*L.* II, p. 328). The latest turn of events, which again strikes so close to his personal circumstances, brings forth the following vehement outburst: 'For I am hostile, hostile, hostile to all that is, in our public and national life. I want to destroy it' (*L.* II, p. 328). Shortly before, he had written to Lady Ottoline that 'we must form the nucleus of a new society, as we said at the very first' (*L.* II, p. 326), but with the latest turn of events that impulse has lost much of its momentum. No matter how bleak the outlook, however, Lawrence continued to hope, as this remark in a letter to Lady Cynthia Asquith shows: 'You learn to believe, in your very self, that we in England shall unite in our knowledge of God to live according to the best of our knowledge – Prime Ministers and capitalists and artisans all working in pure effort towards God – here, tomorrow, in this England' (*L.* II, p. 337). It is only through such an effort, he tells his correspondent, that 'you will save your own soul and the soul of your son' (*L.* II, p. 337). Lawrence is still convinced that only a fundamental change in attitude can bring about the condition necessary for human fulfilment, but he already realises that his is a voice crying in the wilderness: 'You see this change must come to pass. But nobody will believe it, however *obvious* it is. So it almost sends me mad, I am almost a lunatic' (*L.* II, p. 338).

If no one will believe him, then he must try to do something to convince them. In an attempt to enlighten public opinion, therefore, he and Russell agreed on a plan. This is how Lawrence describes it to Lady Ottoline: 'We think to have a lecture hall in London in the autumn, and give lectures: he on Ethics, I on Immortality: also to have meetings, to establish a little society or body around a *religious belief which leads to action* [Lawrence's italics]' (*L.* II, p. 359). Like his previous efforts, this collaboration with Russell was to end in failure, and in the end, Lawrence was forced to try to do something by himself. The confrontation over the 'Lectures', however, led Lawrence to address the question of the structure of government in an ideal state, and while the details are lacking, there is sufficient evidence in the correspondence to grasp the basic principles which he would like to put in place. It is ironic, indeed, to note that Russell, as a member of the established English aristocracy, is the advocate for 'democratic control' (*L.* II, p. 370), and Lawrence, born of the working class, argues for 'an elected aristocracy' (*L.* II, p. 371). Lawrence informs Lady Cynthia that he does not 'believe in the democratic (republican) form of election' (*L.* II, p. 368). What he envisions is a hierarchy of electors, with each group 'voting for that which [it] more or less understands through contact' (*L.* II, p. 368), and a system which 'works up to a Dictator who controls the greater industrial side of the national life' (*L.* II, p. 368) with a parallel system which would 'work up to a Dictatrix who controls the things relating to private Life' (*L.* II, p. 368). In this way, 'the women shall have absolutely equal voice with regard to marriage, custody of children etc.' (*L.* II, p. 368). Writing to Russell, Lawrence restates his belief that 'The working man shall elect superiors for the things that concern him immediately, no more. From the other classes, as they rise, shall be elected the higher governors. The thing must culminate in one real head, as every organic thing must – no foolish republics with foolish presidents, but an elected King, something like Julius Caesar' (*L.* II, p. 371). He also repeats his idea of a parallel female electorate: 'And as the men elect and govern the industrial side of life, so the women must elect and govern the domestic side. And there must be a rising rank of women governors, as of men, culminating in a woman Dictator, of equal authority with the supreme Man' (*L.* II, p. 371). There is no record of how Russell may have responded to Lawrence's proposed form of government, but it is easy to see that his ideas are not carefully considered political views. One could well ask about the relationship between the 'industrial side' and the 'domestic side', and whether these are in fact the mutually exclusive concerns which Lawrence would have us believe. Added to this, we might well wonder whether women would accept the obviously limited role that Lawrence gives them in the total structure. While, on the surface, Lawrence may seem to offer a system of equality for the sexes, closer examination would show this not to be the case. While 'custody of children' is of personal concern to someone like Frieda, since she was still battling for access to her children, what Lawrence calls 'the domestic side' would hardly satisfy the needs of all women for the development of their separate individualities, which Lawrence states is the goal for both men and women. There is, finally, something unsavoury in his adoption of the titles 'Dictator' and 'Dictatrix', which embody the kind of compulsion in personal affairs which Lawrence consistently rebels against.

That a reconciliation of Russell's and Lawrence's views would prove impossible is surely obvious, and by the late summer of 1915, when Lawrence was established at 1 Byron Villas, Hampstead, the plan for the joint lectures was all but abandoned. When Lady Cynthia enquires how the lectures are proceeding, Lawrence sadly answers: 'I don't know if they will ever begin. I don't see how I am to start' (*L.* II, p. 378). Having apparently failed to persuade Russell to give up his idea of democracy, Lawrence continues to insist that 'there are aristocrats and plebeians, born, not made. Some amongst us are born fit to govern, and some are born only fit to be governed' (*L.* II, p. 379). Although this inherent distinction is obvious to him, he could hardly expect the rest of society to accept his view. He tried to argue that 'even the most stupid of us will know how to choose our governors, and in that way we shall give the nucleus of our classes' (*L.* II, p. 379), but the 'question of the incontrovertible soul' (*L.* II, p. 379) is a much more problematical matter than Lawrence would care to admit. He is, nonetheless, forced to admit that he is left 'without associates' in his scheme and, feeling that his friends 'betray the real truth' (*L.* II, p. 380), he decides that 'One must start direct with the open public' (*L.* II, p. 381). His declaration henceforth is as follows: 'I don't want any friends, except the friends who are going to *act*, put everything – or at any rate, put *something* into the effort to bring about a new unanimity among us, a new movement for the pure truth, an immediate destructive and reconstructive revolution in actual life, England, now' (*L.* II, p. 381).

It was in the hope of influencing the 'open public' that in September 1915 Lawrence proceeded with plans to launch the periodical which he called *The Signature*, to be addressed to those 'people who care about the living truth of things' (*L.* II, p. 386). By this time, the break with Russell was irrevocable, but Lawrence still had in mind the eventual creation of an ideal society: 'I only want people who really care, and who really want a new world' (*L.* II, p. 387), and he thought that the ideas which he would expound in *The Signature* would 'start some germ of positive belief and [thus] work towards living, reconstructive action later on' (*L.* II, p. 396). To put it in another way, he planned to write 'the preaching – sort of philosophy – the beliefs by which one can reconstruct the world' (*L.* II, p. 386). He admitted that it was 'a rash venture' (*L.* II, p. 391), but he felt compelled that 'we must do something' (*L.* II, p. 391). He and Russell had 'become strangers again' (*L.* II, p. 392), and the loss of this last vestige of support for his utopian ideal made Lawrence 'feel like going into a corner to cry' (*L.* II, p. 393). Still, he was able to rouse his spirit and declare: 'Nevertheless, though the skies fall, or have fallen, one must go on with the living, constructive spirit – Somebody must' (*L.* II, p. 397).

Besides issuing a periodical, meetings were also planned, and some were apparently convened in the rented rooms in Fisher Street. Not only were there too few subscribers to *The Signature* to make it a success, but Lawrence's essay which he titled 'The Crown' failed to rally any kind of support for his new society. Even his friends, and Lady Cynthia Asquith is a good example, were 'rather hostile' (*L.* II, p. 411) to the latest expression of his philosophy. Lawrence professed that he did not 'want the *Signature* to be a success' (*L.* II, p. 411), but even his limited objective 'to rally together just a few passionate, vital, constructive people' (*L.* II, p. 411) was more than was ever achieved. He had set aside three months as the time which he was prepared to commit to the venture, but after six weeks and three numbers of the periodical, the whole effort was abandoned. On 21 October 1915 he wrote to Koteliansky that he was 'giving one week's notice' for terminating the rental of the Fisher Street rooms, and resigned himself to accepting the failure: 'Everything comes to an end' (*L.* II, p. 413). The Fisher Street tenancy duly ended on 30 October 1915, with Koteliansky being directed to 'carry round to the Bureau the curtains and the carpet' (*L.* II, p. 418); Lawrence would 'come and fetch them' (*L.* II, p. 418) later. As for the general state of affairs: 'At present all is turmoil and unrest' (*L.* II, p. 418).

The Signature was Lawrence's last sustained effort towards establishing 'Rananim', but despite its failure, Lawrence refused to give up his vision. Putting that preoccupation in religious terms, he wrote to Lady Cynthia Asquith: 'The fact of resurrection is everything, now: whether we dead can rise from the dead, and love, and live, in a new life, here' (*L.* II, p. 420). In due course, Lawrence abandoned his objective of changing English society and turned to America, saying, 'I think there is hope of a future in America' (*L.* II, p. 437); 'I shall try to start a new shoot, a new germ of a new creation, there: I believe it exists there already' (*L.* II, p. 438). When he meets several young people, among them Philip Heseltine, Robert Nichols and Aldous Huxley, Lawrence once more sees the possibility of founding a colony, hoping to 'unite with the very young people, to do something' (*L.* II, p. 468). His vision of 'Rananim' in Florida is described for Murry and Katherine Mansfield in these words: 'there we make songs and poems and stories and dramas' (*L.* II, p. 452); and he adds, almost pathetically, 'If only it will all end up happily, like a song or a poem' (*L.* ii, p. 452). The Florida 'expedition' came to nothing, since Lawrence's problems with the banning of *The Rainbow* and with the military service were such that he could hardly expect to obtain permission to leave the country. By the end of the year, on 30 December 1915, when he writes to Katherine Mansfield, he is already thinking about 'Rananim' as a thing of the past: 'I wish we'd had our Rananim – or got it.'[24]

Forced now to remain in England, Lawrence settles in Cornwall, where he tries to convince himself that this 'is the first move to Florida' (*L.* ii, p. 491); but it is not long before he admits to Koteliansky that he is 'willing to believe that there isn't any Florida' (*L.* ii, p. 498). The scheme, which he had described to Russell on 29 December 1915, whereby along with 'six or seven . . . all very young people' (*L.* ii, p. 490) they would 'go and start a new life in a new spirit – a spirit of coming together, not going apart' (*L.* ii, p. 490), the colony of which Russell could be 'president' if he wished, has become henceforth 'like artificial lights that are blown out – one can only remember it' (*L.* ii, p. 498). Even the much scaled down version of the ideal community, where for a time Murry and Katherine Mansfield came to live in a cottage beside that of the Lawrences, where Lawrence had hoped that the four of them together, if only they could 'sufficiently retire' from 'the world outside', could 'create a new world, from the spirit' (*L.* ii, p. 554), even this modest experiment came to nothing. None of Lawrence's list of projects for the two couples – 'learning Greek', building 'a carpenter's bench', 'woodcarving' and compiling 'an anthology of short stories from all over the world' (*L.* ii, pp. 597–8) – none of these ever came about.

Even so, Lawrence was not prepared to give up his dream of utopia. His letters to Koteliansky continued to broach the idea and to insist that the original idea was the right one; originally conceived at the end of December 1914, the vision of 'Rananim' periodically surfaces until January 1926. 'Where is our Rananim?' Lawrence asks on 4 September 1916, and he speculates somewhat wistfully, 'If only we had had the courage to find it and create it, two years ago. Perhaps it is not utterly too late' (*L.* ii, p. 650). When he writes to Koteliansky about two months later, on 7 November 1916, he appears to respond defensively to what may have been a note of scepticism on Koteliansky's part: 'I tell you *Rananim*, my Florida idea, was the true one. Only the *people* were

wrong. But to go to *Rananim without* the people is right for me, &
ultimately, I hope, for you' (*QR*, p. 95).[25] This is a puzzling
remark, because the whole purpose of the ideal colony was to
bring people together, and now the vision admits virtually no one
else. We might well ask, what sort of society can it be, if its
numbers are so limited?

It is January 1917 when Lawrence again mentions 'Rananim' to
Koteliansky. In what were for him among the darkest days of the
war, the dream of a faraway place, where it would be possible to
enjoy some respite from the unhappiness of the war, asserts itself
once more, and for a moment at least the possibility is manifest.
'My dear Kot', he writes, 'when we can but sail for our *Rananim*,
we shall have our first day of happiness. But it will come one
day – before very long. I shall go to America, when I can – & try
to find a place – & you will come. That is the living dream. We
will have our *Rananim*' (*QR*, p. 106). It would be several years yet
before Lawrence could leave England, and when he did, he did
not set out directly for America. From his letter to Koteliansky,
written just four days later, we can see how determined Lawrence
was: 'I shall say goodbye to England, forever, and set off in quest
of our *Rananim*. Thither, later you must come' (*QR*, p. 107).
Koteliansky must have been pressing Lawrence regarding the
details of the plan, and perhaps expressing his impatience at the
delay; he is told: 'Wait, only wait for our *Rananim*. It shall come
quite soon now' (*QR*, p. 108). Whether 'quite soon' was to be
taken as meaning a few months or a few years was apparently not
clear, and so we have an explanation in the letter of 9 February
1917: 'we shall come to our *Rananim* before many years are out –
only believe me – an Isle of the Blest, here on earth' (*QR*, p. 109).

Nothing is heard from Lawrence about his utopia until a year
later, by which time the dream is characterised as something that
was missed, an opportunity which was not seized. 'O my dear,
dear Kot', Lawrence says regretfully, 'why didn't we go to our
Rananim! What a weak-kneed lot we were, not to bring it off' (*QR*,
p. 130). Even as he wrote those words, Lawrence must have
realised that his earlier dream was no longer possible, but he still
hoped for a small measure of happiness, if only for a very short
period: 'Let us have our *Rananim* for a month or two, if we can't
for ever. – One must have something to look forward to' (*QR*,
p. 132). He expressed the same kind of short-term expectation to
Mark Gertler, and although he eschews the name, the possibility

of an ideal society has been scaled down to that of a vacation to be enjoyed together by his friends. The concept is not unlike his suggestion to Jessie Chambers, voiced many years earlier, for a big house in which 'all the people he liked could live together'.[26] Ever optimistic, Lawrence tells Gertler: 'So I always want to have a plan of going away after the war – anywhere that is not England – perhaps Italy – going away and living in one place, all of us, at least for a while. . . . Whatever you think of this plan, we might try it for a holiday.'[27] When he hears about Dr David Eder's trip to Palestine, Lawrence's reformist zeal flares up momentarily as he exclaims: 'I wish they'd give *me* Palestine – I'd Zionise it into a *Rananim*' (*QR*, p. 133), but this is surely only a passing thought.

Nearly a year goes by before he again mentions his former preoccupation to Koteliansky: 'I still have some sort of hope for our *Rananim*' (*QR*, p. 155). There is, however, no elaboration, and the hope is certainly a very faint hope. After three more years, Lawrence still recalls vividly that momentous Christmas in Bucks. in 1914, when the totality of the utopian vision had first manifested itself: 'I too think of the Bucks. Cottage fairly often, and still sometimes lull myself with: "Ranane Sadihkim/Sadihkim Badonoi" ' (*QR*, p. 232). On his way to San Francisco in May 1922, he writes Koteliansky that 'from Sydney we shall visit the South Sea Islands' (*QR*, p. 242), and the thought immediately conjures up the faded vision of his utopia – 'think of our "Rananim" ', he reminds his friend. As the Christmas of 1922 approaches, he is again reminded of the time in Bucks., a memory which he shares with the man who was so instrumental in supplying a name for the vision of a perfect society: 'Do you remember the Christmas in Bucks? – a cycle seems to have revolved since then, and come back to the same place. I feel a *bit* like I felt in Bucks.' (*QR*, p. 250). What the feeling was would be difficult to establish. Was it optimism, once more, that mankind could rejuvenate itself? Was it a glimmer of that 'new heaven and earth' which Lawrence had glimpsed long ago? Was it the belief reasserting itself that one man could perhaps start a whole new way of thinking and feeling and living? Whatever it was, Lawrence can think of no other appropriate word to describe his feeling and can only express himself to Koteliansky by once more invoking the symbolic potency of '*Rananim!*'. Still, nothing endures forever, and Lawrence's dream of utopia is no exception. The man who had so confidently proclaimed, 'Oh, but we are going. We are going to found an Order of the Knights of Rananim' (*L.* II, p. 252), and whose avowed mission was 'to see the social revolution set going' (*L.* II, p. 303), in the end is forced to accept failure. Twelve years later, Lawrence finally admits: 'That *Rananim* of ours, it has sunk out of sight' (*QR*, p. 276).

NOTES

1. Emile Delavenay, *D. H. Lawrence: l'Homme et la Genèse de son Oeuvre (1885–1919)* (Paris: Librairie C. Klincksieck, 1969) p. 665.
2. This account, attributed to May Chambers, is printed in *D. H. Lawrence: a Composite Biography*, ed. Edward Nehls, vol. III: *1925–1930* (Madison: University of Wisconsin Press, 1959) p. 601. The attribution is disputed in George J. Zytaruk, 'The Chambers Memoirs of D. H. Lawrence – Which Chambers?', *Renaissance and Modern Studies*, XVII (1973) pp. 5–37.
3. Delavenay, *Lawrence: l'Homme*, p. 665.
4. *Biography*, ed. Nehls, III, p. 602.
5. E.T. [Jessie Chambers], *D. H. Lawrence: a Personal Record* (Cambridge University Press, 1980) p. 49.
6. *The Letters of D. H. Lawrence*, ed. George J. Zytaruk and James T. Boulton, vol. II, *June 1913–October 1916* (Cambridge University Press, 1981). Citations to this volume will be given in parentheses within the text and abbreviated as *L.* II.
7. 'Study of Thomas Hardy' was published in *Phoenix: the Posthumous Papers of D. H. Lawrence*, ed. Edward D. McDonald (London: William Heinemann, 1936) pp. 398–516. The original typescript from which McDonald printed the text is clearly titled by Lawrence 'Le Gai Savaire'. This title should be restored when the book is edited for publication in the Cambridge Edition of the works of D. H. Lawrence. For some useful comments on the various versions of Lawrence's philosophy, see L. D. Clark, *The Minoan Distance: the Symbolism of Travel in D. H. Lawrence* (Tucson: University of Arizona Press, 1980) pp. 91–111.
8. See Lawrence's letter to J. B. Pinker, *The Letters of D. H. Lawrence*, ed. Aldous Huxley (London: William Heinemann, 1932) p. 414.
9. D. H. Lawrence, *'Fantasia of the Unconscious' and 'Psychoanalysis and the Unconscious'* (London: William Heinemann, 1961) Phoenix Edition, p. 9.
10. H. G. Wells, *A Modern Utopia*, Introduction by Mark Hillegas (Lincoln: University of Nebraska Press, 1967) p. 30.
11. See 'Selected List of Utopian Works 1850–1950', in *The Quest for Utopia: an Anthology of Imaginary Societies*, ed. Glen Negley and J. Max Patrick (College Park: McGrath, 1971) pp. 19–22.
12. Lawrence, 'Study of Thomas Hardy', in *Phoenix*, pp. 399–401.

13. Mrs Henry Jenner, *Christian Symbolism* (London: Methuen, 1910) p. 150.
14. *Journal of Katherine Mansfield*, ed. J. Middleton Murry (London: Constable, 1954) Definitive Edition, p. 65.
15. Beatrice, Lady Glenavy, *'Today we will only Gossip'* (London: Constable, 1964) p. 91.
16. *French Utopias: an Anthology of Ideal Societies*, ed. with an Introduction and translations by Frank E. Manuel and Fritzie P. Manuel (New York: The Free Press, 1966) pp. 250–58.
17. D. H. Lawrence, *Reflections on the Death of a Porcupine and Other Essays* (Bloomington: Indiana University Press, 1963) pp. 210–11.
18. *The Autobiography of John Middleton Murry: Between Two Worlds* (New York: Julian Messner, 1936) p. 322.
19. S. P. Rosenbaum, 'Keynes, Lawrence, and Cambridge Revisited', *Cambridge Quarterly*, XI (1982) p. 257.
20. See Russell's letter to Lady Ottoline quoted in ibid., p. 258.
21. Ibid., p. 261.
22. Ibid., p. 263.
23. D. H. Lawrence, *The Symbolic Meaning: the Uncollected Versions of 'Studies in Classic American Literature'* (New York: Viking, 1964) p. 238.
24. *The Collected Letters of D. H. Lawrence*, ed. Harry T. Moore, 2 vols (New York: Viking, 1962) p. 768.
25. *The Quest for Rananim: D. H. Lawrence's Letters to S. S. Koteliansky 1914–1930*, ed. George J. Zytaruk (Montreal: McGill-Queen's University Press, 1970). Citations to this volume will be given in parentheses within the text and abbreviate as *QR*.
26. Delavenay, *Lawrence: l'Homme*, p. 665.
27. *Collected Letters*, ed. Moore, p. 543.

18

Lawrence as Fictional Character

MAURICE BEEBE

No author since Byron has been depicted in fiction more often than D. H. Lawrence. What we think of as the Lawrence Legend probably owes as much to the peripheral literature that has grown up around his name as to his own writings. Just as his carelessness over copyright made some of his works fair game for unscrupulous publishers, Lawrence himself seems to have entered the realm of public domain. James Thurber's amusing spoof, 'My Memories of D. H. Lawrence' (1937), in which none of the recollections has any validity whatsoever, implies that some of the many memoirs of Lawrence that appeared after his death are fanciful and exaggerated enough to be considered at least partially as works of fiction. Lawrence compounded the difficulties of separating truth from fabrication by including distorted self-portraits in many of his novels and stories, and by collaborating imaginatively as well as literally with people who shared his experiences. Samuel Roth wrote anonymous sequels to *Lady Chatterley's Lover*, and J. I. M. Stewart includes in one of his recent novels a short poem, a *'pensiero di D. H. Lawrence'*, that reads as follows:

> Lost to a world in which I crave no part,
> I sit alone and commune with my heart:
> Pleased with my little corner of the earth,
> Glad that I came, not sorry to depart.[1]

The poem, inserted in *Young Pattullo* (1974) to arouse the curiosity of the hero of that novel and to make him visit Ravello in Italy, is only fictitiously a work by Lawrence, but it is now a modest little addition to the canon of the Lawrence Legend. In addition, there are parodies of Lawrence the man, burlesques of his writings, and film and stage versions of his life, such as Tennessee Williams's *I*

Rise in Flame, Cried the Phoenix (1951) and Christopher Miles's *Priest of Love* (1981), that obviously make use of fictional techniques as well as imagined events. And finally, as we shall see, there seems to be a new breakthrough in creative scholarship that enables inventive biographers to shape their versions of truth in strange ways.

The best-known fictional surrogate for Lawrence is Mark Rampion of Aldous Huxley's *Point Counter Point* (1928). Although both Lawrence and Huxley discounted the adequacy of the portrait, Lawrence finding him 'a gas-bag'[2] and Huxley admitting that 'Rampion is just some of Lawrence's notions on legs',[3] the identification of Rampion as Lawrence in Huxley's celebrated *roman-à-clef* can hardly be questioned, nor its importance in the ideological structure of the novel exaggerated. This is particularly evident when Rampion is seen as a midway stage between two other appearances of Lawrence in Huxley's fiction – first as J. G. Kingham in the novelette 'Two or Three Graces' (1926) and then as The Savage in *Brave New World* (1932).

A simple verbal link helps to establish the relationship of these works. We are told that before she met Kingham in person, Grace Peddley had no prejudices against him in spite of the fact that she had been told that 'the man was a savage'. She knows that 'savages, after all, are more attractive than repellent' (*TTG*, p. 148), and it is not long after their first meeting that Grace finds herself wildly in love with an outspoken and passionate man who provides an extreme contrast to the awful bore she married and the pseudo-bohemian dillettante with whom she has already had an affair. Kingham is introduced as a much-travelled writer with a 'close-cut beard, redder than his hair' and 'a brilliancy, a vividness about him' (p. 16). Scorning all forms of mediocrity, Kingham makes 'a habit of telling all his acquaintances, sooner or later, what he thought of them – which was invariably disagreeable' (*TTG*, p. 142). Like Lawrence, he is known by his initials, and in those rare moments when animation leaves his features, his face becomes 'like the face of a dead or dying Christ' (*TTG*, p. 157). He startles conventional people by not 'keeping a fig-leaf' over his mouth (*TTG*, p. 163), and there are other qualities that make Kingham one of the most Lawrentian of Lawrence surrogates in fiction.

Yet George Woodcock has argued that critics have wrongly 'imagined' Kingham to be a portrait of Lawrence. After all, Woodcock reminds us, Huxley took pains to disclaim the identification.[4] In a letter of 1930, Huxley wrote that Kingham was 'concocted' before he knew Lawrence – 'at least I'd only seen him once, during the War' (*Letters*, pp. 339–40). But if Huxley had seen Lawrence only once before writing 'Two or Three Graces', that one meeting seems to have had an unusually strong impact that was kept alive by Huxley's faithful reading of Lawrence's writings as they appeared.[5] During the eleven years that passed between meetings, one aspect of Lawrence remained particularly strong in Huxley's impression of him – his vision of a utopian colony.[6] Not long after the two young writers first met at the home of Lady Ottoline Morrell in 1915, Huxley wrote to his brother Julian in America that he was thinking of visiting that country himself:

> there is a good man going to Florida, one D. H. Lawrence, a novelist and poet and genius. . . . well, well, this good man, who impresses me as a good man more than most, proposes . . . to form a sort of unanimist colony. The purposes of which are to await a sort of Pentecostal inspiration of new life, which, whether it will come is another question. But Lawrence is a great man, and as he finds the world too destructive for his taste, he must, I suppose, be allowed to get out of it to some place where he can construct freely and where, by a unanimous process, the rest of his young colony might do the same. The gist of all which is that when, and if, I go and see you, I shall very likely go and see him also, to spend, perhaps a little while in his eremitic colony . . . which , I am sure, would be quite particularly medicinal to my soul. (*Letters*, p. 88)

J. G. Kingham also has a vision of a better world as he proclaims:

> The Utopia I offer is a world where happiness and unhappiness are more intense, where they more rapidly and violently alternate than here, with us. A world where men and women endowed with more than our modern sensitiveness, more than our acute and multifarious modern consciousness, shall know the unbridled pleasures, the cruelties and dangers of the ancient world, with all the scruples and remorses of Christianity, all its

ecstasies, all its appalling fear. That is the Utopia I offer you –
not a sterilised nursing home, with Swedish drill before
breakfast, vegetarian cookery, classical music on the radio, and
rational free love between aseptic sheets.   (*TTG*, p. 200)

If the sterile utopia he describes in contrast to his vital one sounds
rather like the society depicted in *Brave New World*, it is now
apparent that this is no accident. Peter Firchow has considered in
detail the many ways in which *Brave New World* depicts a conflict
between values that derive from such utopian writings by H. G.
Wells as *Men Like Gods* (1923) and the more primitivistic views that
may be found in Lawrence's writings about the Indians of New
Mexico.[7] Not the least telling of these associations is the Savage's
puritan revulsion when he sees how love-making is conducted at
the feelies, his preference for Shakespeare and early works of
romantic literature, his love for his mother in a society where
even the word 'mother' is forbidden, and his adherence to
ritualistic ceremonies that owe much to early Christianity. The
Savage is depicted sympathetically, but when he hangs himself at
the end of the novel, the implication is that there is no place in
the futuristic society for a person with deep feelings and old
values.

Philip Quarles, the Huxley-spokesman in *Point Counter Point*,
finds that 'after a few hours in Mark Rampion's company he
really believed in noble savagery'.[8] In a novel in which practically
every character is satirised, Rampion stands out as an admirable,
positive standard by which the deficiencies of the others can be
measured. 'What I complain of', he says upon his first appearance
in the novel, 'is the horrible unwholesome tameness of our world'
(*PCP*, p. 129). He produces a painting that satirises Wellsian
notions that equate evolution with improvement (*PCP*, pp. 289–
91), he is scornful of the scientists and industrialists who proclaim
the glories of material progress, his 'rather Utopian' educational
programme would call for teaching children nothing at all, letting
them grow up like peasants developing their natural virtues (*PCP*,
p. 437), and he has abiding faith that instincts are more important
than is intelligence (*PCP*, pp. 561–2). Philip Quarles rather envies
Rampion, not only because 'he lives in a more satisfactory way
than anyone I know' (*PCP*, p. 440), but also because he has
learned 'the art of integral living' (*PCP*, p. 444). When Philip
ponders, 'Shall I ever have the strength of mind to break myself

of these indolent habits of intellectualism and devote my energies to the more serious and difficult task of living integrally?' (*PCP*, p. 444), he sounds like a good prospect for that 'sort of unanimist colony' that Lawrence thought of starting and that Huxley thought of joining.

A deliberate attempt to turn real life into fiction and then fiction back into real life lies behind Lawrence's appearance as Derrick Hamilton in *Neutral Ground* (1933), a novel by Helen Corke that recounts not only the central dramatic situation of Lawrence's second novel, *The Trespasser* (1912), but also tells how the writing of that book came about. Lawrence and Miss Corke were teaching at different schools near Croydon when they first met during the winter of 1908–9. The following summer ended in disaster for Helen when Herbert Baldwin MacCartney, a married man from whom she had been taking violin lessons, killed himself shortly after they had gone on holiday together on the Isle of Wight. Lawrence returned from his own vacation to find her devastated by what had happened, and he appears to have encouraged her to put distance between herself and her dead lover by transforming the story of their relationship in a work of controlled art. That autumn, she wrote a short memoir of her liaison in the form of what is known as 'The Freshwater Diary'. This is itself a work of fiction, in which the male protagonist is named Siegmund in homage to MacCartney's admiration for Wagner, and the story is filled with lyrical images and musical analogies in a rather self-conscious attempt to make it appear poetic and artistic. Throughout her long life, Helen Corke tried to make sense of her most traumatic experience, incorporating a longer version of the diary-memoir as a quoted insert in *Neutral Ground* (which she finished writing in 1918, though it was not published until fourteen years later), and finally retelling the stories of her friendships with MacCartney and Lawrence in her admirable autobiography, *In Our Infancy* (1975), published when she was 93 years old.

The fact that Helen Corke persisted in telling her own story in her own words would suggest that she must have resented the way in which Lawrence appropriated that story in order to write *The Trespasser*. In composing his novel, originally called 'The Saga of Siegmund', Lawrence relied not only on 'The Freshwater Diary'

and increasingly intimate conversations with Helen about her
experience and her feelings, but also on a willingness to put
himself imaginatively in the place of the dead MacCartney.
Derrick Hamilton of *Neutral Ground* has 'an abnormal power of
psychic analysis',[9] and just as the self-portrait of Lawrence that
appears as Cecil Byrne in *The Trespasser* would like to think that
'history repeats itself'[10] when he goes walking with Helena on the
anniversary of a similar excursion she had made with MacCartney
the year before, Lawrence was to put much of himself into the
character of Siegmund. Helen Corke explained to Harry T. Moore
in a letter of 1951 that 'Lawrence identified himself so closely with
Siegmund that in a sense he lived the experience'.[11] That being
so, Lawrence may well have been offended if Helen, like Helena
in *The Tresapsser*, responded, 'I see no repetition' (p. 286), to his
assertion that history is repeating itself.

Near the end of *Neutral Ground*, the heroine, Ellis, begins 'to
feel some responsibility for Derrick. He had been her comrade,
unsought, self-appointed, through all the weary time since
Domine's death, and the burden of her love and sorrow had been
very heavy upon him. Patiently and strenuously he had worked
to revive the zest of life in her, always hoping that, by and by, she
would turn and see him, and love him with a wiser love than she
had given Rane' (*NG*, p. 274). But his efforts are in vain. He has
provided intellectual stimulation, and the warmth of his platonic
friendship has gone a long way towards purging her of the past,
but his romantic attentions and her inability to respond have only
forced her to recognise the neutral ground of her peculiarly
asexual nature. When she meets Theresa, Derrick's fiancée, that
fictional surrogate for Jessie Chambers feels a 'quick instinctive
jealousy' when she is told that Derrick and Ellis had spent much
time together the preceding autumn. To Theresa's anxious
question, 'Did you enjoy yourselves?', Ellis responds, 'No! we
didn't, really. We were alone together too long a time. We talked
and talked, always analytically, till we'd shredded up the very
strands that tie one into existence.' And when Theresa begs to be
told 'what is Derrick to you?' Ellis says rather grandly, 'He is a
wave. . . . He stimulates me, he swings me on – in a measure he
supports me. But there is no rest in him' (*NG*, p. 305).

Helen Corke's depiction of Lawrence as Derrick Hamilton in no
significant way contradicts the portrait of Lawrence drawn at
greater length in her *D. H. Lawrence: the Croydon Years* (1965) and

in her autobiography. Derrick is 22 when introduced, a young man with 'an extraordinary sensitive and impressionable temperament' (*NG*, p. 192) who has suffered from a chest weakness since early childhood. Entirely without practical teaching experience, he is observed after his first morning at the school striding from the building 'white and tense with irritation' (*NG*, p. 192). The men on the staff instinctively avoid him, partly because 'he had failed signally to pass their tests of capacity both for sport and school discipline', but 'later, when they had had some experience of his intellectual fearlessness and power of passionate argument', they 'paid him a grudging respect and kept out of his way' (*NG*, p. 193). Derrick's devotion to his mother is emphasised, and when Mrs Hamilton appears on the scene she obviously owes much to Mrs Morel of Lawrence's *Sons and Lovers*. It is easy to become confused when Theresa, 'a dark, handsome girl with drooping shoulders' (*NG*, p. 222) appears also, and one tries to untangle the Miriams and Jessies from the Helens and Ellises. It does not help to find in the somewhat fictionalised diary of the Initiation chapter of *In Our Infancy* that Theresa / Jessie / Miriam becomes 'Muriel', whom Helen has known as 'Emily' in the 'Nethermere' manuscript that was to become *Sons and Lovers*. Lawrence's poems to and about Jessie allude to her as 'Muriel'. And before 'Muriel' meets Helen in real life, she has read about 'Helena' in 'The Saga of Siegmund'. The two young women, meeting in reality in 1909, must have felt like fictional characters. 'She may resent my presence – and how detestable if I seem to intrude upon their older connection', Helen Corke writes in the guise of a diary kept at the time in question; 'Yet each of us has David's portrait of the other – I know her as "Emily" of *Nethermere* – she has just read the manuscript of *The Saga*.'[12]

The Trespasser and *Neutral Ground*, worlds within worlds, confusion of multiple identities, real and fictional – the reflexive aspects of the Corke–Lawrence relationship are obvious enough. *Neutral Ground* has long been out of print and is not easy to come by, but it easily stands comparison with *The Trespasser* in the credibility of its characters, the strength of its insight into the psychology of a woman liberated long before her time, and even in the smooth maturity of the writing. Whereas Lawrence's version of Helen Corke's story is all too often heavy-handed, solemnly earnest and melodramatic, *Neutral Ground* is marked by the kind of irony that enables the author to see both sides of all things – even people who trespass on the privacy of their friends:

> Ellis's swift glance warned him. He stopped, instantly humble. 'I beg your pardon! I've an insatiable interest in people – I can't help myself. You've not, I think. You will find it difficult to forgive me.'
>
> 'No!' said Ellis, a little surprised at herself. 'I do not. But you shouldn't trespass!'
>
> 'I'll keep on the high road if you'll walk with me,' said Hamilton lightly. 'But I can't help the opinion that the folk who spoil the countryside with "Trespassers will be prosecuted" notice boards are unjustifiable. The earth, you know, is the Lord's.'
>
> 'Yes!' said Ellis. 'But nevertheless I'm going to reserve the right of building a wall round my garden.'
>
> 'And also,' Derrick surmised, 'of sticking the top of it full of bits of broken glass!'   (*NG*, p. 198)

Not so much Lawrence himself as the Lawrentian type is to be found in the character of James Logan in Gilbert Cannan's *Mendel: a Story of Youth* (1916). Based closely on the life of Mark Gertler, whose path was to cross those of both Cannan and Lawrence at several important intervals, this forgotten novel is a *Kunstlerroman* that takes Mendel Kühler from his poverty-stricken childhood in the Jewish ghettoes of Austria and London to a successful career as a painter whose good looks and talent grant him access to the more fashionable levels of society. More than anyone else, the painter Logan helps to encourage Mendel and to inspire him with notions of greatness, and though Logan may well owe as much to Whistler and other free-spirited bohemians of life and fiction as he does to Lawrence, it is not difficult to see why Frieda Lawrence could recognise some of her husband's speeches in the words of Logan.[13]

When Mendel and a friend visit the studio of the 'great man' for the first time, Logan greets them without a word and rushes back to his easel, working with furious energy until a woman comes out of a door behind him and crosses the studio. He hurls his palette into the air and shouts, 'How can I work with these constant interruptions? Damn it all, an artist must have peace!'[14]

He proves more amiable on subsequent meetings, especially at his bohemian haunts in Soho, and it is not long before he has appointed himself mentor, agent and partner to the more talented Mendel. 'Like a figure of Blake, immense, looming prophetic, beckoning to achievement' (*MSY*, pp. 177–8), Logan stood to Mendel 'for adventure and freedom, independence and courage' (*MSY*, p. 287). Frieda could well have recognised her husband in such proclamations of Logan as this one:

> 'Humanity,' said Logan cheerfully, 'is fast going to hell. It likes it; and as the democratic idea is that it should have what it likes, not a finger, not a voice is raised to stop it. Everything that stands in the way – ideals, decency, responsibility, passion, love – everything is smashed. Nothing can stop it unless their eyes are opened and their poor frozen hearts are thawed.' . . . 'We passionate natures,' said Logan, striding up and down like Napoleon on the quarter-deck of the *Bellerophon* – 'we passionate natures must take control. We must be the nucleus of true fiery stuff to resist the universal corruption. We must be dedicated to the wars of the spirit.' (*MSY*, p. 234)

Unfortunately for Logan, it is his passionate nature which finally destroys him. Mendel comes to realise that Logan is less original than he thought himself to be, and he sees that Logan can never be strong as a painter nor free as a man unless he breaks away from his possessive mistress. That woman, Oliver, in whom Frieda thought she saw something of herself, comes to exist for Mendel 'hardly at all as a person, but as an evil, fixed will set on the destruction of Logan, of friendship, of art, of love, of beauty, of everything that lived distinctly and clearly with a flame-like energy' (*MSY*, p. 388). Finally, in a fit of jealousy, Logan kills Oliver and mortally wounds himself. Mendel visits his dying friend in the hospital, and the novel ends with some high-flown utterances about the dangers of passion and the 'profanation of the holy spirit of art' (*MSY*, pp. 429–30) that could only have annoyed Lawrence. Lawrence was still a young man near the beginning of his literary career when Cannan appropriated him for the character of Logan, and while that portrait may have helped to promote the legend of Lawrence, it is interesting to note that whatever prophecy may lie behind Logan's fate turned out to be false. It was Gilbert Cannan, not Lawrence, whose uncontrolled passions led him from one personal disaster to another and finally caused him to be certified as insane.[15]

To a lesser degree than with the parallels to be found in *The Trespasser* and *Neutral Ground*, *Mendel* demonstrates some of the give-and-take that makes it difficult sometimes to decide who borrows from whom in the developing legend of Lawrence as hero. Lawrence seems to have drawn on Cannan's depiction of bohemian locales in London as well as on his own experience for similar scenes in both *Women in Love* and *Aaron's Rod*, and there is a rather curious passage about two crudely carved African figurines (*MSY*, p. 360) that may explain the appearance of a similar scene in *Women in Love*.

Such give and take seems especially complicated when one turns to Hilda Doolittle's *Bid Me to Live (A Madrigal)* (1960) and considers the tangled relationships depicted not only in that frankly autobiographical novel, but in works of fiction by several other characters in the book. Here are the essential facts behind these people and their works.

In the autumn of 1917, wartime embarrassments caused the Lawrences to leave Cornwall, where they had been staying in a cottage belonging to the musician Cecil Gray, and to move in with Hilda Doolittle at 44 Mecklenburgh Square in London. They spent about six weeks there, from 20 October until December. Captain Richard Aldington, Hilda's estranged husband, was occasionally home on leave during this period, and it was about this time that he started an affair with a young American woman, Dorothy Yorke, who lived upstairs in rooms previously rented by John Cournos, to whom Dorothy had been engaged. Cecil Gray, who may have been sexually involved with Frieda in Cornwall, appeared in London, and it was not long before an attachment developed between him and Hilda. They lived together in Cornwall during the spring and early summer of 1918, and Hilda gave birth to a daughter in March 1919. Cournos, who seems to have thought that Hilda was romantically attracted to him, was out of the country during the weeks when the Lawrences lived at Mecklenburgh Square, but he wrote a fictionalised account of what he knew about Hilda's life in *Miranda Masters* (1926), which Lawrence is known to have read. In *Aaron's Rod* (1922), Lawrence had already described the Hilda–Aldington–Dorothy triangle, and among the heavy satire of Aldington's *The Death of a Hero* (1929) may be found his own bitter description of the two women who had been his wife and his mistress.

Fortunately, it is not necessary to compare at length the four novels that describe the Aldington ménage at the time when the Lawrences resided there, nor to discover the 'truth' behind the fictionalised events; that has been attempted elsewhere.[16] What matters here is the way in which Lawrence's limited role in the madrigal centred around Hilda has been inflated to such an extent that it begins to take on the dimensions of a legend. Unless something of Lawrence lies behind the narrow-chested Mr Bobbe, whose humble origins and malevolent class-hatred make him the Thersites of his day, Lawrence plays no significant role in *The Death of a Hero*. As Richard Somers in *Aaron's Rod*, he is largely only an observer, and his role is marginal in *Miranda Masters*, where he appears as Richard Ramsden, a poet whose frankly pagan verses have scandalised all of England. The Cournos figure of that novel warns the heroine, 'You must have nothing to do with him! He is a great flame, it is true, but a disintegrating flame. Everything he touches falls to ashes in the contact! Frankly I don't like him as a man!'[17]

On the other hand, Lawrence tends to dominate *Bid Me to Live*, and it is precisely his flame, 'the cerebral burning'[18] of his inspiration that lies behind the conception of Hilda Doolittle's work. Just as she and Lawrence maintained a correspondence, exchanging manuscripts of their writings as well as letters, during the several years from the time of their first meeting in 1914 until 1917, so Julia, the heroine of *Bid Me to Live*, has had an intense epistolary relationship with Rico, the Lawrence figure. 'Rico's flaming letters had been no ordinary love-letters', Julia tells us, 'they were written to her in "pure being", as he said' (*BML*, p. 58). She reflects in this way while awaiting the arrival in London of Rico and Elsa, 'his great Prussian wife' (*BML*, p. 58) whose firm-fleshed body could be expected to take care of his other needs while Julia and Rico 'would burn away, cerebristically, they would burn out together' (*BML*, p. 58). Then Rico appears:

> There he sat. He had poured himself, at volcanic heat, into his novels, those heady sex-expositions that nobody would publish, after his last novel had been suppressed. . . . His

poems were written at the same state of molten-lava temperature, but now the lava was cool, ashes fell almost visibly upon them. He was tired out. . . . Soon he would be white and drawn, as he had been the first time she saw him, visibly an invalid, with his narrow chest, his too-flaming beard, his blue eyes. The eyes looked at her, not surprised to see her, as if he had been there a long time. (*BML*, pp. 76–7)

In Elsa's presence, Rico declares to Julia, 'You are there for all eternity, our love is written in blood' (*BML*, p. 78), but the next day, when the two are left alone together, Rico fails a crucial test:

She got up; as if at a certain signal, she moved toward him; she edged the small chair toward his chair. She sat at his elbow, a child waiting for instruction. Now was the moment to answer his amazing proposal of last night, his 'for all eternity.' She put out her hand. Her hand touched his sleeve. He shivered, he seemed to move back, move away, like a hurt animal, there was something untamed, even the slight touch of her hand on his sleeve seemed to have annoyed him. Yet, last night, sitting there, with Elsa sitting opposite, he had blazed at her; those words had cut blood and lava-trail on this air. Last night, with the coffee-cups beside them on the little table, he had said 'It is written in blood and fire for all eternity.' Yet only a touch on his arm made him shiver away, hurt, like a hurt jaguar. (*BML*, p. 81)

Her brief touch and his quick recoil are all the physical contact Julia and Rico have in this novel, and it is clear that for him at least their relationship must remain on the platonic level.

Yet the bond of their love in that otherworldly relationship remains as strong as ever. Julia cannot have Rico physically, but when Vane (Cecil Gray) arrives, she feels that 'it would be madness to reject this gift, this gift of the gods, of Rico. It was Rico who had brought him to the house and it was Rico ironically who had precipitated this . . . "You and Vane are made for one another," Rico had jeered' (*BML*, pp. 120–1). Later, after she has gone to live with Vane in the country, she finds herself annoyed by Rico's prying into the intimate details of her life there, as if he were gathering material for one of his novels:

But I am aware of your spider-feelers, I am not walking into your net. I am not answering your questions, 'What room have you? What room has Vanio?' Not quite so obvious as 'Do you sleep together?' I am not telling you of my reactions, or if there were or were not reactions on his part. A nice novel, eh Rico?

And then, forgetting that she has already put him into *her* novel, Julia proclaims, 'So Rico, your puppets do not always dance to your pipe' (*BML*, p. 164). Nonetheless, *Bid Me to Live* ends with a long letter to Rico that makes it clear that he continues to dominate her thoughts and her artistic compositions. She tells him about a vision she experienced shortly after she arrived at her place of exile:

> When I 'got out' in Corfe (I was in a fever) I went into a little house, quite a simple little house in the forest. You were out cutting wood, like a woodcutter in a fairy-tale. It was the air. I felt cooped-up in that cottage. I was writing the Orpheus sequence for you. But when I 'got out' it was all very simple.
> I was waiting for you.   (*BML*, p. 173)

Vane may serve as a temporary and temporal mate, but it was Rico who 'started this' (*BML*, p. 174), and Julia will continue to think of him as her spiritual 'husband' (*BML*, p. 141).

Until the appearance of Janice Robinson's recent biography of Hilda Doolittle,[19] there seemed no reason to question the accuracy of the Doolittle–Lawrence relationship as it is described in *Bid Me to Live*. In a 1960 interview in *Newsweek*, Hilda admitted that the book was 'completely autobiographical',[20] and such biographers of Lawrence as Emile Delavenay, Emily Hahn and Paul Delany have used the novel as if it were a reliable account of what happened at Mecklenburgh Square. None of the letters that passed between Hilda and Lawrence before 1917 seems to have survived, and unless these letters were to turn up, any attempt to know the whole story of their relationship must remain conjectural. There can be little doubt that Hilda, like other women who knew Lawrence, was deeply attracted to him and saw herself as something of a disciple at the Orphic level.[21] That he profoundly influenced her writings, perhaps even more than did Ezra Pound, is shown by the many parallels of themes, images and allusions traced in Robinson's study. But there is no convincing primary evidence to support Robinson's claims for a much more intimate personal relationship than has been assumed. She implies that Lawrence was deeply involved with Hilda, that *Bid Me to Live* is a cover-up, that Lawrence was perhaps the father of Hilda's baby, and that both *Lady Chatterley's Lover* and *The Man Who Died* were largely inspired by his affair with her. Without the missing letters or other documentary evidence, it seems unlikely that reliable scholars will ever be able to prove conclusively the validity of these speculations, or to refute them, but for now it may suffice to consider the Robinson critical biography as if it were still another work of fiction whose existence in print can only add significantly to the Lawrence Legend. *Bid Me to Live* was thought to be in part about the failure of Hilda Doolittle to achieve a physical relationship with Lawrence. Now, through the alchemy of the confusion that comes from trying to separate works of fiction from the real events on which they are based, it is only a matter of time before some people accept the Robinson thesis as the truth. Then *Bid Me to Live* will be thought to conceal the real story of a passionate love affair that was told more truly in *Lady Chatterley's Lover*!

No wonder Julia could say of Rico, 'He is part of the cerebral burning, part of the inspiration. He takes but he gives' (*BML*, p. 67).

NOTES

1. J. I. M. Stewart, *Young Pattullo* (Boston: Little, Brown, 1974) pp. 304, 310.
2. *The Collected Letters of D. H. Lawrence*, ed. Harry T. Moore (New York: Viking, 1962) p. 1096. See also Lawrence's verses 'I Am in a Novel' in *The Complete Poems of D. H. Lawrence*, ed. Vivian de Sola Pinto and Warren Roberts (New York: Viking, 1964) p. 489.
3. *Letters of Aldous Huxley*, ed. Grover Smith (New York: Harper & Row, 1969) p. 340. References to this book are made in the text as *Letters*.
4. Aldous Huxley, *Two or Three Graces and Other Stories* (George H. Doran, 1926) p. 148. References to this book are made in the text as *TTG*.
5. George Woodcock, *Dawn and the Darkest Hour: a Study of Aldous Huxley* (New York: Viking, 1972) pp. 131–6.
6. There are a considerable number of studies that trace the Huxley–Lawrence connection. Among the better ones are: Pierre Vitoux, 'Aldous Huxley and D. H. Lawrence: an Attempt at Intellectual Sympathy', *Modern Language Review*, LXIX (July 1974) pp. 501–22; Joseph

Goldridge Bentley, 'Aldous Huxley's Ambivalent Responses to the Ideas of D. H. Lawrence', *Twentieth-Century Literature*, XIII (Spring 1935) pp. 96–108; and Jerome Meckier, *Aldous Huxley: Satire and Structure* (London: Chatto & Windus, 1969) pp. 78–123.

7. Peter Firchow, 'Wells and Lawrence in Huxley's *Brave New World*', *Journal of Modern Literature*, V (April 1976) pp. 260–78. See also John Hawley Roberts, 'Huxley and Lawrence', *Virginia Quarterly Review*, XIII (Autumn 1937) pp. 546–57.

8. Aldous Huxley, *Point Counter Point* (London: Chatto & Windus, 1928) p. 270. References to this book are made in the text as *PCP*.

9. Helen Corke, *Neutral Ground* (London: Arthur Barker, 1933) p. 192. References to this book are made in the text as *NG*.

10. D. H. Lawrence, *The Trespasser* (Cambridge: Cambridge University Press, 1981) p. 226. The background of Lawrence's novel is skilfully traced in Louise Wright's 'Lawrence's *The Trespasser*: its Debt to Reality', *Texas Studies in Literature and Language*, XX (Summer 1978) pp. 230–48.

11. Harry T. Moore, *The Priest of Love: a Life of D. H. Lawrence* (New York: Farrar, Straus & Giroux, 1974) p. 134.

12. Helen Corke, *In Our Infancy: an Autobiography, Part I: 1882–1912* (Cambridge University Press, 1975) p. 187.

13. Frieda Lawrence, *The Memoirs and Correspondence* ed. E. W. Tedlock, Jr (New York: Alfred A. Knopf, 1964) p. 207.

14. Gilbert Cannan, *Mendel: a Story of Youth* (George H. Doran, 1916) p. 164. References to this book are made in the text as *MSY*.

15. See Diana Farr, *Gilbert Cannan: a Georgian Prodigy* (Chatto & Windus, 1978). The murder-suicide that ends Logan's life in *Mendel* was actually based on the fate of a painter named John Currie who killed his mistress, Dolly Henry – see ibid., p. 140.

16. Peter Firchow, 'Rico and Julia: the Hilda Doolittle–D. H. Lawrence Affair Reconsidered', *Journal of Modern Literature*, VIII, no. 1 (1980) pp. 51–76.

17. John Cournos, *Miranda Masters* (New York: Alfred A. Knopf, 1926) pp. 175–6.

18. Hilda Doolittle, *Bid Me to Live (A Madrigal)* (New York: Grove Press, 1960) p. 67. References to this book are made in the text as *BML*.

19. Janice S. Robinson, *H.D.: the Life and Work of an American Poet* (Boston: Houghton Mifflin, 1982).

20. Cited in ibid., p. 133n.

21. A revealing letter from Lawrence to Cecil Gray on 7 November 1917 seems rather emphatic in the distinction it makes between the kind of 'Hebridean' relationship Gray had with Frieda and the 'Orphic' tie between Lawrence and some of his women friends: 'my "women" [Esther Andrews, Hilda Aldington, etc.] represent, in an impure and unproud, subservient, cringing, bad fashion, I admit – but represent none the less the threshold of a new world, or underworld, of knowledge and being. . . . You want an emotional, sensuous underworld, like Frieda and the Hebrideans: my "women" want an ecstatic subtly-intellectual underworld, like the Greeks–Orphicism – like Magdalen at her feet-washing – and there you are' (*Letters*, p. 532).

Hilda's name, omitted from the Huxley and Moore editions of Lawrence's letters, was restored from the original manuscript by Paul Delany in *D. H. Lawrence's Nightmare: the Writer and his Circle in the Years of the Great War* (Basic Books, 1978) p. 333. It will be remembered that Julia is writing her Orphic sequence at the end of *Bid Me to Live*. Perhaps the main weakness of the Robinson thesis is the way in which she tends to overlook simple literary influence. Much of what Robinson would like to think is the product of shared experience would appear to derive from Hilda's devoted reading of Lawrence's works over the extended period of years in which she revised her writings.

19

Elegies for D. H. Lawrence

JAMES C. COWAN

When D. H. Lawrence died in Vence on 2 March 1930, the response was immediate and widespread if not quite unanimous. Complaints by Lawrence supporters such as Rebecca West, E. M. Forster and Rhys Davies[1] against the hostile nature of many Lawrence obituaries, although in part justified by negative commentaries in the London press such as J. C. Squire's in the *Observer* and those in *The Times* and the *Evening Standard*,[2] led to the widely accepted but erroneous idea that Lawrence's obituary press was universally disparaging. A recent study by Dennis Jackson of more than 200 obituary notices in Britain, Europe, America and Australia has shown that most obituaries throughout the world were journalistically fair, and that some played the story as a significant news event.[3] Little notice has been taken, however, of the various poetic responses to Lawrence's life and death, to his personality and ideas, or to particular elements of his work, some written immediately after his death, others years after the event. In this study, I should like to focus attention on a group of five poems written in response to Lawrence's death, including Ruth Lechlitner's poetic lament 'Resurrection in Exile: to D. H. Lawrence' (1930); three poems which, in one sense or another, constitute poetic elegies for Lawrence, namely Walter Lowenfels' *Elegy in the Manner of a Requiem in Memory of D. H. Lawrence* (1932), William Carlos Williams' 'An Elegy for D. H. Lawrence' (1935) and Marya Zaturenska's 'In song, the Countersign' (1937), which is inscribed 'In Memoriam: D. H. Lawrence'; and, finally, John Clellon Holmes' 'Dying Lawrence' (1976), which comments on the death from the perspective of distance.

Ruth Lechlitner's 'Resurrection in Exile: to D. H. Lawrence',[4] written in twenty-three lines of iambic pentameter concluding with a single iambic dimeter line, from the setting of a high place in 'the olive-silvered hills' of France, employs nature imagery to suggest Lawrence's death

> From this high place the restless sea is still,
> Each seeking wave is quiet; and the red rock
> That crumbling bared its ragged teeth, recedes
> Through space to purple silence

his struggle for Beauty

> against the wilful blind
> Who prisoned her in walls of stone and steel

his taking Beauty to himself and

> Fighting with whips the rebel's fight, alone
> And fighting Death

and ultimately his apotheosis as his soul speaks from the eternal cycle of nature

> 'Yet is uplifted in me the pure beam
> Of immortality to kindle up
> Another Spring and yet another year
> Folded as yet.'

If the prosody is sometimes slightly irregular, the formal plan of the poem is not, as it presents an elegiac theme in a conventional pattern of imagery, moving from the poet's death, through a reflection on the struggles which preceded his death, to consolation in the life cycle of nature.

Walter Lowenfels' *Elegy in the Manner of a Requiem in Memory of D. H. Lawrence*[5] (alluded to as *Lament* in Keith Winter's satire of D. H. Lawrence and his circle, *Impassioned Pygmies*) consisted, according to the author, 'of lines 4678 to 5184 from Book II of REALITY PRIME'. 'Intended for a choral service, in the manner of a Requiem for a dead man', the poem is marked with marginal abbreviations for voices: 'B, Baritone; C, Chorus; Q, Choir; T, Tenor; S, Soprano; A, Contralto; O, Bass'. As the author's note explains, 'I have had in mind a form of operatic poem: verse, music, moving design, synchronized on a recording instrument: reproduced, from records, privately by the "reader".' In 'the program furnished for the composition of music to the Lawrence section', Lowenfels offers the following detailed statement of the theme:

> Elegy = search for elegy = search for resolution of individual inner drive (toward life, toward death) vs. general outer pressure (toward life, toward death) = how resolve these extremes? the one and the many? Lawrence (poet, creative individual) and the uncreative mass that creates him? concrete reality (the way outer, common things seem) and visions, dreams? (the way outer common things do not seem).
>
> Search for elegy = search for continuity between dead and living = how demarcate between what is creatively alive and creatively dead, now in confusion through lack of creative human acts? = extreme contrast between creative, human aspirations (angels) and 'acts' of biological continuity (insects).
>
> Problem: how resolve this death; how justify this experience?
>
> Resolution: biology, plants, insects, flies breeding maggots out of sacrificial flesh; not creative human acts.
>
> Disintegration, the extreme negation = the human creation.

The elegy is divided into five parts, with a transition between Parts II and III.

Part I, 'In the Valley of the Corpses', introduces the poem with the many voices of choir and chorus and with periodic arias by tenor, baritone and bass. The author's note identifies the 'Symbol: life frozen in winter marshes. The outer scene symbol for inner experience traversed in elegiac search.' The opening passage echoes T. S. Eliot's *The Waste Land* in the apostrophe to the drowned Phoenician sailors:

> Phoenician
> sailors from Tyre
> ghosts of ships that haunt these ports
> you who sought death in strange lands.

The allusion to Eliot establishes a link between *Elegy* and *The Waste Land*, both of which begin with a vision of the modern

world as a generation which prefers death to life. Lowenfels'
moderns, in fact, wilfully seek out death. The alternative is posed
in the figure of Lawrence, to whom the poet refers amid the
imagery of the south of France where Lawrence died. The elegist
himself appears as a disciple who still carries Lawrence's message,
in an allusion to the central images of *The Rainbow*, rainbow arch
and wedding:

> Miles centuries days
> from the heart's land I carry his awkward bow
> like a wedding of despair.

The imagery reinforces the sense of despair ('O Winter in the
cones') as the poet begins his quest for elegy and hence for
renewed, creative life, 'seeking an elegy for him / dead . . . / in this
Atlantis of the mind'. In *The Waste Land*, the speaker asks, 'What
are the roots that clutch?' (line 19). In *Elegy*, the roots are 'rotting',
signalling a further decline. But the poem presents a world not of
archetypal disorder but of impotence and inaction, as in *The Love
Song of J. Alfred Prufrock* and *The Hollow Men*:

> We cannot sink. We cannot rise.
> We freeze. We crack
> to any single thing.

Much of the imagery continues to echo Eliot's, particularly that of
The Hollow Men, as Lowenfels presents a world in which even
pain is unfelt as

> a shadow sweeps us
> like a wing above our rock
> to an immolation we do not know,

and confesses,

> . . . we evade
> the evocation of an instant.

The frozen condition is conveyed as succinctly as Eliot conveys
that of the 'hollow men':

> We are the should be's of the dead
> doomed to winter it among the squids
> fixed in snows of unaspiring centuries
> in the ice-age of our make-believe.

Unable to die a creative death, these moderns – 'who never saw Dionysus in the flesh' – are unable to be reborn in the cycle of life. Dionysus, who will later be identified with Lawrence as the mourned poet Dion, here represents the vitality which the moderns lack:

> Purifier!
> Destroyer! Avenger!
> How call you?

For the problem has now become, as Lowenfels' outline of the elegy suggests, how to evoke 'Dionysian mysteries, religious ecstasy, dream acted out as reality in the flesh', or, in the imagery of the concluding verse paragraph of this section, 'among the corpuscles', 'in the blood'.

The second part of the poem, 'In the Valley of the Poet', isolates from the 'many' the figure of the 'one', the poet, in a series of images of the unremitting cycle of death and rebirth. The opening lines of the section place the source of poetry in the uroboric cauldron of the ocean floor where the dead become the seeds from which new life will arise:

> This is the valley of the sea-spores
> and the rain of dead things drop
> to lay on the sea-bottom
> their eternal floor.

The sea change to which this leads is a series of imagined lives: one who followed the heart which 'rose/like Elijah on a jewel'; another who held 'on the stage/a spot light of soliloquy'; another whose 'time was like an accordion stretching out':

> I aged three score and ten
> too quickly between each shake of the tongue
> for others to know
> coming and going
> how often I died
> to compose another me;

another who by poetry distilled experience and

> . . . showed to others
> the skeleton only
> of what the poem had eaten away.

Instead of the phoenix-flame of rebirth, he knows only

> a flame of egophagy
> purifying to nothing
> but the ash.

From these imagined lives, however, the poet's self emerges, phoenix-like, unique and alone, an identifiable soul:

> Rising I rose
> a chrysalis into change
> and left one drop of blood behind
> from the living heights
> dropping to the sea floor.

The last section of Part II, 'I heard a nightingale among the whales', which has sometimes been printed as a separate poem, functions as a transition to Part III. Moving from the ocean floor to the Swiss Alps, the elegist evokes images of sea mammals, of insects and spiders, and of wild flowers – edelweiss, bluebells, ipakak, hawkweed – as images of the ' "acts" of biological continuity' in the life cycle of nature: 'Now is the land seasonal again.'

Part III, 'Among the Luminals', resumes the elegiac search for the poet who will provide the necessary 'human, creative aspiration' to unite body and idea: 'So I fled into the thing for him.' Without the poet, the elegist must ask:

> Caught trapped
> without a word among the luminals?
> O Master what rituals of what seasons?

Much of the imagery of sea-life and ocean floor is reiterated, followed by the citrus visions of limes and oranges, but the poet is not yet found, the rebirth is not yet effected, and the Dionysian potential waits beneath the sea:

So your human yolk
flowers like a crab with anemone
only inwardly like the crystal of a cancer
and cracks in the shell
for not being born.

As a consequence, in a strikingly Lawrentian image,

the sperm of the mind
struck from its roots
fertilized monstrosities
    among the vacuums.

  In Part IV, 'The Return', Lawrence's death is evoked as a source
of new creative life:

Dion is dead.
We cannot rise. He cannot sink.
  He is the last
none left to carry a choir of song
to sing a last melody.

Hence, he is now invoked:

. . . O master a thousand years away
    lift this dying
into the elegy we missed.

As Lowenfels employs the term, it is elegy that provides the
'continuity between dead and living' and makes creative act
possible. The elegist sees the modern world as Lawrence had seen it:

We are sick.
We are dribbling into death
and the mind's a quack
    curing nothing with quicksilver.

Thus, Lawrence, who is seen throughout as a bull ('Hoofed O
Phoenix') is addressed again in epic epithets:

> Hoof-glitterer! Charger in the sun! From the hilltop
> pawing the cliffs and the wild.

It is the human aspirations that Lawrence represents that will again call forth elegy,

> sweeping in one undying crest
> the elegy's endless wave.

Part V, 'Among the Revelations', is an apocalyptic vision in which 'a voice of burial' speaks with the sound of the wind-tossed forest after 'the voices had departed and the waters rolled above the trees':

> For the many
> just that remains
> of which your christ is oblivious.

Thus, religious revelation becomes meaningless, 'like an ocean in an empty shell'. Moving 'among the pieces', among various images of decay, putrefaction, disintegration, the elegist expresses, as Lowenfels' note to this section indicates, 'Glorification of maggots, life out of death. World as organism. . . . Lawrence's dead body as food for natural process':

> Saprini Sarcophagi
> the master of ghouls
> all workers in putrefaction
> the white bark of them egg-laying
> a white manna of the sea.

As Lowenfels' note explains, 'the extreme experience evokes the extreme humility. "Catharsis." Biological continuity = Jesus among the maggots; Lawrence among the beetles; Orpheus among the corpuscles'. If this reading is not immediately apparent from the imagery, what is clear is that the consolation, tenuous but traditional, depends upon the life cycle of nature as the source of whatever revelation there is.

William Carlos Williams' 'An Elegy for D. H. Lawrence: Died 2 March 1930',[6] although not traditional in form, contains conventions of the traditional pastoral elegy, such as grief for the dead poet, imagery of nature, particularly that of water and flowers, song from nature in mourning, and the relation of the poet's life and death to the movement of seasons.

Set in early March, the time of Lawrence's death, the elegy is structured upon an ironic counterpoint between the fact of his death and the resurrection of spring that he will never see.

> Green points on the shrub
> and poor Lawrence dead.
> The night damp and misty
> and Lawrence no more in the world
> to answer April's promise.

Death, however, reveals some truths that life does not. The second verse paragraph develops the further irony that in life Lawrence had achieved such 'unenglish greatness' that he never answered a letter he once received praising him, whereas now that he is dead 'it grows clearer/what bitterness drove him'.

The third verse paragraph introduces the first of several extended allusions to Lawrence's work, this one to 'Snake':

> The serpent in the grotto
> water dripping from the stone
> into a pool.

This symbol for Lawrence is paralleled with the image of 'forsythia hung with/yellow bells in the cold'. Lawrence, who in the first section can no longer labour furiously 'against waste, waste and life's/coldness', in the fourth section, as in the final period of his literary career, is

> worn with a fury of sad labor
> to create summer from
> spring's decay.

An allusion to Lawrence's travel writings, 'Men driven not to love/but to the ends of the earth', leads logically to the Aztec image of *The Plumed Serpent*: 'The serpent turning his/stonelike head,/the fixed agate eyes turn also'.

The seasonal imagery of early March continues with the image of 'unopened jonquils':

> But for Lawrence
> full praise in this
> half cold half season –
> before trees are in leaf and
> tufted grass stars
> unevenly the dead ground.

A second allusion to 'Snake' recalls,

> Slowly the serpent leans
> to drink by the tinkling water,
> the forked tongue alert.

In the seventh verse paragraph, the pleasant walk of two companions by sea or river bank is contrasted sharply with Lawrence's apocalyptic image of the flood in *The Virgin and the Gipsy*:

> Flood waters rise, and will rise,
> rip the quiet valley
> trap the gypsy and the girl.

The irony of 'Lawrence dead' before the return of spring calls to mind

> the scorched aridity of
> the Mexican plateau. Or baked
> public squares in the cities of
> Mediterranean islands,

places associated with Lawrence through his travels and through books such as *Mornings in Mexico* and *Sea and Sardinia*. 'The sweep of spring over/temperate lands' is contrasted with its slow arrival elsewhere, unknown to Lawrence, who is, for a third time, identified with the serpent in an image which links the imagery of snake, flood, and death:

> The serpent cannot move
> his stony eyes, scarcely sees
> but touching the air
> with his forked tongue surmises
> and his body which dipped
> into the cold water
> is gone.

The 'satiric sun', too, is gone. But nature, through the cricket's 'Greep, greep, greep', sings

> Sorrow to the young
> that Lawrence has passed
> unwanted from England.

The elegy ends as it began, in the ironic contrast between the fact of that death and the emergence of spring in the forsythia and 'the crin-kled spice-bush/in flower'.

Marya Zaturenska's 'In Song, the Countersign' (1937),[7] written basically in iambic pentameter, begins with an iambic hexameter line and varies metrically throughout to include extra unaccented syllables in mid-line and feminine line endings. The poem is not 'about' Lawrence, nor is it, although elegiac in tone, an elegy in any formal sense. The inscription, 'In Memoriam: D. H. Lawrence', and the allusion in the second line to the date of Lawrence's death, suggest that Lawrence's is the poetic or prophetic voice that announces and interprets the spring:

> Again that voice intangible as running light
> On half awakened tree in early March,
> That voice forgotten, heard reluctantly
> In dreams that fear the sun, and waking flee.

The voice is 'beguiling' like the sirens' songs, the symbol of the lure of art, which, unable to flee, the speaker resolves:

> No, let us drown in music and resign
> Our hearts, our souls, our loves, to the wide waters.

If the artist, as James Joyce's character Stephen Dedalus notes in another context, records 'the signature of all things', the song he follows, in Zaturenska's conception, is 'The lost music, life's rich countersign'. The maidens cast their wreaths, symbols of wholeness in love, upon the water of life experience, and the young men follow, 'lifting their voices' in 'one voice, one melody', 'cool in summer's heat, in darkness bright'. But the attainment of love is inevitably followed by the necessity of giving it up, and life and love are processes which, it must be accepted, culminate inevitably in death and loss:

> So are our vanquished bodies cast ashore
> And empty are our eyes, empty our arms,
> And the sharp raptures in our hearts no more.
> Our little deaths are swallowed by the sun;
> Our aspirations, longings and alarms
> Are drawn into sleep's vast felicity:
> Oh, not love's martyrs or life's victims we.

The stanza reiterates some of the central insights of Lawrence's 'The Ship of Death', and the idea of the return of human sexual energy ('Our little deaths') to the sun is Lawrentian by way of Aztec and other primitive religious myth. The drawing of human aspirations and concerns 'into sleep's vast felicity' echoes William Cullen Bryant's *Thanatopsis*.

The final stanza seems to allude directly to Lawrence's role as artist and prophet of sexual love and blood consciousness:

> Recorders on bleak stone, symbols of vaster dreams,
> Lovers of love, expounders of the blood.

Lured by 'the perilous mountains' and 'the remote white voices' of our vision,

> We sink, we drown, in bottomless lost streams.

The poem sustains to the end the elegiac mood in a serious and moving meditation on the decline of sexual love and ultimately on the surrender to death itself.

John Clellon Holmes' 'Dying Lawrence',[8] written four decades later, is not formally an elegy but a retrospective consideration of Lawrence's creative death in contrast to 'The mean deaths of the spirit in this age'. Recognising that Lawrence 'is nothing now', the poet imagines no resurrection or apotheosis but recalls a series of images, some from life, some from poetry, that are associated emblematically with Lawrence's dying:

> behind geranium shutters
>   glimpsing whatever future
> we ravaged consciousnesses have.

What strikes the poet most at this distance is the intensity of

Lawrence's life in contrast to the triviality of life around him:

> The busy dogs of Bandol
>   knew he was intensely among them,
> his high pitch of conscious life
>   burning, and burning up.

In an echo of the 'geranium shutters' behind which Lawrence glimpses our future, there is 'No longer any way to shutter down the eye'. Like William Carlos Williams, Holmes notes, with the clarity of specificity, the ironic juxtaposition of returning spring with Lawrence's death:

> The burden of spring's recurrence,
>   its remorseless fecundity
>   indifferent to his fever –
> he coughed against the knowledge
>   that each year pomegranates swell new.

This seemingly conventional image of seasonal fruition introduces, in the next sentence, what is perhaps the central insight of the poem, namely recognition of what it means to be a fallen creature in a fallen world:

> What broke Lawrence
>   was what he saw
> at the bottom of the garden.

After this turning point, the poet presents, with power and taste, the searing image of Lawrence's brokenness as a symbol for that of man in general:

> Half-a-man with his narrow face,
> charred sticks of walking bone,
> the quick of movement finally blurred,
> the fierce, unveiling eyes –
>   terrier's eyes –
> cornered at last.

One may be reminded of William Butler Yeats' 'tattered coat upon a stick'. One should certainly note that it is in the context of his being broken and cornered that Lawrence turns, with 'an oceanic longing – for death's fathoms', to the concept, presented in 'The Ship of Death', that he is

> To be quite blotted out –
>   taken back into the flow –
> re-wombed in oblivion.

The poet returns to his meditation on Lawrence's dying as Frieda becomes, in effect, the midwife of death, assisting

> . . . his difficult passage out
> his foot in Frieda's hands.

Lawrence's anticipation of 'the imminent mystery' with 'A fearful bliss' as 'Life's consummation / the bridal night to come', is met with a profound ambiguity,

> and death bringing the huge, blue silence
>   like ceremonial gentians
>   to the bon voyage.

Whatever the mystery discloses for Lawrence, we are left with 'a sense of absence – / a fissure in the time'. Returning to the contrast with which he began, between the intensity of Lawrence's living and dying and the triviality of experience today, Holmes' concluding iambic pentameter line sums up the effect of 'The mean deaths of the spirit in this age' that he had observed in the initial line: 'Lord, how meager some men make the flesh'. These two lines perfectly balance each other and bracket a poem structured on a deliberate and fully achieved, but not rigid, balance. The closely observed details, resonant with allusions to Lawrence's life and works, yield a meaning that is both particular in reference to Lawrence and richly universal in its revelation of what it is to be fully human – to live life with intensity and to die.

These five poems, while of varying poetic quality and length, are broadly representative of the elegiac response which Lawrence's death elicited in creative writers. If no one of the poems quite attains the artistic level of the major elegies of English literature, nevertheless their response to the death of a poet is similar to that of earlier elegies. As Lord Byron had lashed out at the *Quarterly* reviewers in 'Who Killed John Keats?', Ruth Lechlitner's 'Resurrection in Exile: to D. H. Lawrence' criticises 'the wilful blind' who refused to recognise Beauty, leaving Lawrence to fight 'the rebel's fight, alone'. Walter Lowenfels' *Elegy in the Manner of a Requiem in Memory of D. H. Lawrence*, as its parallels with Eliot's *The Waste Land, The Love Song of J. Alfred Prufrock* and *The Hollow Men* suggest, attempts to embody the sterility of the modern era as Lord Tennyson's *In Memoriam* had encompassed the essence of the Victorian age. William Carlos Williams' 'An Elegy for D. H. Lawrence', which recalls the season of the dead poet's departure and evokes his major themes, inevitably brings to mind W. H. Auden's greater elegy, 'In Memory of W. B. Yeats'. Marya Zaturenska's 'In Song, the Countersign' uses the memoriam to D. H. Lawrence as the occasion for a more general meditation on death, like William Cullen Bryant's *Thanatopsis*, as the common end of human experience. Finally, John Clellon Holmes' 'Dying Lawrence' finds in Lawrence's death the paradigm of existence which asserts itself creatively, even in dying, against 'the mean deaths of the spirit' that characterises his age. These poems are 'occasional' in the restricted sense of the term, but the five poets, despite their use of established literary convention, had no recognisable obligation to write elegies for D. H. Lawrence. They were, rather, in their several ways, impelled by the testament of Lawrence's life and work to bear poetic witness to what he had meant to them.

NOTES

1. Rebecca West, 'A Letter from Abroad (The Death of D. H. Lawrence)', *The Bookman* (New York) 71 (April–May 1930) pp. 188–95; reprinted as 'Elegy', in *The New Adelphi*, 3 (June–August 1930) pp. 298–309; later reprinted as *D. H. Lawrence* (London: Secker, 1930) and as *Elegy: an In Memoriam Tribute to D. H. Lawrence* (New York: Phoenix, 1930). E. M. Forster, 'D. H. Lawrence', *The Nation and the Athenaeum*, 46 (29 March 1930). See also Forster's further correspondence on the issue in *The Nation and the Athenaeum* with T. S. Eliot (5 April 1930), W. S. Adams (12 April 1930) and Clive Bell (19 April 1930), with replies by Forster. Rhys Davies, 'D. H. Lawrence in Bandol', *Horizon* (London) 2 (October 1940) pp. 191–208.
2. J. C. Squire, 'D. H. Lawrence', *Observer*, 9 March 1930, p. 6. See also John Arrow, *J. C. Squire v. D. H. Lawrence: a Reply to Mr Squire's Article in 'The Observer' of March 9th, 1930* (London: E. Lahr [Blue Moon

Booklets no. 4], 1930). 'Mr D. H. Lawrence: a Writer of Genius', *The Times* (London), 4 March 1930, p. 11. Edward Shanks, 'Death of Mr D. H. Lawrence: Novelist Whose Books English Censor Banned', *Evening Standard* (London), 3 March 1930, p. 10.
3. Dennis Jackson, ' "The Stormy Petrel of Literature is Dead": the World Press Reports D. H. Lawrence's Death', *The D. H. Lawrence Review*, **14** (Spring 1981) pp. 33–72.
4. Ruth Lechlitner, 'Resurrection in Exile: to D. H. Lawrence', *New York Herald Tribune*, 6 April 1930, p. 4.
5. Walter Lowenfels, *Elegy in the Manner of a Requiem in Memory of D. H. Lawrence* (Paris: Carrefour, 1932).
6. William Carlos Williams, 'An Elegy for D. H. Lawrence: Died 2 March 1930', *Poetry: a Magazine of Verse*, **45** (March 1935) pp. 311–15; reprinted in *The Collected Earlier Poems of William Carlos Williams* (New York: New Directions, 1951) pp. 359–64.
7. Marya Zaturenska, 'In Song, the Countersign (In Memoriam: D. H. Lawrence)', *Poetry: a Magazine of Verse*, **50** (September 1937) pp. 302–3.
8. John Clellon Holmes, 'Dying Lawrence', *The D. H. Lawrence Review*, **9** (Autumn 1976) pp. 373–6.

Index

solar plexus, 166, 173
Sophocles, 30
Spender, Stephen, 78–9, 90n
Spengler, Oswald, 118
Spilka, Mark, 142
Squire, J. C., 311, 325n
Squires, Michael, 124n
Stallybrass, Oliver, 160n
Stevens, Wallace, 199
Stewart, J. I. M., 105n, 295
Strindberg, Johan August, xi
sub-culture, vii
Swinburne, Algernon Charles, 68, 189
Symons, Arthur, 182

Tanner, Tony, 92, 104n
Taylor, John Russell, 233n
'tenderness', 129, 263
Tennyson, Alfred, 33; *The Princess*, 33
'theory of relativity', 172
Thucydides, 258
Thurber, James, 'My Memories of D. H. Lawrence', 295
Tiedje, Egon, 212n
Tillich, Paul, 254
Tolstoi, Leo, 30; Tolstoyan ideas, 147
Trilling, Lionel, 248, 264n

Van Goch, Vincent, 16
vernacular drama, 217
Verga, Giovanni, *Mastro-don Gesualdo*, 248
Vivas, Eliseo, 142, 161n

Watson, Jean, 5
Weil, Simone, 252
Wells, H. G., *A Modern Utopia*, 293n; *Men Like Gods*, 298

Wesker, Arnold, 216, 219, 232n
West, Rebecca, 11, 311, 325n
Whitman, Walt, 100, 211; *Leaves of Grass*, 190
Widmer, Kingsley, 161n; *The Art of Perversity*, 91n, 126
Wilde, Alan, 104n
Williams, Charles, 242–3
Williams, Raymond, 214, 221
Williams, Tennessee, *Rise in Flame, Cried the Phoenix*, 295–6
Williams, William Carlos, 'An Elegy for D. H. Lawrence', 311, 318–21, 325, 326n
Winter, Keith, *Impassioned Pygmies*, 312
Woodcock, George, 297, 308n
Woolf, Virginia, 258
Wordsworth, 17–18, 22, 52–3, 55, 65, 67–8; *The Prelude*, 54, 64
working class, 8; working-class culture, vii; working-class drama, 217; working-class novel, vii
world crisis, 170
Worthen, John, 91n
Wright, Louise, 309n

Yeats, W. B., 76, 163, 188, 199, 215, 323; *A Vision*, 163

Zaturenska, Marya, 'In song, the Countersign', 311, 321–2, 325, 326n
Zen Buddhist, 132
Zytaruk, George J. (ed.), *Letters of D. H. Lawrence II*, 293n; (ed.), *The Quest for Rananim*, 123n, 294n